Embodied Utopias

Utopia has become a bad reputation in recent scholarship on modernism, architecture, urban planning and gender studies. Many utopian designs now appear impractical, manifesting an arrogant disregard for the lived experiences of the ordinary inhabitants who make daily use of global, public and private spaces.

The essays in *Embodied Utopias* argue that the gendered body is the crux of the hopes and disappointments of modern urban and suburban utopias of the United States of America, Europe and Asia. They reassess utopian projects – masculinist, feminist, colonialist, progressive – of the late nineteenth and early twentieth centuries; they survey the dystopian landscapes of the present; and they gesture at the potential for an embodied approach to the urban future, to the changing spaces of cities and virtual landscapes.

With essays from a wide range of fields including architecture and urban planning, art and art history, media and cultural studies, communications, geography, philosophy, and gender studies, *Embodied Utopias* makes an important contribution to the ongoing dialogue between cultural theory and the history and practice of architecture and urban design.

Amy Bingaman is Visiting Scholar, Departments of Art and Design at the Cornish College of Arts, Seattle. **Lise Sanders** is Visiting Assistant Professor of Literature at Hampshire College, Amherst. **Rebecca Zorach** is Harper Fellow and Collegiate Assistant Professor of Humanities at the University of Chicago.

THE ARCHITEXT SERIES

Edited by Thomas A. Markus and Anthony D. King

Architectural discourse had traditionally represented buildings as art objects or technical objects. Yet buildings are also social objects in that they are invested with social meaning and shape social relations. Recognising these assumptions, the **Architext** series aims to bring together recent debates in social and cultural theory and the study and practice of architecture and urban design. Critical, comparative and interdisciplinary, the books in the series will, by theorising architecture, bring the space of the built environment centrally into the social sciences and humanities, as well as bringing the theoretical insights of the latter into the discourse of architecture and urban design. Particular attention will be paid to issues of gender, race, sexuality and the body, to questions of identity and place, to the cultural politics of representation and language, and to the global and postcolonial contexts in which these are addressed.

Already published:

Framing Places
Mediating power in built form
Kim Dovey

Gender Space Architecture
An interdisciplinary introduction
Edited by Jane Rendell, Barbara Penner and Iain Borden

Behind the Postcolonial
Architecture, urban space and political cultures in Indonesia
Abidin Kusno

The Architecture of Oppression
The SS, forced labor and the Nazi monumental building economy
Paul Jaskot

The Words Between the Spaces
Buildings and language
Thomas A. Markus and Deborah Cameron

Forthcoming titles:

Colonial Constructions
Architecture, cities and Italian colonialism
Mia Fuller

Spaces of Global Cultures
Anthony D. King

Writing Spaces
Greig Crysler

**Edited by
Amy Bingaman, Lise Sanders and
Rebecca Zorach**

Embodied Utopias

Gender, social change, and
the modern metropolis

London and New York

First published 2002 by Routledge
11 New Fetter Lane, London EC4P 4EE

Simultaneously published in the USA and Canada
by Routledge
29 West 35th Street, New York, NY 10001

Routledge is an imprint of the Taylor & Francis Group

Typeset in Frutiger by Wearset Ltd, Boldon, Tyne and Wear
Printed and bound in Great Britain by TJ International, Padstow, Cornwall

British Library Cataloguing in Publication Data
A catalogue record for this book is available from the British Library

Library of Congress Cataloging in Publication Data
Embodied utopias : gender, social change, and the modern metropolis / edited by Amy
Bingaman, Lise Sanders and Rebecca Zorach.
    p. cm. – (Architext series)
  Includes bibliographical references and index.
  1. Visionary architecture. 2. City planning. I. Bingaman, Amy, 1970– II. Sanders, Lise,
1970– III. Zorach, Rebecca, 1969– IV. Series.
NA209.5 .E46 2001
711'.4–dc21
                                                            2001040810

ISBN 0-415-24813-2 (hbk)
ISBN 0-415-24814-0 (pbk)

Contents

Figures

Notes on Contributors

Amy Bingaman teaches art history at Cornish College of the Arts in Seattle, Washington. Her interests include nineteenth- and twentieth-century British painting, decorative arts, and architecture, as well as gender studies. Her essay, 'The Business of Brotherhood: Morris, Marshall, Faulkner & Co. and the Pre-Raphaelite Culture of Youth', appears in *Nineteenth-Century Artistic Brotherhoods,* Laura Morowitz and William Vaughan, eds. (London: Ashgate Press, 2000). At the University of Chicago, she is currently finishing her dissertation titled 'Furnishing Utopia: William Morris, Hand-Production and the Pre-Raphaelite Economies of Desire'.

Peg Birmingham is Associate Professor and Chair of the Philosophy Department at DePaul University. She is finishing a manuscript on Hannah Arendt entitled *The Predicament of Common Responsibility: Hannah Arendt and the 'right to have rights'*. She has published articles on Irigaray, Heidegger, Foucault, and Arendt as well as on architecture.

Christa Erickson is an interdisciplinary artist and writer who investigates the politics, pleasures, and pains of spaces mediated by electronic technologies. Her individual and collaborative works have been exhibited widely, including galleries in New York City, the bi-national InSITE, the Walker Art Center in Minneapolis, The California Museum of Photography, the Institute for Studies in the Arts (ASU), and the Banff Center for the Arts in Canada. Christa speaks about new media regularly and is Assistant Professor of Art at SUNY, Stony Brook.

Margaret Farrar recently received her PhD from Penn State University and is currently Assistant Professor of Political Science at Augustana College. She is working on her book *Building the Body Politic: Subjectivity and Urban Space*.

Elizabeth Grosz teaches Comparative Literature and English at the State University of New York at Buffalo. She is the author of *Sexual Subversions: Three French Feminists* (Sydney: Allen and Unwin, 1989) and editor of *Becomings: Explorations in Time, Memory and Futures* (Ithaca: Cornell University Press, 1999).

Sharon Haar is an architect and Assistant Professor at the University of Illinois at Chicago. Her projects and articles have been published in various journals including *Architectural Design*, *Sites*, *Newsline*, and the *Harvard Design Magazine*. She is author of 'Coming Home: A Postscript on Postmodernism,' in Christophy Reed, ed. *Not At Home* (New York: Thames and Hudson, 1996). She is currently working on a book titled *The City as Campus* which explores the relationship between urban design and urban universities.

Hazel Hahn is Assistant Professor of History at Seattle University. She is completing a book on advertising and urban culture in nineteenth-century Paris. Her current project is on French colonial history in Hanoi, 1900–40. Publications include 'Boulevard Culture and Advertising in Fin-de-siècle Paris,' in Alexander Cowan, ed. *Senses of Place: the City and the Senses* (Aldershot, Hampshire: Ashgate).

Barbara Hooper is a doctoral student in the Department of Urban Planning at the University of California, Los Angeles, where she is completing her dissertation, 'The Performativities of Space: Bodies, Cities, Texts.' This work is concerned with the body, the city and social order, and focuses on the spatialization of body and mind as regards the production of differentiated urban subjects in specific contexts, i.e. classical Athens, modern Paris, and postmodern Los Angeles. She has published a number of articles on critical urban studies in journals and edited collections.

May Joseph is Associate Professor of Global Studies in the Department of Social Science at Pratt Institute, New York. She is the author of *Nomadic Identities: The Performance of Citizenship* (Minnesota, 1999) and co-editor (with Jennifer Natalya Fink) of *Performing Hybridity* (Minnesota, 1999).

Thomas A. Markus is architect and Emeritus Professor, University of Strathclyde, Glasgow, UK. He is author of *Buildings and Power: Freedom and Control in the Origin of Modern Building Types* (London: Routledge, 1993); co-author with Debbie Cameron, *The Words Between the Spaces: Buildings and Language* (London: Routledge, forthcoming December 2001); editor and co-author, *Order in Space and Society: Architectural Form and its Context in the Scottish Enlightenment* (Edinburgh: Mainstream, 1982); and co-editor with Tony King of *Architext* Series, published by Routledge.

Brian P. McGrath is an architect and the author of *Transparent Cities* (SITES Books, 1994) and research in new technologies of urban representation (www.skyscraper.org/timeformations). He has been an Adjunct Associate Professor in Urban Design at Columbia University since 1992, and an architecture faculty member at Parsons School of Design since 1990. He co-edited *New Urbanisms/New Work: Yonkers Nepperhan Valley* (Columbia Books on Architecture, 2000). McGrath has been teaching and researching at Chulalongkorn University in Bangkok, Thailand since receiving a Senior Scholar Fellowship from the Fulbright Foundation in 1998.

Kelly Quinn is a PhD candidate in the Department of American Studies at University of Maryland, College Park, where she teaches American Studies and Afro-American Studies. Her dissertation examines the history of New Deal housing programmes. She has worked in sheltering and legal programmes for homeless and battered women in Alaska, Maryland, and Washington, DC.

Anthony Raynsford is a doctoral candidate in art history at the University of Chicago where he is completing a dissertation entitled 'Templates and Archetypes: Archaic Cities in the Social Imagination of Postwar Urbanism'. He received his MArch from UCLA and has previously published in the *Journal of Architectural Education* and *Modernism/Modernity*.

Lise Sanders teaches literature, gender studies and cultural studies at Hampshire College in Amherst, Massachusetts. Publications include 'The Failures of the Romance' (*Modern Fiction Studies* 47:1, March 2001) and ' "Indecent Incentives to Vice": Regulating Films and Audience Behavior from the 1890s to the 1910s', in Andrew Higson, ed. *Young and Innocent: Cinema and Britain, 1896–1930* (Exeter: University of Exeter Press, forthcoming 2002). She is presently at work on a book entitled *Consuming Fantasies: Labor, Leisure, and the London Shopgirl, 1880–1914*.

Suzanne M. Spencer-Wood is Director of Women's Studies and Associate Professor in Anthropology at Oakland University. She stimulated the rapidly growing field of gender research in historical archaeology by organizing the first two conference symposia on the subject in 1989. Her publications include an article on urban green spaces designed by nineteenth-century women's organizations in the *Landscape Journal* (1994), and a chapter in *The Archaeology of Household Activities*, edited by Penelope M. Allison (London: Routledge, 1999).

Despina Stratigakos is an Assistant Professor in the Department of Art at Illinois State University. A specialist in gender and architecture, she has published 'Architects in Skirts: The Public Image of Women Architects in Wilhelmine Germany', *Journal of Architectural Education* 55, no. 2 (November 2001) and is completing a book entitled *Unsettling Architecture: Women and the Architectural Profession in Imperial Germany*.

Brent Stringfellow is currently practising as an architect in Boston, Massachu-setts. He graduated from the University of Pennsylvania in 1992 and received the MArch from the Harvard University Graduate School of Design in 1997. 'Personal City' is based on work completed for the thesis project, 'Panurbanism: Tysons Corner, A Case Study' completed with Charlie Cannon, Bogue Trondowski, and David Yocum in the spring of 1997.

Elizabeth Wilson is Professor of Cultural Studies at the University of North London. She is the author of *Adorned in Dreams: Fashion and Modernity* (Berke-ley, CA: University of California Press, 1985), *The Sphinx in the City* (Berkeley, CA: University of California Press, 1993), *Bohemians: The Glamorous Outcasts* (London: I.B. Tauris, 2000), and *The Contradictions of Culture: Cities, Culture, Women* (London: Sage, 2001).

Andrew Wood is an Assistant Professor at San Jose State University. His latest book, co-authored with Dr Matthew Smith of Indiana University South Bend, is entitled *Online Communication: Linking Technology, Identity, and Culture* (Mahwah, New Jersey: Lawrence Erlbaum & Associates, 2001). His research agenda includes the study of world's fairs as contested terrains of ideology, nationality, and gender construction. He is expanding his 1998 dissertation on Disney's planned community, Celebration, to be published as a broader mono-graph on the intersection of world's fairs, city planning, and corporate rhetoric.

Rebecca Zorach is a Harper Fellow and Collegiate Assistant Professor in Human-ities at the University of Chicago. She has taught art history and cultural theory there and at the School of the Art Institute of Chicago and the University of Pennsylvania, and has published essays in *Art History*, the *Journal of Medieval and Early Modern Studies*, and *Wired* magazine. She is currently working on a book entitled *Matters of Excess: Blood, Ink, Milk and Gold in the Visual Culture of the French Renaissance*.

Foreword

This volume has its origins in a year-long workshop culminating in a three-day conference, funded by the Graham Foundation, at the Center for Gender Studies at the University of Chicago. That project, also entitled 'Embodied Utopias', sought not just to study others' utopian visions, but to embody a 'different' everyday practice of academic work. In many ways that aspiration to a 'different practice' was a continuation of the vision of the women's studies centers founded in the 1970s, aspirations that had become less common by the late 1990s. We sought to be more egalitarian than is the norm in academic institutions; we tried to transcend barriers of practical and abstract knowledge; and we tried to engage as much in community-building as in event-production. I am delighted to be able to say that while all such efforts run up against the hard walls of established norms, 'Embodied Utopias' came closer than any other project during the three years of my directorship of the Center in being utopian in practice as well as in subject. The intellectual and organizational initiative, responsibility, and follow-through for the project came from students; the Center's administrative assistant, Julia Coyne Nitti (now Allen), played an important intellectual as well as administrative role; participation in the project ranged far beyond the University; and the conference and book came out of a sustained year-long discussion.

Without the intellectual and political vision, commitment, and energy of three women who were graduate students at Chicago at the time, neither the workshop, nor the conference, nor the book would ever have come into existence. Rebecca Zorach was one of the principal investigators in the project we presented to the Graham Foundation (Katherine Taylor, of the Art History Department at the University of Chicago, and I were the others). The conceptualization and writing of the successful grant application were very largely hers. During the workshop year (during which Rebecca Zorach was absent doing her dissertation research), the other co-editors of the volume, Amy Bingaman and Lise Shapiro (now Sanders), along with Julia Nitti, took responsibility for planning the monthly meetings. The workshop was also sustained by the active participation of both undergraduates and graduate students at the University. They, along with some other students, took on the planning of individual panels for the conference. Finally, without the intellectual energy and expertise in the workshop of two colleagues from the University of Illinois at Chicago, Sharon Haar and Greig Crysler, the project would have been much poorer. Their generosity in fact made possible our efforts to encourage reflection on the built environment on a campus where such work is hindered by the absence of schools of design, architecture, and urban planning.

'Embodied Utopias' was conceived in four temporalities and with four different publics: the one-time intellectual engagement of grant-writing to fund the project, the trace of which is the proposal submitted to the Graham Foundation, and whose audience was limited to that Foundation and the administration of the University of Chicago; the repeated, informal, very engaged but necessarily brief, monthly evening meetings of the workshop of ten participants, of which no enduring record was kept; the one-time, but three-day long and very intense, encounter at the conference itself, in which about one hundred people participated, the trace of which lies in the unpublished written versions of the papers presented, hidden in the authors' files; and, finally the potentially eternal embodiment of that work in this volume, now available to an infinite audience.

This book is important – a statement I can make because my involvement with the project ended with the conference. It makes important interventions in the domain of feminist and gender studies, architecture and urban planning, and analyses of utopian thinking. It is an embodiment of the power and possibility of interdisciplinary discussion. Contributors include students, practitioners and teachers from the disciplines of Architecture, Art History, English, History, Social and Feminist Theory; essays range from the eighteenth century to the present; the geographic terrain is global. Finally, and perhaps most importantly, the essays approach the concept of 'embodied utopia' from very different angles and produce quite different visions.

The theme of gender is central to volume. Two of the early essays in the volume take on the question of masculinism in utopian imaginaries, while others focus on both the construction of a certain vision of womanliness through architecture and urban planning and women's responses to those visions. Thus, the first essay by Thomas Markus questions the possibility of the embodiment of non-patriarchal utopias and that by Barbara Hooper links utopianism, modernity, and masculinist desire in the work of Le Corbusier, while Despina Stratigakos focuses on the impact of women as architects and patrons on the built environment.

A different angle on the politics of architecture emerges from essays focusing on the question of state power and class domination. Three papers address visions of 'Americanness'. Margaret Farrar's essay demonstrates, for example, that Washington DC was designed to produce a certain kind of embodied citizen. Sharon Haar's work on Hull House argues that early Hull House workers hoped to actually transform immigrants' mode of life and instill bourgeois norms by means as varied as the architecture of Hull House itself and cooking and craft classes. Suzanne Spencer-Wood, also writing on the Settlements, provides a more hopeful read, arguing that Hull House represented a vision of the integration of difference in U. S. society rather than the demand that immigrants conform to Anglo-American bourgeois aesthetics of everyday life. This theme reappears in a contemporary context in the work of Kelly Quinn, which emphasizes the ways in which the appearance of a building can make it more or less appealing to its intended users. Through a study of two battered women's shelters in Washington DC, she demonstrates how the seemingly starker building actually allowed more space for its inhabitants' expression than did the 'homier' building, whose hominess was defined by middle-class norms and entailed a rigid control on what tenants could do with the space.

Finally, five articles directly address the intersection of gender, capitalism, and architecture. Brent Stringfellow, Andrew Wood, May Joseph, Brian McGrath, and Christa Erickson, all, in various ways, analyze the ways in which capitalism – whether in the shaping of work environments and rhythms, in providing (or not) the economic means necessary for new buildings, or in encouraging the movement of populations – shapes the ways in which the built environment both structures and is structured by forms of capital. The contexts vary from the transformation in the post-World War II period of unincorporated land in Tysons Corner, Virginia into a commercial center, to the Disney Corporation's planned community, *Celebration,* to an evocation of Hanoi from the past to the present, to synchretic culture in contemporary Bangkok, to the disembodiedness of cyberspace. The volume concludes self-reflexively with essays by Elizabeth Wilson and Elizabeth Grosz questioning of the very desirability and utility of utopian visions. *Embodied Utopias* changes our way of thinking how visions of gender and social justice, and of the nation, can or should be embodied in the built environment, and it offers material with which to rethink the very place of planning itself.

The volume would, in other words, have made an important contribution to our understanding of the world regardless of how it had come into being. I would like to suggest, however, that the history of the book's production also matters. The volume's origins lie in the conviction that those who have moved from being formally charged with teaching need also to learn and that those formally charged with learning need also to teach. That is, of course, a statement made banal by the student movements of the 1960s and 1970s, and although often repeated, it is rarely actually implemented. Most often students are recruited to provide the labor need to test, demonstrate, or substantiate a professor's idea, rather than assisted in finding the resources with which to embody their own visions. This volume, then, while utterly forward-looking and innovative in its content, methodology, and implications, also has connections backward to an earlier (utopian?) vision of how knowledge can and should be produced.

Leora Auslander
University of Chicago

Acknowledgements

Many individuals and institutions have been instrumental in bringing this project to completion. We would first like to express our gratitude to the members of the Center for Gender Studies at the University of Chicago, many of whom worked tirelessly to assist us in organizing the 1999 conference that inspired this collection, 'Embodied Utopias: Gender, Social Change, and the Built Environment'. In particular we wish to thank Julia Coyne Allen, Leora Auslander, Lauren Berlant, and Norma Field for their generous gift of time, energy, and insight. Other mentors and colleagues in Chicago and elsewhere provided essential guidance for the original vision, including Sherry Ahrentzen, Kathryn Anthony, Robin Bachin, Peg Birmingham, Jennifer Bloomer, Greig Crysler, Roberta Feldman, Sharon Haar, Mary Harvey, Paul Jaskot, Laura Letinsky, Katherine Taylor, Anthony Raynsford, Rachel Remmel, Katherine Taylor, and Mark Wigley. The conference could not have taken place without the generous support of a grant from the Graham Foundation for Advanced Study in the Fine Arts, and we would like to take this opportunity to thank the outside reviewers for the proposal.

For lending direction and shape to the book, we wish to thank Archi*text* series editors Tom Markus and Tony King, both of whose comments have proven invaluable, as well as the attentive editorial and production staff at Routledge, especially Rebecca Casey, Caroline Mallinder and Victoria Regan. We also wish to thank Helen Ibbotson and Kathryn Murphy at Taylor and Francis, and Carl Gillingham and Lesley Ann Staward at Wearset. We are grateful for their assistance in refining the collection; any errors that remain are our own.

Amy Bingaman would like to express her gratitude to her co-editors for their insightfulness, wit, and patience; to Leora Auslander, Lauren Berlant, and Elizabeth Helsinger for their sagacity and unwavering support; and to Julia Allen, her colleagues in the Departments of Art and Design at Cornish College of the Arts, and her parents. She also wishes to thank her sister, Betsy Bingaman, who has courageously demonstrated the challenges of embodied alterity, and especially Lori MacIntosh, for her steadfast encouragement and editorial acumen.

Lise Sanders is grateful to Lauren Berlant, Elaine Hadley, Elizabeth Helsinger and Mary Russo, and especially her co-editors, for their wisdom and intellectual sustenance. She would also like to thank the students, faculty and staff in the School of Humanities, Arts and Cultural Studies at Hampshire College, with whom she has had the pleasure of discussing ideas related to this volume. Finally, she thanks Kate Rosen, Allison Smith, and her parents for their unflagging support, and as always, Eric Sanders, for teaching her about the possible.

Rebecca Zorach wishes to add her own warm thanks to her co-editors, to series editors Tom Markus and Tony King, and to Leora Auslander and Julia Allen. She also thanks her parents and Lauren Berlant, Sawad Brooks, Jacqueline Francis, and Sigfried Gold for helping her understand the utopian; colleagues and friends too numerous to name at the University of Chicago for their insights and support; and the collegial communities and resources of the Center for Advanced Study in the Visual Arts at the National Gallery of Art and the Penn Humanities Forum at the University of Pennsylvania.

The Center for Gender Studies at the University of Chicago was the inspiration and setting for much of the work included in this collection. We dedicate this volume to its members, and hope this will be the first of many such commemorations.

Embodied Utopia

Introduction

Amy Bingaman, Lise Sanders, and Rebecca Zorach

The drive to construct or envision ideal societies existed long before Thomas More coined the word 'utopia' in 1516, and has outlasted him in the long-standing hopes of planners, architects, philosophers and social reformers that particular ways of ordering space and designing the built environment might have a salutary effect on society, communities, families and individuals. The notion of the ideal city or ideal place has long existed in most of the world's religious traditions; likewise, throughout history, communities based on the pursuit of shared ideals have separated themselves from their larger social context. It is, perhaps, the secularization and mass application of utopia that might be perceived as a specifically modern, if not specifically western, phenomenon. Perhaps this is also utopia's downfall.

Since the last quarter of the twentieth century, utopian projects have been understood, more and more, to be material impossibilities. The ambiguous roots of the word invented by More – from the Greek *ou* meaning 'not' or *eu* meaning 'happy', and *topos* meaning 'place' – remain today a source of theoretical speculation. Is *utopia* the good place or the impossible place? Is the good place, in fact, no place at all? The essays included in this collection acknowledge the pervasiveness of the desire to create a good place – and the equally prevalent perception that such projects inevitably fail. Operating under the assumption that utopianism is both a social activity and a thought process, we aim first to outline the structures of desire that form the backbone of modern, urban utopian discourse. Secondly, we seek to create a framework for comprehending the failures, revisions and reinvention of such projects, as well as the pessimism surrounding current utopian debate.

While taking utopian hopes seriously, the chapters in this volume incorporate the lessons of recent studies in order to maintain a critical view of such projects (including those that are feminist). How do scientific and engineered proposals for 'real', inhabited places, on the one hand, and utopian political aims expressed in fiction and theory, on the other, converge to bear upon our understanding of 'the good place'? The essays focus on the viability of utopian social projects in terms of the ways bodies (gendered, raced, classed, variously-abled) relate to built environments (from urban spaces re-engineered by colonial conquest or social endeavour to the theoretically anonymous, democratic ideal of the Internet). The collection as a whole therefore addresses the concept of utopia (as both 'no place' and 'good place') critically through the study of architectural history and form, on the one hand, and theories of embodiment, on the other. The concept of 'embodied utopia' may appear to be a contradiction in terms – with the body signifying unpredictability, concreteness and change, and utopia characterized by predictability, abstraction and permanence – yet we remain committed to incorporating the body into future conceptions of utopian theory and practise.[1]

UTOPIAN FAILURES AND ASPIRATIONS

Whereas myths in premodern culture enforced tradition by justifying the necessity of social constraints, the dreamworlds of modernity – political, cultural, and economic – are expressions of a utopian desire for social arrangements that transcend existing forms. But dreamworlds become dangerous when their enormous energy is used instrumentally by structures of power, mobilized as an instrument of force that turns against the very masses who were supposed to benefit. If the dreamed-of potential for social transformation remains unrealized, it can teach future generations that history has betrayed them. And in fact, the most inspiring mass-utopian projects – mass sovereignty, mass production, mass culture – have left a history of disasters in their wake. The dream of mass sovereignty has led to world wars of nationalism and to revolutionary terror. The dream of industrial abundance has enabled the construction of global systems that exploit both human labor and natural environments. The dream of culture for the masses has created a panoply of phantasmagoric effects that aestheticize the violence of modernity and anesthetize its victims.

(Buck-Morss 2000: xiii)

Today, many would argue that no genuine utopian spirit exists. As Russell Jacoby comments, 'someone who believes in utopias is widely considered out to lunch or out to kill' (Jacoby 1999: xi). The belief that the future can transcend the present has vanished. Perhaps this is due, as Jacoby believes, to collapsing intellectual visions and exhausted radical activist ambitions in an age of political retreat, or to other factors not yet explored. What remains, however, is a discourse of social transformation that articulates the relationship between the utopian impulse and the instinct for social (self-)critique. Thus, the essays that follow do not always take the subject of utopia head-on; rather, they often approach the topic by examining of its alternatives: realism, idealism, dystopia. Whether describing historic movements to create an ideal space for diverse populations, exploring the locations of abject bodies in modern urban settings, critiquing extra-urban postmodern planning strategies, or focusing on the unique discourses of racial colonization, all of the contributing authors either implicitly or explicitly propose *discursive* action against the multitude of injuries, wrongs, and inequalities perpetuated by the very utopian desires that strive to correct such injustices.

Most previous scholarship on the subject of utopia focuses precisely on the reasons for its failure. According to Sally Kitsch, the diagnosis of 'utopian myopia' is frequently levelled against utopianists who focus their visions on the lives, experiences, and desires of some individuals while seemingly remaining blind to those of others. Likewise, 'unintended consequences' result from the assimilation of once-utopian ideas; this kind of social reform often produces very different results from those that the utopian planners envisioned (Kitsch 2000: 5, 7). This, too, often seems to be a particularly valid criticism of the genre of feminist and subaltern utopian ideology. Like any ideology, a utopian vision with an eye toward the politics of gender, race, and class is susceptible to the very assumptions it means to challenge, and can often obscure differences amongst individuals. In compiling this volume, we have not only attempted to avoid such pitfalls, but also to explore where they occur and explain why.

The relationship between the individual body and the body politic continues to transform itself in the physical and virtual spaces of modernity. Taken as a whole, the essays that follow analyze interactions among bodies, subjectivities, ideologies and constructions of utopian social space. Throughout the volume, contributors attend to the tensions among criticism of existing structures, the imagining of new ones, and the corresponding coherence or incoherence of political action. The essays examine cultural fantasies of bodily management and appropriation; unpack contemporary mobilizations of nostalgia to illuminate the desires that underwrite them; offer strategies for survival in a dystopian world; and resurrect historical moments of optimism and missed opportunity to broaden the imaginative possibilities of the present with an eye toward the future. In investigating the gendering of space, this collection raises a series of questions about the way different kinds of spaces – public and private, intentional and contingent – embody various types of gendered and sexual identifications. We have been especially interested in utopian visions of spaces which would accommodate bodies and their gendered and sexual differences, and the way systems of representation (architecture, art, literature, cinema, and cyberspace) produce and are produced by the bodies which inhabit and enact them.

GENDER, ARCHITECTURE, AND EMBODIMENT

Recent work in feminist and architectural theory has done much to remind us of the interrelationship of bodies and architecture (or space in general). At first glance this might seem a relatively simple exchange: the organization of space shapes the way bodies can move, and we order spaces so as to facilitate social relations. Yet this relationship is more complex than it appears, as Elizabeth Grosz has pointed out in her influential essay 'Bodies–Cities' (Grosz 1995:

103–10). This volume's interpretative approach to space has been sharpened by Kaja Silverman's notion of 'dominant fiction', defined, drawing on Althusser, as 'the ideological reality through which we ''ideally'' live both the symbolic order and the mode of production' (Silverman 1992: 2). Understood as a dominant fiction, the features of space are made to appear visible or invisible, bounded or porous, according to a set of subtly reinforced beliefs which organize our perceptions of the physical world. We understand these spatial 'facts' simply to 'be' and not only to be but to be obvious: it does not require explanation, for example, that a modern bank or municipal building should be constructed to look like a Greek temple, that it should be adorned with sculpted female allegorical figures, that the streets surrounding it should be wide, straight and clean, in contrast to streets on the other side of town. Spatial boundaries become psychologically coded barriers: walls, gates, one-way and dead-end streets, decaying buildings, parts of the city where 'you' (normative subject) 'don't go'. That the dominant fiction cannot always be sustained, but necessarily creates moments of excess and failure, is a crucial component of Silverman's argument. The critic's work, in part, is to ferret out these cracks in the smooth surface of ideology.

If, for many of its inhabitants, the built environment has tended to fall into the realm of the obvious and hence invisible, scholarly approaches to it have tended to focus on architectural aesthetics, viewing the form of surfaces and plans in their relation to a succession of styles and auteurs. As Diane Ghirardo writes in 'The Architecture of Deceit', formalist architectural criticism views buildings as 'aesthetic objects par excellence' which are 'set like jewels into the diadem of architecture' (Ghirardo 1996 [1984]: 387; see also Markus 1993). Issues of corporeality (and what Gail Weiss has called 'intercorporeality', the social and phenomenological interactions of bodies [Weiss 1999]), have tended to drop out, as have the social and political contexts and implications of architecture. Kent Bloomer and Charles Moore wrote as early as 1977 that 'the human body . . . has not itself been a central concern in the understanding of architectural form' (Bloomer and Moore 1977: ix), and Bernard Tschumi wrote of postmodern architecture that it should concern itself with 'movement of bodies in space, together with the actions and events that take place in the social and political realm of architecture' (Tschumi 1998: 3). Yet within a recent consensus on the significance of the body in architecture, there is strong disagreement among architects about means by which bodies can best be taken into account: whether architecture should be physically soothing, should produce ethical communities of bodies, or should highlight its own disjunctive relationship to bodies as they move through space.

Space that is 'gendered', whether by habitual use or by metaphor, has become a preoccupation of recent study in many different disciplines (sociology and anthropology, art and architectural history, literature). Space can be variously understood as extension, as directionality, as uniqueness, as the layering of memory, as sensuality, as representation, as intersubjectivity. The highly influential work of Henri Lefebvre, with its insistence on the conjunction of physical, mental and social space, has led scholars to view space as the product of social relations and, hence, constantly changing (Lefebvre 1991 [1974, 1984]).

Building upon this notion, several contributors to this collection draw from Michel de Certeau's conceptions of place and space as fundamentally different, though related, entities. As Graham Ward writes, '[de] Certeau distinguishes between "place" (*lieu*) which is definable, limited, enclosed, and "space" (*espace*), which is that which is constantly being produced by the practises of living' (de Certeau 2000: 13n3). Of similar importance to a number of these essays is the distinction de Certeau draws between 'strategies' and 'tactics':

> I call a 'strategy' the calculus of force relationships which becomes possible when a subject of will and power (a proprietor, an enterprise, a city, a scientific institution [a university]) can be isolated from an environment. A strategy assumes a place that can be circumscribed as proper (propre) and thus serves as the basis for generating relationships distinct from it . . . Political, economic and scientific rationality has been constructed on this strategic model.
>
> I call a 'tactic', on the other hand, a calculus which cannot count on a 'proper', (a spatial or institutional localisation), nor thus on a borderline distinguishing the other as a visible totality. The place of a tactic belongs to the other. A tactic insinuates itself into the other's place fragmentarily, without taking over its entirety.
>
> (de Certeau 1984a: xix)

In this formulation, while a strategy may be the province of the powerful, a tactic can be seen as the instrument of the disempowered, and can operate as a critical response to the exercise of power by individuals and institutions.

Architecture has historically had a special relation to economic and political power. Requiring control over enormous resources – whether governmental or capital – buildings also express the fantasies of individuals, the actualization of abstract plans whose meaning (to the builder) may be more symbolic and self-referential than material. Space becomes a phantasmatic medium through which an imagination expresses itself. In this volume, by articulating the relationship between architecture, embodiment, and spatial/political definitions of utopia, we seek to interrogate the ways in which a subject's experience of abjection relative to dominant power structures is understood to affect its ability to imagine alternatives. How do people with the power to control their physical environment project their desires into it? How do those with less control negotiate spaces that are structured by others?

The founding text for the notion of utopia, Thomas More's book of that name, coincided with a period in European history which, as the founding era of modernity, has received a great deal of revisionist scrutiny in the past thirty years. Perhaps too facile an equation has been made between the development of theoretical perspective construction in painting and architecture, the theorization of Cartesian subjectivity, and the mapping and colonizing exploits of European conquerors. Yet the relationship between forms of subjectivity and control over space are made quite apparent in the technological revolutions of the European Renaissance. Physical space, mapped to mental space, came to be practised not only as a set of relations, trajectories, or lived material realities, but as an open field for the projection and playing out of fantasies. The early modern 'subject' – one necessarily possessed (one way or another) of capacious material resources – ranged over physical and symbolic space, controlling by mapping, enclosing and surveying.[2] Crucially, those who shared the same cultural and linguistic apparatus were able to enjoy vicariously the symbolic control they could not practise materially.

The machines of colonial endeavour operate according to an implicit system in which space – with matter, nature, and the Cartesian 'res extensa' – is implicitly gendered feminine. Feminist theorists, most notably Julia Kristeva and Elizabeth Grosz, have pointed to the Greek (and particularly Platonic) notion of *chora* as a primary tool for understanding Western conceptions of space and time. Time – at least the time of heroic historical narratives – is implicitly masculine, while the female-gendered *chora* is matter, receptacle, space – associated with the womb and with nourishment. 'Neither something nor yet nothing,' Grosz writes, '*chora* is the condition for the genesis of the material world, the screen onto which is projected the image of the changeless Forms' – forms which, taken from the realm of abstraction and imposed upon matter, produce the physically perceptible, ordered universe (Grosz 1995: 115).

If the modern approach to space begins with mapping, its culmination might be in the white walls and clean lines of modernist architecture, which make visible the notion of space as a blank field for play. Planning and design, as Bloomer and Moore and others have argued, have been notorious in their failures to take into account the lived experiences, limitations and sheer quirkiness of bodies, the unexpected uses to which desiring subjects put their surroundings. Desire is a necessary element of our project not only because of its connection with bodies but because, in addressing the *utopian* organization of space, we assume the conjunction of space and desires for it. Accordingly the essays included in this collection define 'utopia' through the interface between bodies, desires, and material spaces, and address the specific ways bodies that are marked differently by gender, race, class, age, etc. may possibly (or impossibly) find an ideal relationship to their (cyber)spatialized, constructed surroundings.

The embodiedness left out of the abstract ambitions of architecture might be understood, with several of the essays in this collection, through Kristeva's theory of the 'abject'. Kristeva associates the abject with the maternal body, with the child's individuation accomplished by its rejection of material, viscous bodily sensations, substances – not-quite-objects – of revulsion. Because the subject's symbolic integrity is constantly threatened, he (specifically he) must constantly constitute himself by a continued rejection of the abject identified with other social entities.

Twentieth-century movements to 'restore order' – the City Beautiful movement, the purging of ornament from modernist architecture, the postwar ascendancy of the suburb and its restitution of patriarchy, and, most horrifyingly, the rise of National Socialism in Germany and its effects – demonstrate ways in which the 'purifying' response to personal abjection might play out in spatial as well as social organization on a grand scale. Judith Butler, while questioning Kristeva's developmental narrative (and providing a corrective to its potential essentialism), makes productive use of the concept of the abject by theorizing *zones of abjection*. These zones are symbolically occupied by bodies made unliveable by the enforced impossibility of acceding to viable positions of identity or agency. Actualizing her metaphor, we can consider the *physical* organization of zones of abjection that constitute large portions of Western cities.

In this view, boundary crossings of any kind would constitute both the eros and the danger of distinctions between zones. The bounded subject is reflected in spatial boundaries – rooms, buildings, neighbourhoods, cities, nations – as well as in textual ones. The separateness produced by boundaries not only *disables* certain types of intercorporeality but also *enables* the kinds of spatial representation Foucault refers to as heterotopias, 'effectively enacted utopias' which have the potential to comment on the larger social space in which they occur. Such spaces include the cemetery, the museum, the tourist colony.

Physical zones are read through psychological landscapes of comfort and danger, so that neighbourhoods experienced as the simple – if sometimes frustrating – everyday by their inhabitants are fetishized as unliveable by other populations. Such fantasies of danger normalize neglect and decay, justify the implementation of development plans without the input of neighbourhood residents and regulate bodies marked by race, gender, sexuality and disability, among other things. On the global scale, a corresponding eroticizing of the exotic makes the landscapes of Third World exploitation appear quaint and 'primitive' from the Western tourist perspective, whereas Western cities themselves, in all their luxury, serve as mass-mediated objects of desire in the global market.

Along with the forces of the market, the long history of twentieth-century traumas – colonialism and its aftershocks, world wars and genocide, the threat of nuclear annihilation – provides a backdrop for the urban utopias of the twentieth century, across states and regions. In this context, the transnational communist 'frugality' identified by May Joseph in her essay on Hanoi resonates with the self-disciplining imperatives of Le Corbusier and other projects of hygienic modernism. In the conference from which most of the essays in this volume were drawn, Katerina Ruedi addressed the reactive 'call to order' in Bauhaus architectural education under the early Nazi regime following an earlier period of play with gender norms; and Ellen Nerenberg demonstrated the fascist logics still at work in the spatial and ideological rebuilding of the family in postwar Italy. These authors analyzed the persistent seductions of order that promised to manage trauma, desire, and social and bodily energies.

Transnational space 'embodied' in physical movement, in the global fetishism of corporate signs, and most recently in the Internet, presents new challenges for twenty-first-century subjects. The original conference programme included not only Hazel Hahn's paper on exoticism and degeneration in French Indochina, but also a presentation on Indonesia by Abidin Kusno, now published in his (Architext) book, *Behind the Postcolonial: Architecture, Urban Space, and Political Cultures in Indonesia* (Kusno 2000). In the present volume we maintain a focus on Southeast Asia as (along with Europe and North America) a crucial site for the exploration of utopian urban thinking, with essays by Brian McGrath and May Joseph complementing Hahn's. The brand of 'utopianism' the three chapters survey in Thai and Vietnamese cities is profoundly inflected by European colonialism and latter-day US intervention, but also by the many populations, heterogeneous conquerors, and diverse religions that have influenced the region in its long history. In the long historical view suggested by the work of Andre Gunder Frank, one can read the modern ascension of the West as a kind of temporary parasite on Asian economic power and technological ascendancy. In this light, taking a more Asian-centric view, the exploitation of European colonialism appears as a short though brutal episode in a long history of Southeast Asian cultural appropriation and incorporation of other cultures (Frank 1998). The resulting diversity of practice can be characterized less as the passive-sounding 'syncretism' than as 'localization' (Mulder 1996). Thus the embodied practices of space in Bangkok, Saigon and Hanoi – like those of the Western cities surveyed in other essays – present models of agency that are both local and international.

SPACE AND THE MODERN METROPOLIS

In focusing largely on the 'modern metropolis', we acknowledge the significance of this unique form of social and spatial organization, dependent on material and demographic resources, on technologies of exploitation, communication, speculation, central and dispersed planning, exchange and migration. The metropolis is a place of desire, fear and revulsion, of cultural production and economic devastation, organized into political and commercial hierarchies, into sacred and secular, public and private, 'safe' and risky. It is a site of sensation, of a mingling of bodies and populations; it possesses havens from the crowd and facilitates abandoning the self within it. Suburbs dependent on cities define themselves against them. Colonialism reproduces the western city's forms in contested spaces layered with symbolic resonance, brutal histories, and current conflict. The flâneur and the scholar read its moments of self-representation, its excesses and interstices.

The collection consists of five sections, with two foundational essays that open and close the volume. The opening essay by Thomas Markus asks one of the central questions of the collection in his title, 'Is There a Built Form for Non-Patriarchal Utopias?' Through the architectural lens of form/function/space, he surveys a variety of historical utopias, whether actually built, coherently designed but not carried out, or imagined in fictional form. He finds qualities common to both patriarchal and non-patriarchal utopias, most specifically a disjunction between formal qualities and ideological and social effects, arguing that divisions of land such as the grid are neutral – like language, containing the possibility of oppressive or liberatory uses. He encourages us to think critically beyond prevailing formalist approaches to architecture and design, viewing form in a more complicated relationship with space and function, and with the intractability of bodies.

The essays in Part II, 'Civilization/Degeneration', reveal how utopian visions – of the city beautiful, the colonial paradise, the radiant city – depend upon the presence of dystopic elements. As these essays and others in this volume suggest, utopia by its very nature can often become repressive, authoritarian, losing sight of its ideals within complex networks of power and domination. In analyses of widely differing national contexts, essays by Margaret Farrar, Barbara Hooper and Hazel Hahn illustrate the 'strategic' side of utopian imagining.

Part III, 'At Home in Public', examines late nineteenth- and early twentieth-century concerns about the coding and gendering of social spaces, illuminating how individuals and entire communities occupy and find ways to use and appropriate spaces for the purposes of social change. Essays by Sharon Haar and Suzanne Spencer-Wood give us two perspectives on how American women reformers remade and redefined domestic space, as proponents and activists or as recipients of social improvement programmes. As Peg Birmingham's section introduction illustrates, both authors explore radical redefinitions of the dichotomy between public and private spheres, expanding conceptions of domestic space as private space – so that women might be 'at home in public' – and suggesting tactical responses to questions of women's place in urban life.

Part IV, 'Esprit de Corps and Esprit Décor', consists of two essays that explore the other side of the public/private divide in tracing utopian impulses to create protective spaces for women. Writing on two very different historical and cultural moments of the twentieth century, Despina Stratigakos and Kelly Quinn each suggest the importance of shelter in creating separate spheres for women, with particular attention to architectural and design choices made by the women who used and/or built these domestic enclaves. As each author also suggests, however, the investment in preserving female bodies can undermine the utopian promise of agentive embodiment, revealing the ways in which prescriptive efforts at imagining female community can express their ideological underpinnings.

Part V, 'Embodying Urban Design', addresses contemporary developments in urban and suburban planning, domestic architecture, and urban design. Essays by Andrew Wood and Brent Stringfellow give us architectural perspectives on the central role of images to 'new' and 'pan' urbanisms. They focus particularly on the relationship of community to technology and to capital, and the exclusions that operate in the production of private utopias and communitarian ideals. Brian McGrath's essay synthesizes trends in architectural urban practice in the recent past and presents the concept of 'simultopia' as a new model for conceiving contemporary urban design as a 'hybrid splicing and intertwining of suburban and urban, local and global, primitive and modern, signifying and embodied, faces and bodies'.

Part VI, 'Haunting the City', addresses the constitution and use of such hybrid, interstitial spaces. Essays by Christa Erickson, May Joseph and Elizabeth Wilson suggest the parallel between the user of virtual or indeterminate spaces and the flâneur or flâneuse of the nineteenth century, browsing through a landscape that was itself defined through the process of wandering or browsing. The question of the gender of this wanderer – and whether the flâneuse has truly come into her own at the dawn of the twenty-first century – is a vital one to ask when considering the relationship between gendered spaces and embodied utopias. Indeed, these essays suggest the importance of locating and producing new forms of communication that might keep pace with a new type of space and that might adequately represent this space to itself and to its users.

Elizabeth Grosz's 'The Time of Architecture' concludes the anthology by re-orienting the discussion of utopia, gender and architecture toward the question of time. Though most utopias make an implicit claim of projection toward an ideal future, temporality as a dimension often drops out of the usual conception of utopia as timeless, rational harmony. Utopias, thus, do not account well for the possibility of change over time. As a concluding moment of the anthology, Grosz's essay brings the concerns and approaches of earlier essays into sharper focus around the issue of temporality. She encourages us to view architectural utopias in relation to process, event, experience, the unexpected and unforeseeable, the momentary and fragmentary, the unprogrammed yet still possible.

CONCLUSION

What these essays work toward, then, is a new conception of the very nature of utopia. As several authors in this collection suggest, utopia as 'the good place that is no place', the ideal that does not, indeed cannot exist except in the imagination, can no longer be a tenable model for envisioning the world. As these contributors remind us, utopia may be always already dystopic in presenting a static and idealized vision that oppresses its inhabitants and stifles the possibility of social transformation. Studies presented here by Brent Stringfellow, Andrew Wood, Hazel Hahn, Margaret Farrar, and Barbara Hooper describe the utopic impulses of modernity, but they just as importantly convey the terrifying effects of such visions, revealing that utopia for some may be dystopia for others. The self-interested desires of America's particular brand of global capitalism produce the sprawling 'pan-urbanism' of Tysons Corner, Virginia, while self-protection against the chaotic and uncontrollable modernity of the outside world makes its presence known in the rhetoric of middle-class domesticity in the context of Disney's 'ideal town', Celebration. The utopian–dystopian imperative to produce ordered, regulated lives emerges in a number of these pieces: in the attempts to 'wipe the Washington alleys off the map', and thereby rid the city of their ungovernable populations; in the anxieties of French colonists about the effects of Indochina's climate and culture on an already 'weakened' national body; and in the abhorrence with which Le Corbusier treated those he considered racial and sexual 'others'. Therefore a prominent feature of this collection is the way in which these authors maintain a stringent awareness of dystopia as a constitutive element in historical instances of utopian imagining.

Yet the retention of the word 'utopia' in this collection suggests that many, if not all, of our contributors want to preserve some of the revelatory, and revolutionary, potential of this term. As Frederic Jameson reminds us, 'the question of Utopia would seem to be a crucial test of what is left of our capacity to imagine change' (Jameson 1991: xvi). Several of the essays we include here express the transformative potential of reform efforts whose utopian underpinnings may be unnamed, such as the various club and labour movements of the late nineteenth century that form the context for Sharon Haar and Suzanne Spencer-Wood's studies of American women's reform efforts which rendered women 'at home in public'; similarly, as Despina Stratigakos' analysis shows, related movements encouraged women's participation in the 'rebuilding' of Berlin following the First World War. This emphasis on the radical potential of transformative thought and action is reflected in Kelly Quinn's account of two shelters for homeless women in Washington, DC, which illustrates through a discussion of design and decoration, two stereotypically 'feminine' spheres, the ways in which utopian ideals can become, or can reveal themselves to be, static and conventional realities. Yet other essays, including those by Brian McGrath, Elizabeth Wilson, May Joseph, and Christa Erickson, express the transformative potential of 'indeterminate' and interstitial spaces: the streets of Hanoi and Bangkok, the back side of London's urban fabric, the virtual landscape of the Internet. While each of these contributors remains wary of the ways in which utopian theory and practice might be used to mask social inequalities and perpetuate the harmful effects of cultural discrimination, they also suggest the importance of *tactical* utopian imagining.

The essays in this collection suggest that the form of architectural space may signify differently in different cultural contexts, as, over the course of time, inhabitants find contingent, tactical, ways to make space their own. If the utopias of the early twentieth century now appear arrogant and dangerous, the current place of the utopian, if it has one at all, appears to be a matter of mobility, of wandering amongst, reappropriating and reinhabiting forgotten and interstitial spaces and non-places. A mobile and vigilant perspective seems all the more necessary in that boundary and form (architectural or otherwise) are available for appropriation either by the powerful or, from time to time, by the powerless.

Seen in this context, the concept of 'embodied' utopia that we take as the title for this volume allows us to identify the shifting, contingent and transformative aspects of utopianism. This is, in part, an effort to follow in the footsteps of some of our mentors at the University of Chicago, an effort to make feminism present in theory and in practice, in their words, 'to inhabit a space of concrete utopian imagining.'[3] One of the flaws in utopias both past and present has been their neglect to consider not just places/spaces but also the bodies, indeed the inhabitants and users, that constitute those spaces. The essays in this collection are therefore concerned with social and corporeal practice: following Michel de Certeau, contributors articulate the various ways in which space is 'a practised place', and therefore a product of the social, sexual, and gendered activities that take place within it. The concept of use or practice allows contributors to address the ways in which spaces are mutable, while at the same time reminding us of the vitality of mutability as a mode of imagining. For what, in the end, is an embodied utopia but the act of imagining an alternative to the constrictive and discriminatory spaces of the present, and then enacting that vision in all its materiality? Ultimately, the essays that follow suggest the importance of embodied utopian visions that attend to the specificities of historical and cultural difference, that recognize the magnitude of local and small-scale practices and their effects on the particulars of human experience. To our minds, the concept of embodied utopia offers not the tyranny of the totality but rather the radical possibility of the fragment, and suggests the importance of work left incomplete, unfinished – social transformation in the making.

NOTES

1   We thank Tom Markus for assisting us in framing this contradiction.

2   Along with these material resources, in Michel Foucault's account, disciplinary resources are developed for producing knowledge and, in the same moment, objects of that knowledge thereby made understandable and 'docile'.

3   Lauren Berlant takes this phrase from a collaborative memo written by herself and her colleagues Leora Auslander, Norma Field, Elizabeth Helsinger and Martha Ward, as a response to their frustration with pedagogical and institutional politics in a faculty working group at Chicago. For more on the risks and challenges of being utopian, or '68, in the present, see Berlant 1994: 124–33.

Part I

Chapter 1: Is There a Built Form for Non-Patriarchal Utopias?

Thomas A. Markus

SOME PRELIMINARY COMMENTS

Whether the word is understood as '*eu*-topia', 'the happy place', or as '*u*-topia', the 'non-place' – two meanings which are often conflated since the happy place exists nowhere – what is the point of utopia? Raymond Williams's definition of it as 'the education of desire' is useful: a way of exploring who we are and what we long for. By articulating 'the not yet' it helps us to act in the actual world, defining objectives, giving direction to struggle and resistance, setting a political agenda and opening the door to creative dialogue.

T.S. Eliot is much more sceptical; he sees it as an attempt to evade moral responsibility, to become invulnerable in a cradle of certainty:

> They constantly try to escape
> From the darkness outside and within
> By dreaming of systems so perfect that no one will need to be good.[1]

No definition can obscure utopia's double effect: oppressive, alienating elements coexist with liberating, humanizing ones. These visions are divided by the most fragile boundary from their inverse – dystopia, especially when they become blueprints for social or material action. Many utopian projects have crossed the boundary even when they were on paper. They required, or assumed the availability of, major resources of land, capital, materials, labour, military power or patronage. By definition these are controlled by those with economic and political power, and their projects are 'power over' rather than 'power to'. One is oppressive, one liberating. Historically such 'power over' has been men's, and it is therefore natural to call oppressive projects patriarchal. But not all utopian projects are like this. There have been hundreds of modest experiments, in which groups have struggled to build model societies and settlements. Sometimes these have been movements of resistance to political or military power, as in the case of the women's protest camps at Greenham Common in England, discussed below, where the driving force was opposition to nuclear weapons. Elsewhere, as in the *kibbutzim* of Israel, the Rappites and Zoarites of America, or The Woman's Commonwealth of Texas, they integrated various forms of religious belief (often resisting mainstream religious institutions), social reform (including critiques of the family and gender inequalities), and radical economic relations (based on the community of goods, and new modes of production). Yet in other instances the impetus was ecology – a counter-cultural movement which opposed nuclear energy, the waste created by urban economies and conspicuous consumption – which led to the setting up, worldwide, of countless small communes. Whilst these experiments are initially small, some eventually grow to be large in terms of size and the number of settlements. They may contain the same intricate mix of alienation and liberation as their grand cousins, but in these it is easier to find the seeds for educating desire. They are usually provisional fragments, either because their creators come from a position of resistance and cannot command major personal or institutional resources, or because their ideas inherently call for fragile solutions.

There are some key questions. If the asymmetrical power relation between men and women were not a historical fact *could* men have designed differently; and could they do so in a future where this asymmetry no longer holds? Indeed would there be such a thing as a 'male' or a 'female' utopia? Or is there something intrinsic to male utopias, whatever men's social or political position, and, equally, do women's utopias contain features which men could never create? Do patriarchal designs also have non-alienating and non-oppressive features? Are the less grand visions liberating and, if so, are they gendered? Do women's and feminist designs have alienating and oppressive features? To produce answers would involve going to the heart of the feminist debate about essentialism and difference, and a discussion of utopia might not be the most fruitful way of doing that. But a close look at utopian designs provides some pointers.

If it is the case that both men's and women's, patriarchal and feminist, utopias contain fragments of both liberation and oppression, and if some feminist utopias are a form of resistance to oppressive patriarchal ones, then a simple gender classification of utopias is not very useful. Rather it is more useful to look at the specific types of resistance. It can take three forms. First, theoretical, intellectual argument. Second, the creation of counter-propositions, alternative visions. And third, action, where built territory has been resisted or reclaimed. Women have played a prominent part in all three.

The critical framework set out here is constructed around some salient utopian features, within which a small sample – imagined, designed or built – can be discussed.

BODIES IN SPACE

The 'embodiment' in this book's title plays a dual role.

- First, embodiment suggests the materialization, in the concrete designs for buildings, towns and cities, of the abstract visions of utopian literature. These built forms structure space, and that space is intended for inhabitation by people.
- Second, following from the above, embodiment refers to the location of bodies – human and hence gendered bodies – in these utopian spaces.

So built forms and human bodies are both implicated. It is therefore impossible to think about designed or built utopias without thinking about bodies in space.

An inescapable property of human bodies, except those in cyberspace (an increasingly important 'non-place' discussed below), is that they have to be some*where*, in some real *space* which is articulated by material objects – built and natural *forms*. When people label and use space they inhabit it (that is what inhabitation means) – they give it *function*. A function is, then, inscribed into space by both language and use.

So the built objects have these three properties of form, space and function which are the key discourses of architecture.

All built space inevitably structures social relationships, by creating 'insides' and 'outsides', categories of 'inhabitants', 'visitors', and 'strangers', and it separates those with power from those who lack power. In other words all space is political. Just as utopian texts can educate political desire, so too utopian designs can educate design practice. To see how, we first need to understand how buildings carry meanings, in terms of these three discourses.

THE DISCOURSE AND DISCOURSES OF ARCHITECTURE

Whilst Louis Sullivan's *dictum* 'Form follows function'[2] is widely rejected, the fragmentation of architectural discourse is even more complete than that rejection implies. There are no inherent connections between form, function and space. To answer the question 'What does this building mean?', we need to find answers with respect to *all* its properties in a *common* discourse. The discourse which contains language, values and everything we do (i.e. social practice) is the discourse of social relations. It is there that we should expect to find answers to the questions about meaning. These relations are of two kinds. First, the structures of power – just or oppressive – which are enshrined in law and contracts, and enforced through sanctions or by coercion. Second, the structures of bonds – such as solidarity, friendship and love. All real human space produces and reproduces these two. As utopian vision is concerned with the creation of power relations that are just and rich bond relations, so its architecture (as indeed *any* architecture) can only be understood in terms of power and bonds.

When function, form and space are mapped into that common field of

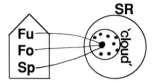

Fu = function
Fo = form
Sp = space

Figure 1.1
Function, form and space
converging to a point or
to a 'cloud' in the field of
social relations (SR).

social relations the meanings may be familiarly convergent, or divergent, in a shocking scatter of paradox and contradiction (Figure 1.1).

Form is the most familiar discourse. Almost everything said or written about architecture is about its forms: criticism and scholarship (drawing on conventional art-historical methods), practice, and debate in the media. Formal discourse is about *physiognomy*, or the *plan*. To analyse utopian designs we need evidence about style and plan. The surprise is that stylistically the *utopian* schemes most radical in function are often clothed in the most conventional forms, so that at first, or even second glance, their architecture proclaims nothing startling. Robert Owen's early nineteenth-century 'New Institution for the Formation of Character' at New Lanark in Scotland has the simple, classical features of a minor late-Georgian country house. Jean-Baptiste André Godin's 'Social Palace' or Familistère at Guise in France, based on Charles Fourier's ideas, for all its radical commitment to liberated relations in industrial production, an 'amorous code', and 'the extension of the privileges of women [as] the fundamental cause of all social progress', is clad in traditional brick with stepped gables. Sometimes this gap between content and form is reversed – radical forms and conservative content. In Archigram's *Walking City*, Soleri's ecological *Arcology* city for 170,000 inhabitants, or Stanley Tigerman's *Instant City*, all from the 1960s, the startling technological forms of vast pure geometries clothe the crudest of social programmes. Such gigantism is alive and well today – as in Mexico's 'symbol of utopia' used for Latin America's most extensive real estate project (Figure 1.2).

It is in film that forms have been most strikingly depicted – but mostly of urban *dystopia*. Fritz Lang's 1926 *Metropolis* was the first dark, monumental and dangerous city on film. Here the workers in the subterranean depths were represented as identical, black-suited automata in a city apparently inspired by Manhattan; this image summed up the widely-held early twentieth-century fear that cities were becoming dehumanizing. H.G. Wells's 1936 *Things to Come*, a cinematic version of Le Corbusier's *Radiant City*, offered a more idealized shining white city, mechanized and scientifically controlled. The dark city of Ridley Scott's 1982 *Blade Runner* – Los Angeles in the year 2019 – is a far cry from Le Corbusier and H. G. Wells. Teddy Jamieson (1999: 14) quotes from Scott Bukatman's critique:

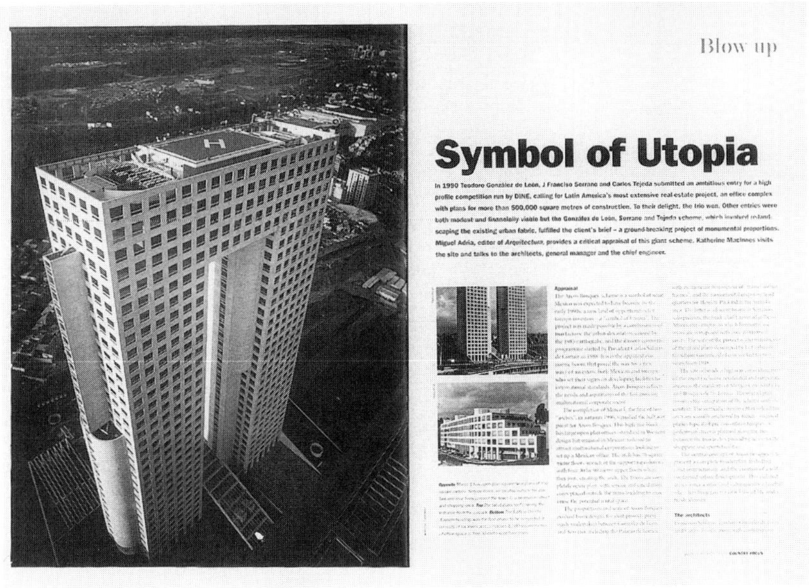

Blow up

Symbol of Utopia

In 1990 Teodoro González de León, J Franciso Serrano and Carlos Tejeda submitted an ambitious entry for a high profile competition run by DINE, calling for Latin America's most extensive real estate project, an office complex with plans for more than 500,000 square metres of construction. To their delight, the trio won. Other entries were both modest and financially viable but the González de León, Serrano and Tejeda scheme, which involved reland-scaping the existing urban fabric, fulfilled the client's brief – a ground-breaking project of monumental proportions. Miguel Adria, editor of *Arquitectura*, provides a critical appraisal of this giant scheme. Katherine MacInnes visits the site and talks to the architects, general manager and the chief engineer.

Figure 1.2
The Arcos Bosques high rise office block in Mexico, 'Latin America's most extensive real estate project . . . a new land of opportunities for foreign investors – a "symbol of Utopia" '. By permission of *World Architecture*, website: http://www.worldarchitecture.uk

> The polyglot architecture of *Blade Runner*'s future urbanism challenges the dream of a rational, centrally planned city. The city is dispersed, boundless, heterogeneous . . . the white cities of *Things to Come* and the 1893 World's Fair and the Futurama of the 1939 Fair have been replaced by a city of darkness, night, chaos and delirium.

Anton Furst's *Gotham City* tried to represent the Hell of Tim Burton's *Batman* (1989). *The Crow* (1994) and *Dark City* (1998) have continued these frightening images of dark, out-of-control cities.

Women designers have sometimes broken the mould, using innovative but unalienating forms for radical functional and production programmes. Alice Constance Austin's plan for *Llano del Rio* (1916) was to create a radical socialist feminist city for 10,000 people to resist domestic drudgery – 'the maiming or fatal, spiritual or intellectual oppression . . . [of] each feminine personality' (Hayden 1976: 301). Her kitchenless houses, organized around courtyards, were constructed using the latest technology. The forms grew out of function, and a concrete panel construction well in advance of avant-garde European industrialized building techniques. Nevertheless the geometry of her city *plan*, with its radiating avenues, circle of public buildings and centre-to-edge hierarchy of land use, is hard to distinguish from age-old totalizing utopian geometries.

Such forms, whether of built projects or of unbuilt proposals, and whether those of dominant conservatism or of radical avant-garde, are rooted in licit construction – sanctioned by law or sponsored by recognized institutions. But the forms of resistance, such as graffiti, or of illicit construction such as squatter housing made of unconventional materials, should also been seen as expressing a vision, a counter-utopia. The analysis of form always raises questions about agency: 'whose forms?', 'whose construction?'. The discourse of *space*, whilst a familiar everyday experience, is barely articulated in architectural texts. The spatial discourse has nothing to do with geometry, and everything with topology – with next-ness. Different spatial structures (syntaxes) create, make possible, or limit, entirely different social relations. A set of descriptive and analytical techniques for this space syntax have been developed by Bill Hillier and his colleagues at University College London.[3]

Using methods of spatial analysis one discovers that some building plans are deep, some shallow. Some have branching, tree-like structures, some have rings. These differences signify quite different relations between users, degrees of freedom in the choice of routes, opportunities for chance encounters, solidarities and possibilities for control and surveillance. In other words spatial maps also map social relations – though perhaps in unexpected ways.

Public buildings such as banks, churches or theatres have their 'inhabitants' (management, ministers of religion or directors) who control the building's programme, deep within space and 'visitors' (customers, congregations or audiences) in shallow space near the surface. They interface at the counter, communion rail or proscenium arch. It is argued that institutional buildings are reversed; the inhabitants near the surface and the visitors (hospital patients, prisoners or school children) deep. Instead of increasing depth signifying increasing power, in the reversed building the most controlled people are in the deepest space. This idea is fruitful for thinking about utopian space.

Not all social relations are embedded in specific local spaces. Hillier and Hanson (1984) propose that Emile Durkheim's organic solidarity is spatial, whilst his mechanical solidarity is trans-spatial (Durkheim 1964 [1893]). Thus members of a family, employees of an enterprise or users of a health centre, related to each other by differences in status, gender and work roles (= organic solidarity), produce their social relations in the local space of the home, the office, the factory or the clinic. Space becomes an instrument in the definition of family membership, white and blue collar workers, or medical staff and patients. On the other hand members of the same sex, profession, academic discipline, or trade union – with equivalent status and roles (= mechanical solidarity), produce their relationships only, or at least partly, *trans*-spatially. Journals, phones, correspondence or the Internet may be more important than spatial proximity. Space is profoundly implicated where differentiation of men's and women's roles and power is strong in organic solidarities. One way of overcoming oppressive social structures such as the strongly gendered roles embedded in local space, is by trans-spatial relationships, as in cyberspace. I will argue that that attempt creates its own paradoxes.

Finally, function. *Functional* discourse deals with questions about activities: where do they take place, when, who takes part, what behaviour is allowed, and who controls change? This programme is *described* and *prescribed* through natural language, and particularly by labels; so classification – a key social construct of language – plays a crucial role. *Prescriptive* texts such as briefs determine the most powerful features of buildings. Categories in such language constitute theories, social practices or social relations. When the language is gendered, space will be gendered.

By examining the text of a brief, where functions are prescribed through labels for activities and space, and these labels are then organized into a classification system, a great deal can be discovered about the underlying ideologies of sponsors or owners. For instance in the Burrell art gallery and museum in Glasgow, the 1970s competition brief set out a classification of art by categories of objects and spaces for their display. The winning designer complied with the brief's spatial, functional and display rules, as did all the 273 competitors, under the sanction of disqualification. This prescriptive text 'designed' the building before the competitors appeared on the scene. A diagram (Figure 1.3) on which each piece of text is represented by a rectangle proportional to its length, shows how certain topics are brief, surface issues and others are deep and elaborated; of the second kind is the schedule of accommodation, in which objects are classified by material (say ceramics or tapestry), date and place. This classification defines similarities and dissimilarities, according to a theory of art history, and hence prescribes the grouping of objects in space, and the adjacency of spaces. Also it is more elaborated for western than for non-western art.

To repeat: we are looking for meanings of form, space and function in the discourse of social relations. If they converge we are in the presence of the familiar, be it liberating or oppressive. If they diverge, the contradiction may be one of resistance or experiment, or simply the result of the more trivial pursuits of postmodernism and deconstruction.

This model challenges two related myths. First that of a coherent discourse of architecture. Secondly the equation 'architecture' equals 'art'. Both are ways of

Figure 1.3
Text structure of the Burrell Gallery Brief (1970).
(Reproduced in Thomas A. Markus (1993) *Buildings and Power: Freedom and Control in the Origin of Modern Building Types*, London: Routledge

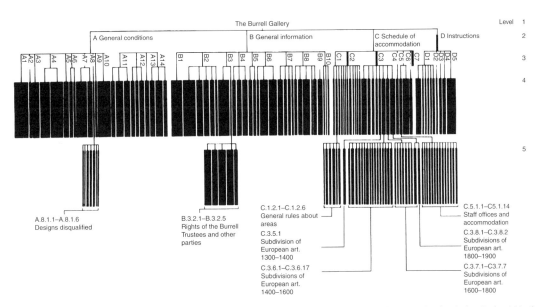

Text structure of the Burrell Gallery brief (1970). At levels 4 and 5 the length of the bars is uniform and their width is proportional to the length of each bit of text. Therefore the area of each rectangular block is a scale representation of the volume of text in the corresponding section. At levels 2 and 3 the text is merely a series of headings and subheadings with the exception of the four marked in thicker lines, which represent a small amount of text accompanying the heading or subheading. Only European Art is classified down to level 5; all other parts of the collection remain classified at level 4. This is the author's diagram, but is based on, and gratefully acknowledges, work by one of his students, Salman Othman, who in his Special Study Project "A Case Study of the Burrell Collection", 1985 (Department of Architecture and Building Science, University of Strathclyde, Glasgow) made the first attempt to analyse the Burrell Gallery brief.

denying the social meaning of architecture. According to the first, the three discourses are convergent, harmonious and internally contingent, whilst the second, the equation, eliminates two and thus any possibility of contradiction. The second is clear in language classifications such as library systems: Architecture is classified in Fine Arts, at Class NA, in the Library of Congress Catalogue, between Visual Arts (General) at N and Sculpture at NB. Fine Arts (N) itself is between Music (M) and Philology and Literature (P). The LCC was influenced by the Dewey Decimal System which has a similar conceptual structure: Architecture at 720, a division of the Fine Arts, 700, is squeezed between Landscape Gardening at 710 and Sculpture at 730. It is therefore unsurprising to find architecture with ballet and painting on arts pages and in media arts programmes. Professional journals, architecture schools, the scholarly literature and bookshops follow suit. Function, reduced by technical language to a 'neutral' issue and thus placed beyond contention, and spatial analysis, are both squeezed out. Building sponsors, by keeping these two discourses silent, are thus liberated to pursue their hidden covert social and political agendas.

When 'architecture' is construed identically by Britain's Prince Charles and tenants of deprived housing estates, across east and west, by women and men – spanning class, space, time and gender – we are indeed in the presence of myth. And when that myth governs the creation of utopian architecture then utopia betrays its critical potential. The task of a liberating vision is first to expose and then to shatter the two myths. Once fractured, meanings can be re-assembled to converge in liberating and unalienated relations embodied in a new architecture. This is the task of utopian architectural discourse.

THEMES FOR A CRITICAL FRAMEWORK

What are the salient features of a critical framework for questioning imagined, designed and built utopias and their inverse – dystopias? Since the boundary between them is invisible and shifting, this history stretches from Plato's Atlantis to Auschwitz. It might be added that few of the cases of utopia considered below have had egalitarian gender relations as their primary objective.

Order

The most striking feature is order. But order is not a simple concept. The order of the ubiquitous and timeless grid shows its complexity. It can be read in many ways. Its beginnings are there in the 9000 year old neolithic town plan of Çatal Huyuk in central Anatolia. The Roman *agrimensores* marked out grids for land ownership and the army for military camps. The grid was the basis of ancient Chinese, classical Greek and Roman, European medieval, and Renaissance cities, as it was for eighteenth-century Edinburgh, nineteenth-century Barcelona, and most American cities.

In land division, the grid is a neutral legal net within which rights of ownership and use are equally distributed. This democratic neutrality is lost by giving it a finite edge, by omitting some cells to form a forum or super-block, by cutting a diagonal route across it, or by differentially widening some streets. Then, as its spatial structure acquires variations in depth, and consequent differences in move-ment density and land values, it can become the instrument for hierarchical power.

The grid has been adapted to a host of ideologies. Plato's ideal cities com-bined the circle with a grid. The square boundary of the Etruscan town, with its four gates connected by the two main axes of the *cardo* and the *decumanus*, and the infill grid, are described by Rykwert (1976).

Reps (1965) has shown how American communitarians used the grid in their often tiny settlements. Le Corbusier's 1925 ideal *City for Three Million People* was gridded.[4] But so too was Leonard Cooke's (Austin's associate) in his plan for her *Llano del Rio* housing, as was Albert Kinsey Owen's in the Mexican city of *Topolobampo* for Marie Howland's late nineteenth-century American Fourierist project for woman and child-centred communities of Free Love (Hayden 1981).

The alternative order is Vitruvius's circle combined with a grid, to produce concentric and radiating space. The militarization of late medieval and Renais-sance visionary schemes, as in Filarete's Sforzinda, created fortified outer walls. In sixteenth-century Palmanova the centre is dominated by the prince's castle and public space. Roads converging onto a centre in star shapes give access *to* power as well as control *by* it as in the great royal and princely estates of Karlsruhe and Versailles. This model, combining defence, hierarchy and civic order, is the form of asymmetrical power *par excellence*, and yet Austin found it usable for *Llano*, deeply influenced as she was by Ebenezer Howard's *Garden City*[5] which had its centre and periphery, radial routes, and specialization of functional zones.

But order is not limited to the neutral grid or to hierarchical centric forms. It has driven *all* architectural creation. A longing for such order is deep within liber-ating utopian visions. In Charlotte Perkins Gilman's *Herland* (1979 [1915]), 'everything was beauty, *order*, perfect cleanness' (19). Marge Piercy's *Woman on the Edge of Time* (1979 [1976]) is struck by the harmony of an environment that, though having no regular, hard, forms, is an orderly balance of nature and culture, living organism and stone. People emerge from

> cornfields, the intensively cultivated gardens, from the fooder to brooder, from huts scattered among the gardens, from the free-form buildings they called just-grews . . . huts crawling with grape vines and roses . . . growth seemed to swarm over the land . . . the joined group of free-form buildings of sinuous curves suggesting a mass of eggs, but with long loops thrown off and high arches and arcades . . . the roof was studded with birdhouses and a pigeon coop built in, as if the masonry broke into lace through which pigeons went fluttering and cooing.
>
> (Piercy 1979 [1976]: 118–30)

Such deep desires can be fulfilled either by suppression in totalizing order, or in the risk-laden acceptance of disorderly freedom, but with very different con-sequences. Richard Sennett in *The Uses of Disorder: Personal Identity and City Life* (1971) drew on Erik Eriksson's psychoanalytic work to explain totalizing suppres-sion. In the adolescent transition from childhood security to adult complexity, we adhere to 'pure strategies' by immersion in powerful and simple schemes – of religion, politics or rock music – lest we disappear in the frightening new world of contradiction, conflict and paradox. Those who cling to this strategy in adulthood, massaging their social relations and their physical environment into a safe and rigid order, are the neurotics. Societies too can cling to pure strategies of fixed social and physical order where nothing unpredicted occurs, no chaos exists, where towns are zoned into single function areas, and traffic moves at predictable speed; these are symptoms of social neurosis. Sennett did not look for differences in men's and women's feelings for order. He might have concluded that fear of chaos and disorder is male anxiety about this difference, and that it is utopia which has taught planners and city *fathers* how to remain dangerously immature.

Urban and Rural

Space flows through both built forms and nature, so has the potential to fulfil the most ancient utopian dream – the harmonization of culture and nature, *urbs* and *rus*. Gilman's *Herland*'s town has not only beautiful, strong buildings – of dull, rose-coloured stone, clear white houses (which are the public buildings), and a fortress of 'great stones' – but these stand in green groves and gardens, like 'rambling palaces grouped among parks, and open squares, something as college buildings stand in their quiet greens' (19). More typically feminist utopias place the urban and the rural in gendered opposition; the degenerate modern city standing for patriarchal destruction. In Gilman's *With Her in Ourland* (1997 [1916]) the heroine compares the American cities, 'such childish experiments . . . poor, miserable, dirty, unhealthy things', with the noble ancient cities of Egypt and Assyria, and longingly recalls the cities of *Herland* where 'a city is the loveliest thing' (145).

Sally Gearheart, in *The Wanderground* (1985) is largely silent about the city; when it does appear it is equated with hard maleness, and though it is also home to the 'Gentles' – harmless men who never touch women – her warm, regenerative images are reserved for rural settings.

In *Woman on the Edge of Time*, the city is the site of all Connie's suffering and pain; and when she accidentally lands in a visionary dystopia, it is a hideous apartment block in New York City.

Language

Texts are pivotal in the making of order. They elaborate in language what appears in designs; sometimes designs are entirely without images, their forms and spaces being only described by text. There could be no utopian design invention without text, even if it is only inscriptions on drawings.

Furthermore, in executed schemes, language is the tool for managing 'perfect' order by behavioural rules. Sometimes these are of spatial exclusion and are even inscribed onto the built object – 'no entry', 'keep out', or 'private', or as rules defining inappropriate behaviour – 'silence', 'no smoking', or 'no food or drink'. Such proscriptions are always space-specific. The power to write, inscribe and enforce spatial rules, all linguistic practices, is one facet of coercive potential based on class, race, sex, age, or even species ('no pets'). Equally, linguistic graffiti, inscriptions of anti-rules, are forms of resistance.

Hierarchies of Gender and Class

Utopian hierarchies are often based on class and gender categories. The hierarchical spatial structure of Ebenezer Howard's *Garden City* has been mentioned. Hierarchy has been deeply formative in planners' thinking, and Hillier has shown that its inability to integrate local with global spatial structure is implicated in alienation, violent crime, ghettoization and other urban pathologies. In Plato's idealized Athens, as in Aristotle's *Politics*, priests, husbandmen, artisans and warriors are identified and segregated. Alberti (1988 [1485]) recommended that each class of people 'should have designed [for it] a different type of building'; whilst some were suitable for 'society as a whole' others were for its 'foremost citizens' and yet others only 'for common people'. Le Corbusier's *City for Three Million People* (1947 [1926]), though having the form of a grid, has a superimposed concentric social scheme, of centre, edge (or margin) and intermediate zones: 'princes of affairs, captains of industry and finance, political leaders, great scientists' to 'occupy the seat of power' at the centre, 'the workers whose lives are passed half in the centre and half in the [peripheral] garden cities' in the middle, and 'the great masses of workers who spend their lives between suburban factories and garden cities' at the edge (1947 [1926]: 100).

Gender hierarchies are constructed less directly – by exclusion from roles and spaces such as 'captains of industry'. Many utopias, feminist or not, have elaborate schemes for communal housework, cooking, eating, laundries and child rearing, but their ability to eliminate gendered work is limited. Robert Owen, in his battle against 'a Trinity of the most monstrous evils that could be combined to inflict mental and physical evil . . . Privilege or Individual Property, Religion and Marriage',[6] intended to release women from domestic drudgery by communal kitchens and dining rooms, but in his communities many did not use them. In Godin's Fourierist Guise, whilst men and women were equally represented in management, women were excluded from industrial production and their roles in the school, crèche, and shop were clearly, and conventionally, defined.

Socialist, communitarian ideas of domestic work were adopted by most feminist utopians. Gilman, in her 1899 *Women and Economics*, long antedating her 1915 *Herland*, is already exploring ideas of the professionalization of cooking, eating and cleaning, and rejects co-operative housework for women; nevertheless her alternative still uses women's labour. Piercy in *Woman on the Edge of Time*, though generally sceptical about technology, resolves the labour question by mechanizing chores like dish-washing and stuffing pillows.

But here is another paradox. On the one hand women are shackled by domestic drudgery to private domestic space. On the other hand the cleaning of houses, clothes and, especially, children's bodies, and food preparation, is seen by some feminists, even at the risk of essentialism, not as imprisoning, but as a unique nurturing contribution to life and health, indeed as a form of resistance to men's destructive public life.

Social hierarchy can be achieved by spatial structure. New Lanark was inevitably quite irregular in form because of the dramatic terrain of steep valley sides and the river; no possibility here of perfect geometries. But spatially there is an outer edge, a 'wall', of workers' housing, penetrated by a gate, intermediate zones of social facilities like the school, Institution and shop, and, spatially deep, the sacrosanct space of production itself – the mills. Given the freedom to plan a version on flat terrain, Owen, for his American *New Harmony*, then gave this same spatial structure an idealized form (Figure 1.4).

Claude-Nicolas Ledoux's idealized 1770s Royal Saltworks at Chaux has the same basic scheme: public buildings (shared by 'visitors' and 'inhabitants') are

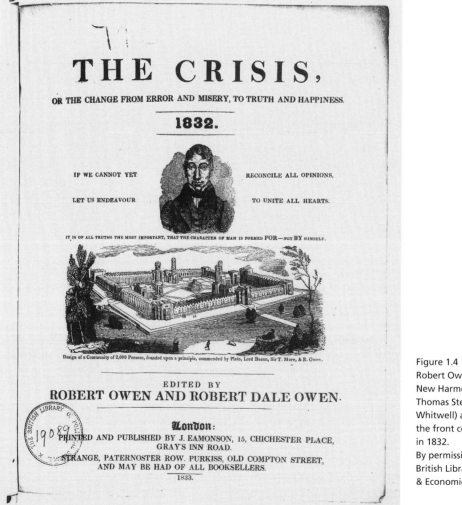

Figure 1.4
Robert Owen's design for New Harmony (architect Thomas Stedman Whitwell) as shown on the front cover of *Crisis* in 1832.
By permission of the British Library of Political & Economic Science

peripheral, in the shallowest space, then a ring of housing for the workers' famil-ies, with their outward radiating produce gardens, and finally, at the deepest level in the centre the two huge production buildings (for evaporating salt) radi-ating from the director's house which embeds a chapel at its core. This is not an 'inverted' institution; increasing depth represents an increase in both power and investment.

Axes

Axes, beyond threading together elements of a spatial hierarchy, have other roles too. The *cardo* and *decumanus* are reproduced in Titus Salt's nineteenth-century production town at Saltaire in Yorkshire. One axis is that of everyday social life – workers' canteen, almshouses, hospital, school and Institution. At right angles is the 'cosmic' axis of God and production – the church at one end, the mill entrance at the other. Their crossing is the 'navel of the earth', the intersection of earthly society and cosmos. From here the housing radiates in concentric 'ripples' of decreasing size, status, and rents; those of managers nearest the crossing, skilled workers further away and the unskilled at the edges, in the smallest houses.

Axes are always cosmic signifiers pointing to their referents – triumphal gates, palace entries, factory gates, churches or altars. One does not have to go to the North–South axis of Albert Speer's Berlin to see axes as power metaphors. In the ninth-century plan for an ideal monastery of St Gall, the axis runs from the entrance, between twin towers, through the basilica's double apse and two altars, between the novices and sick monks' cloisters, and finishes at their two altars in their, smaller, church. This axis links those with least power in the deepest space with the rest of the complex, and creates the spatial inversion typical of an institution.

Purity

Perfect cities need protection from pollution and disorder. Purifying canals, sophisticated sewage systems, and fresh air channels influenced Vitruvius's town plan, eighteenth-century hospitals and prisons, nineteenth-century workhouses and imaginary utopian islands. Baron Haussmann's great avenues meeting at star-like '*places*' in Paris, superimposed in 1853 on an older, disorderly street pattern in the name of rational sewerage, actually achieved, post-1848, total visual control, elimination of dark hiding places, and the facility for cavalry to charge and canons to fire free of obstacles.

Utopian writing envisages systems for dealing with crime and disorder and, since cities were models of the good society, they maintain order by filtering out disorder at the opening in the boundary – the gate. At Chaux the gate is sand-wiched between the prison and the guardhouse – institutions keeping disorder safely at the periphery. Nowadays the elaborate gate-keeping rituals are achieved remotely and electronically.

Mary Douglas (1966) sees the taboos surrounding body openings, which allow food, drink, body wastes or substances of sexual intercourse to pass inwards or outwards, as ritual devices to protect against category breakdown. Apertures in the body's otherwise continuous surface are liminal points at which the distinction between self and other becomes ambiguous and hence dangerous. Marge Piercy, in *Body of Glass* (*He, She and It*, 1991) has Shira wistfully comparing her own body to that of the gentle and beautiful robot Yod: 'Don't I seem rather gross to you, always putting stuff in or letting it out?' (325).

The gate, apart from being ritually elaborate, also announces the interior's ideological programme, whether it is the elaborately sculpted biblical narratives of a Romanesque church portal, or the '*Arbeit macht frei*' motto, which encapsulated the production ideal over the gates of Auschwitz.

Transparency and Visibility

At Guise, Godin applied Fourier's tenet of the desirable correspondence between the brain and the environment. Unless the environment reflected the brain, happiness was impossible; an idea drawing on the popular 'science' of phrenology (Figure 1.5). In his communal housing 'Familistères' the balconies looked down on to a communal court with a glass roof which admitted sun and light. These buildings attempted to reproduce the three zones supposed to reside at the front of the brain which respond to Light, Space and Fresh Air. Little did Godin know that nearly a century later Le Corbusier and his CIAM (International Congresses of Modern Architecture) colleagues would repeat this formula in their 1933 *Athens Charter* for modern architecture: 'The materials of town planning are: the sun, the space, the vegetation, steel, and concrete, in that precise order and hierarchy.'[7]

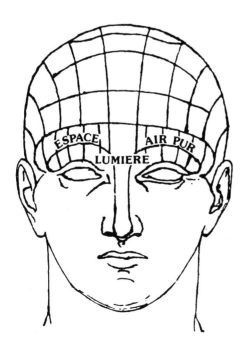

Figure 1.5
Godin's phrenological head.

The emphasis on light, visibility and exposure was but a late manifestation of the Enlightenment desire to reveal the secrets of dark unreason (not least in the self).

Visibility creates another paradox of utopia: control of the gaze is one mechanism for men's control of women, a denial of privacy. Traditional women's roles, exercised in the private space of the home, should give women freedom from control. But this is negated either by visibility, or by using the privacy of domestic space to free men to exercise physical power as violent domestic abuse.

Technology

Just as today's science fiction utopias rely on software technology in cyberspace, those of the past were equally committed to phantasies of technological hardware, especially of transport. William Morris's Thames 'force-barges' in his 1891 *News from Nowhere* were exceptions in being totally non-mechanical. Le Corbusier filled his city centres with aerodromes. The utopian vision of rapid, effortless movement, whose origin, destination and purpose are of no significance, has materialized today in the planners' huge, overriding urban motorways.

The forms of production technology – generators, overhead wires, furnaces and (smoke-free) chimneys – have been inspirational from Sant'Elia, the Futurists and Tony Garnier's idealized industrial city (Figure 1.6) in the early twentieth century, to the stainless steel 'intestinal' architecture of today's industry.

Women writers have favoured the software technology of science fiction, exploring its potential for liberation by the compression of space and time. There are two main genres. One is 'organic', based on an expanded brain capacity, with minimal technological intervention; Gearheart's women communicate thoughts and feelings directly, mind-to-mind, by techniques of 'shortstretch . . . [in a] stretchfield . . . in full retrosens' (= memory). The other, 'high-tech', model

Figure 1.6
Tony Garnier's *Cité
Industrielle.*

uses implants, scanners, and new forms of wave energy. Piercy (1991) owes much to Donna Haraway's 'cyborg consciousness', a common language for women in the integrated circuit', and 'machine dreams'.[8] Piercy not only rejects hard technology, but bodies, incarnation. Mind speaks to mind, the body becomes a mere carrier for infomatic devices, thus avoiding its mess and frailty – as well as its potential strength – it no longer communicates. Yet the created but not procreated, destructible bodies of Yod and the Golem carry a dual message: liberation may be in incorporeal cyberspace and yet it relies on fragile bodies.

The Internet and virtual reality (VR) have brought electronic relationships from science fiction into our real world. But empirical evidence is mounting that, for these to work, the experience and memory of bodies in material space is vital. Mark Draper (1995) has shown that the perception of a VR scene is significantly altered by the introduction of the observer's own body. In MUDs (Multi User Dungeons, or Dimensions) and MOO (MUD Object-Oriented) systems, the role of real space in understanding virtual space is becoming increasingly recognized. Harrison and Dourish (1996) have shown that for players interacting in spaces and places generated by the VR-based real time texts used in Computer-Supported Cooperative Work, the actual spaces they occupy, represent, or remember play a key role.

RECLAMATION

The third strategy for resisting patriarchal environments is reclamation by women of men's territory. The women's anarchist network *Mujeres Libres* in the Spanish Civil War (Ackelsberg 1984) had no visible physical presence. The groups were active in political and sex education, developed a comprehensive employment programme, and set up childcare facilities in neighbourhoods and factories. They continued to live in their original flats and met in any available space. However women's responsibility for child-rearing and domestic work remained unchallenged.

It was different at Greenham Common. This was a group of women's camps set up around the perimeter fence of the major British nuclear bomber base, located in Berkshire. Here the women organized opposition to the military base, and challenged patriarchal assumptions and practices. They built only tents and flimsy shelters. For obvious reasons, each camp was at one of the eight gates of the periphery: this was the land which they were able to claim, for it was impossible to camp within the boundary fence, and since the missiles entered and left the site through the gates, these were the effective points for protest. But they also had a metaphorical significance which relates to the earlier 'purity' discussion. Here is an inversion – dystopia is enclosed, within a boundary, and utopia, a potential realm of peace and love, lies outside. The gates were the liminal points, the dangerous thresholds celebrated and articulated by fragile little ideal communities. But the record shows that conflict, competitiveness and even violence, the roots of the militarism within, also existed in the gate-camps.

The utopian dream is always contaminated, whether by women or men; that liberating ideas and practices survive *in spite* of such contamination ultimately makes it possible to use educated desire in the chaos of the real world.

CAN WE USE UTOPIA?

It is easy to extract from conventional utopian projects alienating, totalizing, even totalitarian elements, and from counter-utopias liberating and humanizing ideas. It requires more skill to find liberation in the former and alienation in the latter. For instance, some feminist utopias have slipped into the same totalizing mode; Piercy's *Mattapoisett* achieved its harmony through a high degree of planning and structure, which she later repudiated in her *Body of Glass (He, She and It)* where she moves to a much less predictable, more fluid and heterogeneous society.

Nor is it difficult to show the destructive influence of utopia on modern architecture and town planning, or its relation to militarism, ecological exploitation and the dream of a perfectly functioning global capitalist economy.

The practical policies which can be extracted from experimental utopias are hardly radical, but nevertheless involve political struggle:

- respect for nature and renewable resources
- scepticism about technology
- spatial freedom, and integration of local with global space
- fragmentary rather than monolithic built forms
- weak functional programmes which allow freedom for spontaneous development
- human scale to towns and buildings
- freedom to choose between public and private space
- a range of living patterns and spaces, not exclusively those of the nuclear family and the individual dwelling
- the possibility of freely-chosen women's-only urban and domestic space
- re-thinking the role of gendered space.

Even to achieve this, politicians, planners and architects – professions dominated by men – would have to learn a painful lesson: that the search for a correspondence between orderly, totalizing visions, and orderly forms and space, is a hopeless dead end. It has had its day.

ONE FINAL IMAGE

To finish. In the mid-eighteenth century Piranesi produced sixteen *Carceri* etchings. They show dark underground scenes of great massivity, complexity and contradiction. The spatial order is subverted by an impossible perspective – staircases which lead nowhere, and bridges which could not connect the spaces on either side of the chasms they span. They anticipate Escher's impossible figures.

There are machines which could be for torture or for construction. There are figures which could be prisoners or their gaolers. In some etchings there is a glimpse of a world above which is light, orderly, rational and obeying the conventional rules of classical design. The *Carceri* are not prisons. As I read them, it is the *over*-ground which is the alienating prison, sitting on a subterranean domain of paradox and free, radical creativity. In the present context we might read the underground as the anti-utopia which is not dystopia, a powerful structureless spatial order of free relations.

NOTES

1   From Eliot, T.S. (1949 [1936]) 'Choruses from "The Rock"' in *Collected Poems, 1909–1935*, London: Faber and Faber, 170.
2   Sullivan drew this conclusion from his analysis of the way nature is expressed in art through structure and ornamentation – a view he articulated in 1924, a year before the end of his life, in *A system of architectural ornament according with a philosophy of Man's powers*, New York, Press of the American Institute of Architects, Inc.
3   The key major works are Hillier, B. and Hanson, J. (1984) *The Social Logic of Space*, Cambridge: Cambridge University Press; Hillier, B. (1996) *Space is the Machine*, Cambridge: Cambridge University Press.
4   The City for Three Million People was exhibited at the *Salon d'Automne*, Paris, in 1922; described in *Urbanisme* (1925), trans. as *The City of Tomorrow* (1947), London: The Architectural Press. Illustrations, a description and quotations from the text are given in Evenson, N. (1974) *Le Corbusier: The Machine and the Grand Design*, London: Studio Vista.
5   Ebenezer Howard's book was first published in 1898 as *Tomorrow: a Peaceful Path to Real Reform*. This was re-issued, with slight revisions, in 1902 under the title *Garden Cities of Tomorrow*. An edition was published by Faber and Faber, London, 1946, with a small paperback edition in 1965, reprinted in 1970.
6   Quoted in Bestor, A.E. (1950), from a speech by Robert Owen at New Harmony, 4 July 1826.
7   Details of the C.I.A.M *Athens Charter* (1933) can be found in *La Charte d'Athens*, Éditions Pion et Cie, 1943; reprinted [1959] Paris: Éditions de Minuit, *Statement of Urban Design Principles Based on the 1933 C.I.A.M Athens Charter*.
8   A list of books and papers by, and about, Donna Haraway appears on the website 'Hyperlink to Donna Haraway', available http://www.asahi-net.or.jp/~RF6T-TYFK/haraway.html.

Part II

Civilization/Degeneration

Desire and Repulsion in the Modern City

Lise Sanders

Modern cities embody a striking paradox: often seen as invigorating environments that facilitate cultural interaction among diverse populations, they also serve as sites of social anxiety and unrest, incorporating varied responses including desire, fear, fascination, and longing. As the essays in this section show, since the late nineteenth century the modern metropolis has been invested with the ability to represent utopian national and cultural visions, but just as frequently reveals the dystopic aspects of such visions. These three essays suggest that utopia and dystopia may not be as easily distinguished as might be imagined, indeed that utopia is in some ways constituted through its opposite. In so doing, they illuminate the complexities of the modern metropolis and help to transform our perception of urban utopias.

Margaret Farrar's essay, 'Making the City Beautiful: Aesthetic Reform and the (Dis)placement of Bodies', narrates the remaking of Washington, DC at the turn of the twentieth century, revealing the efforts on the part of the capital's urban planners to construct a utopian vision of the nation as representative of the body politic and, at the same time, to manage the members of that body who did not fit the utopian ideal by removing the spaces with which they were associated: the alleys which housed the city's poor, often disenfranchised inhabitants. The decision to commemorate Washington's centennial in 1900 with a monumental rebuilding of the city, Farrar argues, reveals the planners' desire to create a 'spatial and moral order' that would embody the ideal of American democracy. The Washington Mall in particular was perceived as 'a large-scale device for civic education, a built space that made visible the values and virtues of its citizens'; as such, it becomes a space that would make citizens through its monuments, erasing ambivalence and plurality and emphasizing a unified national identity. This erasure occurred through an effort to expose and thereby control the inhabitants of the 'unknown territory' in the center of the 'civilized' city. Yet as Farrar's argument makes clear, the attempt to bring the alley populations into public view did not result in increased monitoring of this population; rather, the alley-dwellers whose homes were condemned were simply presumed to have left the city or been invisibly lost within it. Farrar's argument here reveals the limitations of a Foucauldian approach to disciplinary power and instead suggests a new perspective on space and embodiment: using Julia Kristeva's work on abjection to illuminate the revulsion with which reformers viewed the alleys, Farrar argues that the bodies of Washington's alley-dwellers came to be seen as repulsive, feminized, materially different bodies that resisted incorporation into the ideal vision of Washington's representative population.

The usefulness of theories of abjection in investigating forms of symbolization that evolved around the same time is also evident in Barbara Hooper's essay, 'Urban Space, Modernity, and Masculinist Desire: The Utopian Longings of Le Corbusier'. Her contribution examines Le Corbusier's obsession with the sterility of modern space, critically analyzing his search for a form that would embody his valuation of mind over body and his desire to substitute the purity of 'regulating lines' for the twin symbols of modern degeneracy, the modern body (particularly the sexualized and racialized body) and the modern city. Influenced by contemporaries like Adolph Loos, whose 1908 essay 'Ornament and Crime' argued that modern life should be rid of ornamentation and its criminal and degenerate associations, Le Corbusier developed a theory of modernity as the erasure of social turmoil and cultural difference. Yet Le Corbusier's aggressive focus on the 'defective materiality' of the feminine, the primitive and the curve or horizontal line belies his celebration of the masculine, the modern and the straight or vertical; here again we see an effort to control the abject elements of the social body through an ordering of urban space. As Hooper's argument illustrates, the effect of Le Corbusier's writing is to paradoxically valorize the body through its negation, so that architectural visions of cleanliness and hygienic houses depend on a perception of urban modernity fundamentally characterized by its embodiment.

Similarly, Hazel Hahn addresses methods through which the modern metropolis may be reduced to its bodily associations, often with ambiguous effects. Hahn's essay, 'Dystopia in Utopia: Exoticism and Degeneration in Indochina, 1890–1940', examines the exoticism surrounding *Indochina* through travelogues, tourist publicity and fiction, as well as contemporary theories of criminality and degeneration. Hahn uses the picturesque genre to analyze the depiction of Indochina as an exotic and inviting landscape; Saigon in particular, gendered feminine in its nickname 'the Pearl of the Extreme Orient', embodied the utopian colonial vision through its newness and its modern layout and architecture, and like other modern cities (Paris, for example) its monumental aspects were celebrated in guidebooks. However, the exoticist lens through which Indochina was viewed does not simply result in an aestheticized view of the colonial metropolis as a stereotypically feminized space, a charming and exuberant tourist destination. Hahn's analysis of colonial Saigon as it appears in Claude Farrère's 1905 novel *Les Civilisés* reveals the dystopian image of the city as a site of sensual pleasure and moral degradation. Farrère's depiction of Saigon can be read in the context of late nineteenth- and early twentieth-century theories of criminal ethnology and eugenics, which argued that colonization resulted in cultural degeneracy, and used the figure of the métis, or mixed-blood, as an example of racial degeneration. Hahn's argument illuminates the presence of fantasies of social and sexual domination within French colonial visions of the modern city, and highlights their role in the construction of the colonizer as a pathological type, thereby suggesting the complexities of colonial power and its dystopic effects.

In addressing modern strategies of spatial and social control, and the fear, anger, repulsion and alienation that arise from these strategies, each of these authors emphasizes the aesthetics of visual spaces, in particular the sight of the gendered and sexualized body. Farrar discusses the ways in which socially subordinate bodies are simultaneously 'gathered in the full view of the public gaze', and yet remain invisible: in responding to the process of being made forcibly visible, Washington's alley-dwellers are absorbed back into the fabric of the city. Hooper's analysis of the rhetoric of urban hygiene in Le Corbusier and Hahn's discussion of colonial exoticism likewise depend on the drive to see, know and control a given population. The production of visibility – and the resistance to becoming visible – can here be understood as a normative strategy for manipulating populations whose identity is bound up in their bodies.

Taken as a whole, these three essays re-present modernity's continual pre-occupation with the role of the corporeal 'other', whether gendered, raced, or classed as such, in utopian visions of the modern metropolis. Each author articulates the ways in which urban planners in the late nineteenth and early twentieth centuries attempted to bring 'foreign' or 'alien' bodies under control, and also suggests the failures inherent in these attempts to manage the difference these bodies inevitably signified. In highlighting the failure of utopian designs for the modern city and emphasizing the presence of dystopia within utopia, these essays suggest the need, in Barbara Hooper's words, to 'abandon fantasies of mastery and control', and to turn instead to a new definition of utopia, one that recognizes the cultural flux and contingency that characterize the individual body and the body politic.

Chapter 2: Making the City Beautiful

Aesthetic Reform and the (Dis)placement of Bodies[1]

Margaret E. Farrar

> Look down on it in the early morning from the pinnacle of the Washington Monument. The geometric pattern of its streets stretches out in the early sun to a rim of blue water and green hills. From this peephole in the sky it looks like an architect's dream, a World's Fair model turned on by an electric switch, a study in shine and shade and movement, a fabulous and incongruous mixture of long, straight modern boulevards and classical pillared buildings out of Greece and Rome.
>
> (James Reston in the *New York Times Magazine* 1941)

> People bid their wise men. . . to remove and forever keep from view the ugly, the unsightly, and even the commonplace.
>
> (Daniel Burnham on the Senate Park Commission Plan 1902)

How does one build a utopian space? And once one has built this space, how does one then create the citizens who will populate the space as one wishes? After one has planned a perfect city, who then will be allowed to traverse its pristine streets, be qualified to pass its laws, who will litter its alleys, transmit its diseases, commit its crimes, fill its prisons? How does one control the irrepressible, unpredictable, living flesh of the bodies that will surely populate any utopian space?

Far from being mere philosophical abstractions (or impossible contradictions), these questions were at the heart of planning Washington, DC. From its inception almost exactly two centuries ago, Washington was intended to be a tangible symbol of the utopian possibilities for the nation and its urban centres. In addition to the endless technical questions implied in city planning and design, the makers of Washington continually asked themselves broader questions about bodies and cities: How does one build civic ideals – democracy, freedom, unity, and independence – into an urban landscape? And how does one acknowledge that real people (with imperfect, unpredictable bodies) will inhabit this landscape? That city space – no matter how perfectly designed – is always lived space?

In this essay I use the work of Michel Foucault and Julia Kristeva to show how the makers of Washington dealt with this problem utopia embodied, how they built the capital city of the US to reflect a certain kind of body, and how they sought to exclude imperfect, unpredictable, fleshy, faulty, *material* bodies from their corporeal topography.[2] While a Foucauldian description of disciplinary power shows us why alley-dwellers needed to be subjected increasingly to a normalizing medical and managerial gaze, it does not fully explain the policy makers' visceral reactions to alley-dwellers and their homes. Using Kristeva's idea of abjection, we can see how in both their aesthetic reforms (rebuilding the Washington Mall) and social reforms (improving Washington's alleys), Washington's planners wanted to eliminate imperfect bodies from city life and from what Lauren Berlant calls the 'national symbolic landscape' (Berlant 1995: 470). Seeking to organize the body politic around a corporeality that was white, bourgeois, and male, Washington's planners relied on this particular vision of the citizen body as a model for emulation, while at the same time literally building others out of the spaces of citizenship.

MONUMENTAL CHANGES: THE WASHINGTON MALL AND CITIZEN BODIES

When the members of the Senate Park Commission seized upon Washington's centennial in 1900 to rebuild the nation's capital, they already had some experience in building urban utopias. The array of urban design experts who planned the Washington we know today were the same men who were instrumental in designing the White City built for the World's Columbian Exhibition in Chicago ten years earlier,[3] and their plan for Washington bears the imprint of this earlier experiment in city-making. As Washington's centennial approached, a prominent Washington newspaper (*The Evening Star*) and a new national urban planning magazine (*Municipal Affairs*) both proposed that the nation's capital would be the perfect place to actualize the lessons from the White City (Gillette 1995: 90). Washington would be the site for the nation's first comprehensive city plan.

Washington was the ideal place for such an undertaking for two reasons. The first was wholly practical: until this time, Washington's development had lagged behind that of other North American cities. Despite almost universal endorsement for Piérre L'Enfant's original plan for the area, Washington remained a swamp-ridden and relatively small city for most of the nineteenth century. Perhaps the most significant reason for this is that L'Enfant's plan expressed a national unity and a national spirit that simply did not exist through most of the nineteenth century. Divided over issues of commerce and slavery, the states did not put much trust in a national government or much investment in a national capital. Due to Washington's slow growth, much of the area, especially around that of the Mall, was a tabula rasa for future planning efforts (Figure 2.1).

More importantly, implementing City Beautiful ideals in Washington would provide the city with a much-needed national identity. As Charles Moore argued in an article extolling the virtues of Washington beautification,

Figure 2.1
An aerial view of the
Washington Mall,
c. 1900.
Reproduced from the
Washingtoniana
Collection of the Library
of Congress, Washington,
DC

> Any improvements which Congress may undertake in the District of Columbia will be
> made not alone for the benefit of the comparatively few permanent residents, but for
> the much greater number of American citizens who have a just pride in seeing that the
> capital . . . is made worthy of the advancing power and taste of the people.
>
> (Moore 1902b: 751)

By financing Washington's reconstruction, Congress would be building a symbol
of newly expanded federal power in the wake of the Civil War. Moore emphasized that 'after a full century of misunderstandings, and conflict of interest . . .
we were now one people, with common purposes and aims, common ideals,
and a common destiny' (Moore 1929: 116). In their annual report issued that
year, the Washington Board of Trade made this connection between nation, city,
and citizen bodies explicit:

> The bloodshed of the Revolution created the Federal Union and the Capital. The
> bloodshed of the Civil War developed a nation and a national city. The bloodshed of the
> war with Spain washes out all traces of civil struggle, reunites the national elements, and
> expands and promotes the nation and the national city.
>
> (quoted in Gillette 1995: 90)

Yet, paradoxically, by the end of the nineteenth century, this national identity
was becoming increasingly difficult to define. New bodies – those of former
slaves, recent immigrants, and politically active women – were challenging its singularity. Anxiety over these other bodies manifested itself across the country in
compulsory civic education in classrooms, in the institution of more regular city
censuses, and in social reforms aimed at improving the health, housing, and
hygiene of recent immigrants. Washington was at the centre of these new urban
issues. After the Civil War, Washington became an important destination for
African–Americans: while blacks represented about one-quarter of the city's

population until 1850, they represented about one third of the total population by 1870. European immigrants were drawn to Washington as well; the white population in 1850 was around 40,000 but exceeded 100,000 in 1870 (Reps 1967: 53). Learning how to address the problems posed by these new populations was of paramount importance, because (as one reformer succinctly stated), 'Washington should be a model for the nation – not a warning' (Wood 1913: 46). At the start of what would later be called the American century, a rebuilt Washington would make visible and tangible the body of the republic. Beautifying the city would allow it to serve as a built expression of national identity, a body politic not only ideational but also material.

On 8 March 1901, Senator James McMillan, then Chairman of the Senate Committee on the District of Columbia, introduced a resolution authorizing the use of the Senate contingent fund to pay 'such experts as may be necessary for a proper consideration' of the 'development and improvement of the entire park system' of the nation's capital. McMillan's plan, revealed to Congress and the public on 15 January 1902, proposed sweeping changes – one might say monumental changes – to the centre of Washington, DC. Although it took more than a quarter of a century to complete, and certain aspects of the design were never realized, the plan radically altered the landscape of the capital for this (and the next) century.

The plan amplified the tenets of the City Beautiful movement that had been tested in the White City by seeking to impose a spatial and moral order on the chaos of urban life. At the same time, because Washington was not just 'any city', this was to be a spatial and moral order writ large: an ordering of no less than the body politic itself. The centrepiece of the new Washington was the plan to reconstruct the monumental space of the Washington Mall. In marked contrast to other sorts of urban park spaces popular at the time (New York's Central Park, for example), the plans for the Washington Mall were nothing less than majestic: formidable stone buildings and memorials, axial walkways, open plazas and sweeping green spaces, all of which worked in combination to reify the ideals of democracy (Figure 2.2).

In its most conspicuous function, the Mall was a large-scale device for civic education, a built space that made visible the values and virtues required of its citizens. Like the art of the City Beautiful movement generally, the public art planned for the centre of Washington was nationalist art, where a person could encounter his heroes[4] in the sculptures and statues that populated parks and plazas. A strong and vibrant political culture, it was postulated, would inspire a vibrant public art where 'the state, government, the ideals of parties, are no longer abstractions, but are concrete things to be loved or hated, worked for, and done visible homage to' (Robinson 1970 [1903]: 12).[5] In this way, the personal sentiments associated with nationalism and citizenship could be given public and collective form (Berlant 1991: 3). Moreover, the civic lessons built into the Mall were lessons that everyone could read, regardless of his or her ethnic background or level of education. As George Kriehn argued, 'Monuments teach

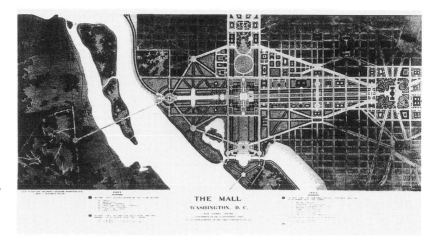

Figure 2.2
The McMillan Plan for
the Washington Mall.
Reproduced from the
Washingtoniana
Collection of the Library
of Congress, Washington,
DC

glory more eloquently than any books', because 'nothing would be a more effective agent in making good citizens of our foreign population than such monuments. Many of them cannot read English books, but they can read monuments which appeal to the eye' (Kriehn 1899: 599–600).

Washington's monumental space, like all monumental space, was not only meant to be looked at but also to be lived. Monuments are not built as inert objects but as effective agents; they are not just symbols to be read by passive readers or spectators, but give form and substance to public memory and provide guides for future action. 'It becomes part of the education of a people', wrote one commentator, 'to have the great events of our history put before them in enduring and beautiful forms, so that ''he who runs must read'' ' (Bush-Brown 1899: 602). Monuments are meant to *make* citizens out of an otherwise heterogeneous, unmanageable population. The monumental space of the Mall was intended to offer every member of the society an image of that membership, a mirror of what it means to be a citizen (Lefebvre 1991: 220).

At one level, this simply means that the stone likenesses of our heroes that occupy the Washington Mall, from the imposing figure of Lincoln to the symbols of American progress that adorn the walls of the Capitol, all reflect – not surprisingly – the bodies of the dominant citizen class in the country: white, bourgeois men. This in itself might not be particularly problematic because as the nation evolves, as more rights are extended to different populations, as the dominant class becomes more diversified (one might argue), the images of important others – whose bodies do not conform to the idealized image of citizenship – should be incorporated into the national hagiography.

The more problematic interpretation, however, is what monumental space itself accomplishes vis-à-vis reinforcing a particular image of citizenship. The images of citizenship that monuments offer us are ossified images that fix the citizen-body and national identity in space and time. Monumental space – at least the City Beautiful variant endorsed by the Park Commission Plan[6] – reflects certitude and finality and disallows for the ambiguity of national space. Monuments 'make space incontestable, both by closing off alternative readings and by drawing people into the presumption that the values they represent are shared' (Pile 1996: 212–13). Monumental space literally writes identity and history into stone; as seemingly timeless and quasi-religious shrines to the nation, monuments erase the ambivalence of history and the plurality of identity. At this second level, then, monumental space in general and the space of the Washington Mall in particular often communicate the importance of a singular, indivisible national identity, and the necessity of producing and policing the nation's symbolic unity.

As Kathleen Jones argues, in the Western political tradition, the signs of (national) authority 'imply a specific corporeality' (Jones 1993: 75), where certain (male, white) bodies are marked as leaders, patriots, professionals, soldiers, and citizens while rendering others invisible, extraneous, or deficient. The production of the symbolic unity of the Washington Mall was in this sense a gendered and raced production; the work of city beautification – monument-building and landscaping – was also the work of gendering and racing the body politic. As its advocates were eager to point out, 'there is nothing effeminate and sentimental about it, like tying tidies on telegraph poles and putting doilies on the crosswalks'; rather, it 'is vigorous, virile, sane' (Robinson 1970 [1903]: 28). In other words, the masculine endeavour of arranging and beautifying public space ('landscape architecture') had to be kept distinct from the traditionally feminine tasks of arranging and beautifying private space ('housekeeping').

In short, making the city beautiful in the case of Washington was an exercise in making the body beautiful: isolating and reifying the virtues associated with the proper citizen body so as to communicate a univocal representation of the body politic. In a very explicit sense – from the 'great white shaft of the Washington Monument . . . to the Capitol itself' (*Century,* 1902: 793) – the Mall was designed to be an expression of spectacular and masculine power, conferring upon the nation an appropriately authoritative symbolic landscape. The symbolic unity of the body politic as exemplified in the Washington Mall was achieved in part through subordinating, repressing, or expelling elements of the citizen-body that threatened to overflow, subvert, divide or undo it. The plan advanced by the Senate Park Commission aimed to materialize and spatialize a symbolic national unity, and to make eminently visible the contours of a proper citizen body.

'PLAGUE SPOTS': ALLEY DWELLINGS AND REPULSIVE BODIES

The idealized citizen body expressed in the space of the Washington Mall found its antithesis in the bodies of the urban poor who populated the Washington alleys at the turn of the century. Although they are frequently treated as distinct (and often opposed) reform impulses in the history of Washington city planning,[7] in many ways, alley and tenement reform paralleled city beautification and mirrored its logic. Despite their often altruistic attempts at improving the living conditions of the alley dwelling population, alley and tenement reformers also had as their goal a city made beautiful by establishing and policing the parameters of a proper citizen body.

The space of the Mall as conceived in the McMillan plan – an open, public space of vistas and vision – could not be more different from the rest of the District. Washington's tall, narrow rowhouses, built side-by-side around city blocks, enclosed alleyways and courts that were often invisible from main roads. While these small back streets were not originally designed for housing purposes, increases in Washington's population, especially after the Civil War, provided ample opportunities for landowners to build inexpensive, often substandard dwellings at the backs of streetside residences to house poor tenants (Borchert 1980: 17). Consequently, these less-than-utopian civic spaces housed a population that did not conform to the City Beautiful's idealized forms; alley-dwellers were (for the most part) black, were often disabled, sometimes sickly and/or elderly, and included many single women raising children. In the 1880s, alley dwelling reached its peak. The alley population was estimated to be nearly 20 percent of the city's total population, and the welfare of alley residents became an important issue in social reform (Figure 2.3).

The alleys posed a problem for the city for many reasons. The most straightforward of these was that Washington's alleys housed the very poorest of the city's poor. The rates of illness and mortality in the alleys far surpassed the rates of disease and death for those residing on the main streets. Beginning in the last quarter of the nineteenth century, a number of studies focused public and political attention on the prevalence of disease and poverty in these areas and called for substantive improvements in the quality of life of the alley residents.[8] Distress over overcrowding, inadequate or nonexistent sanitation,

Figure 2.3
An alley in Southwest Washington, DC, c. 1937. Reproduced from the FSA-OWI Collection of the Library of Congress, Washington, DC

prevalent sickness, and the dearth of pure air pervade these early studies, which describe the deplorable alley conditions in great (and greatly repetitive) detail. In a typical account, an 1874 Report of the Board of Health notes that alley homes often '[had] leaky roofs, broken and filthy ceilings, dilapidated floors, [were] overcrowded, below grade, having stagnant water underneath, no drainage, no pure water supply . . . having filthy yards, dilapidated, filthy privy and leaky privy box[es] . . . [and were] unfit for human habitation' (quoted in Sternberg 1908: 12). In contrast to the sweeping, grandiose language of the McMillan Plan (that of history, heroes, and idealized citizens), the building and health reports of fin-de-siècle Washington catalogued the mundane imperfections of people's daily lives (crowded rooms and leaky privy boxes), and subverted the utopian fantasy of a city made beautiful.

A variety of legislative initiatives at the turn of the century sought to bring the alley problem under control. In 1892, Congress passed legislation prohibiting the future construction of dwellings in Washington's alleys. Ten years later, at the same time he chaired the Senate Park Commission, Senator McMillan helped the Senate Committee on the District of Columbia to create the Board for the Condemnation of Insanitary Buildings, permitting the city to destroy alley dwellings that did not meet contemporary standards of sanitation or structural safety.[9] The result of these initiatives was a significant decrease in the alley dwelling population by 1910. No new dwellings were built in alleys after 1892, and several hundred of the houses, shacks, and huts in these alleys and courts were demolished under the direction of the Board. The number of inhabited alleys shrank, and the alley population was approximately halved.[10] What dwellings remained were, according to the Washington Board of Commissioners, structurally safe, not in themselves unsanitary, and had no reason to be shut down under the red-light district laws of the time (US House 1914: 13, 27). 'We have accomplished all we can accomplish under the existing law', Commissioner Siddons concluded (US House 1914: 18).

Yet the alleys continued to vex reformers. It was not enough that the alleys be relatively safe, or clean, or healthy. Furthermore, the alleys posed no particular threat to the city in terms of crime rates. The records that were available suggested that 'while it is true that there is a certain proportion of the vicious and criminal element in the alleys, it is not a large proportion numerically' (US Senate 1914: 24). Thus by 1914, there were 'a great many houses on alleys that are in pretty good condition and could not possibly be considered a nuisance' (US House 1914: 17). Nonetheless, legislators and social reformers unequivocally contended that

> we should aim to *put an end* to the living of human beings in the alleys and courts of the National Capital. Even where you may find a house that is sanitary in and of itself, we still stand and urge . . . that legislation ought to be enacted by Congress that will forbid, in some reasonable way, the further habitation of the alleys.
>
> (US House 1914: 5–6, emphasis added)

To accomplish this, Congress proposed in the Act of 1914 that the alleys should be declared unfit as places of human habitation (Ratigan 1946: 16). Beginning on 1 July 1918, using any alley building as a place of residence would be considered unlawful (Ratigan 1946: 16), effectively emptying the alley spaces and rendering approximately 12,000 people homeless (US House 1914: 8). While previous legislative and reform activity had focused on broadly defined concerns for sanitation and public health, by 1914 alley dwelling *itself* was the problem; regardless of one's specific circumstances, living in the alleys, the Board of Commissioners argued, was 'always productive of evil conditions' (US Senate 1914: 6). And as influential reformer Charles Weller concluded, this fact necessitated only one outcome: 'alleys are evil[;]. . .their conversion into wholesome streets is quite essential to the common weal' (Weller 1909: 177).

What was it about alleys, specifically, that was 'evil'? (For that matter, what about the main streets was 'wholesome'?) What about alley dwelling made reformers want not simply to improve alley conditions, but (as the magazine *Charities* put it) 'to wipe Washington alleys off the map' (*Charities* 1905: 960), to obliterate them totally from the space of the city?

One plausible interpretation of this excessive response might be found if we examine more closely the connection between visibility and social control.[11] Washington's alleys were a social and political problem because they exemplified the invisibility and anonymity made possible by urban life. Quite simply, Washington alleys and their residents were hidden from the street. Called Washington's 'neglected neighbours' (Weller 1909) or its 'secret city' (Green 1967), the alleys were threatening in part because they were unknown territory in the very centre of (what was supposed to be) civilization. As one housing reformer stated, 'The Washington alley is peculiar, as it is in very many cases hidden from the view of the street, thus giving absolute seclusion to a class of people who are least likely to resist temptation' (US Senate 1914: 22). The horrible conditions of alleys, reformers reasoned, were perpetuated because alley-dwellers could not see the outside world, and were not integrated into life beyond the alleys. 'They have not bearing upon them the restraining influences of the daily observation of their better neighbours. They have no one to inspire them with any better ambition', one reformer argued (US Senate 1914: 19). The problems of the alleys, another continued, could not be solved by keeping these people 'out of sight' (US Senate 1914: 22). Instead, they needed to be 'gathered in the full view of the public gaze' (US Senate 1914: 19).

But bringing the alley population into public view was no easy feat. At the turn of the century, alleys were unmapped and, in many ways, unmappable sectors of the city. First, the definition of an alley itself was problematic. In more than one instance, public officials proposing legislation affecting the alleys could not articulate any standard definition of the term. Housing reformers and census takers often included small streets in their definitions of alleys (Borchert 1980: 18). Alleys were also called courts, or cul-de-sacs, making any strict accounting of them impossible. Furthermore, alley names were unusual and were changed frequently, even capriciously. They were often named by the census-takers, the current residents, or according to the landowner of the block at the time (Borchert 1980: 27; Ratigan 1946: 10). The invisibility of alleys, their illogical names and ambiguous status, disturbed both social reformers and the city police, who had no way to monitor or control alley residents. In short, alleys posed a problem because their inhabitants eluded the gaze of social reformers and of the state.

The invisibility or impenetrability of the Washington alleys allowed alley-dwellers to defy the constraints of what Michel Foucault describes as disciplinary power. Disciplinary power is visually and therefore spatially organized; according to Foucault, the principle of Bentham's Panopticon[12] – that is, the normalizing gaze that combines visibility, record-keeping, and social control – is built into most of our modern institutions, including that of the state. Panopticism 'is a type of location of bodies in space, of distribution in relation to one another, of hierarchical organization, of disposition of centres and channels of power' (Foucault 1979: 205). Modern disciplinary power distributes different populations into schools, prisons, factories, and hospitals, institutions which in turn organize individual subjects by placing them into rows, classes, cell blocks, cubicles, wards, and onto spreadsheets, all of which promote increased visibility and enhanced methods of subjugation. Through observation and classification, people are marked, divided, and distributed in space. Disciplinary power thus 'objectifies those on whom it is applied, to form a body of knowledge about these individuals' (Foucault 1979: 220). Bodies, individually and in the aggregate, are made into students, prisoners, patients, workers – particular kinds of bodies that can be trained into service and habitualized into domination. When disciplinary power is effective, deviant bodies are either normalized (brought up to the standard through corrective training) or they are institutionalized.

Using a Foucauldian perspective, we might argue that reformers' concern for the alley-dwellers was based not only on their lack of modern plumbing facilities, which are elaborately described in so many of these reports, but also on the fact that the Washington alleys baffled the technologies of disciplinary power. The deviant bodies of the urban poor had to be brought under control, and the labyrinthian quality of alley space impeded this process. Instead of spatially and demographically distinct individuals, reformers saw in the alleys anarchic sectors of the city that housed a chaotic, unspecifiable populace, made unmanageable and ungovernable through its invisibility. For this reason, we might postulate, it was imperative that alley residents be made visible, brought out into the space of the main streets and under the full view of the public gaze.

The main difficulty with this Foucauldian interpretation is that it does not explain what happened to alley residents *after* they left the space of the alleys. From 1892 to 1914, approximately 14,000 people moved away from the alleys when their homes were declared unsanitary or structurally unsafe by the Board (US House 1914: 22). A Foucauldian interpretation would imply that these heretofore invisible bodies, now 'gathered under the full view of the public gaze', would be subject to increased monitoring, regulation, or segregation. But, in fact, Washington policy makers and most social reformers at the time were not at all concerned with what happened to the majority of alley-dwellers once they moved out of the alleys. There was little or no attempt to treat or quarantine the sick, house the mad, or send unwed mothers to charitable homes. The people whose homes had been condemned during the previous two decades were not tracked in any way; they were assumed to have either moved out to the suburbs or to have been 'absorbed' by the city (US House 1914: 22). Washington's poor, invisible in the alleys, remained invisible once they left.

Let us return, then, to the question of why it was necessary for reformers not to improve alley conditions, but to 'wipe Washington alleys off the map'. What about the alleys produced these excessive, unreasonable responses? What about the alleys evoked not reform but revulsion? 'Revulsion' is an important concept because it indicates that the policy makers' responses occurred at something other than the level of discursive reason, lengthy reports on health and building conditions notwithstanding. Indeed, this discourse of health and disease very often and very quickly segued from the alley residents' degenerative *physical* conditions and dilapidated surroundings to their degenerative *moral* conditions:

> Our experience in dealing with filth, crowd-poison and disease among these people . . . has taught us that the greatest public economy, viz., the preservation of public health, is defeated by allowing these filthy, worthless, dependent classes of humanity to congregate in the alleys and by-ways out of sight . . . until direful epidemic, incubated and nourished among them, spreads its black wings over the homes of the whole city.
>
> (quoted in Sternberg 1908: 13)

Thus while public discourse about alleys focused explicitly on overcrowding, sanitation, and disease (conditions threatening to the physical body), reformers were quick to associate these problems with the social body, emphasizing that the alleys were 'plague spots', 'physical and moral swamps' that bred both malaria and its ethical equivalents (Weller 1909: 234). Rather than specific concerns for public health or criminality, then, it was the very bodies of the alley population that posed problems for social reformers, because 'such ill-conditioned hovels are culture beds of disease, the germs of which may be carried far and wide by the flies which feed on the rotting garbage and excreta' (quoted in Sternberg 1908: 14).

These are not descriptions based on a normalizing gaze, masked in the neutrality of scientific reason and progress. Instead, these reports appeal to reactions more visceral than visual – reactions to filth, disease, waste, contagion, and infection – fearful, disgusted reactions to smell and taste and touch. While alley dwellings, especially in the detailed health reports of the 1870s, were certainly subject to intrusive inspection, this was an inspection that produced aversion, repulsion, and avoidance rather than the need for medical or political intervention. Alley-dwellers were not to be treated, or assisted, or cured, but *expelled*; their homes were not to be improved but *destroyed*. Reports like these did not only trigger rational/cognitive responses but also physiological/affective ones.

These responses occur below the level of discursive consciousness, in what Iris Marion Young refers to as the subject's sense of ontological integrity (Young 1990: 131); that is, the constant negotiation that occurs between our selves and bodies that are markedly, materially different from our own. Often these negotiations are unsophisticated, unreflective, and unconscious; they seem 'automatic', and attempts to explain them may amount to nothing more than *ex post facto* rationalizations. Some of the most fundamental challenges to our ontological integrity can be understood through the category that Julia Kristeva calls the 'abject'. At the level of the individual body, the abject is material expelled by the body – mucus, bile, vomit, pus, and excrement – while at the same time being a part of it. What is abject draws us in and repulses us all at once; we experience both curiosity and horror at the once-self or almost-self as it serves to remind us of what is bodily, irrational, and animal about us. The abject is, above all, a precarious *spatial* relationship that establishes 'the place where I am not and which permits me to be' (Kristeva 1982: 3). In its proximity to the border of the self, the abject unsettles the self's sense of order; it 'draws [us] toward the place where meaning collapses' (Kristeva 1982: 2).

Utilizing the anthropological work of Mary Douglas, Kristeva contends that abjection also plays out on the level of the social body. The body, Douglas argues 'is a model which can stand for any bounded system. Its boundaries can represent any boundaries which are threatened or precarious' (Douglas 1966: 115). One of the most important ways a social body, like an individual body, gives itself a fragile order is through its ideas of pollution, dirt, contamination, and purity. These ideas codify ambiguous boundaries and reify indeterminate identities into manageable differences:

> Ideas about separating, purifying, demarcating and punishing transgressions have as their main function to impose system on an inherently untidy experience. It is only by exaggerating the difference between within and without, above and below, male and female, with and against, that a semblance of order is created.
>
> (Douglas 1966: 4)

What is considered civilized in a culture – what is appropriate, respectable, and good – is therefore legally, morally, and spatially set apart from that which is considered uncivilized, inhuman, or evil. The space of the social body is marked and guarded against the space of the abject through taboos, rules, laws, and mores. Both personal bodily habits and entire social systems are organized around keeping the abject in its place; that is, away from the space of the self.

The socio-spatial relationship between the self and the abject is also often a gendered relationship. Frequently pollution ideas are meant to mirror and exaggerate ideas about the society's sexual order (Douglas 1966: 3–4); basic material differences are culturally coded, spatially marked, and converted into systems of domination. What is considered a respectable and healthy body – a contained,

controlled body, readily separable from its animal functions – is most often identified in European cultures as a white, male body. Conversely, what is considered
'repulsive' by a culture – what is most closely associated with sexuality, animality,
fluidity, corporeality – is most often equated with women, or femininity.
Women's bodies have been constructed (as Elizabeth Grosz argues) 'not only as
a lack or absence but with much more complexity, as a leaking, uncontrollable,
seeping liquid; as formless flow; as viscosity, entrapping, secreting; as lacking not
so much or simply the phallus but self-containment' (Grosz 1994: 203). Women
of colour, being doubly marked, are accordingly regarded by the dominant
culture as more sexual, more animalistic, more bodily than even white women.

This feminization of the alley population is pervasive throughout reformers'
reports. They were struck by the extent to which, in the words of one reformer,

> woman sometimes becomes the more important member of the family. An inquirer at
> number 27 asks, 'Does Laura Keefe live here?' Her husband Henry is less important.
> Alley folks usually speak of the 'lady who has the room upstairs', ignoring her male
> companion. They refer to Alice Weaver's house instead of Henry Weaver's.
>
> (Weller 1909: 28)

The reason for this was often economic, because 'in many poor families of all
descriptions the woman . . . becomes the more certain wage earner' (Weller
1909: 28). In fact, alley-dwellers were not as isolated from the main streets as
many reformers initially indicate; rather, the primary links to life outside the alleys
were the various services alley women performed to earn money for their families. Alley women frequently took in washing, provided childcare, and worked as
servants for the more prosperous families who lived in streetside dwellings
(Borchert 1980: 113). In one of the 'hidden' alleys, 'the towels of the Senate bar-
bershop were found to be regularly washed and dried. . . . [The Senators] employ
servants who return nightly to these unwashed hovels. Their nurse girls take the
babies for occasional visits to the alley homes' (Weller 1909: 73).

Reformers regarded the feminization of the household as particularly
pathological. In her house-to-house study of four Washington alleys over the
course of a year, reformer Edith Elmer Wood describes the alley population she
studied as

> hav[ing] very much more than their normal proportion of families in which there is no
> male breadwinner. There are a large number of widows and deserted wives. There are a
> large number of old people who are unable to do a full day's work and have no savings
> laid by for their old age . . . There are a large number of the victims of industrial
> accidents and industrial diseases. There are a large number of families in which the
> father is a victim of tuberculosis.
>
> (US Senate 1914: 24)

The bodies she depicts are not only physically deficient, they are also morally and
socially *dependent*. Recent feminist scholarship has demonstrated how 'dependency' became stigmatized over the course of the nineteenth and twentieth

centuries (Fraser and Gordon 1997; Young 1997). As Iris Marion Young argues, 'independence' is the principle virtue of the (male) citizen and property owner in a modern democratic republic (Young 1997: 123). Independence allows individuals to participate in economic transactions and political discussions, and the result of any agreement made by independent (freely contracting, equal) agents can then legitimately be called 'just'. If one does not possess the resources or abilities presumed by the virtue of independence – if one is judged to be 'dependent' – then one is deemed incapable of participating fully in either economic or political life. A dependent person is feminized in the eyes of the state, as one who cannot make choices for herself, and so requires others to make choices for her. The result of 'normatively privileging independence in this sense', Young continues, 'implies judging a huge number of people in liberal societies as less than full citizens' (Young 1997: 125), with very real political consequences. Alley-dwellers, as a dependent class of people, were viewed as incapable of participating in the political process; they were excluded from the parameters of citizenship and deemed incapable of making choices about their health, homes, and lives.

Viewing the Washington alleys through these theoretical lenses of abjection and feminization, we can see that alleys were problematic at least in part because they were sites of permeability and vulnerability in the social body, where the idealized figure of democratic citizenship was contradicted by the realities of bodies cross-cut by gender, race, and class. The ontological integrity of the body politic depended on a unified symbolic space (the Washington Mall). But, as Kristeva argues, the body politic, like any representational system, derives its meanings only through repressing excessive identities or subsuming differences. Coherence, unity, and sameness in the representational space of the nation are achieved only by setting out parameters for the citizen body/body politic and ignoring or displacing elements of the social body that fell outside of those parameters, by establishing a space for the abject and keeping it at bay.

Like all abject spaces, the alleys were not absolutely 'other from' the city; on the contrary, they were integral to it, a structural necessity in so far as they served '*alley* purposes, . . . necessary for the removal of garbage and ashes and bringing in food supplies and other things', as Commissioner Siddons stressed (US House 1914: 13, emphasis added). When the city is figured as a social body, as '[a] spatial system of waste production and elimination' (Poovey 1998: 75), alleys are its intestines, processing and expelling actual and moral waste, while keeping the rest of the city clean and orderly. Yet as abject spaces, the alleys also constantly threatened to exceed or overflow their limits, to seep out into the city proper. Alley women, for example, regularly traversed the boundaries imposed by urban design and undercut the utopian aspirations of Washington's city-builders. Policy makers argued that alley-dwellers had 'got into . . . the heart of the city squares' (US Senate 1914: 12). In contrast to the segregated, functional spaces planned for a City Beautiful utopia, the alleys complicated spaces and collapsed meanings.

In the end, then, it was neither the health nor the criminality of the alley-dwellers that required their removal from the city; instead, it was their potential to un-make the city beautiful by fundamentally challenging the symbolic unity of the body politic. What was important, one reformer reminded the Senate Committee, was not the specific complaints lodged against alley residents but rather

> the necessity for the proper development of the city, for its beautification, for the unification of its plan, all of which comes from the making of the minor streets in the place of alleys, which are bound to be more or less of a disfigurement from any point of view we may look at it.
>
> (US House 1914: 26)

The Washington alleys were abject spaces that needed to be banished from the social system, rendered invisible and kept that way.

MAKING THE CITY BEAUTIFUL

As I have suggested, Foucault's account of disciplinary power does not give us adequate theoretical leverage for understanding policy decisions regarding the expulsion of alley residents from their homes. The bodies of the Washington's alley residents fell outside the institutional parameters that Foucault's analysis presumes. Rather than the docile bodies Foucault describes, alleys housed repulsive bodies: single mothers (that is, illegitimately birthing bodies), black bodies, old bodies, and disfigured bodies. They were untrainable, unmanageable, marginal, extra-disciplinary. Alley bodies were repulsive bodies – disabled, dependent, illegitimate bodies – the feminized excess whose very existence undermined the symbolic unity of the body politic.

Kristeva's concept of abjection shows us how the symbolic aspects of the body politic and the socio-political aspects of city- and nation-building are linked in discourses of urban planning. The Washington Mall and the Washington alley were not only cultural or sociological spaces; the Mall was not simply a 'park' (characterized by the presence or absence of monuments, memorials, and green space) just as the alley was not simply a 'slum' (characterized by certain conditions of disease, mortality, criminality, and illegitimacy which varied across different groups of people). The Mall and the alley were also psycho-symbolic spaces, sites of ontological conflict over what constituted a proper citizen. Recognizing the limits of a Foucauldian body-logic has important ideational and material effects, because while docile bodies can be corrected, cured, or treated, repulsive bodies require (in Elizabeth Grosz's words) 'rituals and practices designed to cleanse or purify the body' (Grosz 1994: 193). Accordingly, policy makers did not recommend institutional intervention in the lives of the alley-dwellers, but rather sought to eliminate them entirely from the space of the city.

At the turn of the century, then, the crisis of inhabited alleys was a crisis in the body politic, and 'making the city beautiful' was not confined to the Senate Park Commission Plan for the Washington Mall. Certainly the reconstruction of the Mall was part of this endeavour, by building into the capital landscape a very particular version of citizenship. This spectacular space of masculinity and authority was to be seen and lived both by the city's population and by the nation's citizens. Yet to impose this singular identity on a space or on a body required rendering residual, contradictory, or excessive elements of this identity invisible. To make the city beautiful, wrote Daniel Burnham in an article promoting the McMillan plan, also meant 'to remove and forever keep from view the ugly, the unsightly and even the commonplace' (Burnham 1902: 620). In this case, 'the ugly, the unsightly, and even the commonplace' were the ambiguous, abject spaces and bodies of Washington's alleys.

NOTES

1 Acknowledgements to *Polity*, where a different version of this essay was first published. *Polity* Volume XXXIII, Number 1 (Fall 2000): 1–23.

2 Washington's attempts at both urban planning and sanitation were by no means unusual. The City Beautiful ideals expressed in the White City (discussed below) and made manifest in Washington were incorporated into the plans of many other US cities (for example, Cleveland, Kansas City, and San Francisco) with varying degrees of success (see Wilson 1989). Similarly, movements to cleanse cities of physical and moral disease are widespread phenomena, as Elizabeth Wilson's description of the 'cesspool city' of London makes abundantly clear (Wilson 1991). Moreover, this sanitizing impulse is not limited to the early twentieth century; Mike Davis's *City of Quartz* (1990) demonstrates how the effort to rid the city of impurities has become increasingly militarized as city officials fight the 'war on drugs'.

3 The White City, as the fully operational model city at the 1893 fair in Chicago was called, is considered to be a turning point in American architecture. Popularly named both for its virtually incandescent appearance and the optimism for urban renewal it conveyed, its sheer scale made it a startling visual contrast to the actual city of Chicago. Actual cities were unpredictable and excessive, intemperate and gluttonous: they consumed unprecedented amounts of energy and people, and expelled equally obscene amounts of filth and pollution. In contrast, the model city featured clean, ordered, functional spaces. Every building erected in the White City served a specific purpose or lauded a specific accomplishment in urban organization, from the Administration and Transportation Buildings to Fisheries or Liberal Arts. Moreover, every component of the city contributed to its total effect: street signs and street widths, plazas and buildings, lamp-posts and bridges, the shapes of the trees used in landscaping and the stones used in construction — all of these were legitimately subsumed under the purview of civic art and city beautification. With its uniform, larger-than-life, neo-classical buildings, immaculate boulevards, green parks, decorative fountains, and state-of-the-art sewage treatment facilities, the White City was, according to one commentator, 'an epitome of the best we had done, and a prophecy of what we could do' (Zueblin 1905: 62).

Through these organizational and aesthetic achievements, the White City helped to alleviate the anxieties produced by modern urban life. Clearly demarcated zones of activity and identity, populated by clean (middle class and white) bodies, were a welcome change from the city's usual ambiguity, anonymity, and alterity. When spaces and bodies were so clearly ordered, the city became less threatening. In contrast to the psychic and bodily threats that urban life posed daily to its citizens, the White City offered its inhabitants the promise of a 'delicious safety', an 'unspeakable and indescribable relief to move freely in the midst of the great throngs and not feel in imminent danger' (Adams 1896: 6).

The architects of the White City were Daniel Burnham (the Superintendent of Construction of the Exhibition); Charles McKim (the neo-classical architect who designed the Exhibition's Art Building), and Augustus Saint-Gaudens (the sculptor responsible for overseeing the White City's municipal art). They were brought together for the Washington project by Senator James McMillan, then chair of the Senate Committee on the District of Columbia, and Charles Moore, McMillan's influential secretary who co-ordinated much of the planning effort. Frederick Law Olmstead, Jr., a landscape architect whose well-known father had been instrumental in the production of the White City, was also included on the Senate Park Commission.

4   The gender-exclusive language here is not coincidental; as I shall argue below, the architecture of the City Beautiful movement produced a ideal of citizenship organized around whiteness and masculinity.

5   Robinson's book, *Modern Civic Art or, The City Made Beautiful* was first published in 1903 and is considered a classic text of the City Beautiful movement. It went through four editions between 1903 and 1918 and was reprinted by Arno Press in 1970 in the series *The Rise of Urban America*. In it, Robinson endorses the Senate Park Commission Plan for Washington as a successful experiment in City Beautiful ideals.

6   This is not to say that all monument space is created equal. Maya Lin's Vietnam Memorial is frequently cited as an example of monumental space that eloquently communicates ambivalence and ambiguity rather than certainty and finality. Another intriguing example of the revaluation of monumental space is in Santo Domingo, where the obelisk-style monument on George Washington Avenue was repainted with the images of three nuns the former dictator had murdered and then was rededicated to their memory. These alternative examples point to the word's origins: a 'monument' is that which reminds or warns; in this sense monuments do not necessarily glorify the past but rather bear witness to it.

7   See, for example, Borchert 1980; Gillette 1989; Green 1967, 1976; and Gutheim 1977.

8   The first studies of the Washington alleys were conducted by the Board of Health of the District of Columbia in the 1870s. After the Board was replaced by a Health Officer in 1878, other reports on health and housing were generated by the Civic Center and the Women's Anthropological Society (1894), the Committee on Housing (1897), and the President's Homes Commission (1908) (see Ratigan 1946).

9   Borchert reports that 'from 1873 until its abolition in 1877, the Board of Health condemned 985 alley shanties, of which nearly 300 were demolished' (Borchert 1980: 45). The Board for the Condemnation of Insanitary Buildings, created in 1906, con-

demned and destroyed 375 alley houses between 1906 and 1911 (Borchert 1980: 46).

10   In 1873 the Board of Health reported that there were 500 inhabited alleys in Washington (Borchert 1980: 23), while in 1914 the Committee on the District of Columbia reported that there were 267 or 268 (US Senate 1914: 5). However, the number of alley inhabitants was a continually contested issue among city officials and social reformers. City officials and members of the Senate Committee on the District of Columbia cite numbers from the police census at the time to describe the number of alley residents displaced during the first decade of the twentieth century. These figures had the alley dwelling population at around 25,000 in 1892 and 11,000 in 1914, with approximately 10,000 blacks and 1,000 whites. However, Rev. J. Milton Waldron, President of the Alley Improvement Association who addressed the Committee in 1914, argued that these census figures significantly underestimated the number of people living in alleys. Waldron stated that there were actually about 2,500 whites and 16,000 people in total living in the Washington alleys (US House 1914: 47).

11   Mary Poovey has argued that the link between morality and visibility is concomitant with the rise of capitalism and urbanization. In his *Theory of Moral Sentiments*, Adam Smith reasoned that individuals are able to remain moral so long as they live in country villages, where their behaviour can be both monitored by and influenced by their neighbours. However, when a country dweller moves to the city, Smith claimed, he is thereafter 'sunk in obscurity and darkness. His conduct is observed and attended to by nobody, and he is therefore very likely to neglect it himself, and to abandon himself to every sort of low prodigality and vice' (quoted in Poovey 1998: 73).

12   Bentham's Panopticon was a design for a prison where prisoners, housed in individual cells ringing a central tower, were observed both from that central tower and by each other. In this way, each individual and his actions could be monitored, recorded, and trained into docility with maximum efficiency. Although Bentham's particular design was never realized in practice, Foucault argues that modern power, what he calls disciplinary power, is organized along the lines of Panoptic space (Foucault 1979: 195–228).

Chapter 3: Urban Space, Modernity, and Masculinist Desire

The Utopian Longings of Le Corbusier

Barbara Hooper

LEFT BLANK FOR A WORK EXPRESSING MODERN FEELING

> Sweep away the refuse with which life is soiled, clogged, encumbered. Let us undertake the tasks of the new civilization.
>
> (Le Corbusier 1987a: 110)

In his 1925 work, *Urbanisme*, Le Corbusier inserted a page entitled 'Left blank for a work expressing modern feeling' (Le Corbusier 1987b: 40) (Figure 3.1). This page expresses the utopian desires with which this essay is concerned: both in its erasure of a problematic past and in its presentation of a *tabula rasa* representative of the new beginning whose existence depends upon this erasure. In expressing these desires Le Corbusier perpetuates a persistent fantasy of modernity and its urbanisms: the production of a pure, clean, rational space – a utopian space – that breaks with, and improves upon, the city and civilization of the past. In this essay I explore the isomorphism between this fantasy and two others: the founding fantasy of western metaphysics that divides an inferior body from a transcendent, superior mind; and the fantasy of a pure clean masculine identity that is spatially and temporally autonomous vis-à-vis a bodied past that it has left behind. The architectural will-to-mastery expressed in Le Corbusier's urbanism draws upon these traditions and raises important questions about all utopian plans and desires – particularly their critical assumption of a negated 'before' and an immaculate, transcendent 'after'.

The larger frame in which I place Le Corbusier's work is an investigation of 'the modern' as a discursive construct that has functioned in the west as a disciplinary strategy directed towards the regulation of subjects defined as modernity's Other. Among the knowledges, sciences, and powers producing the geopolitical order of hegemonic modernity, architecture contributes two important elements: the idea that built forms alter human consciousness and behaviour, thereby transforming nations and populations; and the provision of a method for materializing this order – a 'putting on view' of order (Derrida 1973:

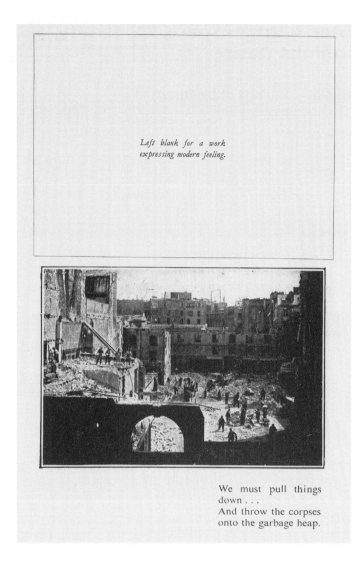

Left blank for a work expressing modern feeling.

We must pull things down . . .
And throw the corpses onto the garbage heap.

Figure 3.1
Blanking out.
Top: Left blank for a work expressing modern feeling.
Le Corbusier, *The City of Tomorrow and Its Planning*, p. 40. New York: Dover Publications, 1987.
Permission: © 2001 Artists Rights Society (ARS), New York/ADAGP, Paris/FLC

Bottom: We must pull things down . . . And throw the corpses onto the garbage heap.
Le Corbusier, *The Radiant City*, p. 96. New York: Orion Press, 1967.
Permission: © 2001 Artists Rights Society (ARS), New York/ADAGP, Paris/FLC

109) – through its formal tactics of hierarchy and division. Like the human body and its performed identities, identities that are socially produced but acquire the aura of the real through association with the body's undeniable facticity, architecture performs to bestow a similar realness upon social constructs. As mechanisms of difference that delineate and divide (e.g. the separation of metropole from colony, male from female, order from disorder); as the named materialization of a time, an epoch, a spirit, an ideal (the Gothic cathedral is the materialization of scholasticism, Cartesianism takes form in Versailles, postmodernity is the Bonaventure Hotel, the modern is a white cube, the primitive is a hut), architectural practices performatively produce the effects that they name.[1] As Mark Wigley suggests, the architectural object becomes 'the most material condition' for grounding and supporting 'the most ideal order' (Wigley 1995a: 12). As what

'controls division' (Ingraham 1998: 10), architecture is an 'idealizing operation' (Derrida 1978: 133) that functions like geometry to purify and petrify the fluidity, indeterminacy, and amorphousness of the real. Le Corbusier's architectural raw materials – space and time, body and city – are the unformed matter with which he hopes to create 'the most ideal order' of the modern, but whose creation is catalyzed by and integral to establishing what is of greater significance: the architecture of modern masculinity and the masculinity of modern architecture.

In a 1913 letter, in the context of describing a painting of two female nudes executed during his travels in the 'orient' (see Figure 3.4, top), Le Corbusier writes:

> The naked man for me is the man who has surmounted himself . . . a complex of firm and rectangular planes. The naked man for me is architecture. When I no longer make architecture, I see everything as women.

(cited in Brooks 1997: 375)[2]

In what follows, within the parameters sketched above, I work towards an elaboration of these seemingly idiosyncratic remarks.[3] My investigative site is Le Corbusier's 'writings'. I mean by writing, following Michel de Certeau, a 'concrete activity that consists in constructing, on its own blank space (*un espace propre*) – the page – a text that has power over the exteriority from which it has first been isolated'; and which 'in its many different forms' is the 'fundamental and generalized utopia of the modern West' (de Certeau 1984a: 134–5).[4] In returning to Le Corbusier, it is my intention to counter two received traditions regarding modernity. The first defines the modern as the product of reason and the second identifies a radical break in the production of space – i.e. the replacement of the monocular, egocentric perspective of the Renaissance with the multiperspectival space of the modern, a space that is also characterized by the terms 'transparency', 'relativity', and 'simultaneity'. Sigfried Giedion (1982), Colin Rowe and Robert Slutsky (1963), and Stephen Kern (1983) are among the authors promoting versions of this tradition. Beatriz Colomina, in her essay, 'Where are we?', similarly suggests, using the example of Le Corbusier, that modern architecture presents a model of perception in which the 'point of view . . . is never fixed . . . but is always in motion' (Colomina 1997: 157). However, the assertion that this 'new' space presents a perspective that is multiple, transparent, and mobile is possible only if one ignores what the view willfully excludes. The strategy of exclusion, of obliterating and eradicating, is in fact the *only* way to produce the idea of the multiperspectival and mobile. Borrowing phrasing from Henri Lefebvre, in producing the modern Le Corbusier aggressively joins 'those forces which make a *tabula rasa* of whatever stands in their way, of whatever threatens them – in short, differences' (Lefebvre 1991 [1974, 1984]: 285).[5]

Le Corbusier's *abattoir* plans for Bordeaux and Challuy provide a *Gestalt* of this violence. Between 1917 and 1918, while Europe underwent the slaughter of world war, Le Corbusier dedicated himself to designing a new Taylorized *abattoir* that replaced inefficient and outmoded versions.[6] Among the first of Le

Corbusier's designs for modern living, the *abattoirs* are produced in the 'clean', functionalist format he was then in the process of developing (Figure 3.7). The *abattoir* can be seen as Le Corbusier's ideal form of the modern: an architecture of rationalized lines, sharp as knives, that simultaneously murder and hide the sight and scent of violence. Like Hegel, Le Corbusier defines architecture as that which 'purifie[s] the external world, and endow[s] it with symmetrical order and with affinity to mind' (Hegel 1993: 90–1). By building an order which is 'the pure creation of spirit' (Le Corbusier 1986: 1), modern architecture lifts humanity out of the 'black disorder' (Le Corbusier 1948: 46) of the present–past and elevates it into the bright white order of the eternal ideal where social turmoil no longer exists. For Le Corbusier matter and the past alike are an 'ugly' accumulation of 'lies', 'manacles', 'traps', 'dead things' (Le Corbusier 1998: 189). In the immutable Corbusian future, all this is left behind, all traces of flesh and death eradicated in a pure white cessation of time.[7]

PURISM AND URBAN HYGIENE

> Any autonomous order is founded upon what it eliminates. . .
>
> (de Certeau 1989: 4)

The modern order Le Corbusier designs is predicated upon the assumption that time and space are unresisting materials, manipulable at will. The utopian city Le Corbusier imagines, then, is impossible from the beginning. His desires reveal, despite his claims for rationality, a will-to-architecture that Kojin Karatani accurately characterizes as the 'irrational choice to establish order and structure within a chaotic and manifold becoming' (Karatani 1995: 17). Nonetheless, Purism and urban hygiene, committed to the ontologization of universal modern forms, are the techniques Le Corbusier invents to accomplish this impossibility. Purism, developed by Le Corbusier and Amédée Ozenfant between 1917 and 1918 – the same years in which Le Corbusier was designing the Purist *abattoir* – is defined by Ozenfant as a 'geometrization of spirit' (Ozenfant 1952: 117). While Le Corbusier applied its ethic and aesthetic to architecture, urbanism, and daily living, Purism was first associated with a style of painting founded in the technological, functionalist logic of the machine – i.e. a logic based, like the *abattoir*, on exactitude and efficiency, economy and precision. In *Après Le Cubisme* (1918), their Purist manifesto, Le Corbusier and Ozenfant criticized what they perceived as developing ornamental or 'rococo' (Ozenfant 1952: 325) tendencies in Cubism, and set forth a scientific aesthetics (Ozenfant and Jeanneret n.d.: 166)[8] for giving expression to the 'Universal and the Permanent' (Ozenfant 1952: 326). Theorized as a science of colours and forms, Purist painting and architecture were calculated to work directly upon bodies and minds, 'rewarding the desires of our eyes' (Le Corbusier 1986: 16) and producing a precise 'symphony' of purifying psychological and physiological sensations (Ozenfant and Jeanneret n.d.: 166).[9] During this same period, Le Corbusier also developed what would remain governing ideas: that of the 'generating' master plan (Le Corbusier 1986: 2–3) and '*traces regulateurs*'. In painting, these techniques consisted of dividing the blank canvas into a geometrical grid that was to master subject matter by rationally ordering its elements. As applied to architecture and urbanism it functioned as it did on canvas – i.e. as a geometric order imposed upon an architectural object perceived as passive: a building, body, city, or nation; a present, future, or past.

Once discovered, regulating lines develop for Le Corbusier Faustian powers, possessing what Walter Benjamin referred to as 'wishful fantasies' both in their 'emphatic striving for dissociation with the outmoded' and their ability to produce a new future (Benjamin 1978: 148). Following Vitruvius and Alberti, Le Corbusier viewed architecture's production of regulating lines as a mental activity that makes possible Man's 'zone of protection' within his chaotic 'natural setting' (Le Corbusier 1987b: 22). Geometry is evidence of this mastery over nature: 'When man begins to draw straight lines,' Le Corbusier writes, 'he bears witness that he has gained control of himself and that he has reached a condition of order' (Le Corbusier 1987b: 37). As 'living beings' 'bred' by humans (Le Corbusier 1998: 192), machines and machine-architecture are geometry incarnate, creations that, ab-stracted from nature, simultaneously ab-ject and transcend it.

> The machine brings shining before us disks, spheres, and cylinders of polished steel, shaped with a theoretical precision and exactitude *which can never be seen in nature itself*. . . . [T]here is nothing in nature that approaches the pure perfection of the humblest machine (the moon is not round; the tree trunk is not straight; only very occasionally are waters smooth as a mirror; the rainbow is a fragment; living beings, with very few exceptions, do not conform to simple geometrical shapes . . .
>
> (Le Corbusier 1998: 112, italics in original)

While western thought has typically viewed nature as a primitive territory to be mastered by masculinist knowledge,[10] in Le Corbusier's writings, this thinking acquires a specificity that accords with a philosophy of history Arthur O. Lovejoy and George Boas, writing in 1935, characterized as 'primitivism' (Lovejoy and Boas 1997).[11] In contemporary thought primitivism is related to what Fredric Jameson describes as 'the philosophy of history for the heroic bourgeoisie . . . [i.e.] Progress' (Jameson 1991: 18); and what Gayatri Spivak names 'the worlding of a world on a supposedly uninscribed territory' (Spivak 1990: 1). In Le Corbusier's primitivist view, world history, essentially the history of architecture and forms,[12] is a series of ascents and declines involving a 'fatal process of selection' (Le Corbusier 1998: 177). Architectural forms per se, the direct expression 'of an epoch and the spirit of peoples' (Le Corbusier 1947: 125), vary in their creative content. Hieratism, of which modern Purist forms are an example, is the highest stage of art: 'the moment when man is no longer pushed about by exterior forces or pure instincts' (Ozenfant and Jeanneret n.d.: 153–4). Le Corbusier's view of history also includes, as is typical with primitivism, a fantasy of contemporary 'savages' living in the present – i.e. unmoderns who are ruled by the forces civilized peoples have overcome.

Adolph Loos's frequently cited 1908 essay, 'Ornament and Crime' – referred to by Le Corbusier in *The Decorative Art of Today* (Le Corbusier 1998: 134) – provides an architectural precedent for Le Corbusier's primitivist views. For Loos, ontogeny recapitulates phylogeny, both biologically and culturally. The sign of this progression from animal to human, child to adult, 'Papuan' to 'Voltaire' is 'freedom from ornament' (Loos 1998: 167). The 'modern man' who tattoos his skin, smears lavatory walls with graffiti, ornaments his house and clothing, is criminal and degenerate. Such individuals are 'stragglers' who 'slow down the evolution of nations and humanity' (Loos 1998: 170). They include, with the Papuan, the African, Slovak peasants, the Persian, and women – for whom ornament is the 'highpoint of their existence, which they have no other means of achieving' (Loos 1998: 174). The aristocrat, 'at the peak of humanity', is alone capable of producing the modern, unornamented future: 'Soon the streets of the cities will shine with white walls! Like Zion, the Holy City, Heaven's capital' (Loos 1998: 168).

Whether borrowed from Loos or simply acquired by living in 'modern times', the theory of the modern as the eradication of the primitive is one of the fundamental precepts in Le Corbusier's architectural arsenal. Within the confines of the binary framework, modern/primitive, Le Corbusier develops his utopian vision of the future and the system of visual diagnostics through which the primitive is recognized as inferior and superfluous. For Le Corbusier ornament, as an excess of matter, provides visible evidence of architectural and spiritual disease and decline; a retrogressive condition that 'thrives as virulently as cancer' (Le Corbusier 1998: 12) and is associated with women, animals, Africans, and 'Orientals'. Ornament is to architecture, Le Corbusier writes, what 'a feather is to a woman's head . . . sometimes pretty . . . and never anything more' (Le Corbusier 1986: 25). Furthermore, ornament 'conceals a defect in construction' (Le Corbusier 1998: 134), presumably the defective materiality of feminine and other primitive humans. Modern hieratic architecture, 'brutal and objective' (Le Corbusier 1986: 26), 'clean and hard,' (Le Corbusier 1986: 47), conversely, has 'nothing to do with decoration': it is 'naked fact' (Le Corbusier 1998: 207), bringing into play 'the highest faculties by its very abstraction' (Le Corbusier 1986: 47).[13]

Primitive forms are recognizable as well by their shape and colour. In *Journey to the East,* Le Corbusier describes the women he encounters there as a 'feast of colour' (Le Corbusier 1991: 54), and colour itself is eroticized and corporealized: 'lemon yellows drowned in dirty greens would have inflamed rotting purples, a swooning of colours, orgiastic palette, cravings of the flesh, hot call of the city, primitive pink, the colour of real flesh' (Le Corbusier 1991: 56). Straight and vertical forms represent the rational, modern, and masculine, while horizontality and curves represent the feminine irrationality of primitive nature. Defining architecture as the 'task of giving living form to dead material' (Le Corbusier 1957: Preface), Le Corbusier theorizes the vertical and the straight as the 'formed' and the curved as the 'formless' – as unformed, de-formed, 'dead material'. 'The straight line', Le Corbusier writes, 'is deeply impressive in the confusion of nature; *it is the work of men*' (Le Corbusier 1987b: 271, italics in original); while the 'curve is ruinous, difficult and dangerous; . . . a paralyzing thing' (Le Corbusier 1987b: 10). Among lines, the 'sensation of the vertical is primary' (Ozenfant and Jeanneret: 166) and signifies the upright posture of men and an 'overcoming [of] the force of gravity' (Ozenfant 1952: 259–60).[14] In contrast, feminine horizontality signifies what is low to the ground like an animal. In *The Radiant City* (1934), Le Corbusier imagines the male as sun and light, the active element that is the 'dictator of life' (Le Corbusier 1967: 78). The female is associated with the formless, with darkness and passivity, with 'parasites, . . . evil vapors, . . . fevers and rotting decadence' – and with the power to 'engulf', 'swallow up', and bring 'death' (Le Corbusier 1967: 80).

The photographs Le Corbusier includes in his texts offer further evidence as to what, and who, he sees when he fantasizes the warring forms of the modern and the primitive. As in Ozenfant's *Foundations of Modern Art*, both *La Peinture Moderne*, co-authored with Ozenfant and Le Corbusier's singly authored, *The Decorative Art of Today*, deploy images of the extravagantly curved, 'fluid', and ornamented-ornamental bodies of the feminized primitive (Figure 3.2) in opposition to those of the hard metallic surfaces and lines of modern architecture and

Figure 3.2
Unmoderns in our midst. Clockwise from left top: Algiers, veiled women. Le Corbusier, *The Radiant City*, p. 230. New York: Orion Press, 1967. Permission: © 2001 Artists Rights Society (ARS), New York/ADAGP, Paris/FLC

Nature–nature. Ozenfant and Jeanneret, *La Peinture Moderne*, p. 44. Paris: Les Editions G. Cres & Cie. Permission: © 2001 Artists Rights Society (ARS), New York/ADAGP, Paris/FLC

Decorative art. Ozenfant, *Foundations of Modern Art*, p. 158. New York: Dover, 1952. Permission: Dover

Zoulou. Ozenfant and Jeanneret, *La Peinture Moderne*, p. 48. Paris: Les Editions G. Cres & Cie. Permission: © 2001 Artists Rights Society (ARS), New York/ADAGP, Paris/FLC

machines. As it did for eighteenth-century architectural historians such as Abbé Laugier, whose histories of form were developed in the context of Europe's 'discovery' of contemporary 'savagery', Le Corbusier's photographs function to authenticate ideas of European superiority and progress and to constitute the modern as masculine, white, European, and advanced. In addition to the white geometrical houses and towering vertical structures Le Corbusier uses to signify the modern, modernity is represented by instruments and machines that, like the *abattoir*, function to dominate or eliminate nature/body/matter. These include the virile tools of modern war and demolition (a torpedo station, warships, tanks and planes); instruments for measuring and controlling time (a speedometer, Lindbergh's instrument board, clocks and watches); machines for conquering space (airplanes, automobiles, ocean liners, dams, and bridges). There are massive phallic factories, airplane hangers, grain elevators, and numerous machines for modern living: turbines, condensers, fuselages, and generators; filing cabinets, calculators, and steel office furniture; iconic toilets and bathrooms. There are several images of surgical equipment and surgeries (e.g., Le Corbusier 1986: xv; Le Corbusier 1998: 88; Ozenfant and Jeanneret: 67). In contrast are the degenerate, excessively ornamented architectures of Versailles and Fontainebleau, and the feminine, breast-shaped huts that figure the primitive in architectural histories from Vitruvius to Le Corbusier (Figure 3.3). There are many photographs of African masks and costumes, as well as photographs of Africans engaged in 'primitive' activities – 'pygmies' climbing trees, a 'Zulu' chief leading his tribe in a dance (Ozenfant 1952: 164); women wearing paint and other ornaments (Figure 3.2). Within the same perceptual frame, Le Corbusier hears in jazz the 'depths of equatorial Africa rise again' (Le Corbusier 1947: 159), a sound in which 'savagery is constantly present, (Le Corbusier 1947: 60) and which calls forth visions of 'naked Negroes', 'tom-toms, massacres, tribes' (Le Corbusier 1947: 160).

While the bodies of black men appear in Le Corbusier's exhibition of modernity's other, female bodies predominate as the signifier of the primitive past architecture's regulating lines must over-write if they are to succeed in creating the modern.[15] As is the case with the verbal and textual images Le Corbusier deploys, this objective is seen in Le Corbusier's female nudes, of which he produced hundreds and all of which he kept hidden from public view (Figure 3.4). Art historian Lynda Nead suggests that the female nude, more than any other art object, 'symbolizes the transformation of base matter of nature into the elevated forms of culture and spirit' (Nead 1992: 2). As this 'base matter' the feminine represents for Le Corbusier what disfigures the orthogonal forms of modern architecture and endangers 'the rule of brute creation by intelligence'. Le Corbusier applies this 'rule' most consistently against women who have escaped masculinist architecture, 'loose' women whose fluid and marginal status in society make them both threatening and desirable within Le Corbusier's white, western, masculinist, heterosexist perspective: i.e. Algerian and Turkish women, veiled women, women from Africa and 'Orient,' peasant women, lesbians and prostitutes.[16] To found the clean and proper order of modern architecture, Le

Figure 3.3
Primitive architecture.
Top: Line drawing of breast.
Ozenfant, *Foundations of Modern Art*, p. 247. New York: Dover, 1952.
Permission: Dover

Middle, left: Negro 'eggshell' architecture. Photo, Marc Allegret. Ozenfant, *Foundations of Modern Art*, p. 145. New York: Dover, 1952.
Permission: Dover

Middle, right: The native hut.
Le Corbusier, *The City of Tomorrow and Its Planning*, p. 18. New York: Dover Publications, 1987.
Permission: © 2001 Artists Rights Society (ARS), New York/ADAGP, Paris/FLC

Bottom, left: The Chapel at Ronchamp.
Le Corbusier, *The Chapel at Ronchamp*, n.p. New York: Frederick A. Praeger, 1957.
Permission: © 2001 Artists Rights Society (ARS), New York/ADAGP, Paris/FLC

Bottom, right: *Icone* (Woman with Candle), 1942.
Richard Ingersoll, *Le Corbusier: A Marriage of Contours*, p. 29. New York: Princeton Architectural Press, 1990.
Permission: © 2001 Artists Rights Society (ARS), New York/ADAGP, Paris/FLC

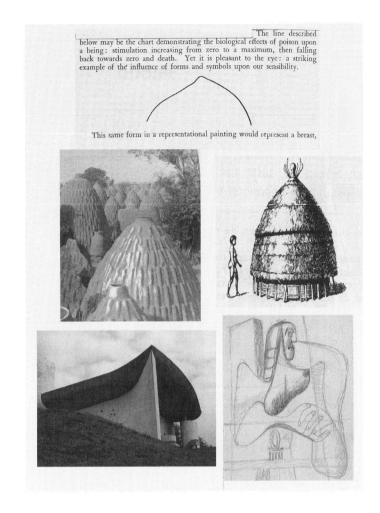

Corbusier abjects the primitive female body, and then, desiring what he has lost, reclaims it with pen and brush. But what has been abjected also invades the public spaces he designs and erects. The body returns in the roof of the chapel at Ronchamp as the breast in *Icône* (Figure 3.3). It returns in the 'organic', curvilinear lines that Le Corbusier first uses in spaces he views as outside and other: in Rio de Janeiro – where, looking down from a plane and seeing 'nature's' curves, the conception of 'a vast programme of organic town-planning came like a revelation'; in Chandigarh, where the roof of the Palace of Assembly resembles a cosmic birth canal; and in Algiers, where his Obus Plan takes on the voluptuousness of the Algerian women painted by Delacroix and himself (Figure 3.5).[17] But it returns most ubiquitously in the aggressive force with which Le Corbusier asserts the need for cleansing and destruction. As René Girard suggests, 'as long as purity and impurity remain distinct, even the worst pollution can be washed away; but once they are allowed to mingle, purification is no longer possible'

When I no longer make architecture,
I see everything as women.

Figure 3.4
When I no longer make architecture, I see everything as women.
Top: *Female Nudes on a Beach,* 1912–1913.
H. Allen Brooks, *Le Corbusier's Formative Years*, p. 374. Chicago: University of Chicago Press, 1997.
Permission: © 2001 Artists Rights Society (ARS), New York/ADAGP, Paris/FLC

Middle: Sketch, a Woman lying with Curtains.
Charles Jencks, *Le Corbusier and the Tragic View of Architecture*, p. 107. Cambridge, MA; Harvard University Press, 1973.
Permission: © 2001 Artists Rights Society (ARS), New York/ADAGP, Paris/FLC

Bottom. *Two Lesbians.*
H. Allen Brooks, *Le Corbusier's Formative Years*, p. 480. Chicago: University of Chicago Press, 1997.
Permission: © 2001 Artists Rights Society (ARS), New York/ADAGP, Paris/FLC

(Girard 1993: 38). It is this fear of contaminating mixtures that Le Corbusier inscribes into the 'body' of the city as a disciplinary regime of urban hygiene.

The city to which Le Corbusier brings his Purist longings is not, as it was for the Futurists and Surrealists, a charged and exhilarating landscape, but a rotting corpse infected by the 'creeping and purulent decay' of the past (Le Corbusier 1967: 178). As Sigfried Giedion suggests, Le Corbusier did not want to fit into an

Figure 3.5
Regulating lines.
Top, left: Obus Plan, Le Corbusier et P. Jenheret, 1932.
Le Corbusier, *Aircraft*, p. 110. Paris: Fondation Le Corbusier, 1987. Orig. 1935.
Permission: © 2001 Artists Rights Society (ARS), New York/ADAGP, Paris/FLC

Top, right: Sketch of Rio, made by the author in an aeroplane, 1929, 'when the conception of a vast programme of town planning came like a revelation.'
Le Corbusier, *Aircraft*, p. 112. Paris; Fondation Le Corbusier, 1987. Orig. 1935.
Permission: © 2001 Artists Rights Society (ARS), New York/ADAGP, Paris/FLC

Bottom, left: Corbusier, Sketch of Nude, Algiers, 1931.
William J.R. Curtis, *Le Corbusier: Ideas and Forms*, p. 123. London: Phaidon Press, 1986.

Bottom, right: Curves. Ozenfant, *Foundations of Modern Art*, p. 145. New York: Dover, 1952.
Permission: © 2001 Artists Rights Society (ARS), New York/ADAGP, Paris/FLC

existing milieu but to conquer it (Giedion 1982: 523). Le Corbusier uses the same oppositional logic delineated above to characterize the unplanned city and his plan for mastering it: mastery means the straight and rational lines of masculine geometry; the city's disease and disorder are associated with the feminine and the curved.[18] As a diseased body the city is described in the same language Le Corbusier uses to define the destructive, de-formative properties of the feminine – e.g. 'rotting decadence', 'stagnation', 'meander', the element that has 'the power to bring death'. The body of Paris is referred to as a 'she' and described as 'old, decayed, frightening, diseased' (Le Corbusier 1987b: 101). Paris is a 'dismal and suppurating zone', its boundaries 'gnawed as though by vermin' (Le Corbusier 1987b: 96). Its colour is that of death and decay, bruised purples, dirty greens, rotting blacks. In *When the Cathedrals Were White*, Le Corbusier laments the present condition of cities via the condition of cathedrals, 'black with grime . . . blackened by soot and eaten away' as opposed to a time when 'spirit was triumphant' and (white) 'people were masters of themselves' (Le Corbusier 1947: 5, 111).

The disorder of the city is visible in its anarchy of curves, associated by Le Corbusier with 'the pack-donkey' and women.[19] As opposed to the rationality of modern urbanism, the pack-donkey's way is 'scatter-brained', the rule of twisting streets instead of vertical lines (Le Corbusier 1987b: 5). The winding road, writes Le Corbusier, 'is the result . . . of heedlessness, of looseness, lack of concentration and animality' [while] the straight road is . . . an action, a positive deed, the result of self-mastery' (Le Corbusier 1987b: 12). The feminine nature and animality of the city are also described by Le Corbusier as a 'thicket' where people live 'like hunted animals' (Le Corbusier 1987b: xxiv). The city reverted to (female) nature is a threatening chaos of 'creepers, its briars and tree-trunks imped[ing] [man] and paralyz[ing] his efforts' (Le Corbusier 1986: 71). In response, 'man undermines and hacks at nature . . . he fights with her, he digs himself in . . . and out of these evils there comes an ordered system of straight lines and right angles' (Le Corbusier 1987b: 24). Like the castrating feminine, the disorderly city 'thwarts us'; it 'humiliates' us and 'wounds our self-esteem' (Le Corbusier 1987b: xxi). To regain control the architect-planner must emulate Rome: 'Rome's business was to conquer the world and govern it . . . if it was brutal, so much the worse – or so much the better' (Le Corbusier 1986: 156).

> The time is past when . . . men of vigour in an age of heroic reawakening . . . can lounge on ottomans and divans among orchids in the scented atmosphere of a seraglio and behave like so many ornamented animals . . .
>
> (Le Corbusier 1998: 192)

The first step in this manly campaign is 'urban surgery', the excision of the city's diseased organs and pathological spaces – i.e. the cleansing that produces the page 'left blank for expressing modern feelings'. Upon this brutally eradicated site that is the Purist canvas are inscribed the regulating forms and lines dictated by the master plan, the masculinist 'tool' that re-forms the city. The ordered city, as it was for Le Corbusier's nineteenth-century model, Baron Haussmann, is based in the ideal of controlled divisions and circulations: the managed flows of traffic, people, and goods; the strictly bordered separation of functions; the production of standardized, clearly differentiated, and hierarchically organized spatial cells.[20] In contrast to the unplanned city with its contaminating mixtures – *abattoirs* and cemeteries mixed with living and breathing spaces, dangerous classes mixed with the bourgeoisie, streetwalkers mingling with family men – the modern city is organized into separate zones for workers and administrators, public life and domestic life, leisure and sport. As a technology of space and time, the utopian city is to regulate the totality of life – its energies, instincts, and behaviours, its reproductions and deaths. There is no extraneous or degenerate matter, nothing overflows or seeps, ornament is strictly policed. All 'type-needs', which are the same for all 'human-types', are architecturally met: 'animal' needs for sun, space, vegetation, light, and air; 'cultural' needs for thought, creativity, and leisure, with creativity as the 'highest possible activity' (Le Corbusier 1998: 74). To achieve this condition requires both correct architectural forms and the strict regulation of nature: the conditioned application of sunlight, air, and greenery within a master-system of thermal, sonic, and olfactory control. The dwelling and its equipment, as what work most directly upon bodies and minds, are particularly important to Le Corbusier's Foucauldian project. Like the city, the house must be purified and cleansed, purged of ornaments and bric-a-brac. The undecorated 'minimum house' (Le Corbusier 1967: 29) is one that is free of all 'dead things from the past' – dirt and disease, dead thoughts, the outmoded and inefficient – and exists as a 'wish landscape' (Bloch 1996: xxxix) from which human unpredictability and 'filth', as taints of the irrational and corporeal, have been erased. The utopian city Le Corbusier imagines as 'freedom through order' (Le Corbusier 1987b: 211) is an elaborate Skinner-box city regulating every moment of everyday life; a still life (*nature morte*) in which behaviours and views are rigorously controlled and living, in its messy materiality, is hidden from sight.[21] Dr Pierre Winter, a regular contributor to *L'Esprit Nouveau* and a member of *Faisceau*, the fascist group to which Le Corbusier allegedly belonged (Boudon 1972: 22), wrote in praise of Le Corbusier's urbanism, particularly the hygienic Corbusian home. In this modern dwelling, Winter writes, 'useless remains are disposed of, life leaves no traces, it does not hoard its waste products, does not wallow in dirt and disease' (cited in Boudon 1972: 24).

In keeping with the twinned goals of purifying life and 'permitting eyes to feast' (Le Corbusier 1999: 46), the colour of the modern is white, the eugenic colour of the surgery or laboratory.[22] As the modern city demands cleansing, it also demands, for Le Corbusier, the 'delicious brilliance of white' (Le Corbusier 1999: 68). White is the purity of blank surfaces on which to write modern living – 'Demand bare walls' (Le Corbusier 1986: 123) – as well as the purity of its spare white forms, while black, like excessive colour, is the colour of the primitive de-formative past.

> In the confusion of our tumultuous times many have become accustomed to think against a background of black. But the tasks of our century, so strenuous, so full of danger, so violent, so victorious, seem to demand of us that we think against a background of white.
>
> (Le Corbusier 1998: xxvi)

Demonstrating the advance upon the past that whiteness represents – a display of an 'ethic different from those who cultivate filth and dust' (Le Corbusier 1947: 47) – Le Corbusier uses opposing photographs to depict the conquering of the curved by the straight, the dark by the white, the primitive by the modern: the round and curving image of an African waterhole labelled 'nomad outpost' set

Here a water-hole ; nomad's outpost (strategy).   **106**

Here finally '' Le Bidon 5,'' nerve-centre on the imperial highway.   The white   **107**
race goes its conquering way. The filling station is a symbol of white civilization.

Figure 3.6
The white race goes its
conquering way.
Le Corbusier, *Aircraft*,
pp. 106–7. Paris:
Fondation Le Corbusier,
1987. Orig. 1935.
Permission: © 2001
Artists Rights Society
(ARS), New York/ADAGP,
Paris/FLC

against the whitened image of a geometricized fueling station, captioned 'the white race goes its conquering way' (Figure 3.6). The moral is clear:

> A heedless people, or society, or town, in which effort is relaxed and not concentrated, quickly becomes dissipated, overcome and absorbed by a nation or a society that goes to work in a positive way and controls itself.
>
> (Le Corbusier 1987b: 12)

The 'Law of Ripolin', Le Corbusier's whiteness credo, demands the removal of colour from exteriors; and of all ornamental hangings, wallpapers, and damasks from interior walls, to be replaced with a clean coat of white paint. When body, house, and city have been purged, there is transparency and illumination; 'Once you have put Ripolin on your walls you will be master of your house and of your-self' (Le Corbusier 1998: 188–9).

The modernization of spirit and the 'rebirth of the human body' (Le Cor-busier 1967: 7) demand, however, not only the passive reception of the purifying actions of white geometric forms upon the body's surfaces, but taking action, trimming the body of extraneous matter, working to harden and straighten it. *Le corps nouveau*, like the new architecture, is pure, rational, and unornamented. In the city 'man has lived in a perpetual state of insecurity, fatigue, accumulating delusions. [His] physical and nervous organization is brutalized and battered by this torrent' (Le Corbusier 1989: 86). Sunlight and bathing, games and sport, are 'the salutary answer to the harmful forces of the past' (Le Corbusier 1986: 198). The modernization of the body requires a corporeal urbanism that 'will revivify lungs, improve circulation, strengthen muscles, and fill [one] with joy and opti-mism' (Le Corbusier 1967: 65). Following this regime, the modern body, like the modern city, 'will re-appear, naked in sunlight – cleansed, muscled, supple' (cited in Banham 1984: 146).

The form of the new human embodies Le Corbusier's dictum that the higher we move on the evolutionary scale, the more we move towards perfect hieratic forms: 'Selection means rejection, pruning, cleansing; the clear and naked emergence of the Essential' (Le Corbusier 1986: 138). This means for Le Corbusier the natural selection of the Essential white male. There are no modern humans whose forms are ornamented or coloured or which can be visibly diag-nosed as female. Women, for Le Corbusier, remain locked in their primitive oth-erness, eroticized objects to be watched, mastered, had. *Der neue Mensch*, in contrast, has three masculine forms: the 'normal man' who is 'typical, standard-ized: two legs, two arms, a heart . . . a man who dreams in verticals and horizon-tals' (Le Corbusier 1998: 33); the modular man, 'measures made flesh' (Le Corbusier 1973: 160), progenitor of an entire universe built to male-scale; and, most perfect of all, the 'naked man' who as the 'naked emergence of the Essen-tial' has rid himself of the past's dark influences.

> The naked man . . . has no need of trinkets. His mechanism is founded on logic. . . . It is reason that brings light to his mind. . . . [He] sets himself to achieve something in the world . . . and focuses his thoughts on what [is] best and most noble . . .
>
> (Le Corbusier 1998: 22–3)

The naked man is, in sum, the pinnacle, the form reached 'when man is strong enough . . . to be able to trace straight lines. In the history of forms, the straight line is the climax' (Le Corbusier 1987b: 37).

As the climax of the straight line, white masculinity becomes architecture, and architecture becomes pure white masculine form. Nakedness suggests for Le Corbusier not nature but the absence of nature, a geometric ideal whose artistry purifies and orders nature. As such it has no defects, no need to cover itself with ornament. As this transcendent being the naked man is autonomous, unmarred by his milieu, a demi-god 'who has grown wings to himself' (Le Corbusier 1986:

123). In *Aircraft*, his homage to aerial *jouissance*, Le Corbusier describes the 'remarkable phenomenon of flying', which produced in him an 'ecstasy' when he thought about it (Le Corbusier 1987a: 5). Flying, for Le Corbusier, 'is the symbol of the new age, at the apex of the immense pyramid of mechanical progress' (Le Corbusier 1987a: 13). It produces an experience similar to the spatial mastery he achieves as an artist and architect, one that produces the sensation of a 'fourth dimension', the '*miracle of ineffable space*' (Le Corbusier 1973: 32, italics in original). As a master of space and flight, Le Corbusier associates himself with 'Aces', 'that dynasty of airmen whose daily sustenance was reckless courage, foolhardiness, and contempt for death' (Le Corbusier 1987a: 7). These men are, Le Corbusier says, 'Madmen. Utopians. The kind of men who century after century lead the world by the nose' (Le Corbusier 1987: 7) (Figure 3.7). The question we must now ask, and whose answer we already suspect, is what kind of architect, practitioner of a material art, will have had as his ideal, not only leading the world by the nose, but an architecture and a masculinity that fly away from their own materiality and whose idea of utopia is a life that leaves no traces?

Figure 3.7
New machines, new men.
Le Corbusier, *Aircraft*,
p. 79. Paris: Fondation Le
Corbusier, 1987. Orig.
1935.
Permission: © 2001
Artists Rights Society
(ARS), New York/ADAGP,
Paris/FLC

Photographs 80–1.
German gliders, 1934.
Le Corbusier, *Aircraft*,
p. 80. Paris: Fondation Le
Corbusier, 1987. Orig.
1935.
Permission: © 2001
Artists Rights Society
(ARS), New York/ADAGP,
Paris/FLC

UTOPIA, DEATH, AND DESIRE

> Behind every frontier that is opened up, the sum total of all female bodies appears . . .
> an infinite untrodden territory of desire which . . . men in search of material for (abstract)
> utopias have inundated with their desires.
>
> (Theweleit 1987: 294)

Luce Irigaray suggests that all western discourse 'presents a certain isomorphism with the masculine sex; the privilege of unity, form of the self, of the visible, of the specularizable, of the erection (which is the becoming of form)' (cited in Grosz 1990: 111). Le Corbusier's discourse on architecture becomes, from this perspective, not only a discourse on the modern as a mode of organizing and controlling space and time, but a discourse on the modern masculinist subject. The threat presented by the feminine to this subject is a bringing to ground, a crash landing of sorts: the fall into the formlessness of indifferentiation that means castration and death. For Le Corbusier, death is the female wounding that must not take place and architecture is what he erects against it.

The wounding Le Corbusier fears is one that has been written into the history of western culture. As carnal flesh and its associated evils; as that which 'overflows or undermines borders' (Grosz 1994: 203); as the abject 'filth' that pollutes social and psychocorporeal order (Douglas 1966; Kristeva 1982); the female body has been produced as what destroys phallic form.[23] When Le Corbusier approaches the city with the intention to cleanse and destroy, he is acting to conquer the destructive power associated with feminine disorder: its fluidity, indeterminacy, and amorphousness. Power explains the persistence of this masculinist fantasy, but there are important psychical realities that fuel it. These are illuminated by Jacques Lacan (1977) in his discussion of the imaginary – i.e. its abjection of influences that contaminate the subject's ideal of self; and by Julia Kristeva (1982) in her analysis of the abject and the two critical borders with which it is associated. These are the social–psychocorporeal border between self and (m)other that the subject, to be a subject, must produce and defend; and the border between the living being and the corpse. In the first instance, the abject is associated with a pre-Oedipal past prior to the subject–object distinction that is phenomenologically and psychically linked with the maternal body and the 'filth' that transgresses its boundaries (feces, urine, spit, blood, milk, mucous, etc.). The fear evoked by the abject maternal body is that of being pulled back into this undifferentiated state. In the second instance, the female body, as signifier of flesh and organic nature, represents the abject future to which every body becomes – i.e. the body become rotting meat. Theodor Adorno suggests that death is the 'absolute anti-utopia' (Bloch and Adorno 1996: 8) and defines death as 'none other than the power of that which merely *is*' (Bloch and Adorno 1996: 10). For Le Corbusier, the power of the abject, and the female body as abject, is precisely this horror of not-being: the collapse of the border between subject and object, and that between the living being and the corpse.

It is this 'horror' that Le Corbusier transposes onto the body of the city as an anxiety about, and a will to control, both the future and the past. To control what-is – a subjectivity that is forever 'dying' in its continual becoming; a body whose form will be disfigured by rot and decay – is both the impossibility inherent in Le Corbusier's will-to-architecture and the impossibility that drives it. The city – as 'frightening', 'rotten', 'diseased', a 'corpse', its borders 'gnawed' – is the body he fears and abjects; the utopian city he creates in its place is the materialization of a future in which the inevitable has been defeated. But these are merely the names, the 'lines' or rationalizations hiding the stakes of Le Corbusier's utopian hopes. The divisions Le Corbusier cuts into the city to order its functions and regulate its flows are iterations of the border between self and other that his imaginary creates in defence of its most ideal order – i.e. a masculine subjectivity that is cleansed of the castrating contaminations of the real. In the same way that geometry projects pure morphological types upon the factual real (roundness becomes a pure circle, a line becomes pure verticality or straightness), Le Corbusier projects his pure masculine form upon the city, abjecting what threatens to disfigure it. To lift the city out of the realm of base materiality, to free it from its 'natural' fate of death and rot, is to lift himself into the Purist realm of the 'Universal and the Permanent'. In the *Interpretation of Dreams* Freud writes that 'flying dreams' are 'dreams of erection'. The 'remarkable phenomenon of erection,' he says, 'around which the human [sic] imagination has constantly played, cannot fail to be impressive, involving as it does the apparent suspension of the laws of gravity' (Freud 1965: 430). Le Corbusier's 'remarkable phenomenon of flying' is of a piece with Freud's remarkable phenomenon. What is achieved in the ideal realms of their aerial architecture is the utopia of ideal masculine being, a cessation of becoming that leaves the climax of the straight line permanently upright, never changing, never dying. For Le Corbusier, as for Martin Heidegger, the ideal form of being is an 'erect standing there, a coming up ... and enduring' (Heidegger 1961: 47). In Le Corbusier's narrative, the mastery of the space–time of the female body, and of the city as this body, are what keep this ideal presence from falling into death.

In Berlin, in the same year that Le Corbusier was writing *Towards a New Architecture* and Walter Gropius was organizing the First Bauhaus Exhibition, Otto Dix executed a painting entitled 'Lustmord', or 'Sexual Murder'. Like the *abattoir*, Dix's painting offers a *Gestalt* of modern architecture and what it is erected over and against (Figure 3.8). The name of the painting is '*Lustmord*', or '*Sexual Murder*', and its imagery of a 'hacked up' female body can be seen as Le Corbusier's 'hacking through nature' to replace its 'evils' with the mastery of straight lines.[24] The ordered vertical architecture of the city that is framed by the painting's interior window exists, as it does in Le Corbusier's narrative of the modern, in striking contrast to the formless flesh and blood of the prostitute whose splayed and ornamental horizontality dominates the foreground. The horror of Dix's painting is that it shows what Le Corbusier's *abattoir*-architecture hides, reveals with chilling explicitness whose murder Le Corbusier's modernity

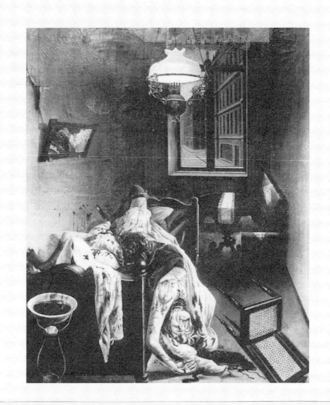

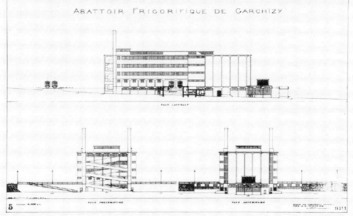

Figure 3.8
Transcending the body.
Top: Otto Dix, *Lustmord*,
1922.
Maria Tatar, *Lustmord:
Sexual Murder in Weimar
Germany*, p. 14.
Princeton: Princeton
University Press, 1995.
Permission: © 2001
Artists Rights Society
(ARS), New York/VG Bild-
kunst, Bonn

Bottom: *Abbatoir
Frigorifique de Garchizy*,
1918.
H. Allen Brooks, *Le
Corbusier's Formative
Years*, p. 489. Chicago:
University of Chicago
Press, 1997.
Permission: © 2001
Artists Rights Society
(ARS), New York/ADAGP,
Paris/FLC

demands, over whose dead body he will erect his phantasmatic utopias. Le Corbusier's obsessive concern with purity and regulating lines reflects not his architecture's rationality, but his murderous irrationality. Because it endangers the hallucination of a pure and inviolable masculinity, feminine flesh is that which must be eliminated. Making the body female/feminine is what enables both reason and masculinity to be purely ideal; killing the female body again and again is what preserves the fantasy. The female body, then, is not an accidental presence in Le Corbusier's narrative. It is that through which, and over which, Le Corbusier founds and articulates his architectural project. It is that in which he resolves his contradictory positions: the valorized mastery of a material art and the simultaneous denigration of materiality; and it is that which, blanked out, is the blank page upon which he writes his desires.

To transcend death, to still space and time, to drive away all contingent presences and see as you will, are actions requiring violence. Le Corbusier's production of the modern as rational and universal is a view that is achieved only by a brutal disentanglement from a larger, more complex and heterogeneous geopolitical reality. It is a view that, like Renaissance perspective, eliminates other views and then hides what is sacrificed outside its frame. Le Corbusier's writing of the modern is, in sum, *abattoir*-architecture, the eradications accomplished by imperialism and industrial capitalism, racism and sexism, reinscribed in his narrative of modern space. The white male, the white race, white walls, the purged city, the hygienic house, the cleansed body, the white canvas, the tabula rasa – all suggest that in Le Corbusier's utopian future, as in his writings, there will have been a radical excision of those bodies he associates with the excessive colour, fluidity, and ornament of the 'primitive' races and the feminine; the 'stragglers' whose 'orgiastic palette' and 'swooning colours' stain the 'delicious brilliance of white'. In his 1913 letter Le Corbusier tells us the form his fully developed utopia will take and what he will blank out to achieve it: 'When I no longer make architecture,' he writes, 'I see everything as women.' Utopia means for Le Corbusier that he will not *have* to see anything at all. Women, with all else that threatens his vision, will have been eliminated from view. In the modern future, 'the desires of [his] eyes are rewarded' (Le Corbusier 1986: 16): thinking against a city of white he sees only himself, naked and supple in sunlight.

What does this mean for utopia today? It means that one should abandon fantasies of mastery and control; that schemes that build with what is and what is becoming might improve upon those operating on the violent premise of overcoming. It means we must be suspect of any plan that posits an eradicable 'before' and a transcendent 'after' and flee any scheme for improving human existence at the first mention of 'rising above'. But these are only the most obvious conclusions to be drawn from Le Corbusier's lesson: conclusions frequently reached in critiques of modern architecture and modern urbanism, modernity-in-general, metaphysics, 'the enlightenment project'. Perhaps less obvious yet more important than what Le Corbusier's writings suggest about the violence of utopian longings are what they say about being human and hence inevitably their prey. From this view, Le Corbusier's most significant lesson concerns the volatility of longing and the desire for things impossible that have little to do with the ideal cities we dream and design – even if we have the power to say they are real and have others repeat it.

NOTES

I thank the editors of this volume for their helpful suggestions and for all their work in preparing this volume. I especially thank Rebecca Zorach for her excellent ideas for improving this essay and also for her unflagging patience as we cut and trimmed (again and again). I would also like to thank Brian Considine for help with the French translation and Kevie Faerkin for assistance with the images. Finally I thank my son, Max Schneider, for help with editing and for pointing out that Le Corbusier's 'the man who has surmounted himself' should read 'sir-mount'.

1   In describing architecture as performative I am borrowing Judith Butler's definition (which in turn borrows from Michel Foucault, and Jacques Derrida). Butler (1993), in her discussion of discursive performativity as it operates in the materialization of sex, defines performativity 'not as a single or deliberate ''act'' but rather, as the reiterative and citational practice by which discourse produces the effects that it names.' Spatial performativity works in similar fashion. I am not positing, ever, an essentialized equivalence between particular forms and meanings; I present these equivalences as constructed by Le Corbusier whose stated architectural meanings rely upon them. As Bernard Tschumi (1998), Spiro Kostoff (1991) and others have demonstrated, an architecturally performed meaning will function only within its specific historical, geographical, discursive context.

2   English translation, Brian Considine, Conservator of Decorative Arts and Sculpture for the Getty Museum, Los Angeles, California.

3   Catherine Ingraham states that because Le Corbusier's writings are so 'idiosyncratic' and 'bizarre' we cannot look to them for illumination of the straight line (Ingraham 1998: 51). Yet Le Corbusier's sexing and gendering of the curved and straight are not deviant within his cultural context. What is perhaps idiosyncratic for the contemporary reader is the unguarded candour of his remarks.

4   I have not conducted an analysis to determine whether users of Le Corbusier's built structures interpret and experience them as modern, transparent, masculine, feminine, etc. See Boudon (1972) for an analysis of the relationship between Le Corbusier's Pessac project as built and its recreations by its users.

5   Le Corbusier's aggression is expressed, among other ways, in his repeated usage of the metaphors of sport and war. See Jencks 1973: 18; Le Corbusier 1967: 150; Le Corbusier 1993: 43; Le Corbusier 1998: 214; Le Corbusier 1999: 16, 37.

6   With somewhat sinister implications, the *abattoir* plans have been omitted from all but the German editions of Le Corbusier's *Oeuvres Complètes* (Baker 1996: 238).

7   Le Corbusier's belief in architecture's revolutionizing and spiritualizing powers is neither original nor unique. Precedents include Plato's *Republic*, St Augustine's City of

God, Sir Thomas More's *Utopia*, Tomasso Campanella's *City of the Sun*, Francis Bacon's *New Atlantis*. Perhaps of more importance vis-à-vis Le Corbusier's work are the architectural and utopian discourses of the eighteenth and nineteenth centuries which posit architecture as a rational instrument of social reform: Claude Nicholas Ledoux (see Vidler 1987), Quatremere De Quincy (see Lavin 1992), Mikhail Bakunin and Peter Kropotkin; utopian socialists Saint-Simon, Charles Fourier, and Etienne Cabet; and city planners like Baron Haussmann.

8   Le Corbusier, perhaps in a move to blank out his personal past, abandoned his birth-name, Charles Edouard Jeanneret, in 1917 – though he continued to produce paintings and articles on painting under the name Jeanneret until 1928.

9   Purism's science of colours and forms was similar to those developed by Charles Henry and Jules Lallemand. These included accounts of rhythmic and non-rhythmic angles and lines (measured by Henry's 'aesthetic protractor') and of colours and forms which soothe and excite. See Von Moos (1987), 218–19, for a discussion of this work as published in *L'Esprit Nouveau*.

10 Examples of this practice include landscape paintings in which the landscape is feminized or those in which the female body, particularly the female nude, is painted 'frontally and horizontally as a kind of landscape' (Rose 1993: 96); the female body constructed as a field to be plowed or blank tablet to be inscribed (Dubois 1988); the colonialist enterprise that constructs the idea of Africa and the Americas as unknown worlds or 'virgin' territories for male conquest and exploration (McClintock 1995: 23); the 'male power fantasy' that sexualizes a feminized Orient for western possession (Said 1979); the use of Tahiti and the Tahitian woman to define an 'alluring or menacing other of Western "civilized" sexuality' (Brooks 1993: 162); women as part of the earth's body that becomes the 'terrain of men's own productions' (Theweleit 1993: 294).

11 The years in which Le Corbusier and Ozenfant developed their aesthetic and architectural principles are within the same period (approximately 1880–1930) in which aesthetic as well as historical primitivism flourished.

12 Le Corbusier states that 'Because its realm is so large architecture may well be defined as general culture' (Le Corbusier 1999: 38) – including furniture, rooms, sunlight, artificial light, air, temperature, the arrangement and function of the dwelling and building, the street, the urban environment, the town, the 'throb of the town', the countryside and its paths, houses, bridges, plants, sky, and 'nature' (Le Corbusier 1999: 32–3).

13 Views similar to those of Loos and Le Corbusier are those of Max Nordau, Walter Benjamin (1999), and Charles Baudelaire.

14 Art historian Heinrich Wölfflin, perhaps an unacknowledged influence on the development of Ozenfant's and Le Corbusier's physiology and psychology of colours and forms, defines architecture as 'upward striving'. In his essay, 'Prolegomena To A Psychology of Architecture' (1886), architecture is presented as 'the opposition between matter and force of form.' The function of architecture is to 'overcom[e] the resistance of formless matter' (Wölfflin 1994: 159) – i.e. of gravity, 'the tendency of all matter to spread out formlessly on the ground' (Wölfflin 1994: 151). Architecture, as

a human endeavour, 'looks upward, not to the ground like an animal' (Wölfflin 1994: 174).

15 This sampling does not begin to represent the numerous instances in which Le Corbusier uses women to suggest the non-modern. *Journey to the East* and *When the Cathedrals Were White*, for example, are filled with graphic references to the 'exotic,' erotically ornamented women Le Corbusier encounters during his travels. When travelling in New York, he is lured by the red light districts and burlesques on Broadway with their 'nude white bodies of beautiful women' (Le Corbusier 1947: 102, 110). When lecturing at Vassar, he 'enjoy[s] looking at these beautiful bodies, made healthy and trim by physical training' (Le Corbusier 1947: 106).

16 Jencks describes Le Corbusier's paintings of 'gargantuan, muscular, and peasant-like' women in the context of Le Corbusier's attempted seduction of Taya Zinkin. When Zinkin refuses, Le Corbusier allegedly responds, 'pity. You are fat and I like my women fat. We could have spent a pleasant night'. Zinkin's response is that 'he took such functional view of sex that it never occurred to him that the act would not carry its own reward for both of us' (Jencks 1973: 104).

17 See Brooks (1993), Colomina (1996), and Çelik (1996) on the relation between Le Corbusier's paintings of Algerian women and the Obus plan for Algiers. For an alternative investigation of modernity and modernization, as well as a discussion of the use of built forms to both materialize and dematerialize (as ruins) the modern in Rio de Janeiro, see Jaguaribe (1999).

18 In *Civilization and Its Discontents*, written three years before *The Radiant City,* Freud analyzed the human condition, setting out the irremediable hostilities between instinct and civilization and identifying females as the 'hostile instinctual force: women soon come into opposition to civilization and display their retarding and restraining influence' (Freud 1989: 59). Le Corbusier was a devotee of this position. See Wilson (1991) for an account of the association between the disorder of women and urban disorder.

19 The donkey, ruled by instincts and 'looseness', is explicitly associated by Le Corbusier with women. He executes a painting of a woman on a donkey, *Vin d'Athos* (Brooks 1997: 273), and includes in *Journey to the East* a chapter on 'She's and He's', the 'young women and the little donkeys of Stamboul' between which he finds 'certain affinities and resemblances' (Le Corbusier 1991: 128). When decorated the donkey becomes even more feminine: ornamented with a 'Persian robe and big black eyes', the donkey, writes Le Corbusier, is like a 'She'. (Le Corbusier 1991: 132).

20 See Hooper (1998) for an account of the spatial politics involved in Haussmann's demolition and reconstruction of Paris.

21 For additional statements on the home consistent with his disgust at corporeality and emphasis on hygiene see Le Corbusier 1967, 1986, 1998, and 1999.

22 See Wigley (1995b) for an analysis of whiteness as a repressed yet 'key subtext' (Wigley 1995b: xv) in modern architecture. While I agree with Wigley that whiteness is an important subtext, and that the white wall is an active mechanism of erasure, I diverge from his conclusions regarding the relation between modern architecture and

fashion – i.e. the idea that whiteness is a 'coat' of paint (the logic of clothing) that covers over the reputed nakedness of modern architecture. For Le Corbusier 'nakedness' is precisely the ideal to be displayed.

23 Yve-Alain Bois and Rosalind Krauss, in their discussion of Bataille's concept of '*informe*', or the formless, define its four characteristics as qualities Le Corbusier associates with the feminine: horizontality, base materialism, pulse, and entropy (Bois and Krauss). However, it is important to clarify that their use of the formless as a 'third term' that stands outside the opposition of form and content is exactly counter to Le Corbusier's usage and its association with the abject.

24 In a disturbing parallel to Le Corbusier's conceptualization of urbanism as surgery, Robert Moses, master planner of New York City, evokes a similar image of violence, one explicitly linked to the *abattoir*: 'When you operate in an overbuilt metropolis, you have to hack your way with a meat ax' (cited in Berman 1988: 290).

Chapter 4: Dystopia in Utopia

Exoticism and Degeneration in Indochina, 1890–1940

Hazel Hahn

From the 1890s to the 1920s, popular French perceptions of Indochina were characterized by conflicting ideologies: exploitative colonialism fed by rivalry with the British empire, the liberal ideology of exporting republican values for accomplishing the civilizing mission, and criticism of colonialism motivated more often by economic than ethical factors.[1] Idealized representations of the effects of colonization, namely material and moral progress, were published in both official and tourists' accounts. Such representations tended to focus on the most visible achievements of colonization, namely the urban layout and architecture of modern colonial cities like Saigon and Hanoi. However, in the realm of the social sciences, strikingly bleak perceptions of the effects of colonization were not uncommon. Such pessimism stemmed partly from disillusionment with the civilizing mission, but was also due to the widespread fear of degeneration in European high culture. Literary obsession with degeneration peaked at the turn of the century following the sensational success of Max Nordau's *Degeneration* (1892), which was translated into French in 1893 (Greenslade 1994: 120). Yet, the idea of the degeneration of civilizations persisted in a wide array of discourses and was also taken up in the 1930s by those who espoused the politics of eugenics. As Ann Laura Stoler has pointed out, degeneration seemed even more threatening in the colonial setting than in the metropolitan one, the sources of degeneration more pervasive and dangerous (Stoler 1995: 102–9). Since degeneration was thought to be an integral part of the evolution of civilizations, not only the colonized but also the colonizer was thought to be vulnerable to degeneration of a different kind. Theorists argued that two different cultures coming into contact could have a mutually destructive influence. European civilization was often thought to cause the demise of indigenous culture rather than successfully create an integrated culture. Certain substances introduced by westerners, such as alcohol and morphine, were thought to cause the moral degeneration of the colonized. Even those who considered certain aspects of Annamese civilization as superior to French civilization tended to agree. The playwright Eugène Brieux argued that before the arrival of the French 'debauch-ery, alcoholism and misery were unknown' in Indochina (Brieux 1910: 132). On the other hand, the most threatening source of degeneration of the colonizers, other than tropical heat, seemed to be precisely the culture of the colonized. This essay rereads the exoticism surrounding Indochina in light of colonial urban plan-ning, theories of degeneration and perceptions of the *métis* (mixed-blood), through travelogues, tourist publicity, literature, theories of criminal ethnology, and eugenics.

THE PICTURESQUE AS EXOTIC

There has been a recent surge in French literature and films on Indochina that reinvents the Indochina of the early twentieth century as a time and place reflected in a nostalgic mirror. Jean Noury's *L'Indochine en cartes postales avant l'ouragan: 1900–1920* (*Indochina in Postcards before the Hurricane*) (1992), complete with covers in pastel hues, reconstructs an Indochina seen through rose-colored glasses. Both nostalgic and sceptical of this very nostalgia, the book evokes a feeling of trying to hold onto a bygone era as a colourful dream, an experiment of ideals. As this book shows all too well, the postcard is a medium well suited for representing the picturesque, containing scenes that are literally worthy of making a picture of. Tens of thousands of such postcards were pro-duced and circulated by the colonial government and private industry partly to attract tourists to Indochina. Through the postcards, the promoters of tourism sought to present an image of an exotic land that was an inviting blend of the different and familiar, a land that provided both adventures and western ameni-ties. Postcards depicted not only ethnic groups, buildings, industries, commerce, the countryside, and diverse aspects of daily life, but also the darker, illicit sides of society, such as prostitutes and corpses of bandits, with the same curious eye that invited spectators partly by jolting them. These images of Indochina contrast with postcards on France from the same period, from which the rougher aspects of society were deleted.[2]

Whereas this photographic picturesque was aimed at both women and men, the literary picturesque was often the only means of representation avail-able to the female colonizer, underneath which, as Sara Suleri has shown about English India, sometimes lay a psychic tension and anxiety that threatened to erupt (Suleri 1992: 75–109). For Indochina the French writer Myriam Harry penned *Petites Épouses* (*Little Wives*) (1913), a picturesque exoticist fantasy. In France, picturesque literature was a well-established genre. The picturesque and the sublime, originally eighteenth-century aesthetic categories for landscape and nature, were increasingly applied to French urban aesthetics in the nineteenth century and used in countless depictions of urban, human types.[3] Since the mid nineteenth century, the picturesque, almost always described as '*pittoresque et curieux*' (picturesque and curious), was a very popular literary and journalistic genre in France, sustained by numerous writers, most of whom were men. By the turn of the century, the picturesque was also used in travelogues to far-away lands, especially by women and for women. Myriam Harry's books were consumed by French women who were attracted to such a genre with a twist of Pierre Loti-like exoticism which emphasized the search for impressions.[4]

The picturesque also worked as a strategy of representation that moulded Asian colonial cities into French categories. Picturesque representations focused on superficial elements such as physical appearances and costumes. One popular topic was the animated atmosphere felt as charming and cosmopolitan. Authors celebrated the harmonious blending of many different types and races on the thoroughfares. What might have complicated this representation – the very facts of colonialism and segregation – was simply set aside. Myriam Harry declared in *L'Indo-Chine* that no other colonial capital could be 'more charming, more serenely welcoming than Saigon', with its large avenues and fragrant gardens, a 'tropical picturesque that's discretely linked to French elegance' (Harry 1912: 74). A significant part of the charm was the heterogeneous crowd of different ethnic groups. The strolling tourist could observe different types amidst the picturesque blend of an 'eclectic and wandering' crowd:

> functionaries, officers, . . . interpreters in blue turbans, . . . mandarins of Laos, . . . pretty *métisses*, . . . Cambodians, coolies with bare chests, . . . pretty Tonkinese women, . . . semi-primitive Annamite women looking at wonderous dolls inside shop windows . . .
>
> (Harry 1912: 75)

Such a representation is reminiscent of the countless descriptions of the eclectic crowd of different classes and nationalities found on the Parisian Grands Boulevards of the nineteenth century, which formed a semi-circle in the right bank. Seen as the centre of the world, due to their heterogeneity and cosmopolitanism, the Boulevards were regarded as a stage of perpetual spectacle, the haven of *flâneurs*.[5] Exotic types increasingly figured significantly on the Boulevards of the turn of the century. Coming from this mode of observation, French female tourists often observed Indochinese street scenes as an exotic, aesthetic and colorful spectrum of ethnic types, a constantly changing kaleidoscope. Others saw the street scenes more as a simple contrast between the eastern and western. Helen Churchill Candee, an American, described Haiphong as a 'French town of villas, churches, public buildings and banks over which spill the population far from French. The Tonkinese have their quarter, too, but there are so many that the bulging quarter overflows. And thus the picturesque is brought into the banal European streets of Haiphong' (Candee 1927: 8). A description like this, with its casual reference to segregation, aestheticized street scenes and organized the hierarchy of identities. Haiphong was considered French because, although its population was not, its infrastructure was.[6]

Serene and animated atmosphere was an element of an almost utopia-like colonialist vision of Saigon. The city's nickname, 'the Pearl of the Extreme Orient', implied something of pristine and exotic feminine beauty, as well as charm and exuberance. The utopic dimension of Saigon also had much to do with the newness of the city and the modern beauty of its layout and architecture. Developed by the French beginning in 1867, Saigon was repeatedly depicted as a modern French city set in eastern settings, a city with 'an absolutely European appearance', with 'long riverbanks, large boulevards, rectilinear and spacious streets, lit with electricity' (Petit 1902: 508, 510). The Frenchness of Saigon was announced to visitors from their first glimpse of the city at the port. For Brieux, the spectacle of arriving in Saigon reinforced the famous description he had heard 'a thousand times', including 'the entry in a deep and large river that flows into the Mekong, its sinuosity, and upon approaching, coming into view, sometimes on the right, sometimes on the left, the towers of the cathedral' (Brieux 1910: 88). French visitors did not greet French architecture in Indochina with universal enthusiasm. By the 1900s such architecture was often criticized as extravagant (Wright 1991: 162).

Just as guidebook descriptions of Paris presented an image of a magnificent city from which unseemly elements – notably the working classes – were often deleted, guidebooks to Saigon and Hanoi focused on their French and monumental aspects. Indigenous parts of the city were marginalized in such depictions. In actuality, the policy of segregation, blatant in residential areas although never completely enforced as in Anglo-India, was much less formal in commercial areas. By the late 1920s frenetic animation, rather than serenity, marked the streets of Saigon. The Annamese, Chinese and Malabars filled the streets amidst Europeans in cars, rickshaws or on cafe terraces (Billotey 1929: 11). In the evening, Europeans took drives around the city. Lines of exclusion were drawn along a combination of race and class lines. As Saigon expanded in the 1920s and 30s, indigenous residential and commercial quarters were relegated to the outlying areas. With different axes for government, pleasure and business, 'powerful and schematic modern buildings' marked the centre, while 'vast colonial houses with verandas' were built in the periphery (Durtain 1930: 102). The amalgamation of the western and eastern tended to be limited to style, as in Boulevard Norodom which evoked 'Asian motifs simplified by the modern line', despite the urban planner Ernest Hebrard's principle to integrate more of the western and the eastern (Durtain 1930: 103).[7] Sometimes, however, buildings that were typically depicted as thoroughly French harboured surprising interiors. The interior of the cathedral in Hanoi, for example, contained elements of traditional Vietnamese temples and shrines. By the late 1920s Saigon was often judged to be too French, which reduced its exotic appeal. To Pierre Billotey the appearance of Saigon as a 'big, pretty French city, in tropical foliage' did much to 'ruin many a description' that he had heard (Billotey 1929: 9).

INDIGENOUS USES OF URBAN SPACES

How did the Annamese use and perceive the city?[8] If the French rhetoric of grandeur and prestige, expressed through monumental architecture, sought to inspire awe and respect in the indigenous population, evidence suggests that rather than seeing such architecture as an urban sublime, the Annamese viewed it differently. The streets of Saigon were 'full of native families from the country-side who came to the city to look'. According to one western observer 'they were obviously enjoying themselves' (Sitwell 1939: 53). When they got tired at looking at all the buildings, they 'just sat down, wherever they were, upon the pavement, occupying the whole width of it. . . . [T]hey rested there for a while, and made green tea, after which they would indulge in a short siesta'. Annamese police officers would try to remove them from the sidewalk in vain, and arguments would ensue. By the time the police threatened to use force, another party would arrive and sit down (Sitwell 1939: 57). Rural Annamese manners constantly intruded and undermined both official and modern ways of navigating the city.

This description comes from a western visitor applying the western cat-egory of tourism to the Annamese. Nevertheless, such a clue calls for in-depth accounts of the ways in which city spaces were used. In the 1920s and 1930s, much of the dramatic action in the streets was staged by the Annamese. In the mid-1920s, the trial of Phan Boi Chau and the death of Phan Chu Trinh, the two most respected leaders of a generation, served as occasions for widespread walk-outs by students. In 1937, when Annamese municipal councillors in Hanoi walked out of a meeting and then resigned to protest the French councillors' refusal to raise the number of Annamese councillors, a large group of Annamese workers gathered in front of the city hall.[9] The strike by the municipal councillors was front-page news in the Annamese press, which saw it as part of a struggle for gaining more rights. The same incident received meagre attention in the French press in Hanoi, which concerned itself much more with global affairs, such as the advance of the Japanese in China.[10] Segregation not only meant different uses of city spaces, but clearly formed two different worldviews and mindsets.

DYSTOPIAN EXOTICISM AND NEURASTHENIA

A significant part of the construction of the colonial exotic was an immense out-pouring of sexual fantasy and domination.[11] Pétrus Durel's illustrated *La Femme dans les colonies françaises* (*The Woman in the French Colonies*) (1898) was a supposed 'study of mores from the anatomical and social point of view' that objectified colonized women. For comparison, it also included objectified depic-tions of European women. It is a singularly anti-feminist treatise, which criticized French feminism and sought to put women in their supposed place. As such, it provokes questions about the place of women in colonial ideology, such as the ways in which women's response to the feminization of the colonies differed from men's, and how the readership of exoticist literature was gendered.[12]

The phenomenal success of Claude Farrère's 1905 exoticist novel, *Les Civil-isés* (*The Civilized*), raises similar issues. Awarded the prestigious Goncourt Prize in 1905, it went through no less than thirty-six editions in three years. This was probably the single most influential novel that shaped perceptions of French colonial life in Vietnam; two books were published by colonialists just to criticize it.[13] It represented French colonial Saigon as a mecca of sensual pleasures that led to the utter dissolution of the moral self. Its view of Asia as a land of sensuality, and Asians as victims of cosmopolitanism, were already clichés well-worn by the novels of Pierre Loti and his imitators. However, in literature, it also marked the emergence of the colonizer as a pathological type. Louis Malleret suggested in 1936 that, although the novel was attacked by later critics as full of 'false exoticism', the novel did raise the issue of 'the pathological aspect of colonial life' (Malleret 1934: 152). This, however, does not signify that Farrère intended to criticize colonialism. The novel did not dispute the value of the civilizing mission. It suggested that current colonizers were incapable of any moral mission because the colony attracted all the degenerate types from the metropole.

Colonial Saigon in *Les Civilisés* is strikingly dystopic. In the novel the tropical setting, with what Malleret sums up as 'languid and beautiful evenings' and 'the heavy scent of plants' (Malleret 1934: 152) is only an exacerbating factor and not the direct cause of moral weakening. Saigon is a corrupt asylum of all the *déclassés* that embody contemporary theories of degeneration. 'The civilized' are inheritors of too long a succession of civilizations (Farrère 1908: 304). The cosmopolitanism of Saigon further erodes the values of civilization, as the encounter between degenerate types only accelerates this dystopian civilizing process. In Saigon, 'the civilized capital of the world', each race's feeling of superiority creates a 'universal license' resulting in 'an incredible progress of civilization' (Farrère 1908: 24).

The very eclectic nature of Saigon's crowds, in contrast to their picturesque descriptions, signifies an utter sameness. 'This is Saigon', Mévil, the debauched doctor declares, 'see women yellow, blue, black, green – and even white'. 'All are for sale, like in Europe' (Farrère 1908: 23). The eclecticism of colonial architecture is likewise criticized: the lieutenant-governor's palace is 'a German temple of new Athens' (Farrère 1908: 180). The ultimate eclecticism is embodied by Dr Mévil, in whose veins 'all the origins were equally mixed' (Farrère 1908: 3). Mévil is a 'pathological case', unnatural both in his youthful appearance and spirit: 'a plant in a greenhouse, modified, deformed, atrophied by a manic culture . . . with speculation instead of instinct' (Farrère 1908: 251). In the novel, Saigon itself is feminized, 'delicate and melancholic' (Farrère 1908: 3), harbouring a constant threat of native riots and an inevitably tragic destiny. Its avenues are suddenly filled with a crowd of colonizers, overcome with 'madness and panic' (Farrère 1908: 281), again feminized as hysterical and alienated from the natives who seem to menace them (Farrère 1908: 280). Saigon is French, but it is an emasculated, unworthy extension of France. Fierce, a marine officer, is the only protagonist able to distance himself from the doomed process of the destructive encounter of different cultures. To him, the idea that the French colonizers could morally improve Asians is 'utopian' (Farrère 1908: 90), as the colonizers are inferior to Asians. He is able temporarily to escape 'a strange malady', 'civilization', because he is seafaring and mobile. (Farrère 1908: 191). Significantly, the possibility of his redemption depends on the pure love of a French woman. In a subsequent novel, *Une jeune fille voyagea* (1925), Farrère depicted a healthy colonizer, a young French woman, as a symbol of the renewal of French colonization. Seen in this context, *Les Civilisés* resonates much more with the fear of white degeneracy in the colonies than a critique of colonialism.

Notably, the success of this novel was largely due to a female readership that would also enthusiastically receive Farrère's other novels (Revon 1924: 6). The colonialist discourse of sexual desire was aimed at native women, not European women who were seen as the bearers of moral, educational and healing missions. The success of this novel makes one wonder if a significant reason for its appeal to women wasn't precisely its exoticism, specifically the unbridled sensualism attributed to European women. The tropical climate, while 'softening and depressing the males, maddened the females . . . with their ardor for pleasure, – all forms of pleasure' (Farrère 1908: 216). Perhaps the novel resonated in the sphere of feminine desire. The attraction of exoticism often had to do with ambivalence, the attraction to the reprehensible as countless fictional representations of European men's attraction to indigenous women suggested (Osborne 1990). What seems to have captured the metropolitan popular imagination was the construction of a colonial existence that seemed to allow extreme experiences that were forbidden in France. The colonial environment was seen as an alternately paradisiac and savage land, and the colonial society was seen as both liberating and claustrophobic. Hence, the appeal of the postcards from the colonies that could depict wilder and darker aspects of life than in France.

In the field of French literary criticism, the inter-war years produced a call for a subtler and more realistic literature – one based on actual experience in Indochina that would replace the tired genre of exoticism. Critics now found earlier works of exoticism superficial and misleading. Roland Lebel designated touristic literature as 'false exoticism', 'superficial impressionism that accounts for no more than the *décor*, costume, what is exterior and strange in the mores of the country' (Lebel 1931: 79). Critics declared that this genre, full of 'prejudices and stupid assertions', had perished (Lebel 1931: 82). Even as these lines were published in 1931, the exotic appeal of Indochina reached its zenith at the Colonial Exposition held in Paris. The centrepiece of the Exposition was a replica of the ruins of Angkor Wat.[14] The government, underlining the importance of Indochina as 'by far the richest and most populated' of the colonies in the empire, emphasized the educational purpose of the Exposition (*L'Illustration* 1931: LIX). Yet the commercial character of the Exposition was manifest in the glamorous image of Angkor Wat serving as the backdrop in advertisements for consumer products such as colonial attire and refrigerators (*L'Illustration* 1931). 'False exoticism' was alive and well in commercial culture, which used the image of Angkor Wat to vaunt the superiority of modern French culture and tech-nology.

In *Les Civilisés*, debilitating climate was associated with moral dissolution. This must have provoked unease in the community of *colons* who frequently suffered from neurasthenia. Considered initially as an urban neurosis, the concept was imported from the US into France in the 1880s (Hacking 1998: 120). In the metropole it was considered a 'malady through overexertion' (Fleury 1930: 106), but in the colonies the illness was associated with 'the loss of the will'. The symptoms of neurasthenia, physical and mental weakness, ruptured the masculine discourse of the colonizer as a physical and mental superior. As Stoler has pointed out, in the colonies the causes of neurasthenia were the reverse of those in the metropolis: i.e. the distance from homeland (Stoler 1991: 77).[15] A typical observation of the effect of this distance was provided in another novel, *La Vie Européenne au Tonkin* (*European Life in Tonkin*) (1901) by Eugène Jung. Distanced from the world of ideas in Paris, and affected by the climate, the *colons* inevitably submit to the desire for lassitude. Along with 'the loss of the will' comes the 'desire for material compensations, and all kinds of sensations and stimulants' (Jung 1901: 245). This loss of the will was often ascribed as both cause and symptom of neurasthenia. The ultimate cure was the return to France, to a 'normal', balanced life. By the 1930s colonial medicine defined neurasthenia as the most common form of psychosis effecting *colons* (Joyeux and Sicé 1937: 334). The native population were not known to suffer neurasthenia at all, and by the 1930s social causes such as isolation were deemed much more important than the climate. Charles Joyeux and A. Sicé clearly saw neurasthenia as a form of mental, as well as physical, debilitation and recommended that only those of 'elite character' be sent to the colonies (Joyeux and Sicé 1937: 335). An advertisement, from the 1931 Colonial Exposition, precisely underlined the difference between the neurasthenia of the metropole and the colonies. It vaunted the merits of a medication that renews energy: 'Modern, feverish and hectic life affects the organism, as much as the extra-European heavy heat. Imitate the colonials!' (*L'Illustration* 1931).

THEORIES OF DEGENERATION AND THE MÉTIS

The idea that different civilizations exert mutually corrosive influence was espoused by Gustave Le Bon as early as the mid-1880s. The arguments of Le Bon, who would gain fame for his theories of crowd psychology, show that a critique of the policy of assimilation did not automatically signify a stance of anti-colonialism. To the contrary, Le Bon discouraged the policy of assimilation for fear that it would weaken the authority of the French colonial regime. At the 1889 International Colonial Conference held in Paris, Le Bon delivered a controversial report on the effects of assimilationist policies on colonized cultures. He was prophetic in his suggestion that giving the colonized a European, liberal education would make them want liberty. The obvious lesson of the French Revolution, for example, would be 'Algeria to the Arabs!' (Le Bon 1887: 455). The last thing that Le Bon hoped for was such an outcome, as he was foremost concerned with the possible weakening of France as a colonial power through the loss of the 'respect' of the colonized. Consequently, he argued for leaving the indigenous institutions on their own. He argued that assimilation was impossible, that 'history shows that two civilizations too different ... never blend together' (Le Bon 1912: 239).[16] One fundamental reason was that 'our civilization is too complicated for inferior people', that 'neither through education, nor institutions, or religious beliefs, or any means at hand, can Europeans exert fast civilizing action on the Orientals, and less still on inferior peoples' (Le Bon 1912: 271, 273).

Fundamental to Le Bon's argument was the principle of the hierarchy of civilizations and races. According to Le Bon there were four types of races, ranging from 'the inferior races' or 'the negroes' who were 'capable of attaining to the rudiments of civilization, but to the rudiments only', to the 'superior races', the Indo-Europeans. Convinced that 'the superior races are wholly unable to induce inferior races to accept their civilization or to thrust it on them', Le Bon admired the English non-interventionist policy concerning indigenous institutions, which was more of a segregationist policy (Le Bon 1924: 27). He cited an English professor who claimed that 'a Hindu, although rarely capable of assimilating our qualities, is to the contrary very apt at adopting our faults'. By his own admission, Le Bon's arguments were immediately criticized by the Indian press and enthusiastically accepted by English colonialists (Le Bon 1887: 449).

Le Bon's theories about decadence also led him straight to a stance of firmer segregation. Using the Lamarckian idea of the hereditary transmission of acquired habits, he argued that 'hereditary dispositions which had required centuries for their formation may be rapidly lost' when the soul of a civilization is dissolved through a large influx of foreign elements. He used ancient Rome as an example, which admitted 'foreigners hailing from all countries' to citizenship (Le Bon 1924: 211). According to him 'analogous causes of decadence threaten our hyper-refined civilisations' (Le Bon 1924: 215). There is an unmistakable affinity between the ideas of Le Bon and Farrère. Le Bon's argument was that different cultures do not blend together, whereas Farrère depicted eclecticism resulting from indiscriminate blending of cultures. Both were fundamentally concerned with the question of French colonial strength. Le Bon implicitly accepted the notions of Renan and Gobineau that the superior races had the right to dominate inferior races.

The tropes of degeneration deployed in *Les Civilisés* were also manifest in the seemingly drier field of criminal ethnology. The prolific and controversial Dr A. Corre in *L'Ethnographie criminelle* (*Criminal Ethnology*) (1894), a work of supposed empiricism based on 'observations and judiciary statistics gathered in French colonies', argued that the rate of crime rose with colonization, that among 'uncivilized milieus' there was less crime than among the civilized. The gravest of the corrupting influence of western civilization on the colonies was the replacement of traditions by 'very degenerative vices' such as alcohol, morphine and opium. He argued that the imposition of one civilization onto another without a carefully manoeuvred transition led to the 'disappearance of less resisting races' (Corre 1894: 596).

Like Le Bon, Corre criticized the aims of the civilizing mission as futile, that 'The French, pretending to be the civilizing force, only add to degeneracy' (Corre

1897: 37). Unlike Le Bon however, Corre also flatly described it as hypocritical. He literally incriminated the act of colonizing as 'criminal' and depicted the colonizer as an exploitative parasite (Corre 1897: 2–3, 37–9). He emphasized the moral vulnerability of the colonizers; among the degenerative vices taken from the indigenous cultures were 'certain sexual habits' such as homosexuality (Corre 1897: 13). Like Le Bon, Corre's ideas were based on both a hierarchy of races and fundamental differences among races. He argued that the *métis* of European and Indian origins, 'a union of two races similar in origin', 'is a satisfying product, likely to help the development of European action'. A *métis* of a white and black races on the other hand, may possess 'nice physical qualities' and a 'brain larger than that of the black', but what appears sometimes as brilliant intelligence turns out to be 'in general very superficial'. Corre judged that hopes pinned on this type of mixed race for social renovation of the colonies were misguided (Corre 1897: 30–1). According to Corre, certain mixtures of races were desirable and certain were not, depending on the influence of heredity and social milieu. He thought that the Franco-Indochinese *métis*, abandoned by their French fathers, were sociologically rather than genetically doomed, 'fatally destined to fall again into the low milieu of the country'. He considered this 'unfortunate, since these people are nice-looking and intellectually gifted', because 'despite more differences, present superior characters, born of two races that are in sum very intellectual' (Corre 1897: 262). This opinion echoed the ideas of A. Mondière from 1886. Mondière also considered Indochinese *métis* as 'physically and morally very gifted'. Mondière encouraged Frenchmen to marry Annamese women in order to enlarge the population of Eurasians (cited in Holbé 1916: 450), an opinion that would become much less acceptable to the French after the turn of the century.

Although Corre implied that certain *métissage* can be inherently degenerative, any association between *métissage* and madness or sterility were absent in his ideas. Others made that association. At the International Colonial Institute held in Brunswick in 1911, M.E. Moresco argued that after a few generations among the *métis* sterility appears, 'unless a new mixing with one of the original races takes place'. This idea was based on the notion that the *métis* do not form a race of their own, and that for them the need and will to procreate and perpetuate their race is weaker than for a 'real' race (Moresco 1911: 453).

By the late 1930s and early 1940s, some eugenicist treatises clearly associated the mixed-blood with inescapable madness and sterility. René Martial, a leading expert on health and immigration, argued in *Les Métis* that one drop of non-European blood, including Semitic and Slavic blood, resulted in symptoms of degeneration that could manifest generations later. He argued that it was proven through the study of blood types in Indochina that the mixture of the Annamese and the French results in an 'instable equilibrium' due to 'antagonistic forces, forces and ideas that are contradictory and confused'. He considered this to be a 'profound, ancient and principal cause of hereditary madness' (Martial 1942: 52–60).[17]

Through the 1930s, the discourse of French law or social policy on the Indochinese *métis* tended to assume that the *métis* inevitably blends into one culture or the other. Medical generalizations of the *métis* characteristics were vague, stereotypical and contradictory. According to some, *métis* children were more delicate than indigenous children; according to others less energetic than Europeans (Gravelle 1913: 32). Social milieu as well as heredity were the focus of the debate. The political consequences of the fates of the *métis* formed the core issue, due to the fear that, rejected by both cultures, the *métis* would turn against the colonial regime. Legal debates from the 1910s through the 1920s gave limited attention to the predicament of Indochinese *métis*, of which only those recognized by a French parent were given French citizenship. The question of how to determine the race of the unrecognized *métis* provoked considerable anxiety.[18] At the French Feminists' Congress at the 1931 Colonial Exposition in Paris, an extensive discussion of the problem of abandoned *métis* took place, ending with a demand for equal rights for them as French citizens (*États généraux du féminisme* 1931: 142). Their perceptions of the *métis* are among the most cheery considered yet. The mixed-bloods were thought to enjoy 'on average good health', and possess temperaments that are a mixture of western animation and eastern calm. Some internal conflict was thought to occur from such a mixture but no disturbing conclusions were drawn (*États généraux du féminisme* 1931: 137). Throughout the discussions, the feminists upheld the view of themselves as the guardians of morality and first saw themselves as French colonialists and only secondly claimed solidarity with indigenous women. Tellingly, the feminists urged the colonial regime to strengthen the censorship of films, in order to prevent any moral corruption of the colonizer or the colonized. While they urged that men take more responsibility for their *métis* children, no mention was made about abandoned indigenous companions. The feminists assumed that mixed children were the result of the lack of white women in the colonies and that many of the abandoned *métis* were born of prostitutes.

Clotilde Chivas-Baron, who reported at the Feminists' Congress on the legal and moral situation of the indigenous women in the French colonies in Asia and Oceania, was also the founder of the Mutual Aid Union of Colonial Women. Her book, *La Femme française aux colonies* (*French Woman in the Colonies*) (1929) was devoted to the works of French women dedicated to the civilizing mission. Her treatment of the theme of the *métis* in her works of fiction reveals more progressive, subtler views than other novelists'. Malleret mentioned Chivas-Baron along with Jeanne Leuba as one of the two most impressive of women colonial novelists of the era. *Confidences de métisse* (*Confessions of a Métisse*) (1927), which condemned the cold, destructive actions of a Frenchman who abandons his indigenous companion and his daughter, was far from original in the portrayal of an alienated *métisse* with a heart of gold and a doomed fate. However, her *Trois femmes annamites* (*Three Women of Annam*) provided a subtler portrayal. The *métisse*, Ginette, a daughter of a Vietnamese woman married to a Frenchman, is more than the sum of her conflicted selves. A spirited character, she is critical of the hypocrisy of the French colonial rhetoric exporting 'liberty, equality, fraternity'. She seems to be able to see through all the schemes and secrets, on both French and Vietnamese sides. She exposes and turns around such secrets, such as the fact that her Vietnamese cousin's French husband was about to depart for France to be married to a French woman, that in fact the cousin had been sold to the Frenchman as a mistress (Chivas-Baron 1925: 207). Although the novel's depiction of the *métisse*'s tendency to act in paradoxical ways – as a result of mixed characteristics – is stereotypical, the novel represented this tendency in a positive light.

Among the picturesque types depicted by Helen Churchill Candee was a *métisse* seen at the theatre, 'a strange flower displaying its exotic beauty – the Eurasian lady of Tonkin', dressed in the latest French fashion and surrounded by the admiring French (Candee 1927: 21). This example of the feminine picturesque set aside any sense of alienation that the woman in question might have felt, even as it contributed to that alienation with the adjective 'strange'. It leads us to the question of how to study the history of alienation and fear. The sense of alienation and the metaphors of pathology for colonial existence were articulated not only in terms of the weakening of body and mind but also of pathological anxiety and fear. Agoraphobia becomes an apt metaphor in the critical analysis of the rules of exclusion and inclusion in colonial cities. Agoraphobia was termed as such by Carl Westphal in 1871. Where neurasthenia entails weakness and exhaustion, agoraphobia is characterized by panic attacks and fear of public spaces and gatherings.[19] Yet from the beginning, agoraphobia was associated with neurasthenia. Freud thought that agoraphobia was found most often among neurasthenic individuals (Knapp and Schumacher 1988: 43). Westphal's suggested cure for agoraphobia differed little from that for neurasthenia: visiting water spas and taking 'healthful water' (Knapp and Schumacher 1988: 40). Those suffering from neurasthenia went to Dalat, the popular hill station built at 1,700 m of altitude, to take fresh air and try to restore their health deemed ravaged by the climate. Dalat might have harboured the agoraphobic as much as the neurasthenic. Fears of public spaces and crowds, leading to panic and a keen, sudden sense of alienation, were described in fiction, as in George Orwell's *Burmese Days* (1934), where an Englishwoman, Elizabeth, senses a sudden sense of alienation and fear and returns home in search of familiar comforts. Life in the colonies, both for the colonized and the colonizer, induced an extraordinary amount of fear. For the colonized, the fear of running into the colonizers could take on phobic dimensions. On the other side were the sense of alienation in a foreign environment, the ideology of segregation itself which stemmed from the fear of physical touch, and the search for the familiar comforts. All of these can be considered as minor forms of agoraphobia, situations and ideologies that perpetuated fear and anxiety.

CONCLUSION

This examination of an array of French texts on the effects of colonization has shown contrasting images: idealization and aestheticization on one hand and pessimistic diagnoses of the mutually destructive influence of different cultures on the other. At the turn of the century, when Indochina remained mostly an exotic and distant colony, utopian and dystopian visions coexisted in travelogues, literature and social sciences. By the late 1920s Saigon and Hanoi began to appear at once as visually too French to be exotic and culturally too Annamese and complex to be even remotely utopian. The appearance of an Annamese middle class and the growth of anti-imperialist activities by the Annamese made colonial existence both much more complicated and suspect. At the same time literary critics, rejecting superficial exoticism, called for authentic colonial literature embracing the complexity of life in Indochina. Yet exoticized images of both the colonized and the colonizer permeated the metropolitan commercial culture of the inter-war years, reaching its peak at the 1931 Colonial Exposition.

The theories that focused on the effects of the civilizing mission gone awry – as mainly seen in Farrère, Le Bon and Corre in their writings dating from the 1880s to the mid 1920s – contained multiple interpretative opportunities for the construction of the colonizer as a pathological type, which might nullify the idea of the colonizer as superior to the colonized. Few drew such a conclusion, and Corre's outright condemnation of colonialism was unexpected, as his argument did not build up to it. However, the texts clearly reveal that all three thinkers perceived colonizers as possessing a range of capacity – or a lack thereof – for colonization. Likewise, theories about the hierarchy of civilizations and races were far from consistent in their conclusions, depending on their interpretation of hereditary and environmental factors. By the early 1930s the discourse about *métis* children in French Indochina seemed to gain a certain rationality. Yet a decade after the feminists advocated for equal rights for unrecognized *métis* children, eugenicist tracts from the metropole – supposed blueprints of an ideal society – would condemn all *métissage* on a pseudo-scientific basis. The perception that the colonizer was vulnerable to both the cultural and genetic influence of the colonized formed one major cause of the fear of *métissage*. An analysis of agoraphobia, as both an illness and a metaphor, would enhance the understanding of this fear, and the broader ideology of segregation, which profoundly shaped the psyche of the colonizer and the colonized.

NOTES

1   For a comprehensive account of the colonization of Indochina, see Brocheux and Hemery (1995). On the idea of the civilizing mission, see Conklin (1998).
2   On French postcards see Schor (1992).
3   See *Les Français peints par eux-mêmes* (1841) and Goncourt et al. (1889).
4   On Loti see Todorov (1993).

5   See Schwartz (1998) and Hahn (1997).

6   Due to indifference, the lack of language skills and the fear of the unknown, few French travellers wandered into the indigenous parts to investigate. Leon Werth, who did, wrote a searing critique of French colonialists in *Cochinchine* (1926).

7   On the work of Hébrard, as well as on colonial urban planning in general, see Logan (1994 and 2001), Le Brusq (1999) and Wright (1991).

8   Here I use the term 'Annamese' rather than 'Vietnamese', following Goscha (1995), since it was the term that the indigenous population used for themselves.

9   National Archives n.1. Hanoi. Mairie de Hanoi E9 383.

10 *Avenir du Tonkin*, 4 December 1937: 7e; 11 December 1937: 4e; 18 December 1937: 4e.

11 See Stoler (1991). On the British case see McClintock (1995).

12 On colonial women, see Clancy-Smith (1998) and Knibiehler (1985).

13 Virginia Thompson claimed that *Les Civilisés* did the single most damage in the French perceptions of their colonialists, that the novel did nothing but affirm existing bourgeois prejudice against the adventurer (Thompson 1937: 405).

14 On the Colonial Exposition, see Morton (2000) and Norindr (1997). On French exoticism of the inter-war years, see Ezra (2000).

15 On neurasthenia in colonial Philippines, see Anderson (1997).

16 *La Psychologie politique* includes *Revue Scientifique* articles from 1886–9. On Le Bon, see Marpeau (2000), Barrows (1981) and Rouvier (1986). Rouvier leaves out the racist and segregationist ideas of Le Bon. Biondi calls Le Bon the more appropriate 'segregationist' (Biondi 1992: 40).

17 Martial tried to adopt the blood-group anthropology, developed in the early 1930s, for screening potential immigrants into France (Schneider 1990: 94).

18 See Stoler (1997). On *métissage* in Réunion, see Verges (1999).

19 On agoraphobia and urban space, see Da Costa Meyer (1996) and Vidler (1991 and 1993).

Part III

At Home in Public

Peg Birmingham

Certainly since the time of the Greeks, Western political thought has organized itself around the distinction between the public space of the city and the private space of the household. This distinction is fundamentally gendered: men as free citizens belong to the public space, whereas women are relegated to the private realm of the household wherein the chief duty is to attend to the needs of the body. Alberti's fifteenth-century treatise, *On the Art of Building in Ten Books*, is unquestionably one of the fundamental texts of this tradition, explicitly offering us an architectural vision of how the boundary between the public and the private ought to be built and maintained. At the same time, it is a treatise on how patriarchal authority ought to be exercised in the household, outlining a particular intersection between the spatial occupations of the husband, always exposed to the outside world, and those of the wife who is sequestered deep in the recesses of the house. Alberti reinscribes the traditional prohibition of any confusion between this gender-space division, whether it be the husband's occu-pation of the house or the wife's occupation of the exterior, public space. The greatest threat is the threat of being in the wrong place, a threat that is always associated with the feminine per se insofar as the woman outside the home is not more masculine, but rather, more dangerously feminine, while a man occu-pying the interior of the home does not become less masculine but rather ominously feminine. Thus, to be in the wrong place is to be threatened with a dangerous femininity.

The following two essays show the ways in which gendered utopian visions of the nineteenth and early twentieth centuries have disrupted the traditional gendered distinction between the public and the private. These essays examine the ways in which the *material dimension* of public spaces confound the very dis-tinction between the public and the private, showing how gendered utopian visions since the nineteenth century have rendered the boundary between the public and the private much more fluid, insisting that we rethink what it means to be 'at home in public'. Indeed, these two essays implicitly show how the feminine utopian vision of the nineteenth- and early twentieth-century social reformers undoes the 'law of the proper place'.

Sharon Haar's essay, 'At Home in Public: The Hull House Settlement and the Study of the City' (from which I take the title of my introduction), examines the ways in which the Hull House Settlement confounds the distinction between the public and the private, calling into question the notion of a home as a private space opposed to public life. Indeed, 'At Home in Public' captures the radical transformation this distinction undergoes with the Hull House Settlement. Examining the architecture of the Hull House as it grows and develops over three decades, Haar convincingly shows how the boundary between the public and the private becomes increasingly fluid and difficult to locate. At the same time, the gendered material practices of the Hull House which are *both* public and private, viz., they take place in a 'household' that explicitly defines itself as public, call into question the location of women's work. Moreover, Haar's focus on the ever increasing expansion of the Hull House Settlement, occurring through these gendered material practices, calls into question the *concept* of the city, that is, the view that the public spaces of city develop out of the visions of city planners whose perspective, like the philosopher-king, is always a view from above. More precisely, the concept of the city relies on a vision that understands public space as rationally organized, and it represses the bodily and material conditions that might pollute this vision. The vision of the city by urban planners is one that grasps the city as a functional organization capable of administration through various well-planned and programmatic strategies. On the contrary, Haar claims that the radicality of the utopian vision of the Hull House reformers lies in implicitly rejecting the vision of city planners, instead grasping the public space of the city as a set of myriad, material lived practices with a life of its own, beyond the attempts at rational organization in which everything has its proper place and function.

Significantly, this changes the usual sense of 'utopian'. Rather than denoting a vision that is without location or *topos* due to its inherently high-flown view, the utopian vision of the Hull House reformers situated itself on the ground, within the material practices of its projects. The 'atopos' here, therefore, has a quite different sense, indicating only that there is no proper place in which to locate these material practices. The architecture of the Hull House Settlement reflects an understanding of the city as a place that is constantly exploding, in which places are woven together in ways that cannot be planned in advance, where heterogeneous and even contrary elements make up its spaces. The Hull House Settlement is an embodied, inhabited public/private place that eludes rational organization and administration. Nothing stays put. The gendered law of the proper place no longer holds sway. Significantly, the maps that Haar refers to in her essay are in actuality maps of urban practices on view through the various rooms and buildings that over time and space materially make up the Hull House Settlement.

Spencer-Wood's essay, 'Utopian Visions and Architectural Designs of

Turn–of–the–Century Social Settlements', also examines the ways in which women social reformers embody their utopian visions through the architecture of their public institutions. This essay also shows how the built environment of these social movements not only confounds the public/private distinction, but actually adds to the public space regulations and occupations once confined to the private. For example, legislative regulations on the conditions of labour came out of these settlements, as did the development of a powerful unionized working class. Of particular importance was the settlements' contribution to the development of women's trade unions. Moreover, utopian reformers created new public professions such as kindergarten teachers and public health nursing.

Most importantly, Spencer-Wood's essay supports many of Haar's claims regarding the city as a set of material lived practices that elude the grasp of a dominant, bourgeois culture. In her essay, she challenges the 'social control historians' who claim that public co-operative activities were anti-revolutionary by teaching immigrants that the key to a better life lay in adopting bourgeois American values. Most generally, the social control historians (Foucault's *Discipline and Punish* would be exemplary of this group of theorists) argue that reformers such as those associated with the Hull House were 'cynically using their utopian vision of pluralistic society which was implemented with programs promoting ethnic culture as just a temporary first step in a homogenizing Americanization program.' Similar to Haar's analysis, Spencer-Wood's account takes issue with this assessment of the utopian vision, arguing that the annual reports of these various settlement houses suggest something else, namely, a commitment *not* to shape immigrant behaviour to the traditional colonial pattern. Indeed, Spencer-Wood points to the elitist assumptions that underpin these claims. The social control historians, she argues, implicitly assume a passive, pliable, and powerless immigrant or lower-class body that can be easily controlled by a 'tops-down' management model. She gives compelling evidence that these immigrant groups were much more unruly and independent than the social control theorists allow. Her argument suggests that the analysis of these utopian reform programmes must take seriously the role the participants themselves played, practices mostly overlooked by social control historians. She argues that the evidence against the social control theorists lies in the everyday practices of these immigrant groups. These practices of everyday life, she claims, reveal that the immigrants themselves determined the effects of these programmes; they tactically decided if and how to use the various programmes developed by the utopian vision. Implicit to Spencer-Wood's analysis is the claim that in analyzing these various social utopian visions it is not enough to simply look at the dominant discourse of the reformers. There is, at the same time, a 'submerged discourse' that takes place at the level of the material practices themselves. These overlooked material practices indicate that the participants have visions and operations of their own which belongs to the lexicon of user's practices.

As Michel de Certeau points out in *The Practice of Everyday Life*, it is not enough to analyze the actual programmes put in place by the social reformers; it remains to be asked what the participants *made* of these programmes (de Certeau 1984: 31–2). Spencer-Wood's essay shows that the participants tactically used these programmes for their own ends and purposes, and in doing so actively transformed the dominant or official discourses in ways not considered by social control theorists. Moreover Spencer-Wood, as does Haar, argues that the architecture that housed these material practices reflects the pluralism at the very centre of the social utopian vision. Both essays in this section therefore suggest the importance of attending to the changing material practices of participants in the social reform movement at the turn of the last century, and help us in our own historical moment to rethink dominant conceptions of the public and the private, the utopian, and the everyday.

Chapter 5: At Home in Public

The Hull House Settlement and the Study of the City

Sharon Haar

In 1909, reflecting on the first twenty years at the Hull House Social Settlement, Jane Addams remarked:

> No effort is made in the recital to separate my own history from that of Hull House during the years when I was 'launched deep into the stormy intercourse of human life' for, so far as mind is pliant under the pressure of events and experiences, it becomes hard to detach it.
>
> (Addams 1981: xvii)

As Jane Addams's public identity came to stand in for Hull House, it was the Settlement's 'community of women' that shaped her ever-expanding vision of reform. Jane Addams's work, the work of those who lived and worked with her, and the Hull House Settlement itself were complexes of overlapping, ambiguous, and sometimes contradictory private and public interests and spaces. As Addams – the person – came to embody Hull House, her own body occupied a diverse range of environments and projects that transcended rigid categories of private and public space, domestic and civic concerns. As a social spheres Hull House was simultaneously private and public. In her various roles Addams lived this simultaneity: until her death in 1935 she served as both the Head Resident of the house and the President of its institutional manifestation, the Hull House Association.[1] At her memorial in 1935 numerous individuals filled the residential courtyard of the Settlement complex, occupying the ground, terraces, fire escapes, and windows. Images show the court filled with bodies other than Addams's. But when the 'restored' house reopened in 1967 as the Jane Addams Hull-House Museum it was Addams's bust that occupied the space of honour, as the urban environment surrounding the building had been cleared of the tenements and immigrants she had come to Chicago to work among.

As a building, the categorization of Hull House as either private or public, home or institution, has limited many attempts to understand its activities and the spaces that supported those activities.[2] Curiously, little has been written

Figure 5.1
Jane Addams's profile
before 1900.
Jane Addams Memorial
Collection, Special
Collections, The
University Library, The
University of Illinois at
Chicago, JAMC neg. 9

Figure 5.2
Jane Addams's funeral,
1935, in Hull House
Courtyard.
Jane Addams Memorial
Collection, Special
Collections, The
University Library, The
University of Illinois at
Chicago, JAMC neg. 520

about the Settlement's architecture, particularly its place and placement within the larger city. Until recently, attention has focused on either typological similarities to a growing network of women's institutions at the end of the nineteenth century or the buildings' stylistic affinities with the Arts and Crafts movement.[3] By contrast, this chapter addresses the urbanism of Hull House, looking at how the Settlement grew over time from a home in the city to an example and way of being 'at home' in the city. In doing so, I intend to illustrate how Hull House undermined the boundaries between its status as a community, as an architectural complex, and as an institution devoted to the study and reform of the industrial city. Much can be learned by revisiting Hull House's history and influence through an exploration of its residents' interdisciplinary approach to the study of and participation in urban life.

'OBJECTIVE' AND 'SUBJECTIVE' VISIONS OF REFORM: JANE ADDAMS'S LEGACY

In conceiving of Hull House as a reform institution, Addams attempted to reinscribe a myth of Lincolnesque democracy into the space of the late nineteenth-century industrial city. The desire to heal the rupture created by the Civil War was an ideal unsustainable in the industrializing, urbanizing nation. Indeed, one can read Hull House as a monument to a longing for an ideal past. But despite a sentimentalizing tone, Addams did not write her narrative as a nostalgic vision of the past, nor did she live her life that way. As William James put it: 'The fact is, Madam, that you are not like the rest of us, who *seek* the truth and *try* to express it. You *inhabit* reality; and when you open your mouth truth can't help being uttered'.[4] The destruction of the Hull House Settlement is only one of many losses to history. But often ignored is Ellen Gates Starr, who co-founded the Settlement with Addams. The almost complete identification of the house as the autobiography of Jane Addams produced further losses. What early feminist scholars found when they started to sift through the rubble of the Settlement was the community that resided there, and with more recent scholarship on immigration, class, and race, the neighbourhood that this community settled within.[5]

Jane Addams wrote of Hull House in binary terms. In her writings she speaks of Hull House as both concept and space, subject and object, a set of activities and a complex of buildings, interdependent with but distinct from the city at large. Hull House as a particular set of buildings in a particular urban milieu was an embodiment of these concepts and activities. But historically, Hull House has come down to us today as an embodiment of Addams and/or, in stronger feminist readings, the 'community of women' (although there were also men) who lived and worked with her. Addams stated that the principle behind the plan, sometimes referred to as a scheme, was to ameliorate the social, economic, and environmental problems of nineteenth-century urban life. As time went on, the focus of their work centred on immigrants, particularly women and children.

These plans were underwritten by particular ideals of American democracy that she sought to uphold and further within the context of the industrial city.

Twenty Years at Hull-House, with its prologue, the tale of Addams's own development into political and representational consciousness, merged the autobiographical and the historical in a spatialized narration. It is the story of many through the ideas of one. In the architecture of Hull House, as elsewhere, notions of political and linguistic representation are extended and given dimension as 'who may enter' is given physical meaning and 'what is spoken' combine to create liminal experience. To scrutinize the writings (broadly speaking) of Addams in relation to Hull House is to do more than simply animate the physical artefact or decipher the inscriptions of a text. It is purposely to conflate the personal and the political, the private and the public, the citizen and the city into lived experience, in space, through time. The purpose of such a project is to bring Hull House back into the ambiguous space that it actually occupied in the first decades of its existence.

Jane Addams was a prolific writer and publicist for Hull House, the most influential social settlement in the United States. Addams's nephew John Weber Linn described her writing technique as requiring a 'paleographic expert' to decipher; as 'some of the sections of the original manuscript were such an interweaving of clippings, and elaborations and insertions and connections' (Linn 1935: 257). Not unlike descriptions of the nineteenth-century city from nineteenth-century critic Charles Baudelaire to early twentieth-century author Walter Benjamin to the contemporary philosopher Elizabeth Wilson, Linn's description is also an analogy for the creation of both the concept of Hull House and its architecture, which grew in response to the needs of its neighbours, the interests of its residents, and the concerns of its network of intellectual, political, and financial supporters. Deciphering the architecture of Hull House presents an archaeological challenge further complicated by the destruction of the complex in 1963. Addams's and the residents' extensive texts provide insight into this exploration.[6]

Much of what might be called the legacy of Jane Addams and Hull House has been brought together in the *Jane Addams Papers*, which consists of 82 reels of microfilm of materials collected from around the world. These documents provide maps to Hull House as an institution in space and the buildings as fluid containers and evolving constructions for activities and people. These papers and fragments of papers – incomplete, torn, often undated, sometimes miscollated – provide snapshots of moments of the house's existence. As one scrolls through the microfilm, linearly, sometimes, but not always chronologically, events unfold then drop off or may be interrupted by other interconnected or distinct events. Archiving produces these narratives imposing linearity to events, documents, people, and buildings. Recollecting, too, is an activity of multiple voices and discourses. To move beyond these textual artefacts of Hull House, we must take account of it as an 'embodied subjectivity' or 'psychic corporeality' as Elizabeth Grosz would describe 'a feminist theoretical approach to concepts of the body' (Grosz 1994: 21–2).

In his foreword to the 1961 edition of Addams's *Twenty Years at Hull-House* (1910), Henry Steele Commager notes that this text is not her autobiography, but the biography of Hull House. He states that she asks us '[not] to consider her, but only the society she served', despite the fact that the text begins with the national history that brought her to Hull House and is interwoven with her own personal history. Commager's reading of *Twenty Years* reinforces one image of Addams as Saint Jane – performing miracles of order within the unruly, untidiness of her neighbourhood – at the same time as it inextricably links her to the house she occupied, objectifying both in the process. But the text could also be considered a feminist autobiography, one that acknowledged the embedded relationship between the residents of Hull House, their activities, and their home.

Twenty Years at Hull-House collects many of Addams' writings, including two of the earliest: 'The Objective Value of a Social Settlement' and 'The Subjective Necessity for Social Settlements'. Addams consistently claimed not to have had any preconceived idea of what Hull House should be; its activities always increased, she claimed, 'in response to demand' (Addams 1969a: 33). As Addams described it in the 'Objective Value' Hull House residents pursued four lines of activity: social, educational, humanitarian, and civic (Addams 1969a: 33). The objective value of the Settlement was to accomplish these aims. Addams had a vision and her writings were often abstractly idealistic; but she was pragmatic, not visionary, in her activities. In *Twenty Years* and other texts she interweaves actual experiences at Hull House as demonstrations for theoretical proposals. Addams's vision was brought into being through provision. Unlike most American utopian projects – a future perfect based upon agrarian communal nostalgia – Hull House was situated in the city and worked with the conditions of existing urban life.

To the woman who saw herself as 'settling in the foreign colonies', Hull House was foremost a home rather than an association, a foothold in the alien environment of the American industrial city (Addams 1969b: 1). Addams, speaking of the beginning of the enterprise as a journey to a strange land, wrote: 'You may remember the forlorn feeling which occasionally seizes you when you arrive early in the morning a stranger in the city' (Addams 1969b: 11). To Addams and her upper-middle-class colleagues the tenement districts of America's rapidly growing industrial cities were colonial outposts teeming with unknown and potentially unknowable inhabitants: recent immigrants to the United States. As alien as the American city was to these new immigrants, the urban-industrial environment was to Addams's 'settlers', as the residents of the Settlement were known.[7] Seeking at first to address issues of relations between the classes and the amelioration of the problems of the industrial city, Addams and her fellow residents developed a multi-dimensional concept of 'alienation' which focused on the problems of immigrants, particularly women and children. Addams' notion of 'settling in the foreign colonies' suggests a reciprocal relationship of otherness inherent in the concept of settlement within immigrant communities.

Hull House's residents, initially all women, were also foreigners to the neighbourhood in which they settled. But the relationship was not equal. The 'settlers' called themselves 'residents' of Hull House, while the inhabitants of Chicago's nineteenth ward were their 'neighbours'.[8] Yet even as the Settlement grew to an ensemble of thirteen buildings occupying a full city block, Addams refused to see it as an institution, arguing for a sustained 'flexibility', adapting as the environment demanded.

Residents' writings attest to the need to reside in the neighbourhood in order to accomplish the Settlement's work. Addams began 'The Objective Value' with a physical description of the house and its context that spoke directly to the inadequate human and social provision characteristic of the urban–industrial conditions that she hoped to improve. Built in 1856 by Charles J. Hull and eventually deeded to the Settlement by his heir Helen Culver, Hull House sat in what was once a suburb of Chicago. By the time the architect Allen B. Pond brought Addams to see the house, Hull and his family had long abandoned it and a tenement district populated by European immigrants – the 'foreign colonies' – had grown up around it. Addams was taken by the transitory and fragile character of the tenement and tenement life, both of which would become the objects of the Settlement's work: 'The site for a settlement was selected in the first instance because of its diversity, and the variety of activity for which it presented an opportunity. It has been the aim of the residents to respond to . . . the neighbourhood as a whole' (Addams 1969a: 30, 32). The objective space was the neighborhood and the city. By 1889 the house was already a relic of an agricultural past eclipsed by industry and tenements. The site itself contained the conflicts between the country's recent rural/agricultural past and its modern urban/industrial future (at least as perceived in 1889), itself embodying the need to reconceive democratic and civic relations.

If the objective value of the Settlement – its institutional purpose – was to work for the improvement of its neighbourhood and its neighbours, the Settlement also met important subjective needs for Addams and the residents, for the most part white, middle-class, college-educated women, who were in need of a space in which to put thought into action. Addams's text, 'The Subjective Necessity for Social Settlements', addressed the purposes that the house served for its residents (Addams 1969b: 6, 22–3). The 'settlers' used the house as both a site for collective living and as a means of forming a community that gave them access to public life (Hayden 1981: 174). Hull House offered its female residents a way to occupy the public space of the city. They created a place that did not yet exist – both physically, by building Hull House, and institutionally, by creating an alternative to the separate spheres of gendered life in late nineteenth-century society.

Hull House was an object and a subject – objective value and subjective necessity – treated as a dichotomy but enmeshed and interdependent. The house negotiated the city; it was constituted by multiple identities, many being theorized and enacted for the first time. In one view Hull House can be seen as an alternative to nineteenth-century women's life options. Addams maintained a coherent image of the house by consistently disclaiming its status as an institution. Yet the house was a contingent object being shaped as new concepts of living in the city were being thought. It is through this ambiguous frame that we may comprehend Hull House as constituting an 'embodied utopia'. Hull House's meaning changed as the relationship between subject and object – resident and neighbour, residence and institution, home and city – transformed in the late nineteenth-century urban environment.

TRANSFORMATION BY DESIGN: READING THE SPACES OF HULL HOUSE

Hull House was built through repetition and iteration; neither objects nor subjects were fixed. So that when Addams spoke of the architects 'harmoniz[ing] everything' (Linn 1935: 209), she was speaking to the way in which they assisted in the constant reorganization of the programmatic and physical components of the Settlement complex, rather than the balancing of distinct and unequal parts. Hull House's skin, the assemblage of Italianate Victorian, Prairie School, and Arts and Crafts architecture common during the time, belies the polymorphous programme. Guy Szuberla writes of the house as functionalist architecture clothed in historicist iconography: 'an embodiment of the complex of progressive ideals: commitment to both a planned future and a sentimentalized past' (Szuberla 1977: 116). Victorian architecture need not compel Victorian lifestyles or values; women residents at Hull House were clearly rejecting Victorian norms. As we shall see, this is the distinction between Arts and Crafts movement author Milton B. Marks's image of the house as a pedagogical object in the uncivilized city and the complexities of residential experience in the spaces of the Settlement.[9] No project illustrated the expansion of the mission of the house better than *Hull-House Maps and Papers*, published in 1895. This document was created by the residents of Hull House out of data collected in relation to social activist and Hull House resident Florence Kelley's work for the United States Department of Labor. A rich and diverse document, *Hull-House Maps and Papers* allows us to see Hull House, its neighbourhood (Chicago's nineteenth ward), and its neighbours at a critical moment at the end of the nineteenth century. The maps offered an image of the geographical distribution of the 'foreign colonies', revealing physical and social interactions in this densely and diversely populated ward. The maps were an attempt at 'a photographic reproduction of Chicago's poorest quarters . . . and . . . an illustration of a method of research' (Holbrook 1970: 11). They reinforced the transitional quality of the neighbourhood, of buildings and residents on the move. Concerned that the documents be taken seriously as social science, resident Agnes Holbrook, who wrote the notes that accompanied the maps, stated apologetically: 'Families also move about constantly, going from tenement to tenement . . . form[ing] a floating population of some magnitude, and a kodak view of such a shifting scene must necessarily be blurred and imperfect here or there' (Holbrook 1970: 13). This blurred image was a highly accurate perception of urban life in which no building or family could claim permanent status.

While 'the aim of both maps and notes [was] to present conditions rather than to advance theories' (Holbrook 1970: 14), they proved indispensable as documents to support the residents' social activism, particularly on behalf of women and children. Hull House residents developed a paradigm for women's participation in progressive reform (Sklar 1985: 677). Working first on behalf of women and children, residents were able to address a series of larger urban and social issues. For Kelley, the house-by-house canvas of one small piece of the city provided an intimate knowledge of urban life and revealed previously ignored components of domestic life. *Hull-House Maps and Papers* uncovered a domestic aspect of the city – the space of feminine life – that had previously gone unexplored.[10] As Elizabeth Wilson and Carroll Smith-Rosenberg have pointed out, as more women appeared in them, cities during this period were increasingly portrayed as unruly and uncontrollable. Through studies such as Kelley's, not only did women begin to appear, they were also represented in the city. *Hull-House Maps and Papers* signified a change in the idea of the Settlement from a model home used as a vehicle to promote civilization in the city wilderness, to an organization working to advance urban and industrial change.

An anthology, *Hull-House Maps and Papers* also contained Addams's 'Sketch of Hull House', a text that she updated throughout the early 1890s as documentation of the work of the Settlement. The day-to-day activities of the house were brought together with the intense exploration of everyday life in the ward. The study of daily life led to theoretical formulations about urban growth and change that led to practical proposals for urban reform. Speaking of the interaction of radical reform and female relationships, Smith-Rosenberg writes: 'Through their efforts to re-form urban America, they created a position of power and legitimacy for themselves' (Smith-Rosenberg 1985: 256). Hull House residents accomplished this by studying the fabric of the city. They brought legitimacy to the study of the urban life of cities, not just its monuments and institutions, recognizing that the city would have to be re-formed to accomplish reform.

Although the architecture and physical growth of Hull House was never documented, it is possible to reconstruct many of the public urban spaces through photographic representations and the documents of activities. Printing 'programmes' conveyed stability, but it also illustrated the ways in which activities were tied to the buildings and the growing network of residents, friends, and neighbours. By the winter of 1891 the entire public space of the house was consumed by the neighbourhood from 9 am until 10 pm. Although opportunities for social contact were paramount, the spaces were also used for a variety of practical and extension courses and services, such as a kindergarten, that were made available to the neighbourhood. The distribution of the 'programmes' formalized the activities of the house, connecting it to the neighbourhood and potential supporters. The house was an extension of the homes of its neighbours

Figure 5.3
Sketch of Butler Art
Gallery and Hull House,
c. 1896.
Jane Addams Memorial
Collection, Special
Collections, The
University Library, The
University of Illinois at
Chicago, JAMC neg. 529

but it was also a forum for civic life paralleling that of the greater city. The pro-grammes showed the need to establish stability, even in the midst of an improvi-sational process.

The 1892 *Programme* revealed a significant expansion over the activities and facilities of the previous year. Activities included extensive lectures, clubs, and classes, as well as a college extension department, an art exhibit room and studio (in the complex's first new building, The Butler Art Gallery), a public reading room, a summer school held at Rockford Seminary, a kindergarten, five bathrooms, a stamp station, a day nursery, and a diet kitchen – not all of which were set within Hull House proper. The individuals associated with each of these activities were identified, credentials that demonstrated their expertise carefully described. The *Programme* detailed both what went on in and around the house but also the activities conducted by the residents outside the house, often in professional capacities that brought them into the city and into contact with its inhabitants. Hull House was also growing through new buildings and expansion into other buildings in the neighbourhood. During this period, as more buildings were added and spaces became more typologically distinct, rooms often changed function.

Hull House's institutional activities had corporeal identities. Addams always attached activities to the individuals who instituted or furthered them. The *Jane Addams Papers* contain several documents listing the residents of the house at various moments until the 1930s. Helen Lefkowitz Horowitz notes that between 1894 and 1929 (the fortieth anniversary of the Settlement's founding) the resi-dential population grew from twenty to seventy (Lefkowitz Horowitz 1983–4: 50). It is through these documents that we can reconstruct the varied residential components of the Settlement complex, how residents changed, moved from one residence to another, co-habitated, married, had children, etc. The image of

Figure 5.4
Hull House entrance,
c. 1913.
Jane Addams Memorial
Collection, Special
Collections, The
University Library, The
University of Illinois at
Chicago, JAMC neg. 528

the Settlement as a 'community of women' cannot be sustained past the early 1890s when men took up residence. So why do we retain that image? Most significantly, Hull House was founded, run, and largely funded by women. But also, in seeking to dismiss the Settlement's institutional qualities, Addams always stressed that the Settlement complex was a house, the physical manifestation of domesticity.

What distinguished the very public Hull House from the private lives that were lived within it? Certainly those who resided at the house were consciously choosing to live a public life; their house was a public space, with the kitchen, dining room, parlour, and upper hall all being used by the neighbourhood at various times of the day. As the Settlement grew, more discrete spaces were created, distinguishing living quarters from public spaces, although some permeable and interdependent spaces remained. Except for the living quarters themselves, most spaces were used for multiple purposes over the course of a day or week. Addams and other residents spoke of the activities of the house, not the buildings that contained these activities, as in the first twenty years both were in constant flux. Although the complex of buildings did not expand after 1907, programmes and activities changed and many spaces were remodelled to accommodate these changes.

Speaking of the growth of the Settlement over the years, Addams wrote: '[The architects] clothed in brick and mortar and made visible to the world that which we were trying to do' (Addams 1981: 114). The Settlement was an embodiment of the political, cultural, economic, and juridical status of its residents, the architecture conceived quite literally as its protective skin. Over the years Hull House grew both in relation to the 'demands' of the neighbourhood, but also as a response to the activities and programmes various residents wanted to pursue. Kelley stated:

> An enterprise, started in warm enthusiasm by a resident, goes on long after that resident has dropped it. Perhaps the form may vary if the neighbourhood need demands a modification of the original plan; but the difficulties of the initial steps having been met by the temporary sojourner, the undertaking remains a real gain.
>
> (Kelley 1898: 552)

As residents brought different orientations, the mission and programme of the Settlement shifted and congealed through the accumulated personalities. As in a city or an educational institution, experiments were tried out in temporary quarters; those deemed successful often required a new facility. Transience was, therefore, crystallized. Curious 'experiments in hospitality'[11] would take root in the civic consciousness and space of the city.

When Elizabeth Grosz writes of 'body writing', the ways in which sexual difference is produced, she likens it to etching, which acknowledges the interaction between message, inscription, and the materiality of the surface inscribed. This is the beginning of a new understanding of how individuals and communities interact in urban space, but further how architecture is more than the trace of these activities (Grosz 1994: 191). We can see this in Pond's description of Hull House's architecture:

> Hull House is plainly rather an aggregation of partially related units than a logical organism. It is, however, only fair that this rigor of judgement shall be somewhat abated for a building or group of buildings that has grown by a long series of wholly unforeseeable accretions to an original accidental unit.
>
> (Pond 1902b: 183)

Hull House underwent an urbanization: from a singular object in the prairie to an object in a dense urban environment, Hull House grew in a manner that articulated a series of changing relationships to its urban context, ultimately becoming part of the physical fabric of the neighbourhood. In 1893 many activities took place in neighbourhood buildings. By the turn of the century the original building was surrounded by new constructions that formed a small courtyard addressing Halsted Street. After the turn of the century with the addition of an apartment building, a music school, and a dining room, a second, interior quadrangle took shape. By this time the Settlement was sorted into functional units that nonetheless retained a great deal of interdependency. While public buildings retained their entrances on the street, residences were entered from the interior courtyard. Pond's articles illustrated these developments most clearly. He focused on the way the combination of buildings, not just the individual buildings and the activities they housed, formed a network of interaction for various programmatic and residential functions and further, how these buildings appeared on, and were accessed from, the streets of the neighbourhood.

The carefully enumerated lists of 'residents' in the house over the years reveal overlapping communities of people and buildings: women living in Hull House proper; men living in men's residences; working women and men living in co-op residences; singles and families living in an apartment building (originally intended to be rented for income); and others living in apartments spread throughout the complex, usually on upper floors and in penthouses. Then there were those who worked at Hull House as either staff or volunteers who did not reside in the Settlement. To think of Hull House purely in terms of a singular community forms too tight a circle around these individuals, and belies the complexity of the Settlement's purposes and residents. It is more appropriate to see the Settlement as an inhabitant of the city. However, as a residential space, as in many of its activities, Hull House was a stratified community reflecting late nineteenth-century class distinctions. The residences and apartments were spaces occupied by largely upper-middle class or professional men and women. The Jane Club, a co-operative apartment building sponsored on the grounds of Hull House, was intended for young, single, working-class women. The establishment, and eventually the building, of the Jane Club clarified the purposes of Hull House proper. A co-operative, residential space, the Jane Club (named after Addams) was available to 'Any self-supporting unmarried woman, or widow without dependent children, between the ages of eighteen and forty-five, who [was] of good moral character', could afford the $3.00/week for board and lodging, and assisted in 'the household work of the Club'. Hull House too was a residence for working women and men whose work was directly connected to urban reform. Both residences provided community support, but on different terms. Hull House was eventually open to men, women, and families whose work was directly tied to the larger goals of the Settlement and specifically chose to live within the Hull House neighbourhood to accomplish their work. The Club provided safe urban residence for women negotiating the volatile environment of industrial labour relations, subject to the vicissitudes of the urban economy, and suspect because of their connections to labour reform and union organizing.

RE-INTERPRETING THE MEANING OF HULL HOUSE

As feminist theory has moved from (re)discovery to (re)interpretation of nineteenth-century women's lives, there have been notable changes in the ways in which Hull House has been studied. The first phase focused on the preservation of the house and the work of Addams and her 'community of women'. This is the important focus of feminist history. Looking retrospectively at her own early research, Smith-Rosenberg writes: 'I began to see how both women and men put the psychosexual and biological richness of the physical body at the service of political intention' (Smith-Rosenberg 1985: 51). This first phase, however, created the possibility for a second in which, moved into history proper, a house can be opened to critique along nationalist, imperialist or assimilationist lines. For example, mismatch between the cultural and class backgrounds and experiences of the residents and their neighbours is embodied in the story of one of their first social interactions:

> In the very first weeks of our residence Miss Starr started a reading party in George Eliot's *Romola*, which was attended by a group of young women who followed the wonderful tale with unflagging interest. The weekly reading was held in our little upstairs dining room, and two members of the club came to dinner each week, not only that they might be received as guests, but that they might help us wash the dishes afterward and so make the table ready for the stacks of Florentine photographs.
>
> (Addams 1981: 83)

As we can imagine that many of these young women were themselves of Italian descent, the reading of Eliot's contemporary English novel, combining a vivid romance in a historical setting, gave the impression of a shared inheritance, as Starr and Addams had a vast touristic knowledge and documentation of Florence. Eliot's gripping tale of love and political intrigue was played out in the streets of the city that Addams and Starr could illustrate with their photography. So why, twenty years later, would Addams insist on telling us that the guests assisted with the dishes? The intimacy of the interaction is an example of the smallest of the many scales of social life in which the social settlement operated: here it is the surface of the dining room table. A plan of the room would tell us little, but the account tells us a great deal about the shifts in roles of the individuals and the function of the room over a short period of time.

The real shift in the Hull House women's understanding of the home took place in the opening of the domestic to the space of the city, the extension of domestic services (bathhouses, coffeehouses, meeting spaces, etc.) to their neighbours residing in tenements without such facilities, and the provision of domestic yet non-familial space for women in the city at a time when their presence, as Elizabeth Wilson notes, was treated with scepticism if not outright scorn and sanction. The communal replaced the familial for the residents. Minutes of a House Meeting of 24 July, 1896, note: 'Moved and seconded that Miss Gernon be appointed a committee of one to buy a suitable butter dish. Motion carried' (Jane Addams Memorial Collection). Those of 9 June of the same year focused on the 'flourishing' plans and funding for the Bowen Country Club. Thus the private and public spheres of the house overlapped in the residents' meetings, and these became one of several sites for discourse and decisions about the directions of the House and its activities (another would be the official meetings of the Hull House Board of Trustees, convened in 1895). But despite the formality of this intimacy it is significantly different from the way in which a Hull House neighbour would use the house, negotiated through programmed activities and interactions.

Hull House challenged the way in which the house – the domestic sphere – was sited within the city. The interior spaces and the exterior form of the container were literally and figuratively porous and permeable. The architecture and urbanity of Hull House shaped, or more specifically reconfigured, the relationship between the public and private spheres, allowing these spheres to coexist, yet protecting their distinctions. By the time the Settlement was completed in 1907, almost every building contained some form of residential space housing male and female residents, staff, visitors, and possibly renters. Similarly, the architecture of the Settlement allowed all these individuals to move between various spaces of the complex both horizontally and vertically as their lives changed. Only a very rigid reading of the architecture would allow us to say that the private and public spheres of Hull House were held distinct from one another. Living, studying, and taking action in the space of the city were all part of daily life at Hull House. The two courtyards of the house imply a growing separation of private and public spaces in the Settlement. The first court, open to the street, provided an official front door, but the interior, residential courtyard was also accessible and was often used for Hull House programming. Pond wrote of the hybridity of private and public programming that the settlement architect had to accommodate in a long list illustrating how social settlements expanded. 'Although the family life and the easy friendliness give the settlement keynote, they are only the framework in which other activities are set' (Pond 1902a: 143).

The modern city transformed the characteristics and boundaries of the home. Addams advocated women's participation in the transformation of the public realm. This concept of suffrage was an extension of the home into the

Figure 5.5.
Hull House demolition, 1963.
Jane Addams Memorial Collection, Special Collections, The University Library, The University of Illinois at Chicago, JAMC neg. 566

space of the city, but it was also a claim for overlapping spheres. Urban society required a reformulation of private and public life, and with it the place of women in both. The modern city created a fluid condition between private and public spheres; here, the civic realm was the home in public. Addams and her colleagues did not desire to recreate nor reconfigure the domestic on either a local or a national scale. They were responding to changes in domestic life already occurring, particularly in growing American cities. Women's wage labour in the homes of others was as problematic as the increase in prostitution made possible by the anonymity of urban life. Hull House as a space and as an object was transvestite, clothed in an architecture that belied its radicality, that requires

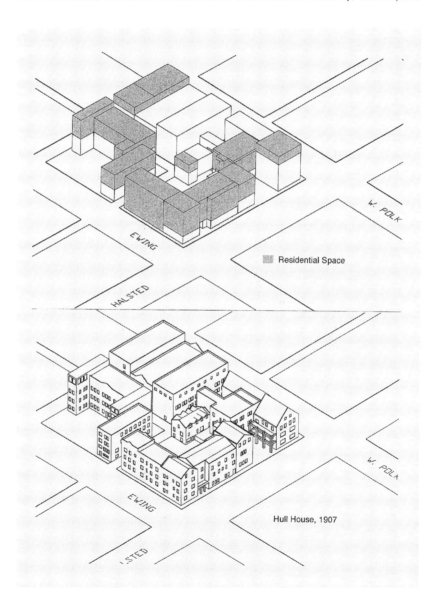

Figure 5.6
Public and private space in the completed Hull House Settlement.

the crossing of fields of study and analysis to comprehend. In her own writings and in the development of Hull House as a space and as a concept, Addams took advantage of the simultaneity of this transitional moment in the development of cities and female identity, capitalizing on but not displaying the cultural, physical, and sexual experiences of the time. The architecture of Hull House provided a space of protection from and infiltration of the developing modern American city. If it was not a space of complete transparency, nonetheless, fixtures, furnishings, and spatial planning were utilized to create distinct, discrete spaces that were continually transgressed through non-architectural programming, daily life in a civic space. To be at home in public was not to occupy two distinct worlds, but to participate in the making of a new domestic and urban environment.

NOTES

1 Recent scholarly work on Addams, Hull House, and the larger community of women and men who sustained the enterprise begins to unravel the complex networks of personal, financial, and institutional support necessary to the work. This includes the close personal and professional relationship between Addams and Mary Rozet Smith. See, for example, Jackson (2000) and Sklar (1990).

2 Hull House's residents' activities both with and for their neighbours were numerous. They started with small social and educational projects, but over the years included the provision of facilities and services to the neighbourhood, social activism on behalf of immigrants, particularly women and children, and urban reform. In this chapter I will detail some of these activities and the architecture in which they took place.

3 The two best known texts are Horowitz (1983) and Szuberla (1977). The most complete discussion of the architecture of the house through 1902 was provided by its architect, Allen B. Pond. His articles will be considered further later in this essay. Jackson's important recent book, *Lines of Activity: Performance, Historiography, Hull-House Domesticity*, addresses Hull House as a context for the performance of domesticity and in doing so adds a great deal to the discussion of the architecture of the Settlement.

4 William James to Jane Addams, Cambridge, MA, 1909, December 13.

5 The phenomenal collection, *The Jane Addams Papers Microfilm*, including its index, has advanced scholarship on Addams by bringing together the extant materials of her life and writings as well as material from the Hull House Association.

6 Indeed, this is the larger aim of my project, for which this chapter serves as an introduction. As is often the case, much of the history of Addams and Hull House have come down through history in textual, not artefactual form. The lack of physical traces of the house, including maps and floor plans, makes it necessary to reconstruct the spaces and context of the house through the narration.

7 The concept of the city as a 'frontier', a 'wilderness', a place of 'disorder', is crucial to the rhetoric of urban growth at the end of the nineteenth century and had a significant impact on both how settlements developed and were perceived by the American public. See, for example, Warner 1972, Woods 1898, and Smith 1995.

8   See my 'Unsettling in the City: The Making of Americans at the Hull House Settlement', forthcoming in *Domestic Narratives of Urban Migration* eds. M. Wilson and P. Kariouk. Princeton, NJ: Princeton Architectural Press, forthcoming, for the complexities of imperialism and assimilation in the Settlement's urban activities.

9   Writing of Addams and Hull House in *Good Housekeeping* ('Conducted in the Interests of the Higher Life of the Household') in 1900, Marks contributed to the domestic mythology of Hull House: 'Hull House, first and foremost, is a home; it is a home of wealth and beauty, a center of culture and refinement – and Jane Addams has been the presiding genius therein for eleven years' (Marks 1900: 213). We should not be surprised to find *Good Housekeeping* focusing on Addams as a good homemaker, but Addams's biographer Allen Davis, among others, has noted her tendency to promote the domestic view of Hull House over potentially more radical analyses.

10 As Carroll Smith-Rosenberg has written, in a different context: 'Women's discussions of the normal events of every day permitted us to endow census data with the warmth of emotional reality. Now we could test the accuracy of prescriptive materials against the reality of what people actually did' (Smith-Rosenberg 1985: 29).

11 Examples include the provision of tubs in the cellar and laundry and the addition of showers in the gymnasium. Both of these projects led to advocacy for a free public bath for the neighbourhood. From a little lending library in Hull House, a Free Public Library developed. What these examples illustrate is that not all activities initiated at Hull House remained in Hull House; many became part of the civic programme of the neighbourhood at large, and often in many neighbourhoods around the city.

Chapter 6: Utopian Visions and Architectural Designs of Turn-of-the-Century Social Settlements

Suzanne M. Spencer-Wood

This chapter explores how nineteenth-century women social reformers materially embodied their utopian visions of society through architectural designs of their public institutions. Reformers made women's public professions and institutions acceptable within the dominant Victorian gender ideology by depicting them as extensions of women's domestic roles (Spencer-Wood 1999a: 170–1). As reformers expanded woman's domestic sphere to encompass man's public sphere, they successfully argued that women's superior morality enabled them to control their expanded sphere, increasing women's power in both the home and the public realm. Unlike their contemporaries, the suffragists, domestic reformers did not directly confront male dominance in the public sphere by arguing that women should have public roles. Nonetheless, the reformers' argument that women would bring a higher moral tone to government was instrumental in gaining the majority of men's support for female suffrage (Spencer-Wood 1991: 241; 1994a: 178–80).

This chapter first presents the context of women's public co-operative housekeeping enterprises, including social settlements. In subsequent sections, I discuss the purposes and effects of social settlements, challenging the social control interpretation through an examination of the diversity of settlement goals and the voices of participants negotiating with reformers for empowering programmes. Finally, I analyse how the architectural designs of two settlements externally expressed reformers' utopian visions of society and internally expressed the actual uses of space for different programmes.

PUBLIC CO-OPERATIVE HOUSEKEEPING ENTERPRISES AND THE SOCIALIZATION OF HOUSEWORK

In public co-operative housekeeping enterprises in Europe and America reformers socialized household tasks, in many cases to assist working women and their families with childcare, food preparation, or housework. In these charitable institutions, predominantly middle-class reformers created new professions for women that, they argued, should be equivalent in status to men's middle-class professions. The professionalization of women's domestic tasks was symbolized and implemented with special, often scientific, equipment and furnishings, and specialized training in professional schools. I have mapped and surveyed over 120 women's public co-operative housekeeping institutions and reform organizations in Boston, including day nurseries, public kitchens, women's social settlements, working women's co-operative homes and clubs, and women's schools for sales clerks, kindergarten teachers, milliners, dressmakers, domestic servants, cooks, and housekeepers. This research shows how reformers challenged male dominance in public urban landscapes with female-controlled public institutions that in some areas physically dominated the built environment either because of the size or height of the buildings women reformers designed or used. Some of these buildings still visually dominate their neighbourhoods, including the Brook House Home for Working Girls, now a clinic, and the Grey Nuns Home for Working Girls, now a retirement home for elderly women, including some of the same women who lived there as working girls in the 1920s (Spencer-Wood 1994a: 184–7; 1996: Appendix A).

THE AMERICAN SOCIAL SETTLEMENT MOVEMENT: CHALLENGING THE SOCIAL CONTROL PARADIGM

The rest of this chapter is concerned with social settlements because they offered the greatest variety of co-operative housekeeping programmes for the working classes within one type of institution. Settlements were communitarian institutions in which social reformers lived co-operatively, hiring domestic servants so that they themselves could volunteer social and educational services to the surrounding poor community. Settlements offered a diverse range of programmes, including co-operative childcare, clubs, gyms, and a variety of classes and social events. Co-operative hot-water laundries and baths facilitated a level of cleanliness that was difficult to maintain in typical cold-water tenements. Co-operative laundries also served as an employment facility for washerwomen (Woods and Kennedy 1911: 106–36).

Many social settlements considered themselves to be melting pots, not for eliminating immigrant cultures, but for combining immigrant cultures with American culture to form a modern utopian social order in the future. Settlements typically offered a wide variety of vocational classes and classes in English, maths, American history, and citizenship that assisted immigrants in becoming economically self-sufficient citizens who could fully participate in American democracy. At the same time settlements offered programmes to help preserve immigrants' pride in their native cultures, including plays in foreign languages, music clubs, ethnic cooking and history classes, ethnic folk dances, and craft fairs where poor women could sell ethnic products that they made by hand from materials provided by the settlement (e.g. Denison House 1912: 10–11; 1916:

28–30; Elizabeth Peabody House 1903: 8; 1915: 5; Lincoln House 1899, 1902; Stanton 1985: 31–2).

Many settlements at least initially followed cultural norms of behaviour that perpetuated social divisions between classes and races (Mencher 1974: 209–10). In Boston, men's settlements more than women's tended to follow cultural norms in having racially segregated classes and/or institutions. Annual reports indicate that most settlements run by women welcomed all races (Spencer-Wood 1991: 265; 1994a: 188, 191). Perhaps the greatest degree of segregation occurred when the men who ran Boston's South End House founded a separate black settlement because they claimed that the local residents required it. They also founded a separate residence for female settlement workers (South End House 1910: 1–2, 4, 26–7). In response to widespread exclusion from Anglo institutions, African–Americans founded their own parallel institutions. For instance, in 1904 six middle-class black women founded Boston's Harriet Tubman settlement to assist their working-class sisters emigrating from the South in finding work in Northern cities (Garcia n.d.).

Some reform programmes and institutions were initially segregated but later became integrated, expressing the utopian goal of cultural integration. The first English-speaking American kindergarten, founded in 1860 by Elizabeth Peabody, was designed for middle-class white children in Boston, to provide her with income. In contrast, kitchen gardens were founded in 1875 by Emily Huntington in New York to teach African–American children middle-class standards of housekeeping using miniature brooms, washtubs, washboards, irons, ironing boards, dishes, tables and chairs (Hayden 1981: 125–8; Snyder 1972: 19–21, 41). However, these programmes were soon desegregated and poor children were given preference in charitable settlement kindergartens (Spencer-Wood 1994a: 191).

Although research by some social control historians has revealed that reformers had a variety of altruistic aims and utopian visions of society, these goals either have been dismissed as secondary or interpreted as rhetoric masking the true anti-revolutionary purpose of reform programmes and institutions in maintaining the social order by imposing middle-class values and behaviours on the working class (e.g. Karger 1987: 137–40; Lissak 1989: 172–81). For instance, the widespread utopian goal of breaking down racial and class prejudices and the barriers between social groups is seen as unrealized from a modern ahistorical perspective, overlooking evidence for decreasing racial and class segregation in women's settlements and programmes (Spencer-Wood 1994a: 190–1, 197). From a social control perspective Lissak (1989: 29–30) unconvincingly argues that Hull House reformers were cynically using their utopian vision of a pluralistic society, implemented with programmes promoting ethnic cultures, as just a temporary first step in a homogenizing Americanization programme.

In the United States Americanization has been considered a primary mechanism of social control that was implemented by settlements and other reform institutions, as well as schools. Americanization can be defined as the processes by which immigrants were transformed into 'Americans' by internaliz-ing normative cultural values and conforming to accepted standards of behavi-our. Americanization was certainly a goal of some settlements, as shown by Karger (1987: 48–57), and was accomplished with varying degrees of success through schools, classes and clubs that taught English, American history, civics, ethics, cooking, and middle-class standards of housekeeping (Stansell 1986: 219).

Diversity in settlement goals

In contrast to the social control thesis, some women's settlements clearly expressed support for a pluralistic utopian vision of diversity. It is difficult to inter-pret the following quotes as advocating the complete assimilation of immigrants into American culture. The 1916 Denison House annual report stated:

> While we interpret the glory of America to these newcomers, let us not fail to interpret their aspirations and endowments to the native born, that the word *Americanization* may cease to mean to the majority of men the impossible task of shaping alien minds and hearts to the old colonial pattern. Let us not rob America of some of the best gifts these foreign-born citizens have to offer her, in our blind efforts to make them over into something too much like ourselves! [. . .] only by the united wisdom of all sorts and conditions of men can we attain to the better social order.
>
> (Denison House 1912: 4; DH 1916: 18)

Similarly the Elizabeth Peabody House annual report of 1914 stated that the settlement stood 'for the affirmation that every man has his value' (Elizabeth Peabody House 1915: 13). These quotes and others suggest that some promi-nent settlement leaders rejected the dominant utopian vision of creating a homogeneous society by forcing immigrants to conform to dominant American behavioural ideals. These reformers did not view American culture as unchang-ing, but instead advocated its enrichment by valuing immigrant aspirations and cultural contributions. These quotes, and programmes in settlements that pro-moted the preservation of ethnic cultures, show that some reformers rejected the one-way acculturation of immigrants implied by the word 'assimilation'. Instead some reformers advocated reciprocal cultural exchange.

American social settlements aimed to create an egalitarian and co-operative community from the diversity of classes and ethnic and racial groups in the surrounding neighbourhood. As the Elizabeth Peabody House report of 1910 put it, 'The basic settlement *motif* [sic] is to awaken neighborhood loyalties: from self-interest to arouse to an appreciation of local needs and to link with this appreciation of general civic good. [. . .] Through all its [the settlement's] group activities runs the aim to awaken its neighbourhood to a consciousness of the neighborhood bond' (Elizabeth Peabody House 1911: 13). The widespread settlement goal of creating programmes to meet the needs of the local poor community was expressed in a quote from the Elizabeth Peabody House report of 1914: 'Policies should spring from local and individual needs as they are made evident and as they are weighted and balanced' (Elizabeth Peabody House 1915: 16). As settlement leader Robert Woods put it, a settlement was '[b]ent upon democratic cooperation with its constituency, having no sort of authoritative sanction over them, and wishing none [. . .] The wishes of the constituency have to be [. . .] always seriously taken into account. Settlement work is endless compromise' (Woods 1923: 49).[1]

Voices of participants: negotiating for empowering programmes

Most social control historians have argued that reformers in settlements and other institutions were not successful in their goals of social control and Americanization because relatively few working-class families participated in reform programmes (e.g. Lissak 1989; Stansell 1986). This 'failure' can be easily explained if, in fact, these reformers were not attempting to force their values and behaviours on the working class, or coercing attendance in programmes. In fact, most settlement workers expressed beliefs that immigrant contributions would enrich American culture (Lissak 1989: 174–5). Some settlement programmes could be useful in small ways to members of ethnic groups who sought to preserve their culture.

American settlements, especially Chicago's Hull House, were considered to be experimental social laboratories fundamental to the development of the philosophy of pragmatism (Seigfried 1996; Spencer-Wood 1997). Because most settlement leaders pragmatically viewed their programmes as social experiments, their annual reports recorded programme enrolments and negative as well as positive responses to programmes. They also recorded changes made to programmes and new programmes created in response to complaints and requests by working-class participants in settlements.

Participants decided if and how to use social programmes, so they played the most important role in determining the programmes' effects. Crocker (1992: 61, 309) and Solomon (1977 2: 7–366) each found that at the local level settlement programmes were important in assisting upwardly mobile members of the working class to achieve their own goals of becoming middle class. Classes that reformers offered in citizenship, English, civics, and American history might have addressed immigrants' own goals of becoming middle-class Americans. Evidence for this claim may be found in a 1902 Elizabeth Peabody House annual report which recorded that there were so many upwardly mobile immigrants 'eager to fit themselves for American life' that over-enrolled evening classes in English, mathematics and American history had to be moved to the larger Hebrew Industrial School nearby (Elizabeth Peabody House 1903: 7).

Contrary to the social control thesis, settlement annual reports show that working-class people were not powerless, passive recipients of reformers' programmes, but rather were active participants who used words and actions to express their responses to those programmes. Many in the working class refused to enrol in programmes that they thought were attempts to force middle-class values or agendas on them. For instance, many refused to attend classes in housekeeping and cooking that they felt simply promoted the bourgeois class-interested agenda of training domestic servants (Hayden 1981: 126; Lincoln House 1905: 44). The effects of programmes were determined by their voluntary use by the working class, not by reformers' stated or unstated goals (Spencer-Wood 1994a: 187–98; 1996: 432–7).

A framework more descriptive of the democratic social process at settlements would include the dialogue and negotiation between social groups. Rather than attempting the hierarchical power of dominance, reformers used lateral powers such as setting an example, mentoring, inspiring, persuading, co-operating, affiliating, and empowering participants in settlement programmes (Spencer-Wood 1999b: 179). Participants in programmes were empowered by the fact that their participation was voluntary, putting them in a powerful position to negotiate for programmes that they felt would be useful in meeting their own social goals. Reformers also empowered participants by responding to their complaints and requests concerning the material content of programmes offered in settlement spaces. The fact that reformers changed their utopian programmes in response to complaints, requests, and amount of participation indicates that they sought to assist the working class rather than control it.

My research has uncovered a number of cases in which settlements changed their programmes or created new ones in response to local needs or participants' requests, which were recorded in annual reports. For instance, at Boston's Jewish Industrial School for Girls, which later became a settlement run by middle-class West European Jews, poor East European Jews requested intellectual as well as manual education for their daughters. At Boston's North Bennet Street Industrial School, which was originally founded for girls, neighbourhood boys succeeded in requesting that space and equipment be provided for a sloyd carpentry class (Spencer-Wood 1994a: 189, 193–6). Lissak (1989: 120) notes that Hull House sought to appeal to local Italian immigrants by shifting from educational and cultural programmes to sports, dances, plays, crafts, billiards, bowling, and a brass band. Public kitchens that offered a scientifically cooked Yankee menu responded to immigrant complaints such as 'You needn't try to make a Yankee out of me by making me eat that' by offering ethnic foods such as spaghetti (Hunt 1912: 220).

Since participation in reform programmes was voluntary, enrolment levels measure the usefulness and/or popularity of a programme among members of the working-class community. High enrolment in programmes indicates that working-class women and their families found such programmes useful in meeting their own needs and goals rather than the goals of reformers. Enrolment figures and positive comments in annual reports show that many settlement programmes and classes were popular, including kindergartens. Reformers appear to have been fairly objective in recording the smaller numbers of negative comments about programmes and requests for new programming, probably because they viewed their offerings as social experiments that they expected to modify and change in response to local needs.

SETTLEMENT ARCHITECTURE AND SPACES

Most settlements were initially established in existing apartments or houses that were rented or bought. But neighbourhood demands for more programmes and higher enrolments led some settlements to raise money to have buildings designed and constructed with spaces and equipment to meet special settlement needs. In many settlements the reformers' living quarters became separate from the settlement building, which often included a theatre or hall for plays, lectures, and concerts, a gymnasium, shower baths, a kindergarten, a roof garden, a play-room, a library, a milk station, medical dispensary or nurses station, clubrooms, and classrooms requiring special equipment for carpentry, pottery, printing, millinery, cooking, domestic science, dressmaking, weaving, and housekeeping. Many settlements also had playgrounds, gardens, and summer camps in the country and organized excursions and picnics (Spencer-Wood 1996: 432–3; Woods and Kennedy 1911).

I have analyzed the architecture and use of space for two Boston settlements and found that the exterior architecture symbolized the reformers' utopian goals and visions of society. In contrast, the size and uses of interior spaces expressed not so much the reformers' ideals as their experiences of the actual demand for different kinds of programmes, expressed in terms of enrolments.

Lincoln House Settlement

Lincoln House was founded in 1887 in Boston as a boys' club by Josephine Allen and Louise Williams, who lived with other reformers in the house until 1899. The reformers stated that '[t]he main purpose of Lincoln House is to provide means through which the better forces of the neighborhood may make themselves effective. It involves co-operation with all good organizations, with churches, school, and most of all, with families [. . .] about the only service the outsider can render is to stimulate the civic spirit and encourage neighborhood initiative' (Lincoln House 1905: 12; Woods and Kennedy 1911: 117–18). This quote, similar to the earlier quote from Woods, shows that these reformers realized that they did not have the hierarchical power of dominance required for social control, but had rather to rely on lateral types of co-operative power that were more democratic.

The new purpose-built Lincoln House that opened in 1905 was specially designed to symbolize and implement a utopian vision of a welcoming community centre (Figure 6.1). At 60 × 90 feet the building was larger than the surrounding tenements, but it was purposely built only three and a half stories high so that it would not be too much higher than its surroundings. The large building provided a utopian example of windows providing light and air from all sides, in contrast to the narrow, deep, rowhouses that had windows only in the front and back and no ventilation or natural light in interior rooms. Good ventilation and access to natural light was considered essential in preventing disease, which scientists thought to be caused by bad air, called 'miasmas' or 'humours' (Winter 1994: 16–17, 54–5).

Figure 6.1
Lincoln House external
architecture.
LH 1903 frontispiece;
1910: 6

Lincoln House visually expressed its permanence and stability by being constructed of dark red brick trimmed with warm Indiana limestone. This configuration of materials was also widely used in public schools, and reformers may have chosen it to express Lincoln House's similar mission of community education. The building materials, as well as Lincoln House's size, expressed its function as a public institution in a domestic neighbourhood of wooden tenements.

Although the size and exterior of Lincoln House was somewhat reminiscent of a school, the reformers sought to minimize the institutional nature of the building by materially symbolizing the act of bringing people together in community in a number of ways, especially around the building entrance. Communitarian Christian values were symbolized by putting the front of the building in physical contact with nature, which the dominant gender ideology associated with the higher moral power of women in maintaining Christian communities in the face of opposition from the capitalistic values of the male public sphere. In front of Lincoln House was a strip of grass, enlarging to rectangles of grass beside the staircases, where shrubs and vines were planted, enclosed with a granite curb and iron railing. Trees were planted along the sidewalk outside the railing, and flowerboxes were placed on the second floor windowsills. These rare green spaces were thought to have the power to morally uplift people in the poor, dirty and therefore 'immoral' tenement-choked neighbourhood by bringing them into contact with nature.

Neighbourhood people were invited into the community centre by a high round iron arch bridging two brick columns topped with granite balls and connected to the iron railings flanking the entrance. This architectural feature materially expressed the settlement's hopes of forming a bridge of common interest between the upper and lower classes, and between different ethnic groups in the old and new worlds. The reformers stated that they purposefully had the building designed to symbolize the character of Lincoln House, which emphasized simplicity, hospitality and the personal, while minimizing its institutional aspect.

A combination of Georgian Revival and Greek Revival architecture was chosen to express settlement values. Georgian Revival architecture hearkened back nostalgically to an eighteenth-century pre-industrial societal order that was largely rural and had little class conflict. Georgian Revival architectural elements also referred to the Roman Republic to symbolically legitimate the American Republic. The Greek Revival style referred to Greek democracy as the earliest legitimating precedent for American democracy. The settlement's architectural styles symbolized its goals of generating republican democracy and social cohesion in order to diminish class conflict. Although Greek, Roman, and American 'democracies' were really democracies only for white men, who owned property and slaves and were the legal representatives of their wives, women reformers had worked to expand democracy to African–Americans and now worked to expand it to women and immigrant groups that often suffered discrimination.

The severely square building was softened by the entry arch and Georgian windows on the first floor, which had elegant round curves in the window, echoed in limestone trim. The largest Georgian windows were flanked by limestone columns and had a false limestone balcony beneath them. These round Georgian arches combined with the recessed entrance gave the building a welcoming feeling of embracing the people enclosed in the little front entrance plaza. A separate staircase led to the large basement auditorium and stage for mixed–gender entertainments, and two regulation bowling alleys (Figure 6.2). Walking up the steps to the first floor entrance could symbolize the upward mobility of members of the poor working class as settlement workers materially realised their main goal of sharing their middle-class privileges to uplift the lower classes (Spencer-Wood 1996: 411–12).

Gender segregation was evident in the designation of a number of spaces specifically for women's or men's activities. However, Lincoln House differed from many schools in having only one staircase. Inside the front entrance one

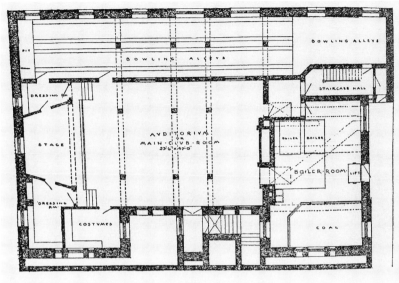

Figure 6.2
Lincoln House basement
plan.
LH 1903: 34

ASSEMBLY FLOOR OF THE NEW HOUSE.

would come first to the directors' offices on the right and the library and reading room on the left. The main hallway across the back of the building provided access on the right to the men's clubroom of 36 × 24 feet, a dispensary and waiting room, stairs and the small men's toilet, while to the left was the women's clubroom of 24 × 29 feet, the larger women's toilet, and the specially equipped domestic science classroom. The different sizes of the gendered spaces suggest that men had larger clubs than women, and domestic science classes were larger than the number of people using the dispensary at any one time. However, the dispensary space seems small for the over 900 people treated there (Lincoln House 1903: 26–8). The larger women's toilet may reflect a larger number of women settlement workers and/or the need for more stalls in women's toilets (Figure 6.3).

The second floor included eleven rooms for gender-segregated clubs and for handicraft classes including sewing, drawing, carpentry, woodcarving, leatherwork, basketry, printing, and clay modelling. The four sewing rooms for women took up about one-third of the floor and were the smallest rooms, suggesting they were the smallest classes. The other craft classes, except for basketry and drawing, were usually for boys. The small size of the women's sewing rooms may be an expression of a continued emphasis on boys, for whom the settlement was originally founded (Figure 6.4).

The top floor was primarily occupied by the gymnasium, 38 × 61 feet with a locker room, eight showers and a lavatory. Boys and girls used these facilities on different days of the week (Lincoln House 1907). This floor also included a coatroom, the kindergarten room, and two adjoining small rooms for individual

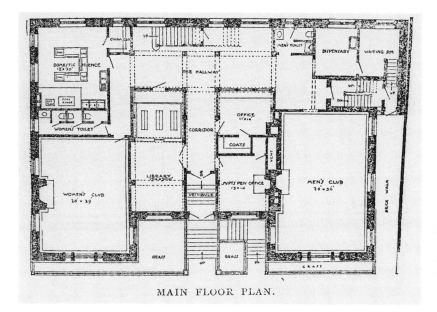

MAIN FLOOR PLAN.

Figure 6.3
Lincoln House first floor
plan.
LH 1903: 35

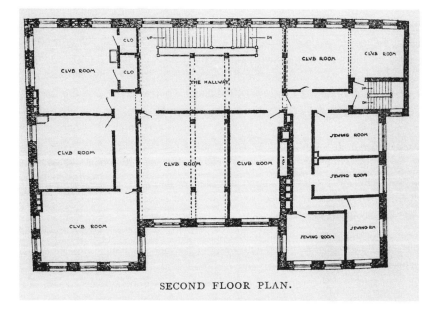

SECOND FLOOR PLAN.

Figure 6.4
Lincoln House second
floor plan.
LH 1903: 36

work and special classes. The 36 × 24 feet kindergarten room had a fireplace symbolizing the home hearth, bringing a domestic feeling to help children feel at home in this large institution. Two skylights provided an abundance of healthy light (Figure 6.5).

A rolling partition in the middle of the kindergarten room permitted it to be flexibly divided into two rooms of a variety of sizes, one with the fireplace and

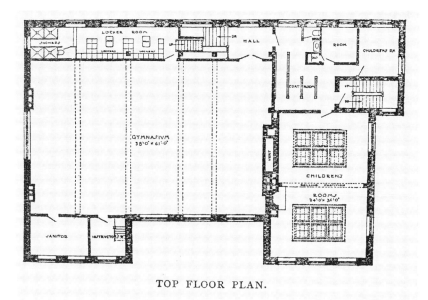

TOP FLOOR PLAN.

Figure 6.5
Lincoln House third floor
plan.
LH 1903: 37

the other without (Lincoln House 1903: 33–8; 1904: 32). The function of this rolling partition is suggested by the Beecher sisters' design of a utopian Christian neighbourhood schoolhouse/chapel: the entire room would be used as a church on Sundays, but during the week the space was designed to be flexibly divided by the screen into a classroom on one side and a living room with a fireplace on the other side (Beecher and Stowe 1975 [1869]: 453–8). The Lincoln House kindergarten room could similarly be divided by its screen into a living room with the fireplace on one side and a classroom on the other. If the settlement followed Beecher and Stowe's utopian model, settlement residents may have used the living room as their communal space, since they did not live in the building.

Lincoln House was similar to the North Bennet Street Industrial School in changing its programmes to meet the changing needs of neighbourhood residents, as indicated by enrolment in classes and programmes and by verbal complaints of club members. The members of clubs could and did change their activities, as when the junior girls' club in 1903 voted unanimously to shift from practice sewing on samples to sewing clothes for a doll. The number of Lincoln House classes grew from one carpentry class in a rented basement in early 1895 to 32 classes in 1903–4. In the winter of 1895–6, a bricklaying class was tried but enrolment was too small for the class to be repeated. In contrast, a class in sign painting started the same winter continued for six years, and a wood-carving class continued until 1905 (Lincoln House 1903: 15, 25–6; 1905: 11; 1906: 40–4). Kindergarten and a wide variety of craft classes were popular, from sloyd carpentry and printing to sewing, basketry, clay modelling, charcoal drawing, and pyrography (Lincoln House 1903: 26–8).

In 1904 a course was added in housekeeping that was discontinued the following year because it only attracted one student. Low or no enrolment in housekeeping classes often resulted from the perception of poor parents that their children were being trained for the low status job of domestic servant. In contrast, cooking, laundry, dressmaking and millinery classes were popular, possibly because pupils used what they learned when they went home (Lincoln House 1904: 31; 1905: 43–5; Hayden 1981: 126). Further, women could apply what they learned in some of the best paying entrepreneurial professions for women, in dressmaking and millinery shops for the upper classes. These domestic classes would have taken place in the large domestic science classroom on the first floor and the four small sewing rooms on the second floor, according to the design of the purpose-built 1905 building. However, it is likely that the actual uses of rooms subsequently changed and more than one subject could be taught in the same classroom at different times, except for the domestic science classroom, which had special scientific equipment that would interfere with other uses.

As stated in 1905, '[t]he organization of Lincoln House has been constructed after the fashion of the most comfortable and homelike dwellings, by additions and modifications to meet the needs and, so far as possible, the ideals of our large family' (Lincoln House 1905: 12). This quote shows that the reformers expected to change their programmes to meet the needs of the neighbourhood, and suggests that they took a domestic view of the neighbourhood as a large extended family. Precedents for this view include eighteenth-century Protestant churches and other early public institutions such as almshouses and prostitute reformatories that considered their populations to be members of a family (Spencer-Wood 2001).

Elizabeth Peabody House Settlement

Another settlement that had its own unique building designed with symbolic architecture and special facilities was the Elizabeth Peabody House. The settlement was domestically viewed as 'a home open to all who come within its influence and for those who live within its four walls' (Woods and Kennedy 1911: 112). It was founded in 1896 as a memorial kindergarten by friends of Elizabeth Peabody, who founded the American kindergarten movement in 1860. Its aims were 'to come in close contact, and be identified with every neighbourhood interest that may affect the welfare of the people in the district in which we are living'. While the Elizabeth Peabody House Association president was a man, the Head Resident was a woman (Elizabeth Peabody House 1913: 3–5; Woods and Kennedy 1911: 112).

In contrast to Lincoln House, the new building designed for the Elizabeth Peabody House settlement in 1912 was a monumental building 77 feet long and 7 storeys high topped by a roof garden. It was twice as tall as the highest surrounding four-storey tenements (Figure 6.6). However, it seems similar to Lincoln House in its attempts to minimize the ability to perceive the towering height of the building by designing the top two floors as dormers in an unusual

Figure 6.6
Elizabeth Peabody House.
EPH 1915: 10

THE ELIZABETH PEABODY HOUSE
*The proposed new building, facing the Charles River
Embankment*

two-storey French Empire mansard roof, topped by a railing for safety on the roof garden. As was the case with Lincoln House, the severity of the rectangular building was softened with rounded Georgian architecture, in the main door, and windows on the first and third floors; the building also included elements of Greek Revival architecture. The eclectic combination of these styles could symbolize the eclectic combination of immigrant cultures under the roof and their contributions to American culture.

The planned uses of the purpose-built Elizabeth Peabody House included residents' rooms on the top two floors, with gender-segregated classrooms on the middle floors and mixed-gender entertainment facilities on the first two floors and the basement. Compared to Lincoln House, Elizabeth Peabody House had more spaces that were used for girls' and women's activities. The seventh floor included rooms for residents (nine women and two men in 1910), a kitchen, a long dining room and other residents' facilities. By renting rooms, resident reformers contributed to the support of the settlement. The sixth floor included the principal living rooms for residents, the Head Resident's room and office, and servants' rooms. The fifth floor housed 'The Girl's Department' consisting of domestic science classrooms, a dressmaking room, a model tenement for teaching housekeeping, and club rooms. The fourth floor included the gymnasium, lighted by tall Georgian windows, separate showers and dressing rooms for boys and girls, and the basketry and carpentry room. The third floor provided 'a large and thoroughly equipped room for kindergarten work; boys' club, a print shop, and a room for men workers'. The second floor was the balcony of a large theatre with a professional stage occupying the first floor. The ground floor or basement included the milk dispensary, the nurses' rooms, and the boys' pool room (Elizabeth Peabody House 1913: 11; Woods and Kennedy 1911: 112).

The large new building was specially designed so the Elizabeth Peabody House could offer more programmes than it could in the old house, originally bought and converted to use as a settlement in 1896. In the old house the residents' pedagogical library, dining room and kitchen were on the first floor, providing residents with much less privacy than their dining room, kitchen and living rooms on the top two floors of the new building. The first floor of the old house also included a reception room. The second floor consisted of one large room used for the kindergarten in the morning and for clubrooms in the afternoon and evening for the older boys and girls, for mothers' meetings and for social gatherings. To facilitate settlement work the room was furnished with a fine piano, pictures and a small but good library for the older children. Likewise, 'the two upper floor[s] [were] furnished attractively in a simple, homelike manner for the resident workers who form the family group, the head worker, kindergartner, and four normal [school] students'. The students came from across the US 'to study in the kindergarten training classes of Boston'. A number of associate workers helped 'to carry on the plans of work in the reading room, clubs, circulating picture gallery, physical culture classes, and socials'. The demand for the kindergarten from the long 'waiting list' of the neighbourhood public schools far outstripped the room capacity, which was limited to 30 (Elizabeth Peabody House 1900: 4–5). The much larger new house constructed in 1912 permitted the settlement to offer more and larger classes, including the larger kindergarten that was the origin and heart of the work.

The Elizabeth Peabody Reports record how in both these different buildings the reformers responded to the expressed needs of their poor neighbours and clients. For instance, when immigrant mothers visiting the settlement's milk station requested English lessons, these were provided in conjunction with instruction in caring for babies and cooking demonstrations (Elizabeth Peabody House 1915:16, 21). In another example, in 1905 the settlement formed a dancing class for Jewish married women 'at the earnest solicitation of the women themselves, and continued until preparation for the Passover completely filled the women's time'. This class, as well as the dressmaking class, basketry classes, and large kindergarten club were all supported by class members from the predominantly Jewish immigrant neighbourhood (Elizabeth Peabody House 1906: 10–11).

The reformers also responded to what they observed were the needs of neighbourhood residents. In 1902 the settlement provided rooms for the Young Hebrew Charities Club and for a class in Jewish history conducted by a young Jewish lady (Elizabeth Peabody House 1903: 8). In 1910 the settlement play director saw that the laws making street play illegal only 'perverted' the natural play instinct into 'dangerous channels'. The settlement proposed gaining the co-operation of other settlements 'to try the experiment of organized street games on one or two non-traffic streets [. . .] to test the theory that if some of the play-ground spirit could pervade street life the bad effects of that life might be greatly lessened' (Elizabeth Peabody House 1911: 20).

Many programmes were well received, from swings in the roof garden, sandboxes, gardens, and kindergarten, to classes in athletics, basketry, brass work, sloyd carpentry, clay modelling, sewing, dressmaking, cooking, domestic science, and clubs for dancing, music and plays (Elizabeth Peabody House 1900: 5; 1909: 10–11; 1913: 3–5). The 1896 report observed that little girls in kitchen garden classes were eager to put the housekeeping 'knowledge gained in the club work into more practical use at home' (Elizabeth Peabody House 1897: 7). The positive responses of parents were exemplified in a 1907 kindergarten mother's meeting where one mother said she came to see 'what kind of teachers we were that had learned her Yetta so many nice things already!' (Elizabeth Peabody House 1908: 25–6).

CONCLUSION

This chapter has analysed how reformers' utopian goals and visions of society shaped the architecture of purpose-built social settlements, while reformers' experiences of the needs of participants pragmatically shaped the design and use of interior spaces for particular programmes. The combination of Georgian Revival and Greek Revival architectural styles symbolized the reformers' utopian vision of a pluralistic American democracy created from the many cultures of immigrants. The eclectic combination of elements from different architectural styles symbolized the reformers' goal that American culture be enriched with immigrant talents and cultural contributions. My research has shown that the social control thesis does not adequately account for the diversity of reformers' stated goals or their willingness to change the programmes they offered in response to falling enrolments or complaints or requests from programme participants.

The design and use of interior spaces expressed the reformers' experiences concerning the demand for different kinds of programmes. Usually the most popular programmes with the highest enrolments were provided with the largest spaces. In both Lincoln House and Elizabeth Peabody House the largest spaces were for the theatre, the gym, bowling alleys or poolroom, and the kindergarten. This evidence indicates that the most popular settlement programmes were entertainments, lectures, sports, and childcare. Clubrooms and domestic science classes were provided with larger rooms that could accommodate more people at one time than could the other classrooms for craft classes. Less evidence about room size was available for the Elizabeth Peabody House than for Lincoln House, but the kindergarten seems to have been the primary public co-operative housekeeping enterprise at both settlements, followed by after-school programmes for older children. Slightly different orientations at these two settlements are suggested by the larger number of vocational classes for boys at Lincoln House in contrast to the larger number of craft classes at Elizabeth Peabody House, possibly because this settlement devoted more space to ideally 'domestic' girls (Woods and Kennedy 1911: 112, 118).

The use of spaces in settlements also expressed some of the new public professions that reformers created for women. The kindergarten room indicates the presence of kindergarten and kitchen garden teachers trained in professional schools. Branches of public libraries in settlements, and the new profession of librarians, were both founded by women's organizations. The medical dispensary and modified milk station for infants led to the development of the public health nursing profession. Settlement residents and reformers who visited poor families created the profession of social work. Classrooms for girls, including for domestic science, scientific cooking, housekeeping, dressmaking and millinery, required professional teachers in these branches of home economics. The new female professions created by reformers were implemented through professional training with special, often scientific equipment, in specialized schools or departments in the new women's colleges, such as nursing, social work, home economics, food science, and library science.

The women's settlements studied here provided more professional employment for women reformers than men. Settlements were public institutions that were important in creating and legitimating women's public professions that were designed to address the needs of working-class women and their families, especially for childcare and education. In addition the municipal housekeeping movement, in which reformers expanded women's housecleaning role into the public household, persuaded male government officials to appoint settlement workers as the first female garbage inspectors, street inspectors, and factory inspectors (Spencer-Wood 1994b: 126).

Women in settlements and other domestic reform institutions, such as day nurseries and public kitchens, demonstrated that women could contribute to the public good and act as public citizens before American women gained suffrage. Settlements were instrumental in increasing the visibility of professional women and their institutions in men's public landscapes. Settlements and other reform institutions that visually dominated neighbourhoods by virtue of their size physically shifted the public built environment toward gender equality before women got the vote.

NOTES

1   Settlements assisted their working-class constituents by supporting trade unions, minimum wage laws, child labour laws, the ten-hour day, and other legislation that Marx, for instance, viewed not as social control, but as significant modifications of the capitalist social system to limit exploitation of workers, increase their power, and aid the cause of radical social change (Rochefort 1981: 577).

Part IV

Esprit de Corps and *Esprit Décor:* Domesticity, Community, and Creative Autonomy in the Building of Female Public Identity

Amy Bingaman

From the nineteenth century to the present day, the degree to which women construct, control, and have sovereignty over the sites they inhabit has been a central concern for architectural theorists, cultural critics, and political activists alike. That bourgeois women in Europe, Britain, and the United States have been considered domestic decorators *par excellence* has implications far beyond the interior aesthetics of their homes. Their domestic dominion has been extended to the moral education of their children and the refreshment of the virtue of their husbands (who were believed to return from work every evening sullied by their exhausting days in the libertine public marketplace). Furthermore, with the rapid expansion of bourgeois consumer culture, as decorators and upholders of morality and virtue, women came to be considered a market force to be reckoned with. The essays in this section deal with the political significance of the production of domesticity from different theoretical and methodological perspectives. But the conceptual apparatus of Michel de Certeau's 1984 *The Practice of Everyday Life* is a common denominator, with its strategy/tactics and space/place dichotomies serving as the foundation on which many of this volume's authors' observations have either implicitly or explicitly been built. De Certeau's core focus is an examination of the gulf between the 'strategic' construction of a site and the 'tactical' appropriation of the dominant ideology's intentions for the site by its inhabitants. The significance of this gulf vis-à-vis gender and modernity is that bourgeois men – producers of 'dominant ideology' and 'hegemonic discourse' – have historically been the builders, whereas middle-class women – similarly understood as mirrors of the tastes and desires of men – have been the appropriators, decorators, and at times even the decorations.

The following two essays show the ways in which traditional visions of an ideal domestic space for women are undone. These essays examine just how the production and use of such spaces not only for women, but *by women,* actually assists in their education as citizens of a much more public realm. Women who strategically produce a space for themselves and female inhabitants of an already existing space who tactically take over its use, disrupt the age-old utopian – but gendered – vision of public sphere ideology.

Despina Stratigakos's essay, 'A Women's Berlin: How Female Patrons and Architects in Imperial Germany Re-Gendered the City', examines how single professional women in turn-of-the-century Germany situated themselves as positive actors in public life, 'actively engaged in the making of their metropolis'. They did this in part by self-consciously creating gender-specific social alliances and designing architecture to house those communities. The alliance-building was as much about the education of a good female citizen as it was about compensating for the sense of loss professional women were perceived to have experienced when leaving a comfortable domestic life for an urban career. These structures and the communities they housed were not replacements for, but rather alternatives to the 'familial' home, responsive to the needs of 'modern' women, and reflective of their individualities. The communal residences Stratigakos discusses simultaneously employed the formal vocabulary of the male public sphere and the more nurturing values assigned to female domesticity. For example, the Lyceum Club's 'clubhouse', designed by member and architect, Emilie Winkelmann, was structurally an industrial-age, unornamented box. Spare, bold, and monumental, it was aesthetically, formally, and stylistically incompatible with traditional notions of what a female architect might design. The values promoted by Club members – and those of other gender-based communities like it – fostered agency and individuality, while simultaneously encouraging collectivity and strength in numbers. In this manner, the group, like the building that housed it, might present a solid, but 'open face' to the city.

Though radically different in membership, the communities of women discussed by Kelly Quinn in 'Endeavours and Expectations: Housing Washington's Women', share several commonalities with those of the collectives examined by Stratigakos. The women of the latter were, invariably, white, bourgeois, and educated, whereas those of the former, while possibly white and perhaps educated, are usually racial minorities and always completely impoverished. Despite the inexorable differences created by the disparate class statuses of these studied groups, the demographic commonality is that they are composed of women who are single and childless (or, in some of Quinn's cases, at least separated from their children). The entry requirements into each community are nearly as restrictive. A member of the Lyceum Club was not only required to be single, but also significantly (and publicly) accomplished in her field; a resident of NEW or NEXT, the two residences studied by Quinn, is required to be single, without children, sober, and demonstrative of a desire to 'get it together'. Thus, neither milieu is a shelter from the world, but rather a place to find personal enrichment and to 'launch' oneself into the public domain. Both depend upon the Enlightenment concept that human beings are rational by nature; encouraged and educated in the ways of reason, they will invariably come to an understanding of the 'common good'. Like the women of Stratigakos's professional alliances, those of Quinn's domestic shelters face a reconfiguration of domestic identity for single women; the residents of NEW and NEXT find in these spaces alternatives not to the 'familial' home, but rather to either an abusive home or homelessness. However, where Berlin's female professionals developed a sense of solidarity out of an already existing sense of independence and individuality, the agency of NEW's and NEXT's women is encouraged to develop out of communality and mutual support. While both environments privilege the experiences of women (as distinct from those of mothers, wives, or daughters), the intended empowerment comes from opposite directions.

Each author underscores the political significance of a woman being able to decorate her residential space as she wishes, even within the context of a communal living arrangement. The women involved with the Lyceum Club and communal households for professional women in Berlin, took a strategic approach to spaces as sites for female empowerment. In all cases the buildings themselves were designed by women with the needs of single, female professionals in mind. Further, women who resided in the gender-based communities were given the option of either having a housekeeper, or doing their own housework, and were encouraged to adorn their private quarters as they wished. This endorsed privacy and individuality, while simultaneously promoting the collectivity that would be vital for women *as a corps* making themselves visible in the public realm.

The women of NEW and NEXT, on the other hand, live in structures with past uses, designed and decorated in large part by more institutionally empowered organizers who believe they have the best interest of the residents at heart. In this context, inhabitants must be tactical in co-opting the space for themselves, and creating a place that is markedly their own. In the building that houses NEW, a spare, fluorescently-lit concrete box, residents are encouraged to ornament the cinderblock walls of their rooms as well as the common spaces. They pin up signs, pictures, photographs, and collages, thus creating a self- or community-designed atmosphere of physical warmth and nurturance – an atmosphere that mimics the ideals of NEW's organizers: a sense of community and mutual support empowers women to be stronger individuals, thus teaching them the skills they need to exist in the public world outside the shelter. From a bourgeois aesthetic point of view, the décor of NEW appears cold, harsh, and distinctly not 'homey'. But, because the creative impulses of the women who live there are supported, Quinn suggests that *as a place* NEW is actually more successful than the Martha Stewart- and Laura Ashley-inspired NEXT. The décor of the latter reflects not the needs and desires of the inhabitants, but rather the desires of the staff and volunteers to re-create an 'ideal' and 'appropriate' home for women. The plush, floral, bourgeois interior, is not, as it turns out, a comfortable space for these women; and, because there are many rules against decorating and rearranging rooms, there is much less opportunity for creative and tactical manoeuvring. Imposing femininity and middle-class domesticity on these women, Quinn suggests, thus impedes or even subverts the stated purpose of collectively educating these women in the values and skills they will require in the world outside the shelter.

Following in the immediate wake of Pre-Raphaelitism in England and Impressionism in France (fundamentally male artistic movements which frequently took as their sole subjects the prescribed docility and passivity of domestic women), and largely contemporaneous with the stereotypically 'feminine' styles of Art Nouveau and the Aesthetic Movement, the female builders of Imperial Germany were deliberate about refashioning both professional and domestic identities for themselves. Similarly, the women of Washington, DC's homeless shelters share an understanding that creative self-expression in a place that is one's own, is one means to autonomy and independence in the public world.

'A room of one's own with a lock on the door': Virginia Woolf's prerequisite for female fiction writers in 1928 is an enduring mantra for seemingly any woman engaged in a bid for public recognition, be it appreciation of her skill and expertise as an architect, composer, physician, or lawyer, or a more fundamental acknowledgement of her visibility beyond the disenfranchised world of the homeless and abused. Stratigakos and Quinn demonstrate that – whether that room is a strategically designed space by and for women, or a tactically co-opted place, both community spirit (*esprit de corps*) and creative autonomy (*esprit décor*) are vital, politically significant components for the agentive education of the 'modern' woman.

Chapter 7: A Women's Berlin

How Female Patrons and Architects in Imperial Germany Re-Gendered the City

Despina Stratigakos

If histories of Berlin mention women and building, they usually refer to the *Trummerfrauen*, or rubble women, who after 1945 literally put the city back together again. Berlin's Town Hall was rebuilt largely by female hands and honoured women's labour with a bronze *Trummerfrau*, who stands today at its entrance. Although she is portrayed as a heroic figure, the *Trummerfrau* is an accidental builder who salvages rather than constructs. Accounts of women as intentional and even visionary builders in Berlin are difficult to find; the professional female builder photographed in 1910 balancing on a ladder above the Town Hall is thus suspended in a narrative vacuum (Figure 7.1). This essay chronicles a

Figure 7.1
A woman builder making repairs to the roof of Berlin's Town Hall.
Illustrierte Frauen-Zeitung 38, 2 (1910): 17

lesser-known history of builders' tools and the female body in Berlin.[1] It explores a feminization of Berlin in the years leading up to the First World War: specifically, how women made their gendered presence felt in the architectural spaces of the city. I focus on interventions in the built environment by women architects and their female patrons that gave form to a vision of a new feminine urban experience. The metropolis was reconceived – and partially rebuilt – as the birthplace and sphere of a new collectivity of modern, urban women. Because this phenomenon was largely a bourgeois response to the industrial metropolis, my account centres on educated middle-class women (*Bildungsbürgerinnen*).[2] In the city's alienating potential – the unmooring of the individual from traditional social ties – these women saw an opportunity to create new communities of self-consciously modern women actively engaged in the making of their metropolis.

BERLIN'S NEW WOMEN AND THEIR URBAN CULTURE

The ascent of the woman builder to the top of Berlin's Town Hall was emblematic of new horizons opening up to bourgeois women after the turn of the century. By 1909, higher learning at universities and institutes of technology was accessible to women in all German states, and in increasing numbers women from the middle classes pursued professional careers in urban centres.[3] Despite conservative social views that too much education was inappropriate and even dangerous for women, a growing minority of bourgeois families permitted their daughters to study for a profession as a safeguard in case they did not find a husband to support them.[4] Once married, however, middle-class women were not expected to work and in some cases were legally barred from doing so. Professional career women were thus perceived to be – and often were – *single* women. No longer 'old maids', they were called 'new' or 'modern' women and were increasingly visible as a new constituency of urban dwellers in Berlin.

A women's guide published in 1913, *Was die Frau von Berlin wissen muß* (What a woman must know about Berlin), marked a profound transformation in the relationship between women and their urban environment (Ichenhaeuser 1913). The guide, intended for long-term residents as well as newcomers, was authored by women prominent in their fields. Twenty-five essays, on topics ranging from high culture to social issues, explored various dimensions of city life from the perspective of what a woman should know. Whether as students, professionals, members of women's organizations and clubs, or contributors to social welfare programmes, the book portrayed women as actors in the urban scene. This represented something new in advice literature for middle-class women. Whereas traditional instructional manuals focused on religion and the domestic sphere, the Berlin guidebook defined women in a secular, public relationship to the city. Rather than inviting women to take their place as mistress of the house, as did traditional advice books, the guidebook suggested a turning toward the city as the new realm of women's activity. There was no longer one exclusive site for women's activity (the home), but a network of sites spanning the city.

What linked these sites was the idea of a public, urban bourgeois *Frauenkultur*, or women's culture. The guidebook to Berlin was both a product of and a contribution to the shaping of this culture, literally mapping it out for its bourgeois readers. This culture can be defined as self-consciously non-denominational, educated, engaged, modern, and feminine. A host of new women's urban institutions welcomed educated middle-class women from diverse religious backgrounds – including Protestant, Catholic, and Jewish – and with varied political perspectives. They thereby provided common ground for a growing discourse on the modern condition of the metropolitan inhabitant. In seeking to influence that condition, bourgeois women envisioned their response as specifically feminine, which to many also meant separate from the male public sphere. Women sought to enter urban public life by expanding their sphere of influence, while nonetheless maintaining its gendered borders.[5]

The idea of a distinct femininity was central to the conception of a women's urban culture. Women, it was thought, brought different qualities to bear on public life than men. Although they did not have the vote – German women received this only in 1918 – they claimed the supposed moral or ethical prerogative of their sex. Drawing upon a traditional understanding of women as the nurturing sex, leaders of the bourgeois women's movement argued that women possessed greater compassion for the suffering of others and thus were well-suited – indeed obligated – to contribute to the well-being of the world around them. Women, they maintained, should foster the progress of humanity by harnessing those special ethical powers and performing public service. From this point of view, women were effective and necessary agents of social change.

Progress was defined not only in terms of social problems – attending to the social ills of the metropolis – but also in terms of urban cultural life. Here, too, women saw themselves as meaningful contributors. The women's guide-book to Berlin encouraged an active female presence in the city's museums, concert halls, and theatres. It also bore witness to the rise of new cultural institutions, such as women's clubs and a women's press. The notion of a women's urban culture was thus also deeply informed by a sense of cultural activism.

A woman was not expected to accomplish all of this on her own, but rather to develop herself in and act together with a community of peers. This, too, marked an important change from traditional assumptions that a woman fully realized herself in her role as wife and mother within the patriarchal family. Single professionals in particular challenged conventional ideas of the meaningful female life. After the turn of the century, various institutions arose in response to the need for new kinds of gender-based communities. In the place of traditional family bonds, they offered *Frauengeselligkeit*, the good company of women. This concept represented much more than companionship; it was about cultivating the self within a same-sex setting that fostered intellectual agency and social commitment. At the same time, these institutions also addressed the desire for a more gender-responsive built environment. Against the patterns and spaces of the old patriarchal home, these new communities helped shape a way of living in the city as modern women. In the rest of this essay, I consider two such types of communities: the German Lyceum Club, one of several clubs for bourgeois women founded in this period, and communal residences for educated, single women. In both of these, women architects played a role in giving visible form to a new idea of urban living.

THE GERMAN LYCEUM CLUB

The Lyceum Club in Berlin, which opened in 1905, presented itself as a novel kind of organization in tune with women's changing professional and social needs and the demands of the modern age (Deutscher Lyceum-Klub 1911: 3).[6] It strove to address the practical needs of single, career women – such as for a place to conduct business or meet friends – while also serving a larger function as a centre of female intellectual and social activity situated within an urban context. Entrance requirements were accordingly elite: Only women with significant accomplishments in their field – such as the publication of a scientific work or musical composition – could become full members (Deutscher Lyceum-Klub 1910: 4). The Club roster represented a who's who of Berlin's female artists, writers, doctors, political leaders and social reformers. Among them were Käthe Kollwitz, Bertha von Suttner, Dr Franziska Tiburtius, Helene Lange, and Alice Salomon, to name but a few of its better-known members.

Eliza Ichenhaeuser, a leading member of the Lyceum Club (as well as the editor of the women's guide to Berlin), argued that women's clubs contributed to the development of an *esprit de corps* (*Korpsgeist*) among women (Ichenhaeuser 1911: 729). Clubs thus had an integrative function, making the individual part of a female collective. Ichenhaeuser also described the clubs as a nurturing place where single women living on their own would find 'a replacement for the lost home' (Ichenhaeuser 1911: 728). The clubhouse was thought to embody these corporative and restorative functions and to symbolize physically this new feminine entity in the urban landscape (Stropp 1913: 256–7).

This collective body was, furthermore, a civic one. Ichenhaeuser maintained that women's clubs were not like those of men – a place to go smoke a cigar and forget the world (Ichenhaeuser 1911: 727). Rather, they were a place to engage with the city and, in the process, to forge an identity as a female citizen. Contrary to Ichenhaeuser's claim, men's clubs in Berlin – their emphasis on leisure and recreation notwithstanding – were also venues for consolidating influence in the public sphere.[7] Women's clubs, however, had to construct the idea of citizenship *and* a realm of influence for their members in the absence of a legitimate political voice. Women's clubs sought to recast their members as socially and politically aware citizens 'enfranchised' by their commitment to and performance of a feminine civic duty. The making of this female citizen involved a personal and collective transformation, and the clubs were seen as the training grounds for the values and skills needed for civic service. Club leaders referred to the clubs as 'small women's states', where women would learn to think democratically and acquire the language of diplomacy and statesmanship (Levy-Rathenau 1910: 3; Salomon 1899: 125). Because of professional and social differences among members, it was thought the clubs combated sectarianism and fostered women's public spirit (*Gemeinsinn*) by allowing the idea of a common good to develop in free discourse (Salomon 1899: 125).[8]

The good company of women, then, represented an ethical flourishing of the individual in community. Writing about women's clubs in the Berlin guide-book, Lyceum Club member Emma Stropp argued that the 'ethical significance of the women's clubs' represented cultural progress and should not be underestimated (Stropp 1913: 264). Since the idea of progress was virtually synonymous with that of modernity, the women's club could claim 'to educate its members to be modern women' (Salomon 1899: 126). For Alice Salomon, a pioneer of modern social work in Germany as well as a Lyceum Club organizer, this meant engaging directly with the 'modern era' and 'modern struggles' in order to contribute to 'general social progress' (Salomon 1899: 126). Thus, an important function of the women's clubs was to bring women into contemporary social struggles. Beyond the women's movement, this entailed confronting issues of poverty, disease, prostitution, alcoholism, and a variety of other urban ills. Lyceum Club lectures and standing committees devoted to social issues were meant to educate members and encourage personal involvement. This insistence on compassion suggests that women's clubs were a consciously gendered model of modern statecraft, one familiar with the language and forms of the male public sphere, but 'feminine' in its values.

The bold sense of agency cultivated by the clubs also extended to the cultural sphere. Against the traditional view of women as passive bearers of culture, women's clubs sought to promote cultural progress directly by playing an active role in the city's cultural life. At the Lyceum Club, standing committees for the arts as well as performances and exhibitions fostered women's cultural participation. In both of these instances – philanthropic and cultural work – women's contributions were conceived as a collective effort in which the agency of the individual was realized through participation in community. The clubs, in short, were expected to heighten the sense of an urban feminine collectivity and contribute to the development of a modern sensibility – one that was aware of and engaged with the life of the metropolis.

The self-conscious modernity of the Club was given architectural expression in the new clubhouse designed in 1913–14 by the architect and Club member Emilie Winkelmann (Figure 7.2).[9] The street façade of the building was strikingly unornamented; the design relied on simple, bold masses for a spare monumental effect. The functional look of the building was in keeping with the style developed by architects such as Peter Behrens to express the modernity of the industrial age. It appealed to the founders of the Club, who conceived their institution as a response to the modern era and the needs of modern women.

The relation of the building to its surroundings is also revealing. The façade

Figure 7.2
The clubhouse on
Lützowplatz designed by
Emilie Winkelmann in
1913–14 for the German
Lyceum Club.
Ilse Reicke, *Das tätige
Herz: Ein Lebensbild
Hedwig Heyls* (Leipzig:
Hermann Eichblatt,
1938), 96

did not incorporate a visible intermediary space, but came out to meet the street. Moreover, the building's exterior walls were regularly pierced with openings: windows, entrance, and loggia. With almost no ornament to obfuscate its form, and with its large apertures, the building presented an 'open' face to the city.

Winkelmann's architectural expression of a new relationship between women and their urban environment was partly self-reflective, for she was herself a new type.[10] When Winkelmann opened her office in Berlin in 1908, she was the first woman architect in Germany to establish an independent practice. In the years leading up to the First World War, women entered the profession in small but growing numbers. Their emergence coincided with a political and economic peak in the women's movement and its forays into large-scale built projects. Women architects found therein an important source of patronage and these visible, 'public' projects helped launch them professionally onto the urban scene.

The collaboration between women patrons and architects represented a complex confluence of both altruistic and opportunistic interests. Women patrons might hire a woman architect out of a desire for an all-female production – partly due to a sense of solidarity but also to show it could be done. Women architects were also expected to be more sensitive to gender-based needs because of their own encounters with the built environment, and therefore to design better for women. For their part, women architects, who were excluded from public works, gained valuable experience designing the innovative, large-scale projects supported by the women's movement.[11]

With many of the leading figures of the bourgeois women's movement among its members, the Lyceum Club served as a site for engagement with architectural issues affecting women. Through the Lyceum Club, Emilie Winkelmann also became involved in the project for a women's hospital in Berlin intended solely for female patients and doctors. Eliza Ichenhaeuser was the head of a standing committee created at the Club in 1909 to support the venture, and Winkelmann was among its founding members. Although private clinics run by women doctors for women existed in Berlin, their facilities were inadequate to the demand (Ichenhaeuser 1910: 613). It was thought that an expansion and centralization of services within a larger hospital facility would better serve the medical needs of the city's female residents (Hoesch 1995: 111). A separate hospital for women was justified by the need to protect the dignity of the female body. Feelings of shame, Ichenhaeuser and others argued, kept some women from seeking help from male doctors, resulting in great suffering and preventable deaths. At public hospitals, poor women were subjected to humiliating experiences, such as being examined by several doctors at once and in full view of others in the ward (Ichenhaeuser 1910: 613).

For Agnes Hacker, a surgeon and the guiding spirit of the project, having a woman architect build the hospital was in keeping with its underlying vision: 'all from women's hands only' (Hoesch 1995: 100). Money for the project was raised through public fund-raising events as well as from private donors, such as Ottilie von Hansemann, the widow of the Berlin banker Adolph von Hansemann. Wealthy women such as she were crucial supporters of women's institutions in the Imperial period. Winkelmann prepared plans for the hospital in 1913, but the advent of war disrupted the project and it was never realized. Sadly, her drawings have not been preserved. One wonders how Winkelmann's design might have given physical form to the desire to make the women's hospital a protective, dignified space for the female body.

In 1912, the Lyceum Club brought its vision of the modern woman to the public's attention in a monumental exhibition called 'Women at Home and in the Professions'. The site chosen was the exhibition halls of the zoological gardens in the heart of the city. Ninety-two displays covered over 9,000 square metres, a new record for these halls. The organizers intended an encyclopedic showcase of women's talents – from A to Z, as one visitor noted – and presented a broad range of occupations, including, for the first time in public as a group, women architects ('E.H.' 1912: 475). The exhibits encompassed all forms of women's paid and unpaid labour, the latter including many branches of social welfare work. In each of these spheres, women were represented as professionals and producers. Rising above the exhibits, friezes decorated the main hall with imagery of emancipated and enlightened women.

In its immensity and central location, the exhibition boldly asserted women's claim to urban space. Concurrently, the breadth of female aptitude on display provided a justification for that claim. The show made manifest a new cosmos, public yet feminine, with the educated, socially involved, and professional woman at its centre.

In her inaugural address, Hedwig Heyl, the exhibition's organizer and co-chair of the Lyceum Club, spoke of making women's accomplishments visible

Figure 7.3
Main hall of the 'Women at Home and in the Professions' exhibition of 1912.
Emma Stropp, 'Die Ausstellung "Die Frau in Haus und Beruf",'
Illustrirte Zeitung 138, 3584 (7 March 1912): 448

and material: 'all this finds witness in these walls' ('Ansprache' 1912: 72). Visibility was, indeed, a recurring theme in the show. In the arrangement of the halls, the show's designers were careful not to obstruct sight lines so that in addition to seeing the displays, the viewers could see each other (Figure 7.3). The theme of visibility was further reinforced by the sponsorship of the German gas industry: The exhibition literally glowed.[12] Journalists marvelled at the spectacular gas chandeliers, which burned with the power of 120,000 candles. An image taken at dusk captures the beacon-like intensity of light emitted by the gas pylons at the exhibition's entrance (Figure 7.4).

While the intended audience was both male and female, the journalist Theodor Heuß predicted that the exhibition's greatest psychological effect would

Figure 7.4
Street façade of 'Women at Home and in the Professions'.
Two gas pylons placed on either side of the main entrance frame the exhibition banner depicting a tree, the symbol of the German Lyceum Club.
Berliner Lokal Anzeiger (14 March 1912)

be on women. Encountering the 'massive impression' of female accomplishments would instill pride and self-assurance in women. A lack of self-confidence, he remarked, was an important hindrance to the women's movement (Heuß 1912: 171). The act of making women aware of their collective potential was perceived by some as political, and it is noteworthy that the exhibition was closely watched by police forces throughout Germany. One police report concluded that the exhibition must be judged political for awakening 'the consciousness of unity'.[13]

Some visitors voiced apprehensive feelings about the exhibition. One journalist, confronted by the apparent self-sufficiency of this women's world, felt the need to reassure male readers that they were not obsolete and about to be thrown on the 'scrap heap' ('E.H.' 1912: 475). A cartoon in the satirical magazine *Simplicissimus* made fun of the pretensions of the exhibitors – portrayed as fashionable ladies – while also suggesting something sinister. Two young women are depicted in conversation, and the caption reads: 'Me? I exhibited the death certificates of my first three husbands.'[14] The German verb '*ausstellen*' plays on the meaning 'to exhibit' the death certificates as well as 'to fill [them] out'. Yet the exhibition was also a tremendous public success, attracting over half a million visitors. It was covered extensively, and favourably, by the German press and for a short while made the new woman and her cosmos a focus of national attention.

COMMUNAL RESIDENCES

While the German Lyceum Club and similar social and cultural institutions concerned themselves with the civic evolution of the new woman, others addressed her domestic transformation. Women's building societies began to appear in Berlin around 1910, and women architects played an important role. According to prevalent social norms, middle-class women exchanged their parents' residence for a marital abode. Unmarried career women seeking an autonomous domestic existence had no place in this formulation. While initially a formidable social constraint, this 'homelessness' – which demanded the creation of alternatives – was simultaneously liberating. Experiments with new forms of same-sex residences thus emerged in response to a growing desire among single women to reconfigure domestic identities. While single women insisted upon their independence, their notion of privacy became intertwined with the idea of an empowering communality; women sought a space of their own but not solitude. For the new woman, the creation of an alternative 'familial' home responsive to her needs and reflective of her person took on tremendous significance.

In the women's guidebook to Berlin, Margarete Pochhammer's essay on living conditions revealed the dearth of choices available to single women. Reputable pensions were expensive and the transitory character of their clientele undermined the sense of a genuine home life. The option of renting a room or apartment of one's own was considered morally suspect, leading to 'uncomfortable situations and false judgments'. The necessity of a respectable address, and the expense of setting up a 'proper' household, meant that such accommodations were unaffordable for many middle-class women (Pochhammer 1913: 236). Nor were single rooms or apartments easy to find, since landlords were reluctant to rent to single women for fear it would damage the reputation of their building and because of women's reputation as burdensome tenants (Mensch 1912: 7–8). The least popular options were institutional-type homes for single women, often run by religious organizations. Their strict rules and mass anonymity appealed little to women who had struggled – and often paid a high price – for their personal freedom.

Attempts to rethink domestic arrangements were embedded within broader discourses about the form of the modern bourgeois family. The search for new types of same-sex communities tended to redefine home life around a notion of peers. Women's building societies envisioned the educated, single, career woman living not in a traditional patriarchal home with its blood ties and relations of authority, but in a freely chosen community of equals. In the various formulations of 'peer' communities – centring, in the examples to be considered here, on academic life, professional careers, and old age – one sees the degree to which identity as a single woman was fluid. Gender was central but not the only variable in structuring a home of one's own.

In 1911, the Association for Modern Dwellings for Women was founded in Berlin as a mediating agency which helped bring together single, educated women who wished to form communal households. Its guiding principle was the formation of 'hearth cooperatives' (*Herdgenossenschaften*), apartments shared by several women. The Association acted as a 'matchmaker' for tenants: Women could register their wishes (regarding area, price, and roommates) at the office, or come to the Association's meetings and be introduced to one another. It also planned to publish a newsletter with information on newly forming groups and other social connections ('Vereinigung' 1911: 7). Women were encouraged to build their hearth cooperatives around a similarity of life experiences (Pochhammer 1913: 236). In addition to social advantages, this arrangement was economical: By sharing kitchen, bath, and other communal rooms, residents had access to more comfortable facilities at a lower cost than they would renting alone. Sharing housework also reduced the need for servants.

The Association initially rented apartments but planned to build residences of its own in various locations in Berlin. To raise money for the venture, it issued two series of promotional stamps. The first series depicted six women in different professions. The second illustrated a proposed building, including views of the exterior, an interior common space, and different sides of a furnished room ('Vereinigung' 1914: 20).

The subjects chosen for the promotional stamps reveal the sense in which the dwellings were considered 'modern'. Their inhabitant, the career woman, was a 'modern' type, as was the design, which was moulded to her new lifestyle. The apartments, moreover, were outfitted with the modern conveniences, such as gas appliances, that she demanded. The stamp series thus made a direct connection between the 'modern' career woman and the 'modern' dwelling. This was reinforced by the location of the Association's headquarters in Berlin's only women's bank, which was itself a novel institution resulting from women's increasing financial independence and the need for capital to fund projects of the women's movement ('Vereinigung' 1914: 20).[15]

In 1914, the Association formed the Women's Apartment Cooperative, which undertook the construction of the new buildings. The board of directors included Germany's first female diplomaed architect, Elisabeth von Knobelsdorff, who was probably responsible for overseeing the design of the new buildings ('Genossenschaft' 1914: 18). Whether the project was realized is unclear: neither the designs nor the locations of the proposed residences are known. A description published in 1916 suggests that the designer maintained the focus on communal dwellings while also incorporating small efficiency apartments for women who wished to live on their own. Large common rooms on the ground floor provided all inhabitants with opportunities for social intercourse (Behnisch-Kappstein 1916: 381). This mixture of self-contained single-occupant and communal apartments, designed specifically for educated, professional women in an urban setting, possibly by a woman architect, and funded by a women's building co-operative, appears to have been unique in Europe.

The Cooperative for Women's Homesteads, established in 1912, had as its focus another kind of new woman – the new female retiree. Bourgeois women who had begun their careers in the 1870s and 80s were the first generation to work their entire lives as professionals to support themselves and were now reaching retirement age. They rejected traditional retirement homes run by religious and charitable organizations. The new retiree wanted to retain in her old age the independence that she had struggled to gain in her youth; she also wished to be with others who understood her life experiences. Furthermore, she sought an environment which she could shape to reflect her needs and tastes ('Frauenheimstätten' 1913: 8–9).

The Cooperative planned to build retirement settlements in Berlin and eventually throughout Germany. The inclusion of several residences and support services at each settlement would make the communities self-sufficient, while careful planning and the patronage of wealthy women were expected to keep rents low. Emilie Winkelmann served on the Cooperative's working committee and designed the first residence, called the 'House in the Sun', which was built near Potsdam in 1913 (Figure 7.5).[16] Externally, this took the form of a single-family home but was subdivided into twelve self-contained apartments. A small dining hall existed for women who did not wish to prepare their own meals, and a resident could do her own housework or arrange to have her rooms cleaned. Seemingly insignificant, this ability to choose contrasted with the regimentation typical of larger retirement homes. Flexibility was also incorporated into the architectural design. Each dwelling, for example, had a loggia which could be transformed from an open-air balcony into an enclosed sun room. Every

Figure 7.5
'House in the Sun' in
Potsdam designed by
Emilie Winkelmann in
1913.
E. von Boetticher,
'Heimstätten für Frauen',
*Berliner Frauenclub von
1900* 3, 10 (July 1915): 6

inhabitant, furthermore, was free to select her own decor, producing a hetero-geneity of styles: 'Modern artistic taste or old-fashioned comfort rule in the different rooms, each according to the character of its resident' (Boetticher 1915: 6). The liberty to decorate according to one's own taste represented a much-valued freedom to women who, having spent years in rented furnished rooms, had hitherto been constrained in this form of personal expression (Ohlert 1912: 238). In this context, being able to hang a picture one had chosen or decorate as one wished was deeply meaningful – indeed, even politically significant.

As she did for the Lyceum Club, the architect created a spare, functional look for the street façade which bespoke the modernity both of the residence type (a product of modern needs) and of its inhabitants. At the same time, the architect incorporated a vernacular idiom in the steeply pitched roof, small flower boxes, and window shutters. Winkelmann's design can thus be seen as a cross between a modernizing functionalism and a comforting vernacularism.

The Victoria Studienhaus (Victoria Collegiate House), a residence for female university students designed by Winkelmann in 1914, represented yet another formulation of a same-sex community founded on the notion of peers.[17] The intended inhabitants were daughters of the educated middle classes (Winkelmann 1914: 2). In its focus on cultivating young women, this institution exemplified the belief in the good company of women and the empowerment of self within community.

Most middle-class women lived with their parents during their studies or, if from another town, with relatives or friends of the family. Those without family accommodations confronted a severe shortage of affordable, decent housing. Student residences were rare in this period and often run by religious organizations with restrictive rules of behaviour. After the turn of the century, several limited efforts were made to found secular residences for women in Berlin. The Victoria Lyceum – the first institution in Berlin to offer academic courses, though not degrees, to women – initiated the project which became the Victoria Studienhaus.[18] With its financial and academic resources and a large donation from Ottilie von Hansemann, it became possible to plan on a grand scale.

The Victoria Studienhaus was conceived as more than mere student housing. Its creators believed that women from different cultural and academic backgrounds would learn from one another by sharing their experiences (Harder 1916: 566). More broadly, they sought to provide women with a sense of academic community from which they were all but excluded at the universities. Significantly, there were no women's colleges in Germany. The Victoria Studienhaus attempted to imitate an American or English women's college campus, particularly in its centralization of resources and its notion of bounded community ('A.P.' 1915: 142).[19] The building and grounds of the Victoria Studienhaus incorporated living quarters for about a hundred women, as well as facilities for instruction, sports, recreation, and cultural events.

The residence presented a stately but reserved neo-classical façade to the street (Figure 7.6). Winkelmann's design evoked the period of the Enlightenment as well as contemporary architectural reform movements concerned with a functional classicism appropriate to the industrial age. Winkelmann thus made reference both to the learning and modernity of the building's occupants, as well as to the educational purpose and novelty of the residence itself. For the interior, she employed the Biedermeier style which had middle-class and urban associations.

Despite Arcadian imagery of private gardens (Figure 7.7), the intentions of the Victoria Studienhaus creators were by no means isolationist. The location of the residence in Charlottenburg was chosen to provide easy access to the city's schools and cultural resources (Friedlaender 1917: 13). A map from a later promotional brochure continued to advertise the Victoria Studienhaus's integration within the broader urban network (Figure 7.8). Agnes Harder, a writer and leading figure in the Lyceum Club, referred to the students as bees leaving the hive to gather the pollen of science, bringing it back to their cells, manufacturing it into knowledge for themselves, and then using it to benefit humanity (Harder 1916: 566). Like the women's clubs, the residence was conceived as a gateway to the city as well as a place apart, where one could prepare for and process this encounter. The experience, furthermore, was expected to benefit not only the individual, but also the greater progress of humankind.

This essay has sketched a significant moment in Berlin's history when the vision of a new way of living in the city as modern women – by reconstructing the self and the built environment through the development of a new female collectivity – flourished and seemed on the verge of realization. Women embraced the metropolis as the new site of a meaningful female life, and their hold marked the urban topography. The First World War began to efface that claim, as the nation – including women – shifted their energies to the war effort.

Figure 7.6
Street façade of the
Victoria Studienhaus in
Charlottenburg designed
by Emilie Winkelmann in
1914.
Undated postcard (after
1945), Landesarchiv
Berlin

When peace returned, Berlin had changed in profound ways. Many of the existing women's projects continued, but the great thrust of building, which had
gained momentum in the years leading up to the war, was never recovered. The
pursuit of a communal feminine experience that had driven these architectural
efforts was ultimately undermined in the 1920s by a different notion of modernity. Nevertheless, women had established a lasting presence in Berlin, and the
city remained a focus for the exploration of the modern female self.

Figure 7.7
View of the garden and rear façade of the Victoria Studienhaus. Undated brochure (*c.* 1930) in the collection of the Heimatmuseum Charlottenburg

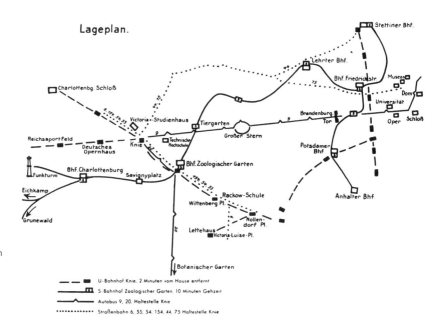

Figure 7.8
Map illustrating the location of the Victoria Studienhaus in relation to other cultural and educational resources in the city.
Undated brochure (*c.* 1930) in the collection of the Heimatmuseum Charlottenburg

NOTES

1   I am grateful to Amy Bingaman, Lise Sanders, and Rebecca Zorach for editorial advice, Peg Birmingham and other participants at the 'Embodied Utopias' conference for stimulating discussions, as well as Barbara Miller Lane, Jane Caplan, Linda Kerber, Leslie Topp, Isabel Bauer, and Thomas A. Lewis for additional comments and contributions to this article. All translations are my own.

2   Women from the working classes made their own spatial claims to the city, and the urban environment was significant in their conception of themselves as modern women. My focus here, however, is on a particular utopian vision that involved the creation of *new* architectural spaces, a phenomenon that required the capital of a wealthier class.

3   During the Wilhelmine period very few students at Germany's institutions of higher learning were from working-class backgrounds, a pattern even more pronounced among female students.

4   Censuses in the mid nineteenth century promoted the perception of a demographic imbalance in the German population consisting of a large number of unmarried women. Concern about these 'surplus' women was strategically employed by the bourgeois women's movement to argue for the necessity of women's higher education and professional advancement. See Albisetti (1988).

5   This phenomenon was not limited to Berlin. For a discussion of women's urban culture in Dallas, for instance, see Enstam (1998).

6   See also 'Der Lyzeumklub', 1905. For a general history of the German Lyceum Club, see Siebenmorgen (1995).

7   On men's clubs in Berlin, see Leopold Walter (1912).

8   Sarah Deutsch discusses similar efforts by women's clubs in Boston in her chapter 'Learning to Talk More Like a Man: Women's Class Bridging Organizations', in On women's clubs in England, see Rappaport (2000).

9   The clubhouse was located at Lützowplatz 8. Building plans are at the Landesarchiv Berlin.

10 For a history of the first women architects in Germany, see Stratigakos (1999). See also the exhibition catalogue by Günther, (1986).

11 Women architects were not permitted to take exams for the civil service during the Wilhelmine period. Elisabeth von Knobelsdorff became the first female government architect in Germany in 1921.

12 Facing increasing competition from electricity, the gas industry saw the exhibition as excellent publicity for winning female consumers; cf. Salomon (1983) 129–30.

13 Report dated 19 June 1912, in 'Die Königlichen Commerzienrath und Fabrikbesitzer Georg Friedrich Heyl und Frau Hedwig Heyl', Pr. Br. Rep. 30 Berlin C, Tit. 94, 10564, Lit. H: 170, Brandenburgisches Landeshauptarchiv, Potsdam.

14 The German text reads: 'Ich? Ich habe die Totenscheine meiner ersten drei Männer ausgestellt.' 'Die Frau in Haus und Beruf', *Simplicissimus* 1912, vol. 16, no. 51.

15 On the women's bank, see Dölle, (1997) 193–220.

16	The current address is Hermann-Maaß-Straße 18–20 in Potsdam. Building plans are at the Amt für Denkmalpflege in Potsdam.

17	The building, which no longer serves as a residence, is located at Otto-Suhr-Allee 18–20.

18	On the Victoria Lyceum, see Albisetti, *Schooling German Girls and Women*, 117–21.

19	Horowitz (1993) examines the design of women's colleges in the United States, for Britain, see M.S. Birney (1993).

Chapter 8: Endeavours and Expectations

Housing Washington's Women

Kelly Quinn

As we probe the meanings of the material world of the modern metropolis, we cannot overlook the living landscapes of poverty in contemporary urban America. Forsaken and vilified, the people who subsist on the streets in major American cities experience the built environment of these places very differently from their neighbours. Homelessness makes manifest the consequences of urban renewal, deindustrialization, the dismantling of the welfare state, and chemical addiction. The existence of people who are homeless represents the shortcomings of capitalism and democracy. Amidst this dystopia, I would like to turn our attention to a transitional housing programme for women that operates two sites in Washington, DC to explore more fully one segment of the population of people who live in poverty. In doing so, I am concerned with the cultural landscapes of homelessness and with the possibilities for solutions. A cultural landscape is a place, bounded by both its inhabitants and its students, through which we may learn about human experience. An examination of the pasts and present of the site offers an opportunity to assess the ways in which the material world enables and constrains human experiences, and the ways in which human experiences enable and constrain the material world (Groth 1994; Hayden 1995; Jackson 1984; Lewis 1979; Meinig 1979). The built environment of homeless shelters reveals a great deal about the meanings of gender, race, and class at the turn of the twenty-first century. Through an examination of such environments, we may also explore the dynamic relationship between artefacts and people. This study suggests the crucial roles that privacy and creativity play in nurturing the development of women who are homeless and in transition from the streets to independent living. This essay asks to what degree does the material culture of a sheltering programme affect its success? Does the traditional vocabulary of domestic architecture instil a sense of 'home' in such a programme? And, finally, what factors contribute to making a shelter a home?

In order to suggest answers to these questions, we cannot rely simply on a formal analysis of the built environment, nor can we rely solely on traditional ethnographies. A cultural landscapes approach enables scholars to apprehend the meanings of a site as well as the people who enliven it. Studies of the built environment that incorporate such an approach enrich our understanding of place. Two scholars have stimulated my thinking about these issues. Jeremy Korr's work on cultural landscape study provides a sound theoretical framework (Korr 1997). His proposal for fieldwork requires scholars to employ a tripartite model for analyzing cultural landscapes; he emphasizes the dynamic relationship between humans, artefacts, and nature. Joan Forrester Sprague's national study of sheltering programmes serves as an example to emulate (Forrester Sprague 1991). She urges her readers to envision shelter programmes as lifeboats for women and children in crisis. Korr's model provided the conceptual framework for my systematic study of these transitional centres in Washington, DC; Forrester Sprague's model inspired me to interrogate the design of what I found on-site.

Sheltering facilities typically provide basic accommodations and social services for residents and visitors: they offer respite and refuge for people in need. Two small sheltering programmes in Washington, DC – New Endeavors by Women (NEW) and New Expectations (NEXT) – assist women who are homeless as they ready themselves for independent living. NEW, the older and larger programme of the two, serves as the umbrella organization for both. Both agencies privilege the experiences of single women who are struggling with alcohol and/or chemical dependency, unemployment, violence, and, in the case of NEXT, pregnancy; the services offered on-site enable women to address these issues and, eventually, to obtain treatment, housing and employment. NEW and NEXT also enrich our understandings of cultural landscapes by challenging scholars to engage the experiences of women in poverty that have previously been overlooked and neglected. An examination of these programmes requires us to consider the cultural and social implications of social service agencies. I agree with social historian Michael B. Katz's estimation that 'The vocabulary of poverty impoverishes political imagination' (Katz 1989: 3). It is my hope that cultural landscape analyses of shelters will begin to enrich our understanding of the experiences of homeless women.

CULTURAL LANDSCAPES OF HOMELESSNESS

Researchers who examine social service agencies may provide insight into various cultural landscapes which constitute American society. Through consideration of social services, we may explore structural differences and power inequalities; we may probe the meanings and notions of social justice and what constitutes a 'civil society'; we may address the histories of public policy, reform efforts, philanthropy and voluntarism, poor and 'marginalized' peoples; we may chronicle the experiences of immigrants and other racial and ethnic minorities; we may assess the gendered and racialized experiences of women and men. Over the past two decades, a handful of historians, urban ethnographers, and sociologists have demonstrated how we assume much, but actually know very little about the values, beliefs, and experiences of America's poor people (Furstenberg 1992; Gordon 1994: Katz 1989; Stack 1974). Moved to respond to the highly controversial works of Daniel Patrick Moynihan and Nicholas Lemann, these scholars engage long-standing debates about the 'culture of poverty' and the state's role in creating, maintaining, and abolishing structural inequalities.

Simultaneously, over the past decade, a number of scholars and design professionals suggest the importance of documenting and explaining sheltering programmes for women ('Bridge over troubled water' 1972; Arcidi 1992; Dandekar 1993; Freedman 1992; Greer 1985, 1988; Hayden 1984; Kozak 1993; Leavitt 1984). In her pioneering project in which she documented the design and services of shelters around the United States, Joan Forrester Sprague argues that housing programmes for women and children serve as lifeboats and represent new types of dwelling. She maintains that this type of housing is a 'new physical environment' that serves as 'signposts toward a better future, solving a seemingly impossible complex of problems by taking an inclusive approach, one that acknowledges and supports contemporary life' (Forrester Sprague 1991: ix). As architect Hemalata Dandekar explains in the introduction to the edited volume of papers from an international conference convened at University of Michigan, case studies that assess sheltering programmes force us to reconceptualize the relationship between gendered expectation for and of women and space. Dandekar asserts,

> [C]ase studies [. . .] provide examples of how the access to shelter, or lack thereof, and its appropriateness in tangible, physical terms, has significant implications for the well-being and development of women. Access to shelter is a lifespan issue for women. From childhood through childbearing and in the later phases of a woman's life, appropriate shelter can help provide the security, safety, accesses, entitlements, power and resources to enable a woman to manoeuvre and negotiate a more rewarding life for herself, her children, and her family. Although the need for shelter can be and is argued to be a basic human need for everyone, a gendered approach [. . .] reveals the special concerns and issues that must be addressed if the development-oriented shelters are to be accessible to women and their dependent children.
>
> (Dandekar 1993: 10)

These scholars urge us to account for the significance of housing and women's experiences, yet they emphasize the housing needs of mothers and children in particular. Access to shelter is also a lifespan issue for women and men regardless of family status. Programmes that cater to women and children – and the scholars who study them – assume that motherhood is a common life experience. Informed both by Dandekar's insistence on a 'gendered approach' and by scholars who write against 'the culture of poverty' tradition, this study focuses on homeless programmes for adult women, a population that has been rendered invisible on the streets and in the scholarly literature.

Despite their limitations, taken together, these two bodies of scholarship challenge us to survey urban spaces and to grapple with their meanings.

Through cultural landscape analyses, we may join the traditional disciplines of ethnography and social and cultural history with architectural and planning history. Much of the literature on urban poverty by historians and ethnographers includes debates over moral categories and sociological phenomena while design professionals tend to concentrate on formal analyses of the built environment. We urgently need to examine the people as well as the buildings in order to comprehend the meanings of contemporary American urban life. Cultural landscape analyses of the contemporary urban built environment of homelessness may enrich our 'vocabulary of poverty', and hopefully embolden our 'political imaginations'.

BUILDING SHELTERING SERVICES FOR WOMEN: NEW AND NEXT

Service providers in emergency shelters in Washington, DC first conceived of NEW in the mid-1980s when they recognized that the existing services in the District of Columbia provided no good options for individual women. At that time, emergency shelters, typically run during hypothermia season (November through to April), offered shelter and minimal (if any) social services to homeless populations of DC from 7.00 pm to 7.00 am. These agencies provided temporary, sparse accommodations in a few scattered locations around the city, for example in the DC Armory. The people who sought shelter from these agencies were not permitted to stay on-site during the day and there were few places that permitted storage for personal items. The emergency sheltering programmes offered only very basic and rudimentary services; they offered no real, viable alternatives for single women who wanted to make the transition off the streets.

Single women faced special problems in seeking sheltering services in DC at that time (and still today).[1] In the mid-1980s, there were a number of reputable homeless programmes and transitional housing programmes for adult men and for female-headed families, but no agency specifically met the needs of single women without children. Most sheltering programmes for homeless people – locally and nationally – assume that children will accompany mothers, not fathers, into shelter: as a result most urban programmes typically offer services either to men or to women and children. Women who either do not have children or who have been separated from their children confront an unexamined bias in the sheltering system that assumes all women have children. In part because of the legacy of American notions about who comprises the 'deserving' and the 'undeserving' poor, most agencies who serve homeless women cater to homeless mothers and their children (Katz 1989). Mothers with children become *the* priority.

The presence of children accompanying parents into shelter creates very interesting dynamics on a practical level, in concrete ways. Accommodating these populations requires agencies to adjust their physical design and service programmes accordingly. Children demand different programmatic considerations than adults.[2] Additionally, on an ideological level, the existence of homeless children in contemporary American society confounds our notions about family life and challenges widely held assumptions about who constitutes 'the poor'. Images of homeless and hungry children resonate with American beliefs about the 'deserving' poor. Both the Right and the Left manipulate these images to advance their political agendas. Consciously or unconsciously, programmes that house children also enlist these images to appeal for financial assistance and community support. Consequently activists and academics regard shelters that house women and children as special places that deserve special attention and support.[3] Homeless adults, especially those who are unemployed and drug-affected, feature prominently in the public's imagination as members of the 'underclass'; this population does not, however, figure prominently in the public's sympathy.

'Discovered' in the late 1980s by social scientists and popular media, the underclass represents the newest members of the 'undeserving poor' (Gilens 1996). Michael B. Katz offers a helpful distinction between the different categories of poverty that emerged in the United States during the 1980s:

> [T]he very poor evoked two different images among affluent Americans. When they appeared pathetic, they were homeless; when they seemed menacing, they became the underclass. Although membership among the homeless and the underclass overlapped, the public discourse implicitly divided them by degree of personal responsibility for their situation. As long as they remained supplicants rather than militants, objects of charity rather than subjects of protest, the homeless became the new deserving poor.
>
> (Katz 1989: 185–6)

Katz's characterization of the 'menacing' quality of the underclass should also include a discussion about what the public takes to be 'deviant'. If women are sexually active, drug-affected, and ostensibly *un*concerned about their children, they also qualify for membership in the underclass. If they entered the public's attention at all, the women of Washington's streets were held to be responsible for their own homelessness. The individual women of the streets and emergency shelters – most of them African–American, some drug-affected, unemployed, and poor – became a part of the underclass. Unwilling to neglect and ignore these women, in 1987, staff and case managers from various sheltering programmes formed a coalition to remedy the paucity of services available to this particular population of homeless people. In 1988, this coalition formed a Board of Directors and acquired use of the property at 611 N Street, NW from the DC Government.

NEW, in its crudest description, is a social service agency in a brick box (Figure 8.1). Located in the Mount Vernon neighbourhood of Northwest near the site of a new convention centre, NEW currently serves thirty-eight individual, adult homeless women at a time in a twenty-four-hour transitional centre. Since it opened in July 1988, NEW has housed more than 1,000 of Washington's women. NEW's attention to women in transition may illuminate our understanding of the gendered and racialized landscapes of homelessness because the

Figure 8.1
New Endeavors by
Women, 611 N St,
NW, Washington, DC,
April 1999.
Photo by author

agency privileges women's experiences, not *mothers'* experiences. From its very origins, the founders of NEW sought to serve women individually: the centre is for women only. NEW's programme consciously rejects cultural expectations that emphasize women's obligations to and responsibilities for their children, partners, and family. As such, NEW's programmes and design reveal a unique service philosophy and building typology. Here, women focus on their own issues in their own space.

In addition to shelter, NEW offers case management, addiction and recovery counselling, employment assistance, help with budgeting and saving money, educational services, classes in independent living skills, housing programmes, legal information, and transportation. From its inception, NEW has assisted women who 'need to get their lives together' (interview, Mary Popit, December 1997). Typically, women arrive at NEW after confronting a dead end in the District's social service agencies. Once referred – usually by staff at other local housing and homeless or food programmes, and sometimes DC jail – women must participate in an interview process to ascertain whether or not NEW is an appropriate placement for the prospective resident. The major criterion used to determine eligibility is whether she is willing to abide by the programme rules during her tenure. If a woman agrees to maintain her sobriety and to 'work the programme', she must sign a contract that outlines the agency's expectations while she remains in-house. As Mary Popit, the current Executive Director, explains, NEW offers a woman 'an oasis in her life, providing some space and an opportunity for her to move further on the road to get it together'.

At NEW, Popit insists, 'women focus on themselves to get back on track' (interview, Mary Popit, December 1997). To this end, the programme expects women to concentrate exclusively on their personal issues. NEW is dedicated as a transitional centre for adult women. While 60 to 75 per cent of the women are mothers, they have been separated from their children perhaps because of drugs, alcohol, or violence. Most often kin – typically mother or sisters – care for their children. The majority of the women who enter NEW intend to be reunited with their children, but the programme requires that before they reconcile with their children, they must first resolve their own issues. Popit explains that the philosophy of the programme recognizes the cultural predilection for women to tend to their relationships before tending to their own needs. She maintains that many women get too wrapped up in the lives of everyone around them; as a result, they neglect themselves. NEW's basic tenet of dealing with women first distinguishes it as an unusual social service agency.

Since the residents of NEW are required to concentrate on themselves during their tenure at N Street, pregnant women and mothers are ineligible for services. To meet the needs of this population, NEW administered a sister programme, New Expectations (NEXT) from 1991–6; they suspended services when federal funding ended. In 1998, after securing another federal grant, NEXT reopened to serve women who are homeless and pregnant as well as postpartum women who are alcohol and/or drug dependent and their infants in a nearby residential neighbourhood. With this grant from the Department of Housing and Urban Development, NEW purchased and renovated a row house at 2801 13th Street, NW (Figure 8.2). NEXT can house up to ten women. Unlike other housing programmes in Washington, NEXT does not have the capacity to assist women who already have children; the major emphasis of this programme is to provide services to expectant women and their infants born to programme participants while in residency. As such, NEXT extends NEW's commitment to women in transition by helping women prepare for motherhood.

Figure 8.2
New Expectations, 2801
13th St, NW,
Washington, DC,
February 1998.
Photo by author

DESIGN AND DECORATION: WOMEN ADAPTING TO SHELTERING SPACES

The design and decoration of the interior spaces of NEW and NEXT reflect two different but related options for sheltering programmes. Both of these sites are adaptive reuse residential facilities: the agency has reworked the interior programmes to suit their commitment to serving women in transition. During NEW's occupation of the site at N Street over the past thirteen years, the staff and residents have coped with major structural problems – like a leaky roof – and also with the larger, more abstract challenge of making a spare, fluorescently lit box of concrete masonry into a successful housing programme. This site suggests the ways in which even a modest housing programme can serve as a home. As the agency revived NEXT, the selection and acquisition of a row house in a residential neighbourhood demonstrated a deliberate effort to house the programme literally in a *home*. My assessment of NEW and NEXT questions whether social service agencies can offer more than simple shelter to their residents.

The arrangement and decoration of NEW demonstrate the ways in which residents – the women themselves – transform the shelter into a home. In the major public space, a felt banner, the cheery yellow walls, and the lace curtains on the glass wall that opens to the porch mitigate the presence of the duct work on the ceiling, the pair of refrigerators, a soft drink machine, the counter from which meals are served, stacks of metal folding chairs, and large tables laminated with woodgrain tops. Here, amid this large, institutional, multipurpose room, the residents actively carve out spaces and sanctify places. For example, during Advent in December 1997, women took over a corner of the room for reflection and contemplation. Drawing wicker chairs into a semicircle, they celebrated the season with an altar of small votive candles, fresh greens, and colourful hand-drawn posters. In so doing, they made the space their own. Similarly, in the semi-public and private spaces of the shelter, the women have made places by naming them – the clusters of bedrooms are announced by titles chosen by the residents like 'The Young and The Restless' and 'The Bold and The Beautiful' – and by decorating with plants, drawings, contact paper, advertisements from newspaper and magazines, and hand-lettered signs that cheer each other on. To be sure, there are contested spaces within the facility: arguments surface about smoking, chores, noise and phone use. Despite these tensions and the sometimes shabby quality of the fortress-like building with its limited fenestration, dimly lit spaces, and second-hand furniture, the women of NEW have made this hand-me-down brick box theirs. Amidst the oddly configured floor plan and the subterranean basement, NEW functions well as a place for women in transition to work out their issues and to experiment with independent living.

Residents identify several specific features of NEW that distinguish it from other centres that operate as 'just a shelter'. The primary distinction that women cherish is the emphasis on privacy. For residents who have lived on the streets or in abusive relationships, the opportunity to have a place of their own, and to control it, is significant. Routinely, women emphasize the importance of having

privacy. When a woman arrives at NEW, she is assigned a room in one of the residential clusters; each is also given a lock for her door. Some residents have
stayed in emergency shelters where 'guests' share a common room and sleep in
rows of bunk beds. A room at NEW ensures privacy, and it also limits the noise
that many women grew accustomed to in other homeless programmes. As she
acclimates to NEW, a resident may rearrange or redecorate her room. One resident likens this experience to being a new resident in a college dormitory. She
notes, 'NEW feels more like a home [than a shelter]. It is as close as you get to
having your own place unless you're in an apartment, a townhouse or a semi-
detached [house]' (interview with Diane, July 1999). Others remark on the comfortable character of NEW; for them, the comfort is directly tied to the privacy.
According to the women, this privacy contributes to a family feeling that enables
them to get 'away from the drama', 'to build up self-esteem', and to ready
themselves for 'real life'.

As a service provider, NEW's other site, NEXT, operates from a similar programmatic philosophy with the goal of preparing women for 'real life', but the
settings in which they operate vary greatly. When NEW reopened NEXT, the
agency administration and staff invested a great deal in the decorative programme; it was overseen and established by the pro bono efforts of a professional interior decorator and the sweat equity of volunteers. As a result, NEXT
opened again with an unmistakable domestic character. Indeed, to celebrate the
opening and perhaps to underscore the importance of the services for pregnant
women, NEW held a 'baby shower' open house to inaugurate the new site. The
colour-co-ordinated carpets, paint, window treatments, furniture, and knick-
knacks reflect the desires of the staff and volunteers to create a comfortable
house for residents in transition. The cozy niches and brightly decorated rooms
suggest an intimacy and aesthetic of which American consumer culture icon
Martha Stewart, the self-appointed doyenne of domesticity, might approve.
While the residence is lovely and comfortable, it is a site that is somewhat less
available to its residents since house rules strictly prohibit women from decorating and rearranging their rooms. For the sake of preserving the suites of
gingham and calico, the programme prevents women from expressing their creativity more fully. NEXT offers shelter and assistance to women in transition, but
it also inhibits their ability to create and maintain a place of their own. NEXT's
vernacular architecture and its location in a residential neighbourhood reflect an
ideal about what constitutes an appropriate home for women and families. From
the arched entrance that welcomes visitors from the exterior to its hand-painted,
stencilled flowers that march along the panelling inside, NEXT exudes a sense of
femininity and middle-class domesticity. This decorative programme embodies
the domestic ideologies of the generous benefactors as it simultaneously
impinges upon the self-expression of the residents.

NEW and NEXT's services enable women to lead lives free of alcohol and
drugs, to obtain housing, to hold down jobs, and to reconcile with family. An
examination of NEW and NEXT also reveals the ways in which physical structures

provide an opportunity for individuals to transform their lives. NEW suggests that humble – even shabby – places can sustain people if the residents are empowered to control their own space. Modest facilities may hold as much promise to promote and nurture change as well-funded, aesthetically pleasing, elaborate accommodations. Especially because NEW and NEXT's architecture is unremarkable, we may assess the power of people to transform places. As an artefact, the form of NEW suggests little possibility for creativity or care: from the exterior, it is an unfriendly, inhospitable site amid the parking lots on N Street. Yet, the ways in which the women of NEW have enlivened the building – from the large, colourful murals on the façade to the small construction paper signs that adorn the private rooms – reflect the power of people to create their own special and significant places.

The women of NEW and NEXT rely on social service agencies to assist them as they move from the dystopian world of the streets rife with addiction, abuse, and exploitation. If these agencies recognize and nurture women's privacy, creativity, and determination, they offer one solution that may represent a pragmatic utopia. As scholars concerned with gender and social transformation in modern urban environments, we may employ cultural landscape analyses of housing programmes like NEW and NEXT to enlarge our vocabulary of poverty, stimulate our political imaginations, and complicate our notions of utopias. With studies such as these, we may begin to reconsider the current configurations of our contemporary urban environments, and begin to imagine cities that are more hospitable and just. As we consider how to shape and reshape the cities in which we live, work, and study, we must first begin to grapple with how poor women endeavour to shelter themselves. If we centre our understanding of the city on the experiences of homeless women, they may offer solutions for housing that ensure dignity and privacy and enkindle creativity. Their experiences may also prompt scholars and social workers to re-examine notions about women and domesticity. A research agenda that includes landscapes of poor women in shelters promises to challenge assumptions about the social and physical constructions of homelessness.

ACKNOWLEDGEMENTS

Kelly Quinn would like to thank the editors of this volume and Melinda Chateauvert, Mary Corbin Sies, David Silver, and Francille Rusan Wilson who carefully read this piece in its various iterations and offered helpful suggestions. She is also indebted to the women of NEW and NEXT who shared their space and their stories.

NOTES

1   The number of available beds in either emergency shelters or transitional centres is inadequate given the need, especially during hypothermia season. When residents of transitional centres are ready to leave these homes, they face an incredibly tight housing market that is hostile to people with low incomes.

2   It is beyond the scope of this essay to explore fully how the presence of children affects the built environment and programme concerns of homeless shelters, but let me offer three examples. First, given that agencies operate with the assumption that women will be the primary care-givers for children, homeless, nuclear families in Washington, DC frequently must decide whether mother and father should separate temporarily in order to gain entry into most programmes. Second, again, since agencies typically expect women to be the single parents, there are very few shelter options for single fathers with children; a local network of churches started an initiative, 'Family Shelter', in 1992, in part to house this population. Through their efforts, church basements and social halls doubled as homes for fathers and their children and for a number of mothers and fathers who chose not to separate. Finally, one example of how children may require special design features includes decisions on the location of open, safe, supervised play spaces in a facility.

3   The works previously cited by scholars and design professionals deal chiefly, if not exclusively, with sheltering programmes for women and children.

Part V

Embodying Urban Design

Anthony Raynsford

Utopias have often been imagined through designs for ideal cities, generally in opposition to a prevailing urban pattern. Actual cities, on the other hand, are rarely built along purely utopian lines. Nevertheless the forms, codes and principles embedded in their designs often have utopian sources, which can ideologically veil the contradictions of the urban landscape or else float as fragmentary signs within a more or less dystopian space. The essays in this section deal with the contradictory results of city building as well as with the utopian ideals, often attenuated and impoverished, which inform their legibility. Brent Stringfellow's essay, 'Personal City', examines what is often called suburban sprawl, here dubbed 'panurbanism', in which green spaces weakly signify Arcadia amidst a tangle of highways, developments and parking lots. Meanwhile, Andrew Wood's essay, 'Re-Reading Disney's Celebration' analyzes the tropes and discourses surrounding the latest attempt to embody a long-standing American utopia: the small town of an imagined, more communal past combined with the technological conveniences of the present. Finally, Brian McGrath's essay, 'Bangkok Simultopia', investigates the overlay of Western urbanistic practices and their utopian assumptions of rational clarity on a city whose inhabitants overturn the logic of these practices through the syncretic coexistence of bodies, spaces and meanings. What links all of these essays is their attempt to come to terms with the resonances and effects of utopian ideals in the contemporary construction of the built environment.

These essays draw from terms and discourses surrounding what, since World War II, has come to be called urban design. On one level, urban design was a mid-twentieth-century reinvention of the architectural planning of cities, codified in theoretical writings since the Renaissance. On the other hand, urban design was a specific reaction, particularly in Western Europe and North America, against the professional authority of urban planning and its numerical abstractions. Urban planners in the twentieth century, an increasingly specialized and bureaucratized class of professionals, have concerned themselves with such issues as land use, density, zoning and transportation, leaving to architects the task of designing individual buildings within the preordained constraints of planning policy. Architects, contesting this division of labor between large-scale spatial policy and small-scale aesthetic intervention, began in the 1940s to demand design control over cities and sections of cities. In doing so architects made the following claims:

1 that the architectural design of cities could significantly improve social well-being and quality of life,
2 that the collective decisions of planners, developers and traffic engineers had produced visual chaos and social distress, and
3 that the qualities of good city design could be studied empirically and reproduced in practice.

In the 1940s and 1950s, the English Townscape movement called for the visual planning of cities, according to sensory, often picturesque qualities. Simultaneously, the call by international modernists for a 'new monumentality' focused on the idea that well-designed civic centres might become platforms for public interaction and communal identity. The founding of the first urban design program in the United States in the late 1950s at the University of Pennsylvania roughly coincided with the entry of new scientific discourses in architectural education, notably environmental psychology and sociology. Along with the new scientific mantle of urban design came a critique of modernist cityscapes as socially and visually dysfunctional and, correspondingly, a valorization of pre-twentieth-century urban forms. The social criticism of Jane Jacobs in the United States and the architectural theories of Aldo Rossi in continental Europe validated, in different ways, the traditional typologies of defined streets, pedestrian scales and mixed uses. From the early 1960s until the mid-1970s, the utopian promise of urban design encompassed both an ecological metaphor of cities adapted to human needs and a rhetoric of place that aligned with local activists over and against forces of abstract homogenization.

One of the most persistent threads of urban design writing has been the critique of suburban sprawl. It may be useful to understand Brent Stringfellow's critique of panurbanism in Fairfax County in relation to the history of such discourses. The term 'suburban sprawl' seems first to have come into common use in England in the 1950s, when the massive decentralization of cities combined with increased automobile ownership produced a landscape in which the categories of city, suburb and country were increasingly difficult to distinguish. Critics feared that the entire countryside would be engulfed in a dystopian landscape of banal homogeneity while the city centres withered away, along with the ever elusive 'sense-of-place.' In 1955, for example, the editors of the *Architectural Review* put together a manifesto against sprawl, which they dubbed 'subtopia,' facetiously combining the words suburb and utopia: 'Subtopia is the annihilation of the site, the steamrollering of all individuality of place to one uniform pattern' (*Architectural Review* 1955b: 371). According to the authors, the phenomenon of subtopia was not merely one of excessive tract housing or destruction of rural space, but rather a fundamental destructuring of cities as defined centres of employment, consumption and domestic life:

> applied science is rendering meaningless the old distinction between urban and rural life; the villager is becoming as much a commuter as the citizen; the old centres of gravity have been deprived of their pull at both ends and in the middle; no longer geographically tied, industries which once muscled in on the urban set-up are getting out of the mess they did so much to make and making a new mess outside.
>
> (*Architectural Review* 1955a: 365)

Such worries and observations were intensified when observers and critics, both European and American, turned their attention to the United States, considered by many to be the vanguard of this phenomenon. From the late 1950s many American architects, including Victor Gruen and Louis Kahn, futilely tried to turn the tide of decentralization and suburban sprawl by offering dense, urban design solutions that also accommodated the automobile. In the 1960s and 1970s, as the critique of suburban sprawl in the United States escaped elite, urban design spheres and entered the environmental and historic preservation movements, Victorian row houses and main streets began to signify in utopian ways that might have been perplexing to those living just thirty years earlier. Such places became refuges of spatial identification, visual anchors, and symbolic 'centers of gravity' in metropolitan areas that, economically, were becoming ever more dispersed and spatially volatile.

As suburban sprawl has come to represent an alienating landscape of loosely tethered spaces separated by ribbons of highway, the traditional, small town, or its simulacrum, has come once again to represent a lost realm of face-to-face contact and everyday intimacies, similar in some ways to the *Gemeinschaft* of nineteenth-century German sociology. In their attempts to critique and reverse the effects of suburban sprawl, urban designers have also reconstituted the wishful idea that configurations of buildings can produce harmonious communities and lively public spheres. This is the broader context which pervades Andrew Wood's analysis of Disney's Celebration and its rhetorical tropes. Above all, Celebration is an example of the so-called New Urbanism, which has emerged in the United States generally and in Florida especially since the late 1980s as a remedy for suburban sprawl. Although most of its ideas, such as promoting density, mixed uses and nineteenth-century building types, date back to the 1950s and 1960s, the New Urbanism has become renowned since the late 1980s for convincing developers to build such projects at the urban fringes. One of the most successful New Urbanist designer teams, Andres Duany and Elizabeth Plater-Zyberk, described the social logic of their urban forms in the following terms:

> *The neighborhood gives priority to public space and to the appropriate location of civic buildings*. Public spaces and buildings represent community identity and foster civic

pride. The neighborhood plan structures its streets and blocks to create a hierarchy of public spaces and locations. Squares and streets have their size and geometry defined by the intention to create special places.

(Duany and Plater-Zyberk 1994: xix; italics in original)

If one understands this description as referring, not to the building out of an existing community, but rather to the manufacturing of a community with no prior existence, then the peculiarly utopian quality of this statement becomes apparent. The idea that a public or a community will materialize, given a convincing architectural setting and but without structural changes in social relations, remains an alluring mirage in American life and certainly underlies the theatrics of Disney's Celebration, an 'imagineered' community with a real-life cast.

Whereas urban designers have clung to a rhetoric of local character and communal identity, much of their patronage has come from the realm of international capital. Two of the largest urban design projects of the 1980s, Canary Wharf in London and Battery Park City in New York are both enclaves, whose formal gestures to 'public space' mainly serve the employees of elite, corporate headquarters. It is this multinational, corporate façade of urban design that Brian McGrath juxtaposes with the syncretic urban culture of Bangkok. As global capital infiltrates Bangkok along with architectural motifs of corporate urban design, both are absorbed and deflected by older patterns of inhabitation and spatial meaning. McGrath's investigation of complexity and simultaneity that resist the utopian simplification of the master plan echoes much critical writing on cities since the 1960s. In the wake of urban renewal and mass housing projects in Europe and North America, many critics cited the apparent distance between the abstractions of the architects and the experiences of those, so to speak, in the street. In the United States, Jane Jacobs critiqued master plans as being hopelessly removed from the complexities of urban behavior. In France, Henri Lefebvre made the all-important distinction between lived space and spatial representations, notably those of architects and planners. More recently Michel de Certeau juxtaposed the static, utopian, visual city, the city seen from above, against the swarming, labyrinthine, tactile city, the city experienced by the pedestrian: 'Their story begins on the ground level, with footsteps. They are myriad, but do not compose a series. They cannot be counted because each unit has a qualitative character: a style of tactile apprehension and kinesthetic appropriation. Their swarming mass is an innumerable collection of singularities' (de Certeau 1984: 97). The narrative tracing of pathways through Bangkok, by suggesting the phenomenological irreducibility of embodied, urban inhabitation, similarly refuses the reduction of urban space to visual form. At the same time, the idea that spaces juxtaposing differing cultures, economic levels and symbolic frameworks, parallels many writings on the so-called postmodern city. Geographers, such as David Harvey, have described such phenomena as space–time compression and uneven development, particularly as they tend to accelerate spatial fragmentation. How Bangkok, in particular, can accommodate the juxtapositions between global and local systems would seem to depend on how the cultures and practices of its inhabitants respond to difference at the urban level.

All of the essays in this section raise questions and issues of what it means to represent social identities and social differences through urban design. How do urban forms become imbued with identifications and desires? How do rhetorical tropes enfold the visual and spatial qualities of designed environments? How do practices of inhabitation confront and assimilate the products of architects, planners and developers? Over all such questions hover the various utopian ideals, the nonexistent elsewheres, whose ideological force variously pervades the urban designers' formal decisions and the inhabitants' spatial vision. This double embodiment, of buildings and citizens, thus takes shape reciprocally through utopian lenses that attempt to filter the fissures and contradictions of contemporary urban life.

Chapter 9: Personal City

Tysons Corner and the Question of Identity[1]

Brent Stringfellow

Tysons Corner, Virginia, is an unincorporated settlement twelve miles west of Washington, DC, midway to the Dulles International Airport. Located in Northeast Fairfax County, Tysons Corner has its centre at the intersection of four major highways – Route 7, Route 23, the Dulles Airport Access Road and the Washington Beltway (Interstate 495). Before World War II, there was little to indicate that a major economic and commercial centre would emerge from this patch of farmland. Remembered as little more than a 'beer joint and a feed store' in 1939, Tysons would come to epitomize the general growth of the American suburb in the postwar years (Figure 9.1).

In addition to favourable housing policy, Tysons Corner and Fairfax County benefited from the paranoia of the Cold War. Decentralization became a

Figure 9.1
'Downtown' Tysons Corner. The Tycon Tower, highest point in Fairfax County, is on the right. Photo by author

significant urban theme, as the threat of atomic destruction clouded the enthusi-asm for life in the metropolis. This was especially true of Washington, DC, where it was assumed that any attack would happen without warning. In 1947, Lewis Mumford advocated that cities should be made less attractive targets with the idea of planned dispersal, while at the same time he argued that substantial gains in the quality of life could be achieved by reducing urban density (Mumford 1961: 482). Though a 1950 plan for dispersing the bulk of the federal govern-ment was not enacted, the concept of dispersal had a strong impact on the area's development, perhaps best illustrated by the creation of the Interstate 495 beltway in 1960. The interstate that was conceived as a rapid transit system for the military quickly became the infrastructure needed to support rapid commer-cial development.

Stimulated by tax policies favouring the ownership of single-family units, the GI bill and the emerging dominance of the automobile, the rapid growth of the American landscape occurred at the periphery of its cities. Between 1950 and 1970, American suburbs grew by 85 million people; the urban cores they were growing out of expanded by only 10 million (Muller 1981). This nation-wide phe-nomenon is underscored by Fairfax County's extraordinary growth from 1950 to 1960, when its population tripled, reaching a quarter of a million people. In 1953, the first shopping centre in the county opened in Seven Corners, just down the road from Tysons. Ushering in a new era of consumerism, the centre was designed to serve 50,000 people and provided parking for 2,600 cars (Garreau 1991: 349). In 1962, Tysons took the first step away from being a typical bedroom community when it began re-zoning land in the area for commercial purposes. Subsequent development in Tysons Corner and Fairfax rapidly became autonomous from Washington, DC; the tie from suburb to city loosened. In 1960, 35 per cent of regional jobs were located in the suburbs. By 1977, the figure was 65 per cent, and is currently upwards of 80 per cent (Garreau 1991: 351).

Currently, Tysons Corner's resident population of 80,000 people has a median household income of $90,000. From nine to five, Monday through Friday, Tysons serves as the Central Business District (CBD; or downtown) for the whole Fairfax County population of 879,000 people, as well as a commercial and retail centre for the greater metropolitan region of 6 million people. Tysons cur-rently ranks as the fifteenth largest business district in the United States, larger than the CBDs of Houston, Cincinnati, Miami, or San Diego. It contains over 20 million square feet of commercial space, 1 million square feet of industrial space, and 5.3 million square feet of retail space. This is the largest mass of retail opera-tions on the East Coast, after Manhattan's. As the economic heart of Fairfax County, Tysons contains 35 per cent of its office space, 33 per cent of its hotel space, and 48 per cent of its service industries. It is also a landscape overwhelm-ingly dominated by the car. 53 per cent of Fairfax commuters travel within the boundaries of the county, while only one-fifth commutes into Washington, DC. 92 per cent of the workforce in Tysons uses a car to get to work.[2]

The product of astonishing growth, Tysons Corner is typical of the environment in which more than half of the American populace currently lives and works. Surprisingly difficult to pin down, it is neither bustling *city*, nor quiet *suburb*, nor rural *town*, but something else. Less the result of any overt urban planning or architectural code, Tysons Corner is the product of shifting demographics, market forces, ambitious development and the universal acceptance of the personal automobile. No longer a suburb economically dependent upon a city, Tysons Corner is simply a new kind of urbanism (Fishman 1987: 184).

Unfortunately, there is little room within existing conceptual frameworks of city, suburb or town that adequately helps us define and understand what is happening on the national scale. Tysons is a density of settlement and a species of urbanism that is both too large to be one place, and composed of too many small elements to be cohesively whole. Cities and towns now subsumed in this ocean of built stuff are mere remainders of specific activity in the larger sea of settlement; they are not centres anymore, but discrete moments of density within a larger fabric. The larger fabric – the sprawling counties full of houses, highways, airports, malls, and office parks – is now the a priori condition of early twenty-first century American settlement. Too diffuse spatially and programmatically to be considered a city, yet too intense commercially to be considered a suburb, this condition can be defined by the term *panurbanism*. Though other labels have been applied to regions like Tysons Corner, notably *edge city* and *exurb*, those terms emphasize a disconnection between a centre city and the periphery. Panurbanism, on the other hand, is a term that attempts to account for the larger fabric – including city centres and rural farmlands. The prefix 'pan' is derived from the neuter form of the Greek *pas*, meaning 'here and there, all over, at random; without order, indiscriminately, [and] promiscuously' and is ideally suited to define the undisciplined development that distinguishes much of the American landscape.[3] Tysons Corner, while not the only example of panurbanism, is perhaps one of the foremost.

As a new incarnation of the city, Tysons Corner in particular and panurbanism in general are distinguished by a number of characteristics that are symptomatic of the dissolution of traditional urban space and its functions. First, Tysons Corner resides in landscape that is both physically open and mythologically filled. Echoing the premise of Leo Marx's 'machine in the garden', the rules established by local zoning ordinances in Fairfax County are designed to maintain physical separation and open space. As a result, Tysons Corner accepts all types of development into the fold – residential, commercial, and industrial – as discrete items, without defining itself as a larger whole. Culturally, the development of large open plots exploits arcadian myths of the frontier, inspiring residential cul-de-sacs and sylvan office parks, where the isolation of space and use is marketed as an amenity. Second, panurbanism is defined less by location than by mobility. Any apparent civic or spatial centre can be defined solely by what is moving through it, whether the cars on the cloverleaf or the goods in the mall. Finally, the operational credo of Tysons Corner is *newness*. In sum and substance, Tysons is a perpetually recycling environment, consistently reinventing itself to remain always in the present and in fashion. The thin material veneer that covers the architecture of Tysons Corner – brickface, metal panel, and stucco – allows for easy demolition and rejuvenation. Consequently, the surface quality of the architecture favours the impermanence of image over the development of any kind of vernacular tectonic.

Spatially, the identity of the traditional city is partially the result of the particular qualities that result from the overlay of various systems, spaces, and functions susceptible to one another, interacting and producing unique formal and social events. In addition, the physical proximity of building in a city promotes a parallel effect in the interaction of the population, as the compressed space of centre cities ensures a bodily interaction analogous to the multi-layered infrastructure of the city itself. But in Tysons, each building is distinctly removed to the centre of its own particular plot, favouring the security of solitude over interaction – in effect, 'a purposeful withdrawal from involvement in and responsibility for the greater politic of the city' (Vanderbilt 1995: 67). The detachment of the architecture from the body of the city is codified in the zoning ordinances for Fairfax County. The Code of the County demands that buildings in a development, upon individual lots, have clear yard space along the entire perimeter of the structure, effectively mandating that all buildings become, or remain, islands (Figure 9.2). In residential zones, the code requires that each house have a minimum front yard of 30 feet, a minimum side yard of 8 feet, and a minimum rear yard of 25 feet. Likewise, office spaces – space that in cities and towns has congregated in clusters – are also centred on their individual sites. An office district requires a front yard equivalent to a 25-degree angle of bulk plane (equivalent to about 25 feet on a 50-foot building), no side yard requirement, and a 20-degree angle of bulk plane for the rear yard (20 feet on the hypothetical building). The demands for clearance around the perimeter of each individual structure are buttressed by a general requirement for open space. In most residential and commercial spaces, 15 per cent of the land must be open; this figure may at times reach as high as 30 per cent. In addition, the requirement for open space is separate and distinct from the requirement for parking, whether structured or open. Parking may use anywhere from 35 per cent to 42 per cent of the total space of a lot. One can quickly see it is very unlikely for a commercial structure in Tysons Corner to occupy more than 50 per cent of its plot. The result of all the codified prodding and squeezing is an architecture that effectively severs the formal and programmatic interaction inherent to an architecture that shares a closer physical proximity. Consequently, any interaction between tenants is discouraged.[4] Ultimately, these zoning regulations create virtual borders before actual buildings even exist in Fairfax County. In *The Death and Life of Great American Cities*, noted urbanist Jane Jacobs details the effects of such borders:

> by oversimplifying the use of the city at one place, on a large scale, [borders] tend to
> simplify the use which people give to the adjoining territory too, and this simplification
> of use – meaning fewer users, with fewer different purposes and destinations at hand –

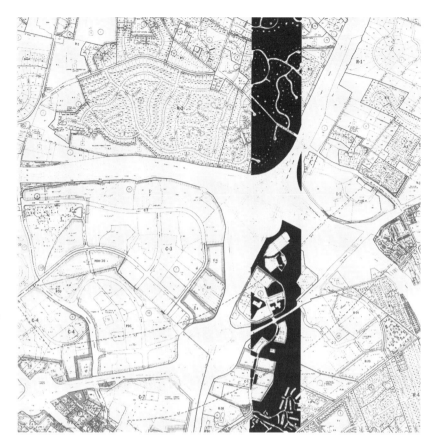

Figure 9.2
Diagram of the centre of
Tysons Corner. Open
space, excluding
highways, are shaded in
the strip on the
right side.
Photo by author

feeds upon itself. This is serious, because literal and continuous mingling of people . . .
is the only device that encourages districts to form in place of fragmented, self-isolated
neighborhoods or backwaters.

(Jacobs 1961: 259).

The iconic example of border that Jacobs cites in her analysis is the railroad track,
and its spatial effects and social repercussions (i.e. the wrong side of the tracks).
Borders exist within Tysons Corner at multiple levels as a result of the zoning
requirements that emphatically divide scale and use. Subsequently, each zone
within Tysons is committed to a single use, so that a commercial zone will only
be occupied from nine to five, a retail zone will be active during store hours, and
residential zones will be active during evenings and weekends. Though not a
characteristic exclusive to places like Tysons Corner (single-use districts permeate
traditional city centres – a typical example is the financial district deserted after
five o'clock or on weekends), the restriction of single-use zones in Tysons
enhances the spatial isolation of each island of development (Figure 9.3).

This spatial and functional isolation has the effect of emphasizing any vari-
ation or difference to a degree that it may be perceived as a threat to the
integrity of a development. As a result, the users of each individual space often

Figure 9.3
Office building and
sidewalk
Photo by author

become preoccupied with discouraging contamination of each island by an outside source. An example can be found at McLean Hamlet, a residential development located in the northern section of Tysons Corner, across the Dulles Access road from the major commercial and retail developments. Containing 512 houses, McLean Hamlet describes itself as providing a 'peaceful life in a quiet setting', along with amenities such as 'mature trees and shrubs, ample colonial-style streetlights, and Shakespearean names for every street'.[5] McLean Hamlet Citizens, a homeowners association, is the primary governing body. In a letter sent to Fairfax County planning officials on November 21, 1997, the committee addressed a proposal to build an assisted living complex for retirees and the elderly adjacent to McLean Hamlet as one component in a new residential development:

> We are strongly against any erosion of the long-standing county policy that the Dulles Toll Road is the dividing line between commercial uses in Tysons Corner on the south side and residential uses on the north side . . . [change in this policy] would degrade the value of these properties and the quality of life in these neighborhoods. We believe that an assisted living facility has many aspects of an institutional and commercial use, and as such, is not in conformance with the surrounding area.[6]

In this case, a private homeowners association (acting in lieu of a government body) reinforces the logic of the zoning code. The primary stated concern of the organization is the building of a structure that violates the divide between commercial and residential use and does not conform to the informal zoning rules that dominate Tysons. It is also worth noting the importance of the Dulles Access/Toll Road in creating and maintaining general separation. However, the fact that an assisted living facility – a *residential* facility – is portrayed as a primar-

Figure 9.4
The centrifugal centre
Photo by author

ily commercial endeavour reveals a distinct bias against the arrival of *other bodies*, notably the elderly and the developmentally disabled. McLean Hamlet is essentially manipulating the ordinances of spatial and functional isolation to enable *social* isolation and exclude no longer productive members of society. While the ideal of Grandmother living down the street may be appealing, the concept of a commercial institution full of grandparents is not. It is, however, interesting to note that now, in 2001, as this volume goes to press, McLean Hamlet Citizens has apparently lost its battle; ground has been broken and this facility is under construction.[7]

This physical and social isolation of the built environment at Tysons Corner simultaneously produces and is a product of an experience of place centred on physical movement (Figure 9.4). The spatial and functional disconnection of Tysons Corner is minimized at high-speed travel – when the overwhelming reliance on the car diminishes the connection of the body to the surrounding environs. The speed of the automobile on the highway compresses topography, as the dispersed moments of building and use are rendered continuous by movement between them. The idea of distance is easily overcome by velocity. It is at 65 miles per hour open space seems logical, allowing one to consider the collection of architectural appearances coherently. By contrast, Tysons Corner from a stationary perspective is 'little more than a swarm of urban bits jettisoning a physical view of the whole, sacrificing the idea of the city as the site of community and human connection' (Sorkin 1992: 8). In this vein, the functional isolation of various neighborhoods in Tysons Corner is remedied by the ability to travel quickly between zones. Precisely because the strict zoning rules of most residential developments prohibit a bodega-like corner store, the five-minute walk to the end of the block is replaced by the five-minute drive to the strip mall.

The process of finding, locating, arriving at and departing from a set of destinations is the central fact of life in Tysons Corner. Acting in parallel with the zoning code is a set of rules that defines the road system hierarchy within Fairfax County. Divided among four categories – Major Artery, Minor Artery, Connector, and Local – the organization of the roads is designed to ease movement through the County.[8] The hierarchy essentially organizes roads in terms of access, limiting certain roads to local access, while designating others as high-speed zones to be used for regional travel only. Consequently, direct travel from point A to point B is impossible, and the movement from local road to connector road to artery is always an exercise that further reduces the impact of physical proximity on the use of Tysons Corner. Richard Sennett writes that the highway engineer creates what could be called 'freedom from resistance' – ways to move without obstruction, effort, or engagement. He further underscores that the desire to free the body from resistance is coupled with a fear of touching (Sennett 1994: 18). This fear of touching is manifest throughout the fabric of Tysons Corner, from the bureaucratic zoning ordinances and road system hierarchies that divide and isolate uses, to the social fear of touching clearly underlying the McLean Hamlet Citizens' letter. Instead of being directly interactive with the city – mingling, as Jane Jacobs says – the body moves passively within the car, the device by which each person in Tysons Corner creates their own personal version of the city. In his book *Bourgeois Utopias*, Robert Fishman notes:

> the true centre of this new city [what he terms *technoburbs*] is not in some downtown business district but in each residential unit. From that central starting point, the members of the household create their own city from the multitude of destinations that are within suitable driving distance . . . all they need and consume from the most complex medical service to fresh fruits and vegetables, can be found along the highways.
>
> (Fishman 1987: 185)

The car enables each inhabitant to customize, and therefore idealize, their own city. Though a walk to the corner store and a drive to the strip mall are functionally equivalent experiences, the drive to the mall can be accomplished in isolation, tucked away within a car, and public interaction is reduced to turn signals and flashing lights. As a result, the highway is an ambiguous realm of public and private interaction – perhaps the nexus of civic life of Tysons Corner. It is on the road where the public gathers most, yet always sealed within the private reality of the car and protected by its sheet metal and velocity. Like the isolation of homes and offices, the car allows for existence in a public sphere that is protected from difference, permitting a user to remain analogously anonymous and detached.

The mobility that characterizes existence within Tysons Corner is also reflected in the perpetual reconstruction of its buildings. The rate at which offices, malls, and houses are planned, constructed and reconstructed creates an environment of continuous spatial re-configuration in which it is easier to locate

Figure 9.5
Typical house
construction.
Photo by author

what is new than it is to remember what was before. Expansion and growth, as the necessary forces behind economic health, ensure that the only certainty is revision. The manner in which contemporary buildings are made – with a thin skin applied over a structurally independent frame – allows for effortless revision of walls, surfaces, and façades (Figure 9.5). Wallpapers, sidings, marble panels, curtain walls, can be removed and replaced for any reason – but usually by a desire for a new atmosphere, a new look or the spatial biases of a new client.

The primary function of architecture in Tysons Corner is appearance, rather than its spatial dynamics. But any one specific appearance is not at issue. It is not what a building looks like that is important, rather, that it look *appropriate* to its function. What matters is not the office building that looks different from the house, but that each is motivated by the same set of determinants – marketability and conformity. In this respect the disintegration at a macro scale – the concise division of the city into zones of functionality – is matched by the deterministic appearance of the architecture. The resulting environment lacks what Lefebvre called the 'conflictual component' – complexity is thwarted at each scale, while the economics of image ends up delineating the architecture of Tysons Corner. Such a reliance on appearance betrays a market-based rationality that both overlooks and minimizes the importance of interactive bodies in the creation of urban space. This contradicts not only the successful urban spaces documented in Jane Jacobs's writing, but even more fundamentally ignores what Lefebvre calls the core and foundation of space – the total body and its physical gestures and movement – in favour of superficial, mural-like depiction (Lefebvre 1991: 200).

Adopting the role of a laissez-faire urbanist, one might be tempted to argue that the panurban condition is a tabula rasa where the dissipated structure becomes an oppressive yet honest collective reflection of the desires of individual inhabitants. In lieu of the spatial unity that defines urban identity in a traditional city, Tysons Corner is a series of discrete objects, each of which fulfils a particular function or appeals to a particular set of desires. One might contend that the lack of overarching urban identity allows for an individual freedom of interpretation and use. Unrestricted by figural identity and its own attendant ideology, inhabitants of the panurban landscape are free to make individual interpretations of the city. As Rem Koolhaas states, 'the stronger the identity, the more it imprisons. Paris can only become more Parisian' (Koolhaas 1998 [1996]: 1248). A city such as Paris is trapped in its own identity, unable to escape the burden of its historically driven urban form. Tysons Corner and other panurban regions are freed from history and hence are more capable of constant reinvention. Likewise, the fact that existence in Tysons Corner is built upon a foundation of personal space – the private home, the automobile – would imply that Tysons Corner specifically and panurban regions in general offer a chance at idealized living through a spatial and social system that allow for seemingly unlimited possibilities of use.

However, the systems that organize Tysons Corner such as the zoning laws – and the homeowners association's manipulation of them – are actually more restrictive than the figural identity of a city like Paris. In contrast to the figural neutrality of Tysons Corner, the iconic buildings, plazas, and streets of Paris are neutral in the sense that they can be modified not only to allow, but also to encourage, different levels of interaction among the population. The dense proximity of a variety of people and places presents an empowering quality not available in Tysons Corner, where the strict rules of zoning and land use discourage spatial, functional, and, subsequently, human interaction. The only exception to this in Tysons Corner might be in the context of privately controlled public spaces, such as the shopping mall, where the interaction is closely monitored and control of the users is absolute.

One might argue that, in terms of appearance, Tysons Corner still represents a neutral field of play where the reduction of panurban space to individual interpretation allows for the construction of a personalized, non-public conception of civic space. The collective images that govern individual desires and subsequently the identity of Tysons Corner manipulate cultural preconceptions along the lines of specific social, economic, and gender models. These preconceptions project a mirage of comfort and facilitate profit. Into the breach left by the physical division of the city and the body, the architecture of Tysons Corner provides a literal and metaphorical armature to sustain a fictional form and image. The fluid veneer is tuned to achieve an environment that is continuously adapting to cyclically fulfil and create desire. Like any other product, Tysons Corner is dependent upon maintaining its value by remaining consistently in fashion – from the style of the perpetually redeveloped residences to the changing face of the mall and its occupants. Panurban regions, as Tom Vanderbilt notes, 'are direct projections of managerial capitalism, places of innovation and obsolescence. Like the outmoded computer chip of last year, they and their Information Age residents will be deemed vestigial as soon as they lose their competitive edge' (Vanderbilt 1995: 67).

The spatial, functional, and scalar relationships of architecture to its inhabitants are dissipated within Tysons Corner to such an extent that the use of image to create an implied identity supersedes the presence of an evolving identity, formed by the interactions between architecture and people. The easily mutable and replaceable architecture is designed to be appealing at one of two levels: first, as a bland copy of that which exists everywhere, promoting a sense of comfort because of familiarity; second, as a glamorous version of Tysons Corner where architectural decorations imply, through their use of certain material or stylistic reference, a lifestyle that might be anything from cosmopolitan to rustic, but in reality does not even exist.

As noted previously, the specific aesthetic of a building is not emphasized, but rather the functional propriety of its appearance. In this respect the office building and the home are each underpinned by the prerequisite that the façade must evoke qualities that are familiar, controlled and recognizable (Sudjic 1992: 269). This consistency, a kind of 'high generic', allows individual newcomers of the same stripe to recognize and accept the conditions they are passing through as 'the right kind of place'. The persistence of these commercial and residential types throughout the country legitimizes Tysons for the people who live and work there, by firmly planting it within the greater panurban landscape. Tysons is an example of the creation of a city from regularized elements, which are able to promote values or themes based upon their individual messages, independent of the structure of the whole city. In Tysons Corner as elsewhere, the banal is maintained to protect the symbolic and financial investment of homeowner and businessperson alike.

Existing simultaneously with the high generic is the tendency to aggrandize the everyday, a transformation of typical elements of daily life into something that implies an exclusive quality. The desire for unique elements that distinguish Tysons Corner from the ordinary attempts to create an attachment to Tysons despite the lack of reference to a specific history or context. As the increased mobility and divisiveness of the panurban fabric blur the territorial and spatial coordinates inherent to the traditional city, the desire for unique qualities that anchor the user to the environment is increased (Huyssen 1995: 7). In Tysons Corner, this anchoring depends upon the acceptance of a set of social values within which personal desires may be subjugated. Like the comfort of the generic, the glorification of the quotidian relies upon the consensus of the market. The sudden arrival of the Ritz-Carlton hotel, with its grand entrance off the 'street' of the Tysons Galleria, brings a whiff of luxury and exclusivity to a shopping mall. Fairfax Square is advertised as the 'Rodeo Drive of Northern Virginia,' with the requisite Hermès, Tiffany's and Gucci, yet it is little more than a strip mall with a substantial investment in a granite veneer exterior.

This type of glamorous architectural veneer is echoed in the print marketing for Tysons Corner Centre, where the imagery also takes on a distinctly gendered tone. The front cover of the store directory depicts a British Royal Guard; his back turned, anonymously occupying a background that is suggestive of some historical and dignified place. More prominently depicted in the foreground is a tall, beautiful woman wearing a stylized outfit that echoes the traditional uniform of the guard behind her, while, not surprisingly, revealing more of her body. It is a puzzling image, seemingly oblivious to the fact it is a cover for the mall store directory. One can extract multiple readings from the cover image, since it is both an attempt to invoke a feeling of international glamour, while reinforcing the notion that while men are occupied with serious business, women are more likely to be shopping. Neither of these are new observations about advertising, but it is interesting that there is no clear functional, or even aesthetic, relationship between the cover and the directory itself.

And as with the brochure, behind the highly ornate façades of Tysons Corner architecture lie wholly unremarkable interiors. Within the office and the home alike, open plan interiors shaped for efficiency and ease of renovation are the norm. In domestic buildings, this gap between exterior appearance and interior function is mediated by ornate decoration. Surfaces are covered with wallpapers, marbles and curtains. As with the exterior, this appliqué plays upon the marketable nuances of normalcy and nostalgia. Appeal to the potential consumer is generated through the exploitation of desire for a mythical past and present lifestyle. Both domestic and commercial structures demonstrate a use of this strategy, with houses dependent upon colonial exteriors and mall stores like Domain insinuating an idyllic lifestyle. A visit to the restaurant 'America' in Tysons Corner Centre offers a commercial case in point. The restaurant's theme is derived from a nostalgic and uncritical view of the American past: on the wall are notably non-ironic quotations and murals about life in America, describing a distinctly non-Tysons vision of small-town America, where neighbours visit each other on their porches and children play in the streets. By invoking a hazy cultural longing for a genuine sense of community, the restaurant's thematics attempt to compensate for what Tysons Corner lacks. Buried within the glib murals is a marketing appeal that implicitly affirms a belief that the past was a superior time, a simpler time, less complicated than the modern world.

The Mayfair Townhouse development, finished in late 1996, is a loose interpretation of typical nineteenth-century Georgetown townhouses. Each three-storey house typifies in price and space the next generation of residential living available in Tysons Corner. Targeted toward absentee professional owners – commuters – its most marketable characteristics would appear to be its location, construction, square footage and resale value. However, Mayfair typifies selling which is based less upon the product of the house – its construction, location, square footage, etc. – than on the implied lifestyle projected throughout the development, and most acutely within the sales model. The interior of the sales model takes the precedent of tasteful and stylish furnishing to a new level. Walking throughout the three-level townhouse, one is slowly made aware of the narrative constructed within the space. The image of a successful nuclear family

Figure 9.6
Interior of Mayfair
Housing development
sales model.
Photo by author

is the foundation; throughout all the rooms is evidence of the mythologized, late twentieth-century version of a 'normal' family (Figure 9.6). Moving through the rooms, one finds a card lying on an end table; on the outside, it reads, 'To a wonderful husband'. Immediately adjacent is a picture of a man in a tuxedo and a slightly younger, well-dressed woman. Other family evidence is laced through-out the model. A dark wood interior and prep school sweater over a desk chair distinguish a child's room on the second floor, suggesting a son at his first year of college. Indications of the lifestyle of the 'resident' are everywhere, from a gardening room (yet there is no yard, only a porch attached to the townhouse) to the wine cellar. Equally, the price tag and luxury additions – Viking stove and wine cellar – clearly suggest the socio-economic position of those who would live here. Through the use of detail, the model townhouse has carefully constructed an idealized rendition of the traditional nuclear family.

The nearly oppressive presence of this successful family sets a clear standard for those who would think of living here, and leaves little room for an alternative conception of home. This is a notion of home that critic Dolores Hayden has called the 'stage set for the effective gender division of labor' (Hayden 1984: 34). The single-family dwelling, as currently manifest in Tysons Corner and the majority of the United States, is the evolution of the early twentieth-century model of domestic living that was organized around a male worker who retreats, after a day of work in the factory, to a private domestic world, where his wife acts as home manager. However, the appeal of places like Mayfair cannot be ascribed simply to the notion that everyone who lives in Tysons Corner is part of a pater-nally organized nuclear family. In fact, the most recent statistics confirm that Tysons, as with the United States in general, has moved some distance away from the traditional vision of the nuclear family. Demographics report 65 per cent of all families are dual-income; a more ambiguous statistic reports that less than 50 per cent of all households are married.[9] The marketing of Mayfair is less focused upon the reality of the potential resident than it is upon the ideal of a lifestyle that such a resident might aspire to, or more likely, feel compelled to achieve. The fact that the marketing of Mayfair is dependent upon a view of a traditional family structure is no accident. The presentation of this family preys upon the modern insecurities that mark the emergence of alternative domestic arrangements. The potential lifestyle of Mayfair may offer an appealing antidote to the anxieties experienced by single-parent households and dual-income households. The selling of Mayfair depends upon the convincing construction of a lifestyle that would seem idyllic to the possible user. Alternately, the presentation may work to discourage non-traditional households from purchasing homes there, essentially excluding such domestic units as single-parent families or same-sex parent couples by subtly persuading them that a Mayfair home – or the Mayfair community – does not offer what they need.

Mayfair's perpetuation of this traditional notion of a family home is consonant with that of the homeowner's association of McLean Hamlet, where the potential arrival of an assisted living home is interpreted as both a commercial venture that threatens the zoning purity of a residential development and an alternative domestic living arrangement that threatens the social integrity of the single-family dwelling. Consequently, Mayfair Townhouses and McLean Hamlet, as representative developments in Tysons Corner, epitomize what Dolores Hayden has referred to as the 'dream house'. Hayden writes:

> The dream house replaced the ideal city as the spatial representation of American hopes for the good life. It not only triumphed over the model town, the dream house also prevailed over two other models of housing, one based on an ideal of efficient collective consumption of scarce resources, the other based on an ideal of the model neighborhood.
>
> (Hayden 1984: 38)

Hayden's contention that the dream house has replaced the ideal city in American hopes is clearly illustrated in Tysons Corner, where it is analogous to the triumph of the private experience over the public one. Mayfair and McLean Hamlet are indicative of a wasted opportunity in domestic architecture, where the social changes that have occurred throughout the last fifty years have had little effect upon the structure of domestic living. There are a few notable exceptions to this in the vicinity of Fairfax County. Eco-Village is a new co-housing project currently under construction in Loudon County, Virginia. Based on the social principles of co-housing and the environmental principles of sustainable development, Eco-Village would appear to be an attempt by a neighbourhood to deal with issues more relevant to contemporary living.[10] However, alternative residential developments have had very little success in Tysons Corner.

Throughout Tysons Corner, the possible expression of individual desire is suppressed in favour of culturally mandated societal norms. The ideology that makes the Mayfair development a successful product is foundational throughout Tysons Corner, embedded within the modus operandi of residential, commercial, and retail architecture. The dominance of these norms throughout both Tysons Corner and the greater panurban landscape is a reflection of a median range of market preferences, rather than an environment that might genuinely empower, or even allow, the marginal, idiosyncratic or individual. Without centre, adjacency or apparent history, Tysons Corner relies on image to define itself and the identity of its inhabitants, using the mechanism of precise delineation of space and programme. Ironically, the appliqué of Tysons Corner depends completely upon the suggestive power of traditional urban and suburban models to represent the social, economic, and cultural based qualities of ideologically dominant notions of personal and public identity, submerging latent characteristics under a constant mirage of possibility.

NOTES

1   *Panurbanism and the Question of Identity* is derived from work completed for the thesis project, *Panurbanism: Tysons Corner, A Case Study*, I completed with Charlie Cannon, Bogue Trondowski, and David Yocum in the spring of 1997 at the Harvard University Graduate School of Design. I am indebted to my co-authors for their work and observations.

2   Facts and figures on Tysons Corner are available from the Fairfax County website (www.co.fairfax.va.us/fairfax.htm) and US census reports (1990 figures). In addition, the Fairfax County Economic Development Authority maintains a website (www.fairfaxcountyeda.org) containing extensive information regarding Tysons Corner and Fairfax County.

3   Definition and etymology of *pan-* from the *New Shorter Oxford English Dictionary* (1993), London: Oxford University Press.

4   All zoning information taken directly from Code of the County of Fairfax, Virginia.

5   See the website: www.mcleanhamlet.org/Information/layout.htm

6   See www.mcleanhamlet.org (May 1998). As of November 2000, this letter had been removed from the website.

7   The buildings, however, must bear no external signage – no indication of this facility's commercial and/or institutional function(s).

8   Information regarding road layouts is taken from the *Public Facilities Manual*.

9   Demographic information taken from www.co.fairfax.va.us

10   www.ecovil.com – from the website. Co-housing is the term for a concept that was first introduced in Denmark. Co-housing neighbourhoods combine the autonomy of living in private homes with the advantages of living in community. People who live in co-housing communities live in their own homes, but may choose to share some of their meals in a common house, which also serves as a recreation and socialization centre. Co-housing neighbourhoods are designed, planned, and managed with a high degree of resident participation. Co-housing communities offer a return to small, close-knit, safe neighbourhoods.

Chapter 10: Re-Reading Disney's Celebration

Gendered Topography in a Heterotopian Pleasure Garden

Andrew Wood

Fanny Burney's first novel, *Evelina* (1968 [1778]), narrates a young woman's search for identity amidst a subtly dangerous cultural landscape. Burney's place-ment of her protagonist in the public locales of eighteenth-century Britain reveals strategies by which the design of public places enacts rhetorical mechanisms of power. Most intriguingly, the unschooled Evelina's visits to various pleasure gardens around London illustrate the sophisticated control of the artless impulse – the supposed innocence of women in a world of men – within a garden of hidden mechanisms and concealed delights, places of institutional power and spaces of potential resistance. For a growing merchant class, pleasure gardens provided a glimpse of aristocracy, while eschewing the formalism of landscape design. For Evelina, however, the social miscues and dangerous liaisons found within the pleasure gardens' dark walks metaphorically state the problematic placement of the feminine within the modern metropolis. Her surrogate father warns: 'the artlessness of your nature . . . unfit you for the thorny paths of the great and busy world' (122), while her female guardian later responds to a nobleman's improper attempts to determine the location of Evelina's home: 'Young ladies, my Lord . . . are *no where*' (275, emphasis in original). More than a mere setting within a typical eighteenth-century epistolary novel, the pleasure garden and its utopian successors illustrate the deceptive 'artlessness' of contemporary strategies through which the feminine is constructed and disci-plined.

In many ways, the Disney Development Corporation's planned community Celebration is a contemporary pleasure garden whose physical and rhetorical construction, like the aristocratic English locales of Burney's *Evelina*, demands a critical response. I propose that Michel Foucault's notion of *heterotopia* provides a useful starting point. Foucault (1986) coined the word *heterotopia* to describe how sites manage crisis and deviance through the inversion of opposing narra-tives (Heatherington 1997; Siebers 1994; Soja 1995). Celebration-as-heterotopia is, therefore, quite different from the modern utopia. Hardly a unified narrative of a better world that is *no place*, Celebration shapes the behaviours of its inhabitants by invoking multiple temporal and narrative spaces within a heterogeneous place. Certainly this paradoxical geography may challenge dominant topologies of discourse (Pile 1994; Price-Chalita 1994; Rose 1993). However, I argue that re-reading the opposing narrative spaces of this community from the perspective of their historical places reveals a particular kind of gendered topography. This topography emerges in the strategies of structure and design within Celebration's homes and layout, recalling historical efforts to shape the movements of women in American and European contexts. As with Celebration's urban predecessors, these strategies do not enact literal practices of control or surveillance. Rather, they are suspended in a subtle matrix of discourses. Like the pleasure garden, Celebration's ideal notion of community and amusement (and, to a lesser extent, commerce) manages neatly to elude critique because of its suspension of contradictory narratives. Yet, as with the pleasure garden, the fissures between these narratives reveal significant implications for the rhetorical construction of (white, bourgeois) women's relation to public life.

Close analysis of these implications is warranted, given that power obscured in generic contexts attains sharp relief when viewed through a feminist lens. The question that motivates my inquiry is simple: what insights may be found from a historical re-reading of Celebration as a gendered topography? Following a brief overview of the town, I will explore the contours and fissures of this topography through its paradoxical invocation of privacy, arcadia and nostalgia. What is uniquely feminist about this reading is the attention paid to both/and rather than either/or articulations of these dimensions. Within Celebration, privacy represents a contested terrain, both affirmed and denied through literal and figurative screens. Privacy does not discipline the feminine through some monolithic gate – but, rather, by blurred boundaries, like the greenzone surrounding the community. Similarly, arcadia offers an organic suburb that suspends itself within, not in contrast with, the utopian horizon. Celebration is a city of curves that enacts a feminized rhetoric of home without eschewing the linear narrative of technological utopianism. Finally, nostalgia emerges as partial and incomplete, rather than a wholesale memory subject to critique. Celebration's promise of multiple pasts offers a rhetorical playground whose props and tropes enact a *paradoxical patriarchy*, one realized more through its absence than its presence.

CELEBRATION: PROTOTYPE COMMUNITY OF YESTERDAY

Not an 'organically' developed community, Celebration reflects overlapping and incomplete histories of urban design. As a product of the Disney Development Corporation and its allied distribution network of media and properties, Celebration invokes Walt Disney's unfinished dream of an *actual* Experimental Prototype Community of Tomorrow. Before his death in 1966, Walt planned to build an ideal and singular community for which optimism and progress would provide rhetorical foundations:

> It will be a planned, controlled community; a showcase for American industry and research, schools, cultural and educational opportunities. In EPCOT there will be no slum areas because we won't let them develop. There will be no landowners [aside from Disney] and therefore no voting control. People will rent houses instead of buying them, and at modest rentals. There will be no retirees, because everyone will be employed according to their ability. One of our requirements is that the people who live in EPCOT must help keep it alive.
>
> (quoted in Mosley 1990: 287)

The strict manner of control in Disney's conception of EPCOT emerges from his plan to turn the community into a hybrid exposition/theme park/profit centre whose exhibits just happened to be residents. In other words, tourists and planners would observe the community in action. As a result, clothing, hairstyles, and cohabitation would be carefully monitored; residents would be under the same kinds of restrictions as Disney 'cast members' in this modern incarnation of the world's fair (Sorkin 1992). The EPCOT Center that exists in Florida today represents an admission that Disney's dream of a hermetically sealed city with draconian laws of personal conduct was ultimately impractical. More a distant cousin than direct offspring, Celebration is a culmination of the modern blurring of social experiment and theme park inspired by the 1851 Crystal Palace Exhibition and the various 'white cities' and 'cities of tomorrow' that would follow. An architectural hodgepodge of multiple styles, from Victorian through Art Deco to postmodernism, Celebration is strikingly similar to the world's fairs of the last two centuries in one respect: it invokes a rhetoric of potentially global narratives whose fragmentary natures forestall coherent critique.

Of course, with all of the discussion and debate over this experimental community, people continue to be surprised to learn that Celebration is indeed a real place: an ungated, planned community located in central Florida, south of US 192 along Interstate 4 in Osceola County. Not including the greenbelt that surrounds the community, Celebration accounts for nearly 4,890 acres of Disney property which, prior to construction, included pasture land and transmission line pathways (Sedway Cook Associates 1990). The planned development of the Celebration project includes 2,034 acres for residential space, 350 acres for office space, 350 acres for retail space, and 210 acres of industrial zoning. This, along with a school, medical centre, golf course, 5,000-seat performance centre, 810-room hotel, and 1,290 acres of open space (Annual Report 1997). The first residents moved into Celebration in the summer of 1996. Two firms, Cooper, Robertson & Partners and Robert A.M. Stern Architects, provided the master plan for the community while independent firms designed specific buildings including the preview centre, bank, town hall, cinema and post office.

Despite the cost and complexity of this experiment, Celebration appeals to

Figure 10.1
Fountains dance in front
of the Celebration
Theatre.
Photo by author

a desire for simplicity, for the elusive sense of 'place' in the lives of upper-middle-class Americans. As such, the town represents simply one example of an architectural and planning movement called New Urbanism (also, Neo-Traditionalism). New Urbanist planners and their advocates reject the suburban 'vacuum at the centre of American life' (Kunstler 1993:119). In their germinal *Wilson Quarterly* essay on the subject (reprinted in *Historic Preservation Forum*), Andres Duany and Elizabeth Plater-Zyberk (1995) decry the failure of American postwar urban planning as auto-centric and anti-community and propose an alternative:

Building real towns will require changing master plans, codes, and road-building standards, and, above all, attitudes. The mindless administration of rules enshrining the unwisdom of the past half century must cease; the reign of the traffic engineers must end. Americans need to be reacquainted with their small-town heritage and to be persuaded of the importance of protecting the human habitat every bit as rigorously as the natural habitat.

(Duany and Plater-Zyberk 1995: 45)

In contrast to Disney's antiseptic EPCOT, Celebration was idealized as a 'typical southern small town' that featured mixed-used zoning, pedestrian-friendly design, and an emphasis on community spirit. One finds an illustration of this sentiment in Celebration's *Downtown Celebration Architectural Walking Tour* (1997):

Celebration is designed to offer a return to a more sociable and civic-minded way of life. It is a walking town. The town plan places special emphasis on restoring streets and sidewalks to the public realm on the assumption that streets should belong to people, not cars . . . In Celebration Village, it will be possible to pick up a quart of milk or step out for a quick cup of coffee without getting into a car. The town centre is intended as a primary focus of the community.

(*Downtown Celebration* 1997: 2)

An architectural response to turn-of-the-century angst, Celebration had little problem attracting residents and visitors – with the key exception that almost all residents are white (Weeks 1999: C01). In this chapter, I seek to examine the process through which this locale shapes the behaviours of Celebration's temporary and permanent inhabitants. Specifically, how is white bourgeois femininity constructed within this heterotopian locale? Initially, I turn to the invocation of privacy in Celebration that affirms, even as it destabilizes, the feminized space of domesticity.

PRIVACY: AFFIRMATION/DESTABILIZATION OF THE FEMININE

As with Burney's pleasure garden, the rhetorical construction of privacy within Celebration produces a problematically gendered topography. Concentrating on the role of public and private in Celebration, therefore, introduces a critical element to this discussion (Benhabib 1992; Lange 1979; Mazey and Lee 1983; Rosaldo 1974; Rosenberg 1982). Thus, I address the discourses that shape female agency. To paraphrase Walter Ong, Celebration is a technology that reifies human relations through a paradoxical articulation of public and private space (Ong 1982, 1986). Ong concentrated on the way in which thought is restructured through writing. I propose that narratives written into the structures of Celebration do not redesign relationships. Instead, they enact privileged domestic spaces while refuting their validity within public life, as promotional documents for potential residents emphasize the complementary and harmonious nature of Celebration's spaces.

As heterotopia, the physical home of Celebration enacts not one, but two kinds of space, according to Disney planners: constructing community and protecting privacy. *The Celebration Pattern Book* (1995) emphasizes the manner in which homes serve this dual role:

> As in traditional neighborhoods, the houses of Celebration will mediate between the public and private worlds of its residents. The back yards will be the focus of the private, family-oriented world. The Front Façade with its porch, loggia or veranda, will provide a comfortable transition between the resident's private world, and the public, community-oriented world of Celebration. In addition, the Front Façade will help define the community space of the neighborhood street or square.
>
> (*Pattern Book*: A–2)

Rhetorically, *home* is marked by both its façade and its interiors. The walls – reminiscent of the manner in which the original Celebration preview centre was entered through a painting of a house that served to conceal an otherwise utilitarian corporate space – communicate the dual meaning of entrance and closure, open public space and closed private space.

The *Celebration Pattern Book* notes the roles of proportion and order in the maintenance of this relationship:

> Celebration Houses will create community space as well as enclose the private realm of the family . . . House façades, visible from streets and public spaces, will have the scale and character of traditional houses with porches, well-proportioned windows, and 'correct' traditional detailing. The back yard of the houses will be the focus of the private world of the family. The form and placement of each house will screen this area from public view.
>
> (*Pattern Book*: A–4)

Consider the power of the word 'enclose'. One finds a simultaneous sense of security and liberation. The domestic realm is protected by the façade through the astute invocation of scale and detail. Written into these elements is the orderliness and linear assurances of proportion and control. Within the public sphere that is enacted through the screen of architecture, one finds a world that is visible and thus subject to institutional regulation. Within the domestic sphere, the private realm is shielded by an unspoken definition of family. Such a definition has no voice because it is separated in an existential manner from public life.

In this manner, the 'screen' serves as both door and window, again reminiscent of the Florida way of living. The screen door has the potential to collapse the difference between public and private, but also the power to maintain that difference. Within Celebration, public and private spaces are said to exist harmoniously. However, as the *Pattern Book* emphasizes, this harmony is a device designed to ensure their continual division. To step within a Celebration home is to invoke a sense of 'other-ness', an alien space that is beyond the control of town authorities. Such a space is feminized when it serves the role of refuge, the site of private encounters that are not known or recognized in the public sphere.

At once, the supposed balance of alternatives reveals an underlying domination of masculine-dominated public space over feminized private domesticity.

The role of technology as a cornerstone to this heterotopian suspension of public and private becomes even more important from this analysis. Early articles on the power of fibre-optic cable to shape human relationships within Celebration tended to concentrate on the fact that these lines of communication are literally buried, separated from public consciousness. However, editors of the *Celebration Chronicle* (1997, Winter) cannot fail to note the impact of technology within the goal of community building:

> Over the past decade, the technology explosion often has caused the sense of community to be eliminated, keeping people at home networking in isolation with their laptops. Not so with the Celebration Community Network, designed to provide residents, alliances, business and students with resources to become involved in the community – drawing them outside of their homes into the community.
>
> ('Community gets connected': 8)

This relationship is not a reciprocal one. Unlike an Internet, communication in the Celebration *intranet* is strictly internal; one cannot easily access the Celebration neighbourhood network from outside. More importantly, the idea that technology draws people 'outside of their homes' rests upon an essential dislocation of home from the public sphere. This dis-placement, the sense that home is negative to the positive space of 'outside', returns us to the central thesis of this essay: Celebration's sense of community depends upon the enactment of isolation. From a feminist perspective, such isolation is historically the site of women's activity; as such, the rhetoric reaffirms the apparent lack of value of domestic space.

On a larger level, Celebration itself enacts a private space, distinguished from a nearby public highway known for its tacky tourist traps and multitudes of restaurants. In this way, Celebration's locale – and separation from the urban spaces that line its northern boundaries – is remarkably similar to the description of Walt Disney World provided in the *Comprehensive Plan of the Reedy Creek Improvement District* (Sedway Cook Associates 1990):

> Because of the District's large size and the character of a large part of its land, Walt Disney World has always been physically perceived as a free-standing community, buffered by forested open space from the surrounding agricultural and urban areas. The community's setting enhances the sense of arrival for visitors and screens the community from development that might interfere with its image.
>
> (Sedway Cook Associates 1990: 2–3)

A greenbelt composed of golf courses and wetlands screens Celebration from surrounding communities. One might find this method of division more desirable than a gate or other security measures. What is more significant, however, is the use of organic and natural space as a rhetorical boundary. The greenzone becomes a liminal space – both garden for play and machine for protection.

To summarize to this point, I propose that femininity within Celebration relies upon a division of public and private spaces that is strategically blurred. The home and community require both, but clearly assume that public space is far more important than private space. Two final examples will suffice to illustrate this section's claim. A *Chronicle* article called 'A place Walt would call home' (1995) notes Disney's dream to locate the raising of family within community instead of the home. Similarly, a *Chronicle* article called 'Lakeside park offers fun and relaxation' (1996) describes a garden near the downtown area as an 'oasis' – a site of renewal found outside of the home. Within Celebration, home-space is defined as private, beyond the realm of public life. This home re-constructs a gendered divide between public and private whose implications for women include the construction of lawless sites which, like the pleasure garden described by Burney, enact technologies and practices of risk and control.

This section has illustrated that the gendered topography of the public sphere as the site for agency is reaffirmed within Celebration. Along the streets, on the porches, at the door, one finds the sphere of activity and regulation. One might assume that such a sphere is democratic, embodying the liberal conception of the individual regardless of gender. However, as with the pleasure garden, public space depends upon the existence of private domesticity where social rules are not strictly enforced. In those spaces, in the knowledge that they exist, the raw reality of masculine power expresses itself. The feminine within the city, destabilized, must be re-articulated – and discursively bound – by the simultaneous construction of a frontier, and the ritualistic forgetting that such a frontier exists. Within this paradoxical notion, Celebration becomes a feminized arcadia bounded by a utopian horizon.

ARCADIA AND THE RE-ARTICULATION OF THE FEMININE

Utopian and arcadian rhetorics exist in heterotopian suspension. Each enacts absence to destabilize the dominant narrative, while *deploying* absence to deconstruct the reader. In his re-reading of More's *Utopia*, Marin fastens upon the playful and ironic absence of location – utopia depicting a happy place not present – along several dimensions, most notably the anticipation of a future without money (Marin 1973). In his reading of Poussin's *The Arcadian Shepherds*, Marin points out the semiotics of absence in a depiction of a tomb of Arcady, noting the death of ego through the negation of an observer (Marin 1980/1998). In both utopia and arcadia, Marin argues that situated discourse negates the ideal. Such a 'degenerative utopia' emerges most forcefully in Marin's re-reading of Disney's Tomorrowland. Allowing that Marin had since distanced himself from some of his original invective, Hill writes that 'Marin plays the role of Malice in Disneyland, treating Disneyland as a [counter] utopia in which fiction has given way to representation, immobilizing itself in ideology' (Hill 1982: 176). A critique of Celebration can build on lessons learned from the criticisms of Tomorrowland and EPCOT Center. Drawing from a Foucauldian emphasis on the *site* of representation, I will first situate the spaces of arcadia and utopia within the American contest of garden and machine. Following this explication, I propose that Celebration constructs a gendered topography that simultaneously celebrates the feminized garden while placing it within the bounds of the masculinized machine.

Utopias of the last two centuries frequently rest upon the power of the machine. Leo Marx describes the machine, epitomized by the locomotive that cuts a sharp path through the landscape, as the metaphor for industrialization in America and its utopian promise (Marx 1964). In a 1988 interview with Judith Yaross Lee, Marx wrote: 'the general faith . . . was that things were going to get better and better – not only materially but also morally, politically, and socially – and this predominant view assumed that advancing technology was a sufficient basis for that progress' (Marx, in Lee 1988: 35). In his autobiography, Henry Adams (writing in third person) describes the almost spiritual power of the machine-as-progress, illustrated by a dynamo he discovers at the 1900 Paris Exposition:

> To Adams the dynamo became a symbol of infinity. As he grew accustomed to the great gallery of machines, he began to feel the forty-foot dynamos as a moral force, much as the early Christians felt the Cross. The planet itself seemed less impressive, in its old-fashioned, deliberate, annual or daily revolution, than this huge wheel revolving within arm's reach at some vertiginous speeds, and barely murmuring – scarcely humming an audible warning to stand a hair's-breadth further for respond of power.
>
> (Adams 1918: 380)

From this perspective, power becomes meshed within the gears of the machine, and the man who runs it. In contrast, the garden remains as a pastoral counter-site. In his interview with Lee, Marx contrasts this notion of machine-utopianism with the pastoral, illustrated by the garden: 'there was a belief that we could resolve our deepest problems by building a simpler world combining the best of art and nature' (Marx, in Lee 1988: 36). Roger Aden writes that even the base-ball field, with its green pasture and cyclical promise of a return home, illustrates the pastoral ideal in public life (Aden 1999). The pleasure garden and its nine-teenth- and early twentieth-century descendants – most literally illustrated in Ebenezer Howard's Garden City Movement – illustrate the popular notion that the pastoral garden offered an essential response to the machine-city that is clearly feminized. In his book, *The Geography of Nowhere*, James Kunstler makes plain the gendered topography of the pastoral myth. Unlike the seventeenth-century conflict over the simultaneous sin and beauty of the New World, the uncultivated land in the nineteenth century contained the seeds of renewal in every sense.

> The rural landscape was . . . the abode of nature, but a new version of nature, neither a wild untamed force nor a cold scientific curiosity. It was a safe, green, warm, sheltering, life-giving realm, full of fruit, grains, flocks of sheep and fowl, its hills and valleys feminine in their voluptuousness and ability to nurture. It was a sweet homeland, at last. Most of all, it was an antidote to the atrocious new place called the industrial city.
>
> (Kunstler 1993: 42)

Figure 10.2
A crane and obelisk
form horizontal and
vertical axes.
Photo by author

From this theoretical foundation, a question emerges: in what way does Celebration balance arcadia and utopia to construct a gendered topography?

An initial response reveals the strategies in which the feminized pastoral is bounded by the utopian machine. Philip Morris describes this machine as a mechanistic grid asserting itself from the air:

> A high aerial photograph of Celebration, just emerging from its green and blue Florida setting, brings the wholeness home. Below the sweep of I–4 and then the new tollway, the streets and blocks emerge. But rather than the usual random pattern of most suburbs, a clear hierarchy can be seen. The neat, tight order of the town centre makes firm edge for the lake. Running perpendicular to the lake, the principal street wraps a square and then extends as a grand boulevard between residential districts to either side.
>
> (Morris 1997: 39–40)

One finds in this passage a fairly literal sense in which the lived place of Celebration retains a strict mechanism of control through the invocation of 'neat, tight order'. The *Celebration Pattern Book* further outlines the manner in which the garden is shaped through the structured ordering of physical place.

> The houses will be designed and built by many different builders and individuals. In order to *create* community space, the design of each house will be required to respond to the individual character of the street, park, or square which it faces. This calls for a co-ordinated approach to designing houses, in which front façades and all parts visible from public spaces are harmonious with each other and with Celebration's goal of building a community.
>
> (*Pattern Book*: A–1, emphasis added)

The mechanism through which gendered topography is subtly enacted through the regulation of artifice emerges most completely in the *Declaration of Covenants*, a document that must be accepted by residents prior to their owning property in Celebration. According to the section entitled 'Architecture and Landscaping', any enhancements undertaken by homeowners must meet standards set by a community review authority: 'Each Owner acknowledges that determinations as to such matters are purely subjective and opinions may vary as to the desirability and/or attractiveness of particular improvements' (*Declaration* 1997: 12). Subsumed within the sentiments of chance encounters and fluid spaces is a strict and firm set of regulations that are not easily read by outsiders. Celebration's impulse to resist the modern city remains suspended within a heterotopian balance of garden and machine. In this way, Celebration avoids falling into Marin's trap of degenerative representation by not appearing to adopt a dominant narrative-ideology, but seeming to enact multiple standpoints.

However, the apparent suspension of garden and machine becomes problematic when one examines the suburban ideal historically as an architectural response to urban unrest and the growing women's suffrage movements in Europe and America at the turn of the century. Placed in the arcadian country, the suburb might be considered the architectural opposite of the City Beautiful movement which sought inspiration from the Crystal Palaces of nineteenth-century world's fairs (Wilson 1989), and the social opposite of reform movements which proposed the introduction of communal living spaces, childcare facilities, and cooking areas to the metropolis.

To men in positions of institutional power, this alternative ordering of space represented an ideological and political challenge. Levy notes that 'male leadership denounced the communal nature of the reformists' domestic arrangements, implying that non-nuclear-family living was foreign and unnatural' (Levy 1992: 33). In the United States, the federal government promoted the suburb for working men and activist women who might otherwise become susceptible to the growing and convergent threat of unionism and feminism. Displaced from the city centre and isolated in the gothic machine (explored more fully below), women in the suburbs confronted the reality of the arcadian metaphor: distance from the city meant distance from power. Hayden recalls that 'the growth of manufacturing meant that while the rest of society appeared to be moving forward to socialized labor, the housewife, encased in woman's sphere, slowly became more isolated' (Hayden 1981: 13). In this sense, arcadia represents the architectural construction of private domesticity.

Responding to what Robert Putnam has called a decline in social capital (Putnam 1995, 2000), New Urbanism follows the same garden path imagined by its suburban predecessors – and manages to earn the same rebuke Lemann heaped upon the Putnam thesis as locked within a race- and class-based structure (Lemann 1996). However, Celebration repositions gender, race, and class within a sophisticated grid of discourse and design. Celebration resembles one of Joel Garreau's edge cities, the final draining of the metropolis into the suburb, where the rare appearance of persons of colour occurs in the community shops in which they are employed (Garreau 1991). An online essay from the La Jolla Institute emphasizes these class- and race-bound edge cities are post-historic; unlike cities which possess multiple layers of demographic history, edge cities hasten to create spaces of community in a vacuum where none have emerged organically (La Jolla Institute 1999). Themed restaurants and faux-architecture offer partial-pasts in environments too busy to allow real ones to form. At this point, however, the edge city comparison weakens. Unlike post-historic cities that sprout along the intersections of interstate and commercial centres, Celebration reaffirms a specific topography through its invocation of arcadian discourse.

Thus, in Celebration, one finds sites such as Arbor Circle within the *Pattern Book*: 'The elliptical configuration of the street around it and the adjacent Arbor Court create a number of uniquely shaped large lots that can accommodate gracious houses' (*Pattern Book*: B–4). Within the illustration, one finds a circle of homes that wind around a green oasis of trees, a continual return to the neighbourhood as in the suburban cul-de-sac. One also discovers the 'gracious' Southern mystique laden with race- and class-based narratives. However, when one pulls further away from this scene, one rediscovers that mechanistic utopia, that grid of *neat, tight order*. This frontier, like the edge of the American West – ceremonially 'closed' at the 1893 Chicago Columbian Exposition – simultaneously dis-places itself as the wilderness becomes tamed and re-establishes itself as the final horizon of the future, untouched by domesticity.

Throughout this section, I have proposed that the topography of Celebration is gendered by enacting, then apparently hiding the frontier. I have argued that the rhetorical architecture of the town is built on a fault line between the arcadian vision of eternal return and a utopian vision that promises infinite horizons. Throughout Celebration, arcadian spaces become edged, bounded, bordered, and constrained by utopian places. As I've argued, this process of gendered topography obscures overt power within the metaphoric garden whose historical foundations require excavation. This excavation reveals fragments of partial pasts whose paradoxical narratives replace the feminine within the community that is *home*.

NOSTALGIA AND THE RE-PLACEMENT OF THE FEMININE

In building the homes of Celebration, Disney reacts to a perceived need in American society through the rhetorical and architectural construction of nostalgic discourse that subtly affirms problematic assumptions of gender. Buttimer describes nostalgia – in this case, for small town life – as a refuge for victims of 'mobile and fragmented' urban milieus (Buttimer 1980: 166). A videotape playing until recently at the Celebration Preview Center promised '[a] new American town of Fourth of July parades and school bake sales . . . spaghetti dinners and fireflies in a jar' (Williams 1995: E7). Disney brochures define this community as 'a hopscotch-and-tag neighborhood to be viewed from front-porch swings' ('Disney's sinless city' 1996: 60). Ironically, this innocent time cannot be revisited; it is discovered in the process of playing in a technologically sophisticated future. A promotional sign epitomizes this blurring of past and future: 'Imagine how great it would have been ... to live fifty years ago with all the neat gear you have today' (Flower 1996: 33). Like the idyllic Hill Valley in the *Back to the Future* series, Celebration promises the best of both worlds.

Celebration homes represent a haven of instantaneous communication and high-bandwidth data transfer, each connected to a state-of-the-art fibre optic network designed to supply residents with an almost staggering amount of online interactivity. Residents seeking to visit an age of organic ritual and cyclical return do so upon a foundation of buried technology. The *Celebration Pattern Book* describes the complicated nature of this relationship:

> Conceived as a small Southern town, Celebration is being developed with an understanding of the community design methods used to create some of America's best neighborhoods and towns. Rather than reconstructing the past, Celebration will carry forward the best town-making traditions into the 21st century.
>
> (*Pattern Book*: A–1)

The small Southern town provides a nostalgic refuge to those who fear the unknown of the twenty-first century. Nostalgic discourse often affirms dominant modes and practices of power (Dickinson 1997; Ley 1989; Mills 1993). As Stephanie Coontz argues in her book *The Way We Never Were*, nostalgia is often used to justify gender-specific practices (Coontz 1992). Here, though, the home assumes a new role, as a façade for its wired foundation. Like the home 'page' of the World Wide Web, this home exists as both private domain and network-node (Wood and Adams 1998). As such, the historical implications of Celebration become hidden.

A paradoxical balance of technological progress and nostalgic playfulness challenges any critique of the gender roles invoked by Celebration's assumptions. Kept within the Preview Center, the *Pattern Book* provides a textual orientation of the community philosophy, description of the four major lot types (Estate, Village, Cottage, and Townhouse – Garden Lots have since been introduced). It also describes six home architectural patterns (Classical, Victorian, Colonial Revival, Coastal, Mediterranean, and French). Of all the housing styles, the Victorian is most revealing:

> Celebration's Victorian Style builds on the traditions embodied in a series of Pattern Books used by builders in the second half of the nineteenth century. These grew out of the chapters of a number of architects favouring naturalism in architecture and landscape design ... In most Southern towns, these houses provide a contrast to the dominant classical style houses. They often have contrasting combinations of rich or pastel colours and exotic ornament.
>
> (*Pattern Book*: C-7)

Figure 10.3
A Celebration streetscape
lined by freshly painted
houses.
Photo by author

The role of exotic ornament within the Victorian home illustrates a larger theme of gendered topography. That which is 'other', alien, beyond the safe cosmos of urban life becomes domesticated through its playful, yet strategic, invocation within the home or upon the house.

The Victorian reflects an age that deified the 'expert' and celebrated the potential for technology to execute more efficiently the process of social definition. The structures of these homes, enclosed spaces which isolated upper-middle-class white women who might otherwise seek entry to the public sphere, inspired household product companies to employ mass-media campaigns to sell heightened standards of cleanliness and the technology necessary to achieve them despite the inefficiency of these housing designs (McGaw 1987). As with the 'real' Victorian homes of the nineteenth century, the gable roofs, stencil-cut wood ornaments, and strategic use of asymmetrical design of many Celebration houses attempt to play with otherwise simple and functional design conventions without altering their historic foundations.

Celebration's cornerstone of 'health' provides another illustration of the town's paradoxically nostalgic rhetoric of 'home'. A brochure entitled *Blueprint for Health* invites readers to 'imagine an old-fashioned hometown that cultivates the mental, physical and spiritual wellness of its residents. And imagine a health-care system that combines personalized attention with powerful technology (Blueprint 1997)'. The heterotopian rhetoric of nostalgia and progress appears to subvert the popular conception of healthcare as a bureaucratic domain, making it more homelike – even as Celebration Health makes the home more *healthy*. Celebration Health depicts both institutional strength and personal touch by describing its resources: a 60,000 square-foot health activities centre with over a hundred healthcare professionals, 'and a doctor who knows all the words to Itsy-Bitsy Spider' (*Blueprint* 1997). A *Celebration Chronicle* article entitled 'The Doctor is in' introduces the reader to one such doctor, Dr Frank J. Stone, and his wife who delights at being home, keeping 'her hands full taking care of their children, ages 14 months, 6 and 8' ('Doctor' 1996: 6), a nostalgic domesticity that apparently naturalizes her gender identity.

The simultaneous invocation of nostalgic and progressive imagery constructs a gendered topography: heterotopian yet subtly masculinist. The construction of a technologically sophisticated community affirms the rhetoric of The New, epitomized in the various postmodern forms throughout the downtown (most notably, the post office and the town hall). Outmoded social orders, progressive ideals, and the mastery of cultural biases ensure the masculine promise of the open frontier (Slotkin 1992). Yet, the frontier is simultaneously settled as the nostalgic home, 'a special place for families' situated in a 'time of innocence' (Lawson 1995: C1). As with the pleasure garden, Celebration displaces its technique of control within ersatz nostalgic spaces. The production of the beautiful city (if not the City Beautiful) employs the architecture of ornament and bric-a-brac, 'spaghetti dinners and fireflies in a jar', to reproduce an unspoken masculine order affirmed through architecturally rendered temporalities through the paradoxical intersection of narratives of progress and nostalgia.

CONCLUSION

Sweeping changes in US national construction – from agrarian to industrial to post-industrial economy, with all of the attendant upheavals in crime, unemployment, and community dissolution – result in a similar cry to that heeded by residents of Celebration: go home to a simpler time. Thus, as Craig Wilson notes, Celebration is 'billed as a 19th-century town for the late 20th century, harking back to a time when lemonade stands, not crime, were on every corner' (Wilson 1995: A1). Of course, no such time existed without some contradiction. In a relative sense, each age bemoans the clash between its reality and ideal state. Failing at utopian pursuits, we settle for pleasure gardens of amusement, commerce, and controlled risk. In these gardens, many seek to reconnect with apparently deeper cycles of the human psyche. From a modern standpoint, these solutions may be 'fixed' as both timeless and impervious to physical alteration (Blair, Jeppeson, and Pucci 1991; Lefebvre 1991; Toulmin 1990). Yet even these representations are sexually, racially and economically bound and, as such, limited in their efficacy.

Thus, Celebration merits attention for more reasons than the fact that, as Andrew Ross has noted, there are more published articles about Celebration than there are residents (Ross 1999). Ethnographic studies, such as the Ross text and Douglas Frantz and Catherine Collins' *Celebration U.S.A.*, reveal tensions in a corporate empire's attempt to fashion public life in such a direct way (Frantz and Collins 1999). Contributing to this dialogue, I have sought to employ a critical feminist perspective to analyze the construction of gendered topography on this site. The dimensions I chose – privacy, arcadia, and nostalgia – were tactical and temporary (Ono and Sloop 1995). Each served momentary purposes; they are not fixed any more than the undulating, green borderland surrounding this planned community. The operations of institutional power in Disney's Celebration succeed because of their fluidity and paradox. No longer enclosed in the sealed dome of an imagined city of tomorrow, Celebration domesticates itself in the fresh air and open spaces of a private and arcadian nostalgia for a peculiar past.

Chapter 11: Bangkok Simultopia

Brian P. McGrath

The neologism 'simultopia' was coined to describe the unique social and spatial organization of contemporary Bangkok. It is an ambiguous term. While '-topia' means place, 'simul-' implies both simultaneity – occurring at the same time – and simulacrum – a copy with no original. Both associations apply to Bangkok. While syncretism provided a mechanism for pre-modern Siam to overlap animist, Hindu and Buddhist influences from neighbouring kingdoms and cultures, in modern Thailand the social practice of 'face' has facilitated the absorption of successive penetrations of both Western and Eastern capitalisms. Together syncretism and 'face' produce Bangkok Simultopia: a hyper-modern milieu of surfaces and signs without an authentic centre or origin over-occurring within the same space of ancient beliefs, practices and rituals.

FIELD NOTES: THE SYNCRETIC ECOLOGY OF 'FACE'

An amplified wail drifts with the morning fog on Khlong San Sab. A taxi-boat engine competes with the call for prayers echoing off the surface of the canal, its wake breaking along the crowded settlement hugging the mosque. Across the *khlong*, mango trees, full of tropical birds, shade wooden bungalows at the end of Soi Kasemsan. An unseasonable rain has cooled the air and hatched millions of flying insects to the delight of the birds and frogs croaking in the gardens below. A slight breeze releases a sweet aroma from saiyoot blossoms before being engulfed by the foul stench brought up from the brown waters below. A moving string of lights crosses the canal as the skytrain silently glides along its concrete viaduct high above Sapan Chang – the old Elephant Bridge – at Sra Pathum Palace. Red lights blink atop dark skyscrapers beyond.

Crossing at Sra Pathum, a monk enters the narrow *soi* under the viaduct, leaving behind the noise of Pathumwan Intersection. Barefoot, he follows the L-shaped lane, a shortcut and refuge from the busy crossing of two multi-lane boulevards. He gathers his saffron robe and lowers his bowl. Two prostrate women offer fish and balls of sticky rice, carefully avoiding body contact with the monk. They next make offerings to a spirit house fronting a cavernous ware-house: rice and fruit placed in a *khratong* boat fashioned from a banana leaf, and an open Coke bottle with a plastic straw. The monk follows a long wall before passing two substantial houses with gardens. The homes seem lifted from an American suburb except for a traditional, four posted, wooden *sala* fronting one. One house owner and her maid place a floral garland on a bust under the *sala*'s tiered roof and come to their gate with offerings for the monk. The two houses frame a high-rise apartment condominium stacked atop a multi-level parking deck. A security guard snaps his military-shine shoes together and salutes stiffly as a Mercedes Benz exits. To the right, in an open factory shed, several men meticulously oil printing machines. In front of the condominium, uniformed cleaning women place more rice in the monk's bowl before he turns left at the elbow of the lane.

Along the next stretch of the lane, four-storey shophouses form a synco-pated rhythm of concrete interrupted by dead-end alleys. The misaligned pattern is not by design, but the result of small-scale property speculation some thirty years ago. House owners placed a small alley, lined with row houses, up the centre of their property with room left for shops along the main *soi*. Some shops are open to the street: two flop houses for young working men who watch TV, eat, drink and sleep together crowded on the floor; others are more private, like the university women's dormitory or the guest houses serving Japanese students on holiday. Businesses invariably contain Chinese ancestor shrines on a back wall, aglow with sombre red lights. In one such shophouse, three-foot blocks of ice filling the ground floor emit a cool fog. The proprietor pays her respects to her ancestors before returning to her accounts. Within this micro-zone blending arctic and tropical climates, a dozen men work. Amulet necklaces protect their bodies; elaborate tattoos on their chests, backs and arms empower their labour. The blocks are axed in half and placed into a metal chute. Ground ice empties into gurney sacks, which are then loaded onto the front carriages of *samlors* heaped beyond the eye level of the drivers. Finally, the deliverymen bow-leggedly pedal preposterous loads of dripping ice-sacks down the *soi*.

The monk continues beyond the shophouses where open cooking on the street attacks the nasal passages and fried chili peppers sting the eyes. Bangkok street vending is an elaborate micro-organizational achievement. An intricate bustle of activity blossoms from the paraphernalia of streetside restaurants in a minimum amount of space – here, some two hundred feet long yet barely three feet wide. Washing stations contain aluminium basins, followed by wooden food preparation slabs, clay stoves for charcoal fires, carts for staging prepared food, and finally rows of folding tables under colourful beach umbrellas. The pattern is repeated three times, with minor variations, each a separate business operated by an intergenerational family of rural migrants. The monk always rests amidst this flurry of activity under a huge banyon – a spirit tree – draped with long gar-lands and containing small figurines of angels, spirits and guardians. Mobile vendors push two-wheeled carts with local market fruits. *Palad khik*, small wooden penises, productivity charms, dangle from their baskets. Two houses across have been converted to restaurants serving the tourists who flock to the inexpensive hotels and guesthouses on the lane. One hotel has a more local clientele. Its ground floor is filled with curtained parking spaces assuring the privacy for the car owners who rent rooms by the hour.

The lane ends around the corner from where it began, at congested Pathumwan Intersection. More vendors crowd the sidewalk here, selling drinks, fruit, and lottery tickets. A family sits on the sidewalk braiding meticulous jasmine and rose blossoms into garlands to sell. Macho motorcycle taxi drivers, wearing numbered neon-coloured vinyl vests, ask threateningly: 'bai nai?' – 'Where are you going?' as they play checkers or lounge on their motorcycles. All the sense organs, opened and soothed by the array of sights, smells and sounds of the *soi* are suddenly attacked by an onslaught of traffic. Eyes, ears and nose shut down defensively; the face turns from an open plate of receptive sense organs to a defensive mask. The only stationary figures in the intersection are the trim, brown-uniformed traffic police wearing helmets covering their heads and ears, white gauze cloth covering their mouths and noses, sunglasses covering their eyes. The skytrain overhead is supported by massive rows of single concrete columns under cantilevered prefabricated beams twisting and bending in three directions; pedestrian walkways interconnect its stations with four enormous shopping, hotel and office complexes. Car and taxi drivers are protected in their journeys as well. Like the boats traversing Bangkok's canals, their prows – in this case rearview mirrors – are draped with amulets and garlands, and their ceilings are inscribed with sacred Pali verse. Both the monk and the ice deliverymen cross, undaunted, silently, gingerly tracing human-powered paths at odds with the rushed mechanized traffic, unforgiving to slower trajectories. Whether protected by Buddha, karma or spirits, they somehow make it across every day.

A bird's eye view of the monk's circuit reveals a network of neighbourhood spirits and guardians. Alleys branching off the lane each contain a spirit house at their terminus, while several other shrines are located on corners, in driveways, vestibules or roofs. A vaulted shrine housing *Phra phom si naa* – a small yet commanding golden figure of Brahma with four faces and eight arms – sits at Pathumwan Intersection gesturing elegantly to the traffic and pedestrians that flow around him. He looks calmly in the four cardinal directions, seated on his right leg with the left dangling. Seven hands hold sacred objects: staff, wheel, vase, mirror, conch shell, scriptures and rosary; the eighth hand lightly grazes his chest (Majupuria 1993: 91). These shrines are unique to Thailand, and offer indigenous representations of the city/body in contrast to Henri Lefebvre's Western archetype:

> St Peter's in Rome is the Church itself: the Church 'entire and whole' – body and
> countenance – 'fastening upon her prey' – the prestigious dome represents the head of
> the Church, while the colonnades are this giant body's arms, clasping the piazza and the

assembled faithful to its breast. The head thinks; the arms hold and contain. It seems that one might justifiably speak here, without overgeneralizing, of a culture of the façade and of the face. As a principle along with its complements (masks) and supplements (dress), may certainly be said to determine ways of life.

(Lefebvre 1991: 273)

In contrast to this unitary body, Brahma's four faces and eight arms look and gesture towards a multiplicity of simultaneous bodies and worlds coexisting in Bangkok: a syncretic ecology, the superposition of animism, Hinduism, and Buddhism, and an urban system of tolerance, coexistence and ephemerality.

This crowded urban lane can be conceived as a domestic realm, although within a Thai tradition of extended households as multifunctional and productive compounds, and the Sino-Thai tradition of the shophouse as an intergenerational home. Female house and business owners preside over the many labourers on Soi Kasemsan. Younger unmarried women – mostly students – are more sheltered, while young male labourers live in an open relationship to the street. Every social relationship is modelled on the family structure of older sibling hierarchy; every social situation has a 'higher' and 'lower' partner. Hierarchy and deference are polite behaviours – transitory and situational – not markers of essential inferiority. Respect for status is more important than gender or ethnic difference. Age, wealth, honoured professions – such as teachers or doctors – all deserve respect and deliver merit. 'Differences in status of rank, based on merit, are more important than gender and consequently many women rank higher than many men. For Thais gender is a secondary concern and status and power receive primary consideration' (Tannenbaum 1999: 244).

However, it is the penniless, shoeless monk who is at the top of the status pyramid and outside domestic structures. Most men enter a monastery for at least a short period of time, and detachment from materiality and sexuality presents a composed and restrained masculine image for all Thai males (Tannenbaum 1999: 245). According to Van Esterik, Buddhism dictates a dualism linking women with fertility, nurturance and attachment and men with supra-mundane power and detachment (Van Esterik 1999: 5). '[B]ecause girls cannot be ordained, daughters cannot repay the debt they owe their parents for raising them and so are under a continuing obligation to support the family. This is in contrast to sons, who can become ordained as monks and ritually transfer the karmic merit they accrue from this act to their parents, so absolving them of filial moral indebtedness' (Tannenbaum 1999: 247).

On this small *soi*, status, ethnicity, gender and body politics intersect within an intricate Thai social organization of 'face' based on a hierarchy of polite deference. Writing on China, Andrew Kipnis (1995: 120) describes 'face' as 'an adaptable discourse of social surfaces' both to dispel the Orientalist stereotype of 'face' as a marker of inscrutability and dishonesty and to analyze how 'face' remains an important modern social mechanism. The flexibility of 'face' in modern society appears in discussions on the fluidity of gender and the tolerance of diverse sexualities in Thailand (Jackson 1995; Morris 1994). According to Jackson, the West's history of criminalizing homosexuality and stigmatizing non-conforming gender expressions has never been present in Thailand. He attributes the culture of tolerance to the long tradition of syncretism. For Morris, 'the concepts of *Kaeng cai* (deference expressed, agreeability displayed) and *naa* (face, front surface, honour or propriety) enables a great mobility and fluidity of practice, preserving the rights of individuals to pursue whatever pleasures, desires or fascinations they choose' (Morris 1994: 37). 'Face' is a convention of harmony, politeness, and agreeability minimizing conflict in an unpredictable world. For Mont Redmond (1998) Thai 'face' offers the freedom from being criticized in contrast to the West's notion of the freedom to criticize.

Maintaining 'face', however, is a richly embodied practice. The body itself is divided into symbolically higher – the head – and lower – the feet – parts that must be continually re-positioned in differing hierarchical relations to other bodies. Van Esterik writes,

> Thai exhibit extraordinary bodily awareness, allowing men and women to control the movement of their bodies with consummate grace. Foreigners are painfully obvious on Bangkok streets as they trip off curbs, lurch into other pedestrians and bump into immovable objects. This lack of control of their bodies and lack of awareness of how they move through space illustrates westerners' different orientation to their bodies. Thai appear to be much more 'in' their bodies than do westerners, further suggesting that the core of the Thai self is strongly embodied.
>
> (Van Esterik 1999: 283)

While Van Esterik's observations are confirmed on Soi Kasemsan, she is wrong to identify a 'core' 'Thai self'. Thai self-*presentation* is strongly embodied as result of highly codified, culturally constructed, embodied practices.[1] 'Face' can only be maintained by bodies trained to be graceful. The Therevada Buddhist meditation practice of Vipassana teaches a comprehensive form of body awareness. Contrary to Western perceptions of meditation as a withdrawal from the body and world, Vipassana quiets the mind so that the sense organs open up to direct experience mediated as little as possible by the activity of consciousness. The technique also teaches walking meditation where each step and gesture is felt completely. An advanced meditator perceives the body as a flowing atomic structure, arriving at an ultimate awareness of a 'body without organs' connected to a universe of movement and change. Thai 'face' is an embodied social practice of constant readjustment of self-presentation to changing circumstances and milieus. But equally compelling is Van Esterik's accurate portrayal of the collapse of Western corporal co-ordination. Where lies the fundamental difference?

UTOPIAN FACIALITY AND SIMULTOPIAN FACE

Gilles Deleuze and Felix Guattari's 'abstract machine of faciality', outlined in *One Thousand Plateaus* – their schizo-analysis of Western capitalism – contrasts sharply with Thai 'face'. 'Faciality' is described as a regime of signs relying on the production of two semiotic systems – public representation, which they refer to as 'the white wall of the signifying capacity', and private self-consciousness, referred to as 'the black hole of subjectivity' – and their wholesale collapse into one another (Deleuze and Guattari 1987: 170). In the overdetermination of the two systems, public display and the meanings of 'self' cannot be separated in the West without putting into crisis ideologies of 'truth', 'authenticity' and 'essence':

> This machine is called the faciality machine because it is the social production of face, because it performs the facialization of the entire body and all its surroundings and objects, and the landscapification of all worlds and milieus. The deterritorialization of the body implies a reterritorialization of the face; the decoding of the body implies an overcoding by the face; the collapse of corporeal coordinates or milieus implies the constitution of a landscape.
>
> (Deleuze and Guattari 1987: 181)

Faciality is a semiotic of disembodiment in which expressivity can only be symbolically performed with the face. The 'self' is disconnected from its situatedness within a surrounding environment, which itself becomes 'facialized' into scenic landscape. Nothing could be further from Western faciality[2] than Thai cultural values of 'face' where public display is held apart from private behaviour and Buddhism teaches the illusory nature of the self. Thai 'face' is an embodied social practice that is not based on a notion of expressing an interior, individualized self; Western 'faciality' detaches faces from bodies in order to construct a symbolic, essentialized self-identity. This section explores the effect of this axiomatic cultural and philosophical difference on the social organization of gender and bodies in modern urban space.

As an architect and urban designer, I write with two objectives: to provide alternative interpretations of Bangkok urbanism, and to analyze strategies towards dismantling the semiotic system produced by the abstract, globalizing machine of Western capitalism.[3] Urban life has become imagined as a scenographic backdrop for personal performance, redundantly acted within and viewed by an asocial self – *The Truman Show* with Truman as the lone audience (and cast) member. Urban design emerged as an attempt to re-embody the city following the abstractions of modern city planning,[4] yet the body was reconstituted into a symbolic construct, a façade, rather than engaged within embodied social practices. My thesis is threefold: that the discipline of urban design was constituted when late capitalism could no longer reproduce embodied ways of urban life; that contemporary urban design practice, as a primary technology of Deleuze and Guattari's abstract machine, uncritically assists in the collapse of all social meaning onto the signifying capacity of individual subjectivity; and that a critical urban design practice must be engaged in order to assist in the dismantling of this machine through newly invented and rediscovered embodied urban ways of life.

Urban design, typically practised as a division within large-scale corporate architecture firms, emerged as a defined profession during the Reagan/Thatcher era and the new political economy of globalization in the 1980s. Urban design as a discipline controls large developments by codifying and formulating uniform design guidelines for exterior building wrappers. In reaction to this *form* of practice, architectural theory has avoided the term 'urban design' altogether, instead appropriating the term 'urbanism' from social theory and applying it to the architecture of the city. In avoiding the very words 'urban design', rather than critically examining the practice itself, architects repress the active character of their own roles in the physical shaping of urban space, preferring the more passive sounding 'urbanism'.[5] This repression is shared by 'post-urbanists' in defining their role as adrift among the forces of late global capital and 'new urbanists' in their disingenuous relinquishing of design control to the popular forces of 'democracy' through carefully choreographed community design charrettes. This section seeks to redirect architecture theory away from this semantic avoidance by 'siting' urban design within the discursive fields of post-structuralism and post-colonial theory and by critically engaging urban life as a force in dismantling the homogenizing forces of faciality and landscapicity.

Writing critical of the modern city by European architects in the 1960s and 1970s prefigured the recent standardization of the professional activity of urban design. The reconstruction of the postwar European city according to utopian pre-war modernist city planning principles drew severe reproach from architects writing in Italy (Rossi 1982), France (Grumbach 1978), Germany (Ungers 1982) and Luxembourg (L. Krier 1980; R. Krier 1979). This critique resonated in America, where the destructive forces of urban renewal and suburban sprawl on American cities were beginning to be acknowledged. Jane Jacobs's writing (1961) prepared the way for the questioning of American urban planning practice, but it was American schools of architecture in the late 1970s that reformulated old rules and codes for rebuilding the American City according to the lessons rediscovered from fifteenth- to nineteenth-century Europe:

> facades were harmonized to create perspectives; entrances and exits, doors and windows were subordinated to facades – and hence also to perspectives; streets and squares were arranged in concord with the public buildings and palaces of political leaders and institutions (with municipal authorities still predominating). At all levels, from the family dwellings to monumental edifices, from 'private' areas to the territory as a whole, the elements of this space were disposed and composed in a manner at once familiar and surprising which even in the late twentieth century has not lost its charm. It is clear, therefore, that a spatial code is not simply a means of reading or interpreting space: rather it is a means of living in that space, of understanding it, and of producing it.
>
> (Lefebvre 1991 [1974, 1984]: 47)

The legible codes of façade and perspective were held up as ideals, and schools of architecture established graduate urban design programmes, such as at Cornell under the direction of Colin Rowe and Koeter (1978), to formulate the argument. The graduates of these programmes became instrumental in design-ing the organizational machines for the management of the new global economy. They produced huge high-tech building complexes wrapped with post-modern urban codes of neo-traditional brick façades, gallerias, colonnades, and public promenades. While New York's Battery Park City and London's Canary Wharf remain the archetypes of this new formulation, the building types and design methodologies evolved and spread globally. The more poetic and nuanced aspects of Rossi and Rowe's arguments were forgotten by the 1990s as the Clinton administration embraced the Kriers' more mechanistic urban formu-lae reborn in America as 'New Urbanism'; the abstract codes of faciality and landscapicity became public policy exported to the new economy city centres and suburbs.

The relationship between, on the one hand, the utopian imagination's reliance on collective meaning arrived at through an ideal of consensus, and, on the other, faciality's collapse of signification and subjectivity, can be gleaned from Dolores Hayden's (1976) and Frances Fitzgerald's (1986) studies of the American utopian tradition. While Hayden's portrayal of early American religious utopias paints a sympathetic portrait of social communitarians constructing refined autonomous urban complexes, Fitzgerald's more contemporary analysis points to the exclusionary homogenization of ideal communities. In contrast to Bangkok's syncretic ecology, American utopias transformed from religious settle-ments (monocredism) to exclusionary suburbs (monoclassism) that later became mono-generational (Sun City) and even mono-sexual (San Francisco's Castro in the 1970s). It followed that baby boomers felt they had earned their own new urbanist utopia: 'the good life' produced by the symbolic display of 'family' and 'community' harmony through the repression of difference.

In recent history Bangkok has moved in the opposite direction, embracing greater and greater heterogeneity, as the embodied practices of 'face' and syn-cretism have proved adaptable to modern circumstances. The Thai economic bubble – from the mid-1980s to the mid-1990s (Pasuk and Baker 2000) – pro-duced a huge array of American, Japanese and Hong Kong-style residential and commercial complexes across a vast landscape. But by reapplying the traditions of syncretism and 'face' in modern urban society, Bangkok has productively (mis)appropriated the artefacts of contemporary urban design practice into what I conceptualize as a *simultopia*: hybrid splicing and intertwining of suburban and urban, local and global, primitive and modern, signifying and embodied, faces and bodies.

As an embodied practice, simultopia eludes traditional forms of representa-tion. While Marc Askew argues that 'Historically Thais have not really been really interested in comprehensively documenting their principle city, it is interesting that this is a Western imposition' (Askew 1994: 38), my research shows that this has not been true. From temple murals, to the ancient Nagaram diagram from the ancient treatise on the art of war, *Phichi Songkhram,* to the formation of the Royal Survey Department in 1885, to the most advanced technologies in remote sensing (National Research Council 1991), Bangkok has compiled multiple representations of itself as Buddhist cosmology, war machine, garden city metropolis and fertile ecosystem. Askew's observation does point to the fact that, in everyday life, Bangkokians prefer to think of their city as a loosely connected collection of meaningful localities rather than as overall, comprehensible totality. I would restate Askew's argument: multiple urban mapping techniques have been long available in Bangkok, but these technologies are strategically deployed to defray the imposition of a singular Western mapping *mentalité*. There is a general indigenous knowledge that the single map is not the territory and the simultopian city cannot be systematically planned or designed in a Western rational manner.

Thongchai Winichakul (1994) argues that indigenous maps and mental images of the Kingdom of Siam – as an unbounded network of autonomous kingdoms – was displaced by a conception of the bounded Nation of Thailand as a 'geo-body' created by modern mapping techniques. I would instead argue the two systems were overlaid with local animist conceptions of urban space as a spirit-filled landscape. Bangkokians' mental image of their city is *simultopian* and 'experts' have not provided the mapping technology that can convey this.[6] Today, Bangkokians prefer seeing themselves as adaptable parts of a dynamic topology: both local and global, primitive and modern, facialized and embodied. The city founded by the Chakri Dynasty at the end of the eighteenth century could not be represented because the city itself was a simulacra of Brahmin and Buddhist cosmological order and an incarnation of the mythical capital, Ayudya, from the Indic epic Ramayana (Ramakien in Thai). The city is also a symbolic reconstruction of the ancient capitals of Siam: Sukhothai and Ayutthaya, as well as an inheritor to Angkor. Media representations of the city abound today; Bangkok is continuously re-presented in the news, movies, soap operas and advertisements as ancient royal capital and modern global city.

SIMULTOPIA: A NEW PARADIGM FOR URBAN DESIGN

On an oppressively hot day or during a sudden monsoon rain, the clever pedestrian can meet her date across Pathumwan Intersection without stepping outdoors or encountering traffic. Aer's journey takes in an entire history of Thai commercial real estate and adapted urban design practices. From the eighth-floor health club of the Patumwan Princess Hotel, she takes the elevator to the second floor of Mah Boon Krong Center. The Japanese-style mall – a seven-storey flea market specializing in knock-offs of foreign fashion – is packed on the weekend with Bangkok's youth. School uniforms have been exchanged for the latest Hong Kong and Tokyo styles. Overlooking one of the malls mirrored atria, four young men have discarded their pressed black shorts and white dress shirts and are sporting 'Miss Kitty' fluorescent hot pants, halter tops and platform shoes, updating the traditional Thai 'third sex' (Morris 1994). They debate whether to go bowling or take in a movie on the seventh floor. After walking the length of the mall, Aer leaves by the second floor skytrain exit at Tokyu Department store, boarding the BTS for one short stop before disembarking at Siam Central Station. Below is Siam Square, a grid of shophouses developed as a shopping area in the 1970s and derived from small American downtown prototypes. Still popular, the shops contain restaurants, local designers, and second-floor English-language schools for TOEFL preparation, all served by diagonal on-street parking. The skytrain mezzanine connects directly across into Siam Center. The atmosphere here is more upscale, dominated by Western and Hong Kong designer boutiques. Aer rides the atrium escalators to the fourth floor. A group of Thai boys with their heads shaved send mixed signals. Although they may be mistaken as recent novices from nearby Wat Patumwanaram, they are really Michael Jordan fans checking out Nike. At the other end of the mall a glass bridge crosses to newly opened Siam Discovery Center. This caters to a more mature luxury goods client, with floors devoted to leisure, lifestyle, women's fashion and the gadget-filled 'men's tech'. Western market techniques of targeting audiences by gender norm runs into some contradictions in Bangkok. Aer's clipped haircut and men's clothing identify her as a *tom*, a masculine-identified woman. She prefers to ride down the glass elevators that face the open plaza between Siam and Discovery Centers. The silent descent cuts a moving vertical section through the city: from the skytrain above to the street level coffee shop where her girlfriend awaits with mochacinos cooled with ice from Soi Kasemsan.

On more pleasant days, a different route can be taken passing through a network of exterior spaces, left over and planned, that animates the commercial developments. These plazas, bridges, platforms, sidewalks and bus stops are populated by commercially sponsored fashion, music and dance events introducing new products and lifestyles. A full mix of income levels cross in these spaces, with new rural migrants gaping at the modern clothing and behaviour of those that arrived only last year. Malls in Thailand have become the staging areas for the new bodily performances of modernity, and this commercial zone has an even wider audience in that advertisements, music videos and soap operas are continually filmed in its stores, atria, restaurants and plazas. The new body and media performances include lovers staging affection or arguments in public and the sexy self-conscious 'catwalk' – a new form of walking meditation implying a display of self-centred individuality oblivious to protocols of social deference. Public affection and coupling between members of the opposite sex afford socializing options in addition to long-standing rules for modesty and privacy between sexes and affectionate homosociality within large groups.

These performances repeat earlier stagings of modernity that took place nearly one hundred years ago in this same place. The water lily gardens of Sra Pathumwan and surrounding palaces and gardens served as an impetus to urban expansion and modernization and became the preferred centres for social life in Bangkok of the Sixth Reign. King Rama VI (1910–25) presided over the decline of the polygamous order of the Grand Palace's Inner Court. Modernity and monogamy were first tested, 'probed', here in a 'European' garden city, the periphery of the old capital.

> Although King Vajiravudh and top government officials debated marriage reform, they stopped short of legislating sexual behavior. Instead, the king relied on the power of rhetoric and representation, promoting new forms of gender relations through his numerous essays and plays, and through the example set by the social circles close to the palace. This emphasis on representation rather than legislation parallels the king's approach to promoting Siamese nationalism, which could be analyzed as having been staged or performed, both in small-scale plays and extravagant public spectacles.
>
> (Fishel 1999: 154)

Here ideas of traditional gender and sex roles were gently challenged through play and performance in newly reconstructed urban realms as they are again today. The vertical mall architecture of Pathumwan Intersection introduces 'horizontally' ordered social strata targeting audiences by gender, age and income, as opposed to the intergenerational and mixed income organization of the horizontal *soi*.

John Hoskin has reiterated a gendered stereotype of the modern city as indecisive woman: 'Bangkok seems to run through an anthology of city personae like a party-going woman trying on dresses as it continually defines its modern self' (Hoskin 2000: 1). Commercial leases and tastes in architectural styles both last from five to ten years, so the malls and stores are in a constant state of refurbishment. However, Western consumerism and the culture of the cosmetic neither threaten nor constitute Thai society. The notion of mutable identity feminized by Western thought is not a key to understanding Bangkok or modernity; it is, in fact, a fundamental and ancient Buddhist principle, the precept of impermanence in all things, the world and our selves. A belief in permanence and essence is part of the Christian faciality machine: 'Peter, upon this rock'. Western urban design is structured on symbolic permanence – lasting values monumentalized in masonry. However Buddhism alone does not explain Thailand. Buddhism teaches moderation while Bangkok is a city of excesses – a legacy of Hinduism – and of sensual pleasure – animism and primitivism will not fade away.

A skytrain journey lifts the skirts Hoskin's words project onto Bangkok. Elevated above the concrete face of ribbon development we can see the canal side settlements, monasteries, old palaces and *sois* of the city. Beyond Siam Center still sits Sra Pathum Palace, now the home of Crown Princess Sirindhorn. Beyond Siam Square and MBK stands a huge canopy of trees shading Chulalongkorn University. The commercial face of Pathumwan Intersection disguises the fact that the mall owners lease royal and institutional land. These commercial complexes may be interpreted as a royally sponsored extension to palaces and institutions for higher education. It is also a very green city from up here. This low, mechanical birds-eye view helps Bangkokians to re-imagine their city from new vantage points along moving transect parallel to the ancient canal. The crisscrossing vertical circulation systems of the malls provide glimpses through the complex topology and layered ecology of Bangkok.

However, it is back on the ground where this new knowledge can be applied.

> The restoration of the body means, first and foremost, the restoration of the sensory – sensual – of speech, of the voice, of smell, of hearing. In short, of the non-visual. And of the sexual – though not in the sense of sex considered in isolation, but rather in the sense of a sexual energy directed towards a specific discharge of flowing according to specific rhythms.
>
> (Lefebvre 1991: 363)

Lefebvre's comments point to an urban design practice that is embodied, fertile and potent, not merely a visual coding of symbolic uniformity for the alienated individual subject. Thai animism and Deleuzian 'becoming animal' present an awe and respect for nature and earth, a materialist belief in the sacredness of all things. Hinduism is a pantheism, a polyvocality, a living with multiple gods, not a condemnation of degrees of difference from the Christian White Man's 'selecting and judging face, an instrument of subjectification in *the computation of normalities*' (Deleuze and Guattari 1987: 178). Buddhism promotes detachment, a breaking of Michel Foucault's technologies of the self, a philosophy of non-being, a 'self'-destruction opposite to Western schizophrenia. The restoration of the body in urban design or in city life involves dismantling faciality and recoding bodies and environments. Urban design is ultimately located within the experience of the city itself. Its semiotic is not logocentric, but *environmental*, in that it takes in *that which surrounds us*. The urban text is a sensorial as well as a symbolic environment, encoded within physical experience and material existence. It is therefore an embodied semiotic, available to all the senses, with the face restored to the body as the receptive plate of sensory organs instead of merely a surface for the projection of signs.

> To the point that human beings have a destiny, it is rather to escape the face, to dismantle the face and facializations, to become imperceptible, to become clandestine, not by returning to animality, nor the head, but by quite spiritual and special becomings-animal, by strange true becomings that get past the wall and get out of the black holes, that make faciality traits themselves finally elude the organization of the face. Yes, the face has a great future, but only if it is destroyed, dismantled. On the road to the asignifying and asubjective.
>
> (Deleuze and Guattari 1987: 171)

Thai 'face' is a modern practice that dismantles Western faciality and landscapicity. Its strategy is not one of resistance to outside influences, nor a return to an ideal of tradition, but of multiplicity, polyvocality, and simultaneity. It is necessary to engage an 'expanded field' of urban design analysis in order to reconfigure the discipline to meet the challenges of the modern metropolis. Rosalind Krauss (1983) located embodied art practices from the 1970s within the larger conceptual framework of architecture/sculpture/landscape in order to liberate art production from the confines of faciality: market, museum and gallery. An expanded field of urban design would draw from gender and body politics, as well as ecology, sustainable economics and technologies (McGrath and Weisz 2000) with similar goals. Urban design reconceived within the simultopian paradigm could engage the social role of 'face', rather than the individuating machine of 'faciality' and its decoding of the body. The deferential codes of 'face' are displayed in an embodied urbanism engaged in a deterritorialization process that is the opposite of the one described by Deleuze and Guattari: faces and architecture are neutral until attached to the bodies and activities that make them expressive. Western urban design is conceived within a utopian imagination, as a fantasy of making a city outside time and place. Instead, Bangkok suggests an urban design practice based in a simultopian imagination within the syncretic ecology of social tolerance and the embodied practice of 'face'.

Leaving the skytrain after nightfall at National Stadium behind MBK mall, hundreds of coloured fluorescent lights – a displaced Dan Flavin installation – dangle from palm trees encircling a grid of tents. A stage is lit with a *luk thong* performance: the eclectic staging of soulful Northeast ballads. Young women dress in elaborate Vegas costumes of their own design while the singer croons over his love lost when she moved to work in the big city and was seduced by its dazzling attractions. Many of the citizens of Soi Kasemsan sit in rapture in the audience, the vending families and women seated in front, the ice deliverymen and motorcycle drivers drink whiskey slightly off stage, hoping to catch the eye of the performers. Opposite in the plaza of Mah Boon Krong Mall, a fashion show is being parodied with audience members invited to accompany famous Thai supermodels on stage. Awkward teenagers and migrant labourers strut down the catwalk. The embarrassing results of this crash course in the signification of embodied subjectivity delight the audience.[6]

NOTES

1   Part of my work has been directed in this effort employing new computer technologies. See www.skyscraper.org/timeformations
2   If it is possible to assign the faciality machine a date the year zero of Christ and the historical development of the White Man it is because that is when the mixture ceased to be a splicing or an intertwining, becoming a total interpenetration in which each element suffuses the other like drops of red-black wine in white water. Our semiotic of modern White Men, the semiotic of capitalism, has attained this state of mixture in which significance and subjectification effectively interpenetrate.

(Deleuze and Guattari, 1987: 182)

3   My academic research in urban design in Thailand has been conducted at the Faculty of Architecture, Chulalongkorn University as a Fulbright Senior Scholar in 1998–9, as a visiting researcher in 2000, and as a visiting professor in 2001. My interest in daily life comes from living half time in Bangkok with a Thai partner since 1996. This has

brought me through Pathumwan Intersection from my home on Soi Kasemsan to Chulalongkorn countless times.

4   Thanks to Anthony Raynsford for elucidating this point.

5   Personal communication, Rebecca Zorach.

6   My work has been directed in this effort employing new computer technologies. See www.skyscraper.org/timeformations

7   Thanks to Deborah Natsios and Grahame Shane for their careful readings and suggestions.

Part VI

Haunting the City

Rebecca Zorach

This final section and Elizabeth Grosz's closing essay begin to address the question: 'Where do we go from here?' The essays in the preceding section have already made plain the demise, or at least the deep questioning, of a certain brand of twentieth-century utopian dreams, the disintegration of notions that urban design and architecture might produce socially 'useful' results. Assimilating this critique, the essays in this section, 'Haunting the City', describe a landscape we might almost call postapocalyptic, with their wandering protagonists picking their way through the rubble of modernity. They are like the viewer Beatriz Jaguaribe describes, in an essay on Rio de Janeiro whose implications may be generalized to the global postmodern, as 'the contemporary viewer who contemplates the wreckage of decayed modernist architecture at the end of the twentieth century' (Jaguaribe 1999: 298).

Among the many symbolic moments we might select to highlight the 'wreckage' of modernist architecture is the failure of the Pruitt-Igoe housing complex in St Louis, unveiled in 1955 to design accolades – and demolished in the summer of 1972, as the last American troops left Vietnam. The end of Pruitt-Igoe marked a kind of end to utopian hopes that innovative Corbusian design would somehow produce better kinds of people. In Peter Hall's analysis in *Cities of Tomorrow* he blames the failure on the fact that Pruitt and Igoe were designed for the wrong populations:

> The design, like that of most public housing down to the 1950s, was for the deserving poor. Most heads of households were to be employed males. St Louis in 1951 was a segregated city: Pruitt was all-black, but after public housing was desegregated by decision of the Supreme Court, the authority tried to integrate Igoe. To no avail: whites left, and blacks – including many welfare-dependent, female-head families – moved in.
>
> (Hall 1996 [1988]: 237)

According to Hall, families conforming to the normative model of white patriarchal nuclear family structure might have done perfectly well in the complex because they would not have felt helpless in it. '[T]he Corbusian city of towers', he argues, 'was perfectly satisfactory for . . . middle-class inhabitants . . . The sin of Corbusier and the Corbusians thus lay not in their design but in the mindless arrogance whereby they were imposed on people' (Hall 1996 [1988]: 240). Hall appears to accept the notion that these families were intractably deviant; he is ambivalent about the power of physical surroundings to shape subjectivities in any active way. Yet the notion of public housing for a patriarchal nuclear family contains a kind of paradox in which state paternalism that takes upon itself the role of 'head of household'. Hall's blithe association of masculinity with agency begs the question whether the women and children would have been better off with men at the 'head' of the family anyway – whether in public housing projects or in conventional houses or apartments.

I use this example to highlight the question of agency raised by the essays that follow along with others in this book. If it is precisely the overriding power of the planner, architect, designer, or philosopher, strips the 'ordinary' person of the agency to shape her own surroundings, what then? As space appears less and less of a 'medium' on which we can act, and more and more occupied, what type of agency may be theorized for those of us – most of us – who live in spaces ordered and arranged and built by others? As Ani Difranco sings, 'Who says I like right angles? These are not my laws, these are not my rules' (Difranco 1992).

Where do we go from here? In the conference out of which this volume developed, Elizabeth Wilson's notion of 'interstitial spaces' proved a defining concept to which we returned again and again. All of the essays in this section deal with the interstices of architectures and their official histories and the tactics – not strategies – by which we negotiate them, as inhabitants, as visitors, as 'surfers', as 'flâneuses'. Wilson writes that 'nothing was hidden in utopia': it presents itself as a technology of transparency. These three authors look with the view of the tactician, a necessarily partial view; in de Certeau's description of tactics they are the means available to those who do not have a complete view, who do not command a 'visible totality' (de Certeau 1984a: xix). The city is a palimpsest (as in Joseph's title), layers of strata and traces of a series of political, economic, and social forms. Urban space is apprehended by a body in motion, rather than being framed by a touristic gaze seeking *sights* – or the bird's eye view of Le Corbusier the airman – or of de Certeau himself atop the Empire State Building. We call this position that of the flâneur, a position most explicitly presented by Erickson's notion of the cyberflâneuse.

Then there is the ghost. The modern urban form, with its sedimented memory, history, display, fetishism, flaking surfaces, palimpsests, has become a haunted place: haunted with the utopian dreams of planners, developers, architects past – and walkers, bikers, drivers, and strollers past. Strikingly, the sites of each of these essays are marked by *wars,* both hot and cold, by the large-scale destruction of bodies. Elizabeth Wilson's London is marked by the Second World War, the Blitz. In 'Against Utopia', we see 'bomb sites left from the Second

World War'; we watch, via Dickens, 'an eerie scene of a scavenger dredging the Thames for dead bodies'. The ruins of Cold War frugality (and the Vietnam War) provide the backdrop for Joseph's essay, the same Cold War that produced the Internet. In Joseph's 'Frugality and the City', the 'solitary bombed-out hull of a rooftop remains a lingering reminder of a violent hovering past'. Christa Erickson shows us 'personae such as ghostBorgGirl [who] haunt this place' where 'this place' might be Diane Bertolo's F2K, or it might be the Internet as a whole. The sites Erickson cites are already part of cyber-history, existing in multiple locations, archives, and as ghostly sites whose 'last update' might be, in the dog-years of the Internet, ancient history. The ghost might be viewed as the after-effect of the traditional split between body and mind (or 'spirit'). The spectre is a visible spirit, as Jacques Derrida points out in *Specters of Marx*, and this is a 'paradoxical incorporation', a certain 'phenomenal and carnal form' of the supposedly disembodied spirit (Derrida 1994: 6). We might want to (mis)appropriate Derrida's concept and use it to describe not the ghosts of the past but the ghosts of the present – embodied, mobile figures. As Rebecca Schneider writes of performance artists, 'bringing ghosts to visibility, they . . . expose not an originary, true, or redemptive body, but the sedimented layers of signification itself' (Schneider 1997: 2).

Erickson addresses the utopian hyperbole surrounding the 'early years' not of the Internet *per se* but of its popularization, its increasing availability to the general (Western) public through the advent of graphical user interfaces (GUIs) and user-friendly Internet service providers. Messianic rhetoric promised a widening of democratic expression, a freedom of speech that might carry with it freedom from one's body and from one's locatedness in a particular place. It presented the 'space' of the Internet as a frontier, with all that that implies. As Erickson shows, a variety of artists have parodied and mimicked this rhetoric, and, later, the commercial sites that 'settled' the frontier. Taking the approach of the bricoleur along with the flâneur, the 'virus of the new world disorder', they have also made viewers aware of the tensions (sometimes productive ones) between 'real' and 'virtual' space.

The position of the flâneur is not an unproblematic one. Leo Ou-Fan Lee has suggested that the position of flâneur was not available to *modeng* (modern) Chinese writers who, in their ecstatic appreciation of the city of Shanghai, found no room for the flâneur's detachment (Lee 1999). And flânerie is intimately connected with the class-inflected capacity to travel the streets (a woman who does so is a 'streetwalker'), the voyeuristic consumption of views, of the life of the city. The flâneuse, then, accepts the challenge to turn her energies to an active and vigilant questioning.

Joseph's narrative voice bears some relation to this critical flâneuse. While she is open to the visual richness of experience she is also attuned to the layering of ideologies – and the cracks in them. Taking a global view of mid-century modernist building projects, she identifies a dialectic of expenditure and frugality, excess and restraint, operating both *across* the capitalist/communist divide and *within* both types of cultures and economies. Joseph sees the modern building projects of the 'Second World' as 'laboratories of utopic organizing unfolding through varying degrees of instrumental rationalization'; in this view they are not unlike Pruitt-Igoe. Today Hanoi is paradoxically characterized by the weight of the past and by the speed with which it assimilates fashions. It is 'a hum in motion, afloat in speed and change'. Yet in the 'dead space of the imagined nation', the monumentalized version of Ho Chi Minh could hardly be further from Ho's wish 'that he be cremated and his ashes spread so that the impulse to deify would not be there'. Motion and stasis remain in constant tension.

Rather than seeking the clarity of utopia, Wilson looks for the 'hidden and secret aspect of urban life where traces of former worlds and lives may be found'. She points us to tears in the urban fabric where the 'backs of buildings', the cracks in the 'dominant fiction', are visible. She seeks out places of inattention and disrepair that escape the tourist gaze. She is interested in wandering the non-places of the city, though these are not Marc Augé's non-places of hyper-mediated supermodernity – superhighways and malls and airport lounges. Wilson, a writer on the city, draws her inspiration from other writers on the city, and this might lead us to examine the position of the writer – or the writer-as-flâneur. To do the kind of work these essays do is to imagine writing, whether academic or essayistic, as utopian – a qualified or contingent utopianism, perhaps better identified as *desiring*. Do we give up on the idea of utopia, or reclaim it? What figures can we put forward – the ghost, the flâneuse, the cyborg – as alternative figures to Utopos, the designer of More's *Utopia*? How porous are the boundaries of our own heterotopias? How transformative are they? These are questions our authors invite you, the reader, to continue to pose.

Chapter 12: Networked Interventions

Debugging the Electronic Frontier

Christa Erickson

During the closing decade of the twentieth century, the Internet, popularly called cyberspace and the information superhighway,[1] became *the* utopian space. In the few short years from 1995 to early 1999, roughly the time period this essay examines, its mythology bombarded American popular culture to such a degree that non-techies became familiar with formerly obscure technical nomenclature like www and dot-com. Promises touted by corporate advertisers, politicians, and cyberfanatics alike were staggering: empowerment, convenience, global democracy, wealth, communities unfettered by geography, mutable identity, and even the erasure of gender and race. Everything was new and better in the e-world and its gold-rush economy.

The hyperbole that has surrounded this global phenomenon has begun to ebb in the closing moments of 2000, as I complete this essay. The Internet is now an ordinary part of life in the US and other developed nations. This assimilation of virtual spaces into the everyday requires that we take seriously the politics of the Internet as a 'place' with real stakes. To this end, this chapter looks at the metaphors and language that surrounded the Internet's formative years. It focuses specifically on the implications of this space as the 'electronic frontier' of popular imagination, and also considers the idea of a 'network' as both a political and a technological structure.

In keeping with the linked and associative structures of the Internet itself, this chapter connects a series of insights suggested by several artists' Internet-related projects that address abstract cyber-utopian claims. Many artists treat the Internet as an electronic street corner and use their work to critique public discourses around it. Many were also informed by the critical public art produced in the 1980s and 1990s that attempted to engage spatial politics.[2] Just as public artists work within and against the architectural structures and materiality of the city, subverting the use of public spaces, net artists work within and against the spaces and structures established by the technological infrastructure of the virtual network. In particular, they address the politics of use. Statistics suggest a vast 'digital divide' (USNTIA 1999) between those who can and cannot partici-pate; thus, class, race, gender, and the relationship of actual and virtual bodies are all taken up by these artists' projects.

It has not escaped these artists' critical attention that corporate capital is a fundamental part of this infrastructure. Some of the projects employ parody and humour as tactical practices, spoofing the visual conventions of commercial web-sites. Some projects take up the personal narratives suggested by individual homepages. Some push the bounds of what is possible with this still limited, but expanding technology. Others create mysterious interfaces, which must be explored to be understood. All of these projects exemplify a practice of writing and rewriting a specific moment.

Just as these artists borrow from urban spatial practice, I will borrow from analyses of the modern city. I suggest the 'cyberflâneuse' as my paradigmatic Internet subject and my approach as author. Although my cyberflâneuse resem-bles the historical 'flâneur' from the late nineteenth century, the spaces she wanders are different – as are her modes of inhabiting those spaces. Similarly, the artists I discuss operate in Internet space in a critical and subtly seditious manner, observing and reinventing it.

For Charles Baudelaire and, following him, Walter Benjamin, the 'flâneur' was the archetypal modern subject, strolling the streets of the city, surveying its contents with a mobile view (Benjamin 1968: 172–5). Contemporary scholars of the modern city, like Janet Wolff (1991), note that the male flâneur has no female equivalent (no 'flâneuse'). In the nineteenth century, women's realm was the domestic, and a female 'street walker' meant something else entirely. Women on the street might become the object of the flâneur's gaze, but the commanding anonymity of the flâneur was simply not available to them. When individuals like the writer George Sand were able to access this privilege, it was only by masquerading as men.

As with the flâneur's city, the virtual space of the Internet has its privileged travellers and its excluded populations. The term 'digital divide' has been used to describe the disparity between those who travel often and in style on the Inter-net and those who lack the tools and access to do so. 'Virtual class' (Kroker and Weinstein 1994) is now in common use for the privileged class of people who work online via various communications technologies. Any trip through a major airport reveals this mobile class wielding laptops, PDAs, and cellular phones. Several Internet scholars refer to themselves as flâneurs of cyberspace (Mitchell 1995: 7); the anonymity and privilege of the flâneur certainly translates to these wanderers of cyberspace. At least at first, they were – like the flâneur – largely male.

The cyberflâneuse might be a cyberspace wanderer with a purpose, adopt-ing a set of 'tactics' for subverting cyberspace. In *The Practice of Everyday Life*, Michel de Certeau (1984a) theorizes ways to transform the planned agenda of a place (*lieu*, a fixed and owned site of power), or its 'strategy', into the embodied practice of space (*espace*, space as produced by the practices of everyday life) through 'tactics'. His work focuses on the ways in which space is actually used, rather than the ways in which places were planned; he is concerned with the reader or pedestrian, rather than the writer or architect. Reading and walking become potentially subversive tools of living and engaging space: 'Everyday life invents itself by poaching in countless ways on the property of others' (de Certeau 1984a: xii). The cyberflâneuse explores the cracks in the virtual sidewalk and might plant a garden in an abandoned virtual lot, haunting the space. She engages people in virtual cafés, disrupting their virtual and bodily lives. Most of all she remembers the complex problems of the material world, rather than being seduced by the easy promise of utopian virtuality. She might even be a he. Like the flâneur, s/he might wander through spaces previously unavailable, fracturing meaning and materiality with 'her' very presence.

NEGOTIATING ELECTRONIC 'SPACE'

Although there are many philosophical and theoretical reasons why one might consider the Internet a 'space', the most obvious one is simply that people treat it that way. Much as William Gibson characterized cyberspace as a 'consensual hallucination' in his seminal novel *Neuromancer* (Gibson 1984: 51), a tacit consensus has emerged to describe the Internet as a space. The language used to describe the Internet and people's interactions within it draws upon spatial metaphors: 'information superhighway', 'surfing the web', 'web address', or even 'homepage'. The very word cyberspace owes its name to the word cybernetics (and cybernaut), coined by Norbert Weiner in 1947, its roots connected to a notion of navigation from Greek origins meaning to pilot or steer. Early writing on cyberspace imagined three-dimensional representational technologies, often termed virtual reality technologies. Although VRML has emerged as a three-dimensional web display technology, most Internet navigation is still two-dimensional; this has not impeded the conception of the Internet as a space.

The physical experience of navigating the Internet through the graphical portion known as the web explains some of the spatial invocations. Despite some similarities to 'channel surfing', it differs from the way people relate to television. As when driving on a highway, people see the web through a window – a seemingly limited view. This view is, however, only a fragment of a larger sense of space that unfolds over time. One navigates the terrain via a set of abstracted instruments that rely upon simple, easily learned bodily movements, or basic voice commands. The small-scale, two-dimensional computer screen and its minute point-and-click gestures imply sensations quite different from physical motion through a space. Yet one retains a sense of control in the ability to direct movement and extend one's exploration through time. The interplay between user and web interface bridges the spatial divide between the virtual and physical worlds. Switching from one web page to the next or one e-mail window to the next might suggest spatial discontinuity; after all, one might be moving from a page originating in Japan to one from New York or Mexico. However, the virtual experience is more like that of montage, cutting from one context to another. The interface becomes a prosthesis, or phantom limb, and the subject an information-space wanderer.

The experience of wandering in virtual space while remaining stationary in physical space can create boundary confusions. This is the subject of *INVERTIGO* (1997), a project that I developed along with Sawad Brooks and Beth Stryker. It included a video installation in a gallery driven by a swing 'interface' that could be manipulated by users, and a corresponding website. The piece staged a literal and metaphoric swing between the physical space of the art gallery and the public space of the web to explore a confusion of presence/absence, real/virtual, and near/far. The swing acted as a physical editing device for a large video projection on suspended translucent scrims. Cinematic cuts at each swing apex evoked a sense of movement and boundary confusion that disrupted the 'swinging' participant's sense of seamless physical experience, as in the experience of wandering by jump-cuts in information space. Suggestions of the presence of someone in the other space (the physical or the virtual) passed back and forth – their physical bodies never touched, but their interactions left traces in the mechanism on 'the other side'. From the web, 'presence' in the gallery could be seen via spy-cameras mounted atop and behind the swing. It was also suggested by a number on a page, analogous to a web page counter, that increased by one with each physical swing in the gallery. In the gallery, 'web presence' was indicated two ways: a rush of male and female bodies in the video projection and the numbered IP addresses[3] of the website visitors on the monitor behind the swing. When many people were 'visiting' the website, the visual accumulation of these numbers gave an indication of the volume of web presence.

The idea of 'connecting' with others in different geographical locations is part of the allure of the Internet. Portions of the Internet have social aspects that are part of the ways in which it is conceptualized as a space. The suggestion of 'place', where one might 'go' to meet others, came early on in the form of mediated areas like chat rooms, MUDs, and MOOs. With the proliferation of Instant Messenger services one is informed if a contact on one's predefined list of people is also 'there' – and communication can take place in 'real time'. Through the ability to design a 'profile', post an image, or create a 'homepage', people have mechanisms for presenting themselves (or the selves they choose) to others. These gathering spaces provide for both social interactions and forms of manipulation. A.R. Stone has documented some fascinating stories of such spaces with telling social implications (Stone 1995: 65–81). For some people, these interactions are an extension of the real, and the attributes of their lives appear as present as they might be in any social setting. Others use the seeming anonymity of meeting online to create a persona to act out alternate identities. Other users move between the virtual and the physical, meeting people within the ostensible safety and anonymity of online interaction but eventually deciding to take the relationship offline. It is significant to note that although corporations build some of these gathering spaces, many originate independently from within existing communities of people.

Even though we may travel 'there' every day, the virtual space of the Internet is not a place as we typically understand the word. Yet the city is still a productive spatial metaphor for the electronic network. William Mitchell, for instance, titles his book on the subject the *City of Bits: Space, Place, and the Infobahn* (Mitchell 1995). Certainly in both the physical city and on the Internet, people meet, carry out work, gather information, shop, and sightsee, or as the case may be, site-see. Marshall McLuhan suggested that every new medium is a rearview mirror to its recent historical past (McLuhan 1964: ix); and, indeed, patterns of cities are enacted online. Many sites are slick and glossy flat façades with flashing banner advertisements, functioning like a mall or the Las Vegas strip. The Internet's notorious 'red-light' zones might be thought of as corresponding city districts, but they are more closely associated to *each other* by numerous 'links' than they are to any other 'neighbourhoods'. While structures and materials are different – bits and files versus bricks and mortar; coded information versus buildings; and links and search engines versus streets and subways – the two worlds remain linked. Industries familiar from the 'real world' are visible to the web wanderer, though their web architectures may differ dramatically from the corresponding physical space.

It is also useful to consider a few differences between the Internet and the city based on construction and time. Basic websites can be made by anyone with computer access and a few simple skills. Although this does not equate to 'democracy', as is sometimes claimed, it does mean that one need not have corporate backing to create one's own web-space or critique another's. In fact, I teach students to make their first websites in only a couple of hours by stealing other sites and modifying them. This time scale is vastly different from the years it may take an architect to see a design built. The compressed sense of Internet time is often likened to 'dog years' – an apt metaphor given its rate of change. The years 1992–4 saw the birth of the first popular browser, Mosaic, and the mark-up language that produces web pages. By 1996 Mosaic had died out, replaced first by Netscape and then, increasingly, by Explorer. Through these stages, the web has undergone a visual transformation from grey pages with crude imagery to sophisticated layouts and animation, including the more recent streaming of audio and video.

COLONIZATION OF THE ELECTRONIC FRONTIER

Since its beginnings in the late 1960s, the Internet has been referred to as a frontier. The first network was developed in a decentralized way as a result of Cold War paranoia, so that if one computer were attacked the others would not be disrupted.[4] With its origins in the American southwestern desert, its militaristic past, and this lack of central authority, the frontier metaphor and attendant Wild

Figure 12.1
Diane Bertolo, FT2K,
1997.
http://www.turbulence.or
g/Works/FT2K

West gunfight and computer cowboy imagery is not surprising. Its legacy includes notions of an untamed space that has only recently undergone 'civilizing' by US governmental regulatory efforts, like the Communications Decency Act of 1996, to make it 'safe' for women and children.[5] Commercials for the search engine about.com (1999) play on this imagery: a vast imaginary desert territory that their service helps you navigate without peril. The frontier metaphor suggests a number of problematic associations and several potentially productive ones. The dominant association is that of colonization, with virtual space providing expansion for multinational corporations, American culture and products, and the English language. However, the sense of newness and lack of structure provide space for imagining other possibilities.

Diane Bertolo's piece *Frontier Town 2000,* or *FT2K* (1997), is an intelligent and visually lovely explication of Internet gathering spaces which juxtaposes the Internet to the city. The setting, an electronic frontier town, alludes to the desert of the American southwest, where the Internet began, and to popular western mythology, in its reference to computer hacker cowboys and gold-rush dot-com opportunities. In Bertolo's critique of the rhetoric around global villages and online 'community', we are told that these spaces are really 'ghost towns', 'memory palaces', or tourist 'theme parks' for the disembodied. Buildings are all single-image flat façades attached to wire-frame models. During our tour we encounter 'realistic re-enactment' games, arcades for 'authentic experiences', corporate trademarks, shoot-outs, and profiles of inhabitants that mimic personal homepages. We are shown fictions of presence and place – no-one really 'lives' here, after all. Yet traces of the past and of known spaces abound.[6] Visitors can send postcards to friends as souvenirs of their visit; personae such as ghostBorgGirl haunt this place, suggesting the presence of the 'cyborg' – a

hybrid subjectivity, human–machine, proposed by Donna Haraway, who calls on feminists to get into the 'belly of the monster' (Haraway 1991: 9).

The historical connotations of the word 'frontier' have not escaped artists Guillermo Gomez-Pena, Roberto Sifuentes, and James Luna. As demonstrated in their 1995 collaborative performance *Shame-Man and El Mexican't Meet the Cyber-Vato*, in the American West, the dream of the white European frontier town meant genocide for the indigenous people who were perceived to interfere with the settlement of the supposed 'untamed' and 'empty' spaces. Their performance work inverts and enacts stereotypes of race and gender along what Gomez-Pena calls the 'new world border' of cultural misunderstanding (1996). Many of this group's recent performance works have been generated from, among other sources, a web-based *Temple of Confessions* (Gomez-Pena and Sifuentes 1996) in which visitors are asked to confess race-based fears and dreams. The venomous tone of these online confessions has shocked even the artists. They attribute the tenor of hatred to the seemingly anonymous quality of posting on the Internet: social niceties drop away as unfettered racial animosity displaces the utopian fantasy of a bias-free space (Gomez-Pena 1998). Their work also makes the point that the information superhighway bypasses the barrio and the ghetto, further keeping the frontier safe for a largely white virtual class.[7]

The new media artist Antonio Muntadas explores another form of colonization on the electronic frontier, the colonization of world languages by English, with his site *On Translation*. The bulk of Internet communication, over 80 per cent, is in English (Tehan 2000). Thus, it is not surprising that a Cisco Systems' 1998–9 advertising campaign featured children from around the globe, all of them speaking English, and declaring the promise of the Internet: 'Are you ready?' English is undeniably part of the reality of global modernization. At the same time, many of the world's languages cannot even be represented as text on the Internet due to the technical limitations of the communications software architecture based on ASCII, the American Standard character set.[8] Muntadas's

On Translation visually reveals the diversity of forty-five different languages. Seeking to overcome and simultaneously draw attention to the Internet's inherent language biases, many of the languages in the piece are actually rendered as images instead of text. The site is based on the initial phrase: 'Communications systems provide the possibility of developing better understanding between people: in which language?' The process of creating the visual translations was modelled on the children's game 'telephone'. In Muntadas's version, the phrase is translated into another language before it is passed on. The resulting process reveals difficulties of translation in the quest for meaningful exchange: language is presented as a never-ending spiral of differences which viewers scan to see the different languages/translations.

CYBERFEMINISM AND GRRL OUTLAWS

Differences in language usage and communication styles have long been areas for feminist research. In an essay by Critical Art Ensemble, media theorist Kathy Rae Huffman is cited for her joke about one of the possible benefits of Internet communication for women: 'In cyberspace men can't interrupt you' (Wilding and CAE 1998). The asynchronous nature of early networked conversation may have allowed a woman to complete her thought; yet on a larger scale, women's participation lagged behind men's in the mid- to late-1990s. The Guerilla Girls, an activist collective known for their critical parody of art world hegemonies, produced a 1995 poster stating that: 'The Internet was 84.5% male and 82.3% white until now'. This statistical illustration explains in large part why the presence of women's voices was and still remains somewhat limited (Bennett and Palmer 1997).

The last fragment of the Guerrilla Girls' poster, 'until now', along with their tongue-in-cheek activism, suggests the character of many cyberfeminist voices. A visible minority claim to be geekgirls with an attitude. The frontier metaphor suggests some of the more potent imaginary subject positions for this breed of grrl: pioneer and outlaw. The pioneer occupies a space considered new or unknown. She is a homesteader, a squatter, occupying a space and making it her own. The outlaw plays by rules of her own choosing, armed with knowledge, challenging conventional norms.

In response to the male-centred culture of the Internet, a visible 'cyberfeminism' emerged in the 1990s, particularly within the arts and culture sectors. It is based in part on Haraway's dense cautionary writings from the late 1980s, including the particularly influential 'Cyborg Manifesto' (1991). She writes, 'Cyborg writing is about the power to survive not on the basis of innocence, but on the basis of seizing the tools to mark the world that marked them as other' (Haraway 1991: 175). Her notion of a critical feminist engagement with technoculture caught many women activists' imaginations. The writings of Sadie Plant in the UK, particularly her *Zeros and Ones* (1997) and some early interviews at the popular ezine[9] 'geekgirl' from Australia, also provoked women to engage.

Plant plays with cyberspace as feminist utopia, recuperating and celebrating the history of women's pioneering past with technology, including the story of the first programmer, Ada Lovelace, and another significant programmer, Grace Hopper. Plant seeks to counteract the truism that technology is a male prerogative. In fact, Plant suggests that 'masculine identity has everything to lose from this new technics. The sperm count falls as the replicants stir and the meat learns how to learn for itself. Cybernetics is feminization' (Plant 1996: 132). This tactic provided inspirational to visual artists who embraced the digital arts over art practices like painting that have a long and very male history. Some draw correlations between the collage or bricolage of cyberfeminist works and other more traditional practices such as weaving. Bricolage, the appropriation and stitching together of whatever is at hand, can be compared to the practices of the cyber-flâneuse or the cyborg.

One of the first, most visible, and most vocal groups of these geekgirls was the Australian VNS Matrix (1991–7). This fragment of their manifesto suggests their mission:

> . . .
>
> we are the virus of the new world disorder
> rupturing the symbolic from within
> saboteurs of big daddy mainframe
>
> . . .

Like an electronic Calamity Jane, they went into conferences about the electronic frontier and played at being one of the boys, disrupting the conversation in brash and unladylike ways. They digitally resurrected the cunt imagery of the early 1970s and brought bodily flesh, fluids, and uncompromising queer sexuality to the clean chrome and circuits of the machine. They relished their outlaw status, inverted cultural stereotypes, and played with the language of sexual domination and control that is embedded in much technical jargon.

HOSTILE TAKEOVERS

Despite the efforts of these trouble-making women, the fantasy of a global tech-notopia for women has little material likelihood, particularly given the economic inequality that segregates the vast majority of the world's women from the basic technological and educational infrastructure required to make web access a reality. Zillah Eisenstein's *Global Obscenities: Patriarchy, Capitalism, and the Lure of Cyberfantasy* (1998) reveals disparities made ever greater by multinational capital. 50 per cent of the world's population had never made a telephone call as of the 1998 publishing date of her book (Eisenstein 1998: 98). Literacy rates and proper healthcare for women world-wide are equally low. Large numbers of third-world women of colour work under oppressive conditions to produce electronic and other goods for the mostly white and mostly male virtual class.

It is virtually impossible to escape the signs of the corporate occupation of the web – almost every commodity and its advertisement lists a web address. In the period between 1996 and 1998, the web became something of a cross between a mall and the yellow pages. Flashing banner ads crept into most sites with any significant readership. 'Free' e-mail and web services abound, but they now come with a commercial element attached. Citizens of developed nations have become accustomed to spending money online. Once again, artists are and were aware of this dot-com world and have parodied and even exploited it, purposefully employing the slick visuals or structural tropes of corporate websites to their own ends.

Bodies Incorporated (1996) is one such site. Artist Victoria Vesna spoofs the promise that online we can all chose the body we want. In order to begin your fantasy, you first have to accept the lengthy legal terms of your purchase. Once you have made your choices, your body can wander through various spaces like the 'gated community' called 'home'. You can even kill off your body and leave it cast aside in the necropolis in favour of another. The site's corporate logo is a spinning head with a copyright symbol on its forehead. This is a particularly suggestive image for several reasons. The head with an extra eye reminds one of the heralded abandonment of the body in favour of the rational, disembodied Cartesian eye/mind. The logo/copyright calls attention to our cultural obsessions with property and their attendant legalisms, even within this immaterial realm. The third eye also hints at the watchful strategies of many dot-com advertisers and their information collection mechanisms for target marketing.

My own *neighbourhood WATCH* (1999) makes reference to such corporate surveillance of consumer behaviour in the electronic neighbourhood, as well as contemporary culture's more general obsession with watching. It reveals 'rear window' web views of three randomly selected web cams from around the globe, as well as the network hostname or IP address of the visitor, on its opening page. The three disparate views exemplify a possible non-contiguous, non-geographic form of space as described earlier. Visitors fill out a form, much as they might on many sites, which asks them about their own watching habits and fears of being watched. The piece stores these in its 'vicarious database' and exposes random fragments from it on another page. The data collection/distribution suggests that the seeming anonymity of online identity is not always so anonymous and that submitted data is not so private.

Vesna's title, *Bodies Inc.,* hints at another aspect of the collision of capital, Internet space, and language: the name of something is both its identity and also its spatial address. For most corporations, the desired name would be the corporate name. Language itself has become a commodity on the Internet. A very simple art piece by Heath Bunting, *Own, Be Owned or Remain Invisible* (1997), makes this point quite effectively. The piece consists of a page of text, ostensibly describing the exploits of the artist. Each word on the page is a link to the website which has co-opted that word as www.thatword.com. So if you follow a word, you might be horrified to discover that someone owns www.be.com or www.where.com. Some words that were not owned when I discovered the site a

Figure 12.3
RTMark mutual fund
mechanism, 1999.
http://www.rtmark.com

couple years ago are now functioning websites. Thus, *Own, Be Owned or Remain Invisible* traces the commodification of language over time.

Internet 'squatting' has been going on, too. Some people have purchased the rights to a domain name for the purpose of selling it to a company or other interest that might want it. This is rather like real-estate speculation. Registering a name with an agency that handles these was not a costly proposition, about $70 during this time period. Sales of already registered names can be high, though, when the buyer is determined to get the name they want and the seller recognizes the value of it. For instance, Steve Forbes bought www.forbes2000.com in 1999 for $6,500 (Ladd 1999).

Another site, rtmark.com (1997–), also plays with 'domain name' issues. RTMark realized that in the global economy, corporations have most of the legal rights of individuals, but none of the responsibilities. So it became a legal corporation whose business is perpetrating playful, well thought-out corporate sabotage. It has undertaken numerous large and small-scale projects, including the now infamous Barbie Liberation Organization's *Operation Newspeak*.[10] It uses the trading-post model of exchange to create a web-based mutual fund mechanism for activism. This allows individuals to invest in specific sabotage projects they want to support, or to lend a hand in carrying one out. It supports other activist-minded projects, too, and is establishing its own art action network.

RTMark has numerous franchise sites, all parodies of corporations and political figures like McDonalds, Shell Oil, and then-candidate George W. Bush. At first glance one might not recognize these sites as parody, due to their seamless design; a little investigation reveals an ironic, pointed, and informative difference. The ultimate example was a collaboration between RTMark and Zack Exley at the parody site gwbush.com. The candidate's lawyers issued them a cease-and-desist letter for using the name. However, because you cannot trademark a personal name, there was no real case. Then Bush filed a complaint with the Federal Elections Commission, asserting that Exley had violated election laws by not registering as a political committee. In the meantime, Bush himself purchased, or 'warehoused', numbers of such domain names, like bushbites.com and bushblows.com, in an effort to prevent further political parodies. Bush was so incensed by gwbush.com that he publicly called Exley a 'garbage man' and said, 'there should be limits to freedom'. The fact that Bush recognizes the important role that the Internet has begun to play in American politics is clear. However, Bush missed the big picture and caused himself a public relations backlash: through the media attention on his actions, he turned a small site that cost a total of $210 for its first two months of existence into an international profile site with over six million visits during May of 1999 (Ladd 1999). Bush's official site only had about 30,000 visits a month at the time. This incident suggests how the Internet might function as a site of intervention on a global scale.

TACTICS IN THE NETWORK

The networked structure of the Internet might increase the scope of tactics and practices that have long been employed by activist organizations. Traditional forms of collaboration and the spread of critical information through grassroots phone trees and pamphlets have expanded easily onto the Internet, as demonstrated early on by the Zapatista FloodNet and others. Traditional culture-jamming tools have expanded to include sophisticated programming borrowed from hacking. However, Ricardo Dominguez, from Electronic Disturbance Theatre, draws distinctions between such activism and hacking, saying, 'we call for disturbances, and distribution, not destruction' (Krempl and Dominguez 2000).

Networking is a traditional feminist tactic that has gone online in a fairly straightforward fashion. Given the shoot-'em-up, boys-with-big-toys character of the frontier, the necessity of these networks is obvious. There are a number of employment-related sites like webgrrls.com that help women train for the tech world. There are also websites which function like artists' networks; for instance, old boys network (OBN) (1997), queerarts (1997), and Face Settings. Face Settings (1997) blends Internet resource sharing, an international event calendar, and traditional physical meetings and dinners. The twenty-something ezine network called chickclick (1997-) originally boasted 'girl sites that don't fake it'. Because several of the linked ezine sites had loyal readership and the umbrella site had such a clever tag line and hip graphics, all were able to garner large 'hit counts', or numbers of visits, and help route readers to each other's sites; they also won the attention of advertisers in search of new markets. Within a year, some of the sites even received significant income from banner ads, allowing their creators to focus on producing the ezine rather than their 'day jobs'.[11]

Artists are using the medium of the web to think about 'networks' within individual art pieces as well. The database or information archive is a structure intrinsic to websites. Such mechanisms particularly foreground the fluid possibilities of Internet space. Muntadas made one of the first such works, *Fileroom*, in 1994. It began as a collection of instances of censorship, inviting visitors to add to this record and creating a partial, fragmentary, and ever-changing global history of censorship and its effects.

Another archival work is *dissemiNET* (1998), a visually dynamic project by Sawad Brooks and Beth Stryker. The site establishes the electronic network as a diasporic memory repository, images and texts floating across the screen. The artists began the piece with stories of disappearance and displacement during the civil war in El Salvador, placing a local political situation in a global context to preserve memories of the event. Now ideas and examples of witness and testimony of many kinds can be submitted to the site's repository and later searched as a form of recall. All the stories are cross-referenced to make connections between them.

Shu Lea Cheang creates an archive and expands on traditional forms of networking in the piece *Brandon* (1998–9), a one-year multi-media hypertext event. The project is organized around the true story of Brandon Teena, whose life is also recounted in the critically acclaimed film *Boys Don't Cry*. The website uses his story as a vehicle to explore the broader issues of gender identity and Internet phallocentrism; it interrogates discourses around the intersections of bodies and identities, both offline and online. The fantasy of gender swapping on the Internet is problematized in its juxtaposition with the story of Brandon's struggle as a female-to-male transsexual who attempted to pass as male in a small town in rural Nebraska, and was consequently raped and murdered. Shu Lea Cheang's website functions as a network, an organizing mechanism for fragments of text, history, and debate; its production has brought together numerous artists, writers, scholars, institutions and even legal analysts into a visual hypertext. As such, the site evokes discussions about the Internet as a global community. Some of the resulting discussions ended up on the website, while

Figure 12.4
Shu Lea Cheang,
Brandon, 1998–9.
http://brandon.
guggenheim.org

some conversation occurred in performance debates. These debates included one titled 'The Body Under the Knife of Medical Technology' that linked the Guggenheim Museum in NY through the web to the Theatre Anatomicum in Amsterdam; another debate connected the Harvard Law School to global 'netizens' who acted as jurors for the cases argued, on such topics as online harassment and virtual rape (Dibbell 1993). By dissecting the phantom nature of gender, Cheang relentlessly interrogates the anonymity of the Internet, demythologizing it as utopian space.

CONCLUSIONS

The utopian rhetoric of the electronic frontier has been tempered in the short time since I originally wrote this text, in part because so many people have become familiar with it. The frontier has largely been 'settled'. Computers are now reported to be in 60 per cent of US households. As of July/August of 2000 in the US, women are reported to be using the web with as much frequency as men (Austen 2000). Although it had a limited presence for some time, Internet art has become normalized within art world institutions with the inclusion of websites in the 2000 Biennial at the Whitney Museum of American Art.[12] As with any new cultural phenomenon, the fantasy of the Internet as a hitherto unknown space has passed into the everyday.

Corporations initially rushed at the Internet opportunities for global expansion and their mallification of the Internet grew at a dramatic rate. However, some of the euphoric glow of the gold rush has now faded; tech stocks are no longer quite so overvalued and dot-com roadkills are innumerable. Although e-commerce has finally become a reality, grossing almost seven billion dollars in the US during the third quarter of 2000 alone (USDC 2000), it is still only around one per cent of estimated consumer retail sales. It is significant that the growth of e-commerce and the mass entry of women onto the Internet coincide. This pattern was seen in urban spaces at the end of the last century and is described by Anne Friedberg in her book *Window Shopping* (Friedberg 1993: 36–7). She notes that women's entry into public life came through consumer activities allowed by changes in the urban spatial configurations that created department stores.

Not surprisingly, the online world reflects the offline one. On a global scale, the material effect of the Internet has largely been to create a greater disparity between information 'haves' and 'have-nots'. Domain name real-estate stakes are higher than they were a few years ago with sales of names going into the hundreds of thousands of dollars. Big corporations have used their financial weight to sue smaller owners of names related to their interests. One of the most infamous examples sparked what is now called the ToyWar. eToys, the online toy e-tailer, demanded that the artist's group etoy give up its domain name. RTMark and other activists staged protests of this bully-like gesture and later claimed responsibility for the public outcry and the plunge in stock prices of

Figure 12.5
Nancy Paterson, *Stock Market Skirt*, 1998.
http://www.bccc.com/nancy/skirt.html

the toy company that as this essay goes to press, is close to going out of business. Although heralded as a victory for Internet democracy, without solid legal protections, corporate bullying continues and many smaller interests are forced out of existence (RTMark 2000).

As corporate occupation has transformed the web and the corporate website has become the undisputed dominant settler on the frontier, the overzealous democratic rhetoric of only a few years ago begins to take on a different tone. Although they still seem naïve, these utopian democratic fantasies are now necessary to envision the Internet as a space where 'choice' and 'debate' mean more than just what product or stock to buy. Activists, artists, writers, and other cultural workers are a part of such a project. Notably, activists have begun to use the Internet to coordinate a network of groups into worldwide protests of multi-national interests.

Two artists reiterate important points. Nancy Paterson's *Stock Market Skirt* (1998) is a humorous but pointed examination of virtual space's effects on even seemingly unrelated parts of our lives. The ebb and flow of the stock market, translated by a computer and mechanical mechanism, raises and lowers the hemline of a skirt as a real time feedback of the activities of the system. But there is no subject, just an old-fashioned dress-dummy, wearing this disembodied dress, no visible agency involved. On the other hand, Regina Frank's performance *Hermes Mistress* (1994–6) depicts an active subject who stitches together fragments of the texts she finds through her laptop, transcribing them into the pattern of her oversized red dress one bead at a time. This subject integrates elements of the electronic space into the fabric of her life, blending age-old technologies with the new and actively editing in the process. The task ahead of her, like the scale of the dress, is immense. It will take time and perseverance and can only be achieved through small, sustained gestures.

In both instances these works suggest the inevitable presence of technology in people's lives, particularly women's lives. Paterson's piece suggests the fickle nature of public investment in the now volatile and less golden stock

Figure 12.6
Regina Frank, *Hermes Mistress*, 1994–6 Spiral, Wacoal Art Centre, Tokyo.
htp://www.regina-frank.de

market. Frank's piece is a poignant image of Haraway's cyborg and the cyber-flâneuse I have suggested. She might also be considered an icon for the only possible embodiment in the virtual space of the Internet. Frank's task mirrors our own attempt to disrupt dominant paradigms and make spaces for ourselves, whether they are physical spaces, virtual spaces, or some combination of both. Only numerous small gestures over time can add up to political change.

NOTES

1   Precise definitions of these terms are not exactly the Internet, but popular use elides them. Cyberspace suggests a larger space mediated by a range of technologies. The information superhighway was originally applied to a specific larger bandwidth media stream proposed by the government.

2   Such artists include Alfredo Jarr, Hans Haacke, Barbara Kruger, Antonio Muntadas, Krzysztof Wodiczko, Repo History, and others. Such art movements as dada, the Situationists, Fluxus, and conceptual art influenced them.

3   An IP address is the unique set of numbers that identifies a computer in the network.

4   Ironically, this decentralized structure and its geographical dispersal make regulation of this space more difficult than a medium like television, although not impossible since it also provides a sophisticated array of mechanisms for surveillance in a technical panopticon.

5   See the *Time* magazine issue on cyberporn from 3 July 1995. The illustrations alone are telling.

6   Elizabeth Grosz (2002) reminds us in her arguments elsewhere in this collection that utopian projects represent the past and the present as if they were the future.

7   A survey from 1998 revealed Internet inhabitants in the US to be 87 per cent white (GUV 1999).

8   An interesting discussion of the technical difficulties of representing languages is addressed in the *New York Times' CyberTimes* essay 'Language: Final Frontier for the True Global Network'. It should also be noted that in picture form, the Internet could also be used to preserve languages that are quickly becoming extinct.

9   The term zine was coined to describe an independently produced magazine. Such independent publications proliferated on the web and came to be called ezines.

10 Don't miss the videotape that documents 'Operation Newspeak', the 1993 media event where the voice boxes on 300 talking Barbies and talking GI Joes were switched and the altered dolls were reverse shoplifted into stores just before Christmas (Barbie Liberation Organization Newsreels, dir. Igor Vamos, 1994; distributed by www.Vtape.ord). It has been broadcast on PBS and seen at many festivals.

11 By the end of 2000, the site was run by a corporation full of men rather than the original women (Heidi Swanson and her sister for the first year) and had lost some of its racier content and catchy tag line.

12 So, of course, RTMark proceeded to sell its tickets to the exclusive artists and bigwigs reception on ebay.

Chapter 13: Frugality and the City

Hanoi Palimpsest

May Joseph

Utopias are sites with no real place.

Foucault

TERROR OF THE HAT

Crisp severe and formal it sat, the cadre hat on the basic wooden table. A sign of a time passing away, token of history's experiment gone awry. Souvenirs of the city stir as kitsch gecko sounds and tube lights spasm. Hip young women cadres in crisp Khaki uniforms and an almost casual air about them attend arrivals at Hanoi airport. I had heard about the forbidding array of armed, sunglassed and uniformed cadres but was unprepared for this disarming entourage of immigration apparatchiks. Their rigid hats by their side on the table made communist

Figure 13.1
Ma May St (Rattan St),
Old Quarter.
Photo: Geoffrey Rogers

paraphernalia look chic and almost a flavour-of-the-day trend that belonged to the streets of SoHo. This striking presence of women cadres as representatives of the state at immigration checkpoints is symptomatic of a trend that is visible along the class spectrum of Hanoi's public spaces. Fashionable working women, students, workers, peasants, hip teens, middle-class women all partake of the daily workings of the city.

The people of the city meet you before the city does, in a teeming flow of socialist modernity. Scooters, cyclos, minibuses, bicycles, pedestrians. Dreams deferred. Khmer towers, Cham balustrade and Soviet architecture unfold a flat city transforming. The heightened presence of women commuters on the streets of Hanoi catch my eye. Women on two-wheelers with kids standing in front, women with large bundles of goods on the front and back of scooters, women with their mothers on the back and baggage in front, women on mopeds and bikes, the city of Hanoi is a hum in motion, afloat in speed and change. The roar of the scooter engines cumulatively create a sphere of noise and drone in keeping with the city's surging thrust forward. No one here is looking back. The fix is on the future.

Uncle Ho's conservatism on clothing for the nation has given way to adventure and style for women on the street. Fashion has never been more important, with tight SoHo flared pants and strapped tops with the bra-straps showing. Impossibly daring shoes occasionally shock amidst the largely sensible display of footwear.

Social change begins with the feet, and this is what the shoe stores seem to be saying, as innovative designs of balsam wood shoes and extraordinarily inventive platform shoes stare at passersby in the old quarter. Straps, heels, wedges, pumps, slides, spikes, boots, clogs. Reinventing the flatness of the city,

Figure 13.2
Hang Bong St (Cotton St),
Old Quarter.
Photo: Geoffrey Rogers

Figure 13.3
Hang Dau St (Beans St),
Old Quarter.
Photo: Geoffrey Rogers

these plastic and wooden vehicles of mobility arrest my gaze. Hanoi is a city discovering a passion for foot adornments. Its streets pulse with the throb of intensity.

THE CITY BETWEEN THE RIVERS

The aura of Hanoi is rooted in the myth of resistance. A fishing and agricultural village by about 2000 BCE, 'The City Between The Rivers', Ha-Noi emerges by the eleventh century as a city of dykes with the given name of Thang Long (Soaring Dragon) with roots as a regional capital from the third century BCE. The ruins of Co Loa Citadel are an evocative reminder of the dramatic defeat of the Chinese in 218 BCE by a local military leader whose famed victory imbues Hanoi with its legendary aura as a historic city of resistance against foreign invaders.

The contemporary city of old Hanoi is the remnant of the Market Town of Thang Long, which was located outside the Royal City, and known as the Commoner's City or 'Kinh Thanh'. Old Hanoi is structured around the ceremonial lake of Hoan Kiem, with the Ho Tay (West Lake) and Song Hong (Red River) framing it to the north and east, the To Lich River to the west, and a number of lakes stretching south. An eleventh-century anonymous description of the ancient capital describes its topography as resembling 'a coiled dragon or a crouching tiger' (Sidel 1998: 1–4).

Despite its watery location, the contemporary historic city has the condensed structure of an inland feudal city, whose imagination is centred south towards the ceremonial lake rather than on all sides towards its watery borders. One of the older cities in Indo-China, Hanoi bears the mapping of many similar cities traumatized by colonial occupation. Its geography moves from the internal logic of mercantile trading zones of the old quarter to the artificially imposed grid-like structure of modern Hanoi designed by the French between 1884 and the early twentieth century, to the post-revolutionary Vietnamese aesthetic which organizes the rest of Hanoi with the heavy hand of Soviet planning and architecture embossed upon the city's visage through the design of Ho Chi Minh's Mausoleum, the redesign of Ba Dinh Square, and the Soviet–Vietnamese Friendship Cultural Palace.

The avenues of Pho Tran Tien, Pho Hai Ba Trung, Pho Ly Thuong Kiet and Pho Tran Hung Dao remain tactile legacies of the French grandiose vision of a colonial Hanoi for French functionaries begun in 1884 that made little concession to native logics and imaginations. These four boulevards mark the horizontal axis of the former French concession, with Pho Tran Tien demarcating the segregated boundary of the 'native city' of Thang Long to the north. As Gwendolyn Wright elaborates, the arrival of the Beaux-Arts-trained architect Ernest Hebrard in 1921 initiated a new phase of French colonial architecture in Indo-China. Hebrard's loose conception of a federated Indo-China, a colonial invention, inspired him to eclectically mix Buddhist, Hindu, Khmer, Confucian, Japanese Shinto and other elements from different regional and national traditions, ignoring the cultural and religious specificity of the decorative motifs and structuring logics being incorporated. His imprint on Hanoi with the construction of the Ministry of Finance (1927), the Institut Pasteur (1930), and the Museum of the École Française d'Extrême-Orient (1931) demonstrates his search for a new semantics in colonial French architecture. These experiments disregard indigenous architec-tural forms while arguing for a new regionally specific French urban design that assimilates its 'Asian' locale (Wright 1991: 207).

Critical to Hanoi's future was the fact that Hebrard had no interest in indigenous urban traditions. He ignored the architectural vernacular of existing Asian cities such as Hanoi. Hebrard's vision for Hanoi included the massive relo-cation of the city's natives to peripheral worker's towns mostly across the Red River, leaving the centre open for French development. The segregationist logics of French urban planning fortuitously left the surviving City of Thirty-Six Streets largely intact. Hebrard's disinterest in attempting to understand how the system of streets (*pho*) worked within the indigenous city led the French to tear down the protective walls of the Commoner's City to create the artificial semblance of a unified but segregated Hanoi (Wright 1991: 206–10).[1]

The eleventh-century Commoner's city was organized into guilds (*phuong*) and streets (*pho).* The *phuong* functioned as an urban district, providing civic and administrative services. Streets or *pho* were organized by trades, particularly in the area known as the thirty-six guild streets within the Commoner's City. For one who meanders through the bustling streets of the City of Thirty-Six Streets in the summer of 2000, the minutiae of detail floods the field of vision as move-ment, human activity and everyday life unfold on the antique sidewalks of the eleventh-century trading city. People gather on the corner of streets by sidewalk cafés for snacks and communal meals. Women in transit to the marketplace carry loads of fruit and vegetables in hanging baskets balanced intricately on either side of their shoulders. Children cycle to school, deftly manoeuvring the dense traffic. Plants on bicycles driven by women en route to the florists, pink upholstered cyclos jostling pedestrians, scooters and cycles. The ear sees and the eye blurs, as a suffusion of bi-pedal intensity and dense living draws the traveller into a place of habitation filled with the machinations of a throbbing Asian city. Food smells and intense sounds interrupted by the roar of two-wheeled transport creates a moving theatre of sensations at once distinctly grounded in this particular city, and simultaneously invoking the comforting mnemonic trace of other trading cities traversed, Cochin, Mombasa. Dense, seductive, intoxicating.

Hanoi is a city of historical junctures, colonial and postcolonial, utopian and modernist, nationalist and postmodernist. A portal to understanding the logic of simultaneity and interconnectedness that shaped socialist cities like Dar es Salaam, Cairo, Dakar and Sarajevo, the city bears the scars of its violent modernity in ways reminiscent of strategically important medieval cities transformed by their brutal histories of feudal, colonial and nationalist struggles. Poignantly caught in the threshold space of what were formerly imagined as 'Second World cities', Hanoi's visage embodies the performance of frugality, where political figures, ideologies and strategic location of place as a city of resistance combined to create specific utopic sites. It is a quickly transitioning monument to the movements of scarcity and frugality that shaped a sphere of modernity during the twentieth century.

THE FRUGAL CITY

For socialist cultures of the last century, the frugal city bears a special place in the Second World imaginary. It is a city filled with the ghosts of its history, and the spectres of 'ours' – that is, of the First World. The frugal city was a utopic city, what Foucault calls 'a site with no place'. It was the space of the ideological phantasmatic, a city quietly resilient in its conviction to survive all odds.

A city of fragments – Hanoi is such a utopic city, lacerated by its dystopic realization. Repressed, buoyant, resilient, seductive, restrained, proud, Hanoi demands submission to be read. For the itinerant traveller, only an epidermal reading of Hanoi's layered history is possible. There are the clearly delineated spaces of the transitioning modernist capital city where the space of trade, the space of health and the space of the nation are geographically and somatically intertwined by the trace of the ancient city. Today's old quarter is the vestige of the former marketplace or Commoner's City, while the area around Ho Chi Minh's Mausoleum marks the borders of the ancient citadel walls, now marked by the solitary One Pillar Pagoda.

Then there are the more inchoate triggers of perception that cities like Hanoi allow the traveller as new buildings and roads are built over the ashes of old. It is the familiarity of having traversed a similar layered landscape of historic past and surging modernity in another space and time. Of having come of age amidst the vestiges of a changing economy in another continent, as transitioning political ideologies collide. The visual signs of fervent entrepreneurialism most embodied by Ho Chi Minh City juxtaposed with obsolete forms of communal farming remind me of Tanzanian and Indian transformations towards agrarian modernization. The circumspect commercialism surrounded by a revitalizing sphere of individual entrepreneurial spirit is exciting after the jaded greed of New York City's Wall Street. Old-fashioned communal generosity encounters capitalist drive in ways that are lost forever in the suburban sprawl of America. Yet, 'America' looms large as Vietnam's sign of the modern, as Vietnamese–Americans like the Los Angeles-based Alain Tan return to Vietnam with entrepreneurial innovations in fast food, such as the protean noodle dish, the 'Pho', described as the Vietnamese answer to McDonalds (*Saigon Times* 2000: 23; *Saigon Times Weekly* 1999: 423).

Frugality in the twentieth century was mobilized within the now defunct imagined space of First, Second, and Third World as a structuring concept that simultaneously expressed the different ends of the spectrum of expenditure. In the United States it was mobilized through the aesthetics of 1930s Depression, 1950s minimalism, the international oil crisis of the 1970s, and the ecological and environmental movements, invoking images of a depleted earth in the interests of planetary sustainability. Socialist experiments such as the Fourierist-inspired utopic housing projects like Brook Farm in Massachusetts and Red Bank in New Jersey in architecture, minimalism and solo performance in the realm of cultural practice, combined with vegetarianism and recycling, marked this self-conscious move toward a selective frugality through lifestyle choices in the United States.

But the structuring logic of a three-world system which shaped relationships of exchange in cities like Cairo, Dar es Salaam, Vientiane and Hanoi during the colonial period of the first half of the twentieth century, and later the Cold War, operated under a different logic of frugality. Colonial exploitation of local and national resources was followed by postcolonial attempts at failed utopic social engineering. For emerging states crippled by the history of colonialism, socialist and communal forms of social organizing offered a radical reconceptualization of power, society and space on what appeared to be modern and utopic terms. These reformist-turned-totalitarian experiments offered a way out of feudal, monarchical and tribal forms of social organization. Socialism was a means of addressing a post-independence transition crisis. The postcolonial city offered a heretofore unknown space for modern self-invention to 'indigenous' subjects. It also brought, along with its modernizing regimes of control and policing, new forms of surveillance, fear and conformity – often etched onto the façade of the city. For Hanoi, as for Asian cities like Djakarta, Eastern European cities like Riga or the former East Berlin, the physical layout of the capital city mirrored the ideology of the state (Kusno 2000: 49–70). Socialist housing, public monuments and statues of Lenin and Ho commemorating the communist state

Figure 13.4
Lenin Park, Hanoi.
Photo: Geoffrey Rogers

and its citizens delineated the horizontal perspective of the main transportation arteries and junctures linking the medieval city to the colonial city and the post-revolutionary city in Hanoi.

Frugality as a state policy and self-reliance as a logic of physical culture deployed through youth camps, state holidays and national parades, institution-alized the utopian ideal of socialist transformation and materialized it as coercive, dystopic social control. Drawing upon communist and Confucian philosophies of frugality, whereby mass education and self-subsistence became the vehicles for redistributing resources by the state, Vietnam went the path of utopic social organizing, followed shortly after by Kerala and Tanzania, among other utopic experiments. Hanoi, Trivandrum and Dar es Salaam were in a space of simultaneous imaginings, parallel laboratories of utopic organizing unfolding through varying degrees of instrumental rationalization.

While these now historically defunct and socially catastrophic experiments have proven to be colossal travesties with far-reaching human consequences, the spheres of social imagining metabolized within these societies are only beginning to be articulated. The urban expressions of such state ideologies of frugality produced particular experiences of twentieth-century modernity. Socialist cities such as Dar and Dakar in Africa, Sarajevo in the former Yugoslavia and Vientiane in Laos, link the International Style with Marxist urban planning in the Second World space of the mid twentieth century. Often marked by postwar socialist housing, signs of urban decay, eroding residential buildings, and nineteenth-century graciousness converted into twentieth-century overcrowded housing, these cities bore an aura of frugality through the public staging of urban neglect.

The frugal city, the city that combined mass housing with minimal expenditure, redefined Bauhaus style as proletarian. The minimalism of Bauhaus merged with the frugality of socialist policies and generated a new post-independence framework of uniform housing that was rational, devoid of character, and productivity-driven. The resulting mushrooming of mass housing in the form of micro-cities such as the Tanzanian '*ujamaa* village' became a sign of modernization in Second World cities. It generated new perceptual frameworks of frugality in relation to efficiency, economic need and aesthetic minimalism.

Frugality was an international modernist project, linking structures of modernity from Havana to Hanoi, from Chandigarh to Zanzibar (Bissell 1999).[2] Its aesthetic springs from the conjunction of a three-world system and a bi-polar logic of excess or scarcity, capitalism or socialism that structured the Cold War era. Operating on a transnational logic, frugality manifested the negative side of expenditure, the alternative economy to spending, the underbelly of conspicuous consumption. Frugality and nationalism linked rhetorics in the modern city, as rights to the city and rights of the individual merged with interests within public policy. Less space, more housing. Less horizontal expansion, more verticality. Less spending, more thrift. These dictums worked on either side of the capitalist/socialist divide and gave way to more complex networks of privatization and gentrification, complicating the relationship between less and more.

Frugality emerges as a set of relations of exchange, between abstinence, enjoyment and expenditure as well as a structuring logic between states. In the United States, frugality became linked in the mid twentieth-century with a notion of restraint, quiet wealth, old money and measured expenditure that denoted expendable capital, and assumed specific historic relations to the production and censorship of pleasure in the modern American city. To consume through elaborate expenditure of vision and aurality opened up newer fields of consumption than the mere exchange of money would permit. Modern cities such as New York come to embody new forms of austerity, simultaneously visual (modernist minimalism), tactile and visceral. The arrogant skyline of steel, glass and concrete in conjunction with the modern grid of streets permitted new forms of social life where the banker and the street vendor, the real estate mogul and the homeless coexist in a maelstrom of change. The frugal becomes an obsessive condition as insatiable desire and the ability to consume vicariously distorts the cycle of urban need marked as the sign of 'America'.

On a different visual register from the verticality of Manhattan's minimalism, the horizontal frugality of Hanoi's visage is a set of social and psychic practices determined by the extraordinary history of resistance and revolution that has shaped the geography of this city's imagination. It hovers around Hanoi like a tangible presence, embossed on people's bodies, faces, the physiognomy of the city. Soviet modernist architecture, Indian-made trains, 1930s French urban planning, 1950s experiments in suburban sprawl, Buddhist minimalism, Communist restraint and austerity propelled by Five-Year plans and an increasingly beleaguered economy.

CITY OF THE SENSES

On the Street of China Bowls, the cock crows a foetid dawn, as comforting sounds of the street sweeper scraping the refuse of yesterday's excess, leaves, plastic, paper and mortality, echo off the intimate streets of the City of Thirty-Six Streets. A little girl takes her first bicycle ride as women on bicycles, long coats and conical hats weave their way through cool damp roads, where satellites atop eroding rooftops beam dreams of France and Hollywood, odourless fantasies, grasped in the stronghold of greed and gluttony, consumptive desire in its ecstatic trance, self-devouring.

Paper devotions, embers of wealth, lie resplendent in commodities of appeasement on Hang Ma Street or the Street of Ghost Money. Here, a candle for graceless death at the corner of the street make paper ghosts a respite for bodies that cannot be retrieved. Incense, red candlesticks and cardboard mausoleums on Hang Quat Street (Fan Street) offer solace for loss and desire as unspoken dreams drift in the myriad lights of smoke and fragrance. Silver and red tinsel monuments burn reminders of troubled spirits and reconciled souls. Fragrant vapours suffuse Thuoc Bac Street (The Street of Herbal Medicine), as herbs, seeds, twigs, leaves and traditional medicines arrest one's olfactory senses. Vermilion, magenta, fuchsia and saffron silks drape the store fronts of Hang Gai Street (Silk Street), rousing the skin to a panoply of colour and texture. Fine laquerware and ornate paintings lure one's eye.

The old quarter hugs the north-eastern part of The City Between The Rivers like a medulla oblongata (Sidel 1998: 4). It is distinctly medieval in its non-gridded compressed labyrinth of winding streets and alleys and remains a mnemonic link between the historic and the modern, a palimpsest of multiple spatial frameworks and temporal materializations. Now an eclectic mix of commodities and desires, the City of Thirty-Six Streets was built as a commercial and residential centre on the periphery of the forbidden city for the commoners as well as for soldiers and administrators of the Royal palace during its eleventh-century emergence. The market town continues to link the different trades, commodities and services in an ever-changing network of relations of exchange. Called the *cité indigène* during the French colonial occupation, the old city bears residues of its former trading economies and artisan commodities such as Han Muoi (The Street of Salt) and Hang Bac (The Street of Silversmiths). These trade and artisan logics have transitioned with forms of modern consumption from old trades of bamboo, rattan, hemp and cotton to new trades of plastic, aluminium, polyester and Internet cafés. Old trades give way to new desires. Hang Bong or The Street of Cotton now sells art, plastic and electronics, while Chan Cam or the Street of Stringed Instruments sells art, tourist bric-a-brac and some musical instruments.

The City of Thirty-Six Streets demands a reworking of space on a more compressed human scale of movement, rather than the modernist, grid-like spaces determined by the size of the automobile that circumvents this medieval space of mercantile logic. It is a self-enclosed universe of dense social life that offers an alternative structure of daily life to the rest of the pulsing city. Tight-knit social spaces generate compact multipurpose public uses. Here, tailors, launderers, shoemakers, hair dressers, restaurateurs, confectioners, bakers, beauticians, fish mongers, fruit vendors, and herbalists work and live within the same space, proliferating the possible distractions in this revitalizing city of the senses. Tube-like dwellings create intense proximities (Sidel 1998: 55).[3]

The verticality of this space allows for at least four levels of everyday activities – the street, the pavement, the rooftops and the fourth interiorized space of everyday social activity. Across the rooftops of the old quarter, space expands in a myriad of uses, roof gardens, clotheslines, balconies of children's paraphernalia. The solitary bombed-out hull of a rooftop remains a lingering reminder of a violent hovering past. A girl stretches in languorous ease in the searing light of dawn. These dense outer spaces offer an array of public social life that complements life on the streets, where corner eateries, cafés and street level hang-out joints allow for a variety of informal gathering points on the street. The smell of roasting fish wafts across the cool of the Hanoi night on Cha Ca Street (Street of Roasted Fish). Shadows linger in the curves of the tree-lined streets as women of the market return, now unburdened of their baskets heavy with watercress, mint and scallions, local economies, fast disappearing.

LAKE OF MEMORY

Shaped like a fluid heart, the expanse of serene water called the Hoan Kiem Lake stretches south of the old quarter. It borders the southern most streets of the old city like a blue gauze, thick with memory and history. The centrality of this immensity of water to the city's imagining is marked by its few remaining historic monuments marking the city's struggle for sovereignty. The Tortoise Pagoda in the middle of the lake is crowned symbolically with a single red star; the Ngoc

Figure 13.5
Hoam Kiem Lake, Hanoi.
Photo: Geoffrey Rogers

Son Temple (Jade Mountain), an eighteenth-century construction located at the northern part of the lake and accessible by the red wooden Rising Sun Bridge, imbues the lake with a ceremonial memory of sovereignty and health. The Ngoc Son Temple resonates as an anti-colonial sign of the victory of the Vietnamese against the Mongols in the thirteenth century. The temple is also dedicated to the patron saint of physicians, La To, concretizing the plethora of uses to which the inhabitants of this city put this span of water.

From morning till dusk the Lake of the Restored Sword is a space of healing, an intense physical inhabitation. Hoan Kiem lies serene amidst the young trees and new concrete park structures of the urban *corniche*. It is a space filled with multiple crossings, old and new, fraught and passionate. As dawn rises early morning, the elderly engage in qui gong, others practice Tai Chi, the young involve in physical exercise, some jog and others push hands. Some meditate, others walk or sit and chat. In the afternoon, groups of men play checkers or gamble huddled by the stone balustrades, while food vendors, herbalists, paper vendors, T-shirt vendors, fruit sellers, retired army officers, women with weighing scales, street children and groups of young men stroll, wander, saunter or sit on the stone benches. Meditation, romance, play, intrigue, camaraderie, all unfold around the periphery of this magnetic sweep of water.

A space born of legend, the lake is the heart of reunified Vietnam. It grounds Hanoi geographically and is the mythic originary space of modern Vietnamese nationalist identity. Legend goes that with the help of magical sword received from the celestial skies, the fifteenth-century ruler Le Loi drove the invading Chinese out of Vietnam. After the reclamation of the city, a giant turtle is said to have risen out of the depths of Hoan Kiem Lake and reclaimed the heavenly weapon from the King.

FORGETTING HO

It is said that Ho Chi Minh never wanted to be buried or hagiographed. He explicitly requested that he be cremated and his ashes spread so that the impulse to deify would not be there (Sidel 1998: 61). But the city of Hanoi bears the burden of Ho's fear, that he would be mummified and made monumental. Like Walter Benjamin, Ho was profoundly opposed to monumentality. He dreaded petrification, as the master of strategy and vigilant protean self-invention. Dead monuments and archaic forms of devotion embodied the excesses of accumulation, and emancipation lay in freeing the state from static manifestations of capital.

Figure 13.6
Hang Bong St (Cotton St),
Old Quarter.
Photo: Geoffrey Rogers

Ho Chi Minh's Mausoleum is a monstrously unfrugal tribute that is at once stultifying, bizarre and unnerving. Its Soviet-designed realization is in contradiction with the graceful lines of Ho's own house on stilts, which he preferred to the Presidential residence while in Hanoi. Ho's own simple aesthetic of bamboo and wood clashes with the cold remoteness of the marble mausoleum that houses the earthly remains of this most protean of revolutionaries. Wrapping its way silently around the inarticulate monument, an astounding serpentine trail of people arrests one's gaze. The unforgettable and infectious power of thousands of people standing in humble veneration to pay their respects to a serene effigy of revolution begs a reconsideration of the power of freedom to fire the imagination of people of Vietnam today. This space of secular pilgrimage is peopled by a remarkable range of devotees, a moving and powerful testament to the inspiring power of a frugal man who defied the limits of possibility. From peasants from the provinces and travellers from the interior, to hip students from southern cities dressed inappropriately in tight shorts and high heels, the winding line of respectful travellers transforms the banality of waiting to an exercise in national reification, where the space of the nation and the line of people in waiting converge in a momentary enactment of national belonging. This is a utopic imagined space of nationness on the move. And yet, it is simultaneously a deadly ossified space of the death of freedom embodied by the static monumentality of the carceral architecture of Soviet modernism.

The event of visiting this dead space of the imagined nation is a contradictory one. It contrasts the live nationalist sentiments and devotion of peoples across generations with the monumental ennui of dead architecture. People move in attitudes of curious deference, winding their way across the cold cryptic spaces of the eerie mausoleum. Static monumentality devours the macro-scale human motion of people lined up to pay their respects to the mummified representation of modern Vietnam's architect. The event is at once a process of forgetting Ho and marvelling at one of the last extraordinary public performances of modern nationalist sentiment – the voluntary and involuntary veneration of a national hero as tourist site, a vestigial spectacle of the last century.

NOTES

1   Hebrard's arrival in Indochina in 1921 initiated a whole era of colonial architectural experimentation in the main cities of Indochina. His city plans for cities like Hanoi, Saigon, Phnom Penh and Haiphong disregarded the structure of the existing indigenous cities.

2   Bissell argues for the category of 'historic' to be assigned to the area of Ng'ambo, Zanzibar, where the East German inspired low-income housing projects of Michenzani pose the visual and conservationist problem of how to designate specific areas as historic. He points out that socialist modernism has not yet become a commodity of marketable nostalgia.

3 The distinctive 'tube houses' of old Hanoi are long and narrow constructions, two to four metres wide and two stories tall. These residences are fronted by a shop facing the street. The middle rooms contain manufacturing or assembly facilities while the interior spaces are residential domestic quarters. Some of these 'tube houses' were originally built with small inner courtyards, sometimes enhanced by water pools or fountains.

Chapter 14: Against Utopia

The Romance of Indeterminate Spaces

Elizabeth Wilson

In her first published novel, *Under the Net* (1954), Iris Murdoch wrote that 'some parts of London were necessary and some were contingent' (1982 [1954]: 24). This was a philosophical in-joke of the period, but when I first read it, it seemed to me to represent a profound truth not only about London but about all great cities. At the time – I first came across the novel when I was an undergraduate – I believed that the 'necessary' parts of London – the old, central districts of Soho and the Law Courts, the sophisticated shopping streets in Knightsbridge, and the gracious parks and romantic residential districts such as Hampstead and Maida Vale – represented its essence. The contingent parts – suburbs, industrial estates, rubbish tips, railway sidings, dead ends, unused bits of land – were not the 'real' London. When travelling abroad, the parts of cities a tourist had to traverse before reaching the centre were even more contingent and one must mentally bracket them off in order to enjoy to the full the impact of the 'essential' city. The planless mess around Paris, the industrial wasteland of Mestre before crossing the lagoon to Venice, the suburbs of Amsterdam, were unfortunate accidents on the way to the transcendental experience that was the truth of these cities.

The search for the 'necessary' city is part of the operation of what John Urry has termed the 'tourist gaze'. As he points out, 'the gaze is constructed through signs . . . "the tourist is interested in everything as a sign of itself. . . . All over the world the unsung armies of semioticians, the tourists, are fanning out" ' (Urry 1995: 133) in search of the 'necessary' experience, the experience, that is, that is adequate to its imaginary anticipation. Urry suggests that 'it is not the pedestrian flâneur who is emblematic of modernity but rather the train-passenger, car driver and jet plane passenger' (Urry 1995: 134). In fact, though, the majority of journeys *to* tourist destinations are produced as non-events, while wandering around the cathedral on foot is 'the real thing'. This is particularly true of journeys by air, since both in airway terminals and during the flight itself, everything conceivable is done to give the impression that nothing is happening at all. On the plane, although the passenger is en route from departure point to destination, there is *nothing* in between, the journey itself is a kind of limbo. The whole journey is 'contingent'; it is the 'historic quarter', the 'old city', that is the necessary object of desire.

Only many years later did I come to understanding that this selective tourist gaze represented a very restricted view of what a city is. What Iris Murdoch meant by the 'necessary' parts of cities have increasingly become those parts that are cleansed, sanitized and rearranged for the delectation of the tourist gaze. François Maspero, in his book of a journey through the *banlieux* of Paris, *Roissy Express*, suggested the 'real', living Paris now resided in precisely the despised and even dangerous peripheral estates, suburbs and shanty town surrounding a core Paris that, he said, has been wholly 'Disneyfied'.

The idea that I might choose the – in Iris Murdoch's terms – 'contingent' aspects of the urban to write about explicitly first came to me during a train journey from Brighton to London. During the latter part of the journey the train snakes round the back parts of Southwark, Bermondsey, the City of London and Blackfriars on its way to King's Cross: a journey through some very old parts of the metropolis, which have been destroyed and rebuilt many times. The viaduct passes over these areas and as it does so the traveller catches sight of the backs of many different buildings, both important and obscure. There are glimpses of alleys, decayed pubs and offices, new apartment blocks, old warehouses and even a few remaining bomb sites left from the Second World War. The bird's-eye view from the railway line above the urban maze reveals the way in which these buildings have accumulated like geological strata, sedimented one on the other, so that the sight provides an awareness of a city almost organically developing over time: the Blitz still visible over the Edwardian world of pubs and dockers and tenements; this landscape in turn covers a still faintly discernible Dickensian world, the world of *Our Mutual Friend*, his late novel which begins in this area with an eerie scene of a scavenger dredging the Thames for dead bodies; and beneath all this, traces even of the medieval world still survive. Then the train suddenly breaks free from this agglomeration of buildings to cross the Thames with a panoramic view of St Paul's cathedral and the new skyscrapers of the financial mile.

Originally I wanted to call this essay 'The Backs of Buildings', and I even planned to make a video of the journey – until I realised that Patrick Keiller's *London* was such a film on a much larger and more imaginative scale than I could ever have achieved. Then, though, I found a flyer for an exhibition which announced itself as a project about 'non-places' and invited its readers to send in their own accounts of non-places – such as underpasses – in which they had had what they felt to be a significant experience. This made me think about the meaning of 'non' or indeterminate places and spaces, and the significance – to me – of the journey through the back lands of inner south London, a journey which had given me a more intimate awareness of the history of London than the well-known vista across the Thames to St Paul's.

An interest in the obscure, forgotten, hidden parts of the great cities of modernity is not new. These lost corners had an enormous romantic charm for the flâneurs of the nineteenth century. Writers such as Dickens, Baudelaire and his friend Alexandre Privat d'Anglemont provided a counter-chorus to the reformers and planners who wished to reshape the city and thereby to banish dirt, disease and crime. Indeed Dickens and, to some extent, Privat d'Anglemont spoke at different times with both voices.

An interest in these spaces, which have been termed interstitial spaces, may represent a rejection of or at least a suspicion of urban space as utopia. I would acknowledge, however, that the term 'utopian' may be used in more than one way. The utopianism I particularly reject is that of literary utopias – from Thomas More onwards – all of which have tended towards the authoritarian in their prescriptions for every detail of life, so that the cities they envisaged became merely a part of a much grander plan for human economic, social and cultural life. No part of human experience was to left unregulated in the majority of these plans. Above all, *nothing was hidden* in utopia. Historically, utopias have been barren of secrets and of anything resembling an alternative world. Françoise Choay in her book *The Rule and the Model* (1997 [1980]) demonstrated that historical architectural treatises closely resembled utopian literature, and this was certainly true of Le Corbusier in *The Radiant City* and other works, in which life was to become perfectly regulated among eugenic and rational lines.

To me, therefore, on the basis of my reading of this literature, and also on the basis of visits I have made to model villages in England, the utopian concept is a largely negative one. To reject utopia outright does nevertheless presents a dilemma because a rejection of utopias can easily turn into a rejection of planning per se, especially given the problems of the high-rise projects in the postwar period which were, at least to some extent, equated or associated with Le Corbusian and other utopian ideas, often of a socialist nature. Yet I am not opposed to planning; planning is the search for urban solutions. Plans that are put into practice often represent a compromise between conflicting views or needs, and democratic planning, which takes into account the views and wishes of local communities, is an incredibly laborious and long drawn-out process, but a very necessary one. It is important therefore to differentiate the exploration of indeterminate spaces both from some postmodern celebration of the fragmentary and from a post-Marxist rejection of planning. So planning is necessary and indeed desirable, yet there is a part of me that resents the fact that it at least seems to leave so little room for the unexpected – in other words, the *unplanned*. How can one reconcile the need for an ordered and liveable environment with this need for the spontaneous? For this spontaneity is also necessary; it is often in these unnoticed places that creativity occurs.

There is a second use of the term 'utopian', in which it appears not as prescriptive rigidity, but rather as a gesture towards the intimation of other alternative or redemptive possibilities in our chaotic contemporary world and contemporary cities. In this use it has a visionary aspect; it is about aspiration rather than perfectibility. However, it is still not quite the right term for the interstitial places of *unspecified possibility* that I wish to describe.

What are 'non-places', interstitial or indeterminate spaces? The panorama of the backs of buildings from Blackfriars to King's Cross is the wrong side of the fabric of the city, a hidden and secret aspect of urban life where traces of former worlds and lives may be found. It is in spaces like these that, in Michel de Certeau's words, the dominated weave a language as they make a path through the city, or their fragment of the city, the place in which they 'poach' on the preserves of the powerful and manufacture a silent or surreptitious resistance. Although de Certeau's influential article 'Walking in the City' (1984b) is over-romanticized, it does identify a way in which individuals make their parts of cities their own.

Whereas most theorists distinguish place from space by describing the former as a specific historical and geographic location, as opposed to a space which is abstract and in a sense empty, for de Certeau space is a 'frequented place', 'an intersection of moving bodies'. It is the pedestrians who transform a street into a space – space therefore implying movement and interaction.

Marc Augé, in his book *Non-Places: Introduction to an Anthropology of Supermodernity* (1995), has identified a third kind of location: non-place, or non-places. He writes not of postmodernity but of a 'supermodernity' in which non-places not only become increasingly common but increasingly characteristic. Non-places are spaces such as airports, 'that space outside real time and space' (Maspero 1994: 7) and supermarkets; they are also the relationships such spaces enjoin. They have the peculiarity that they are 'defined partly by the words and texts they offer us: their instructions for use, so to speak' (Augé 1995: 83). Persons in these non-places are meant to interact only with texts; so, for example, the motorway networks of France (or Britain for that matter) no longer pass through towns, but lists of their notable features – indeed whole commentaries – appear on big signboards nearby. 'Motorway travel is thus doubly remarkable: it avoids, for functional reasons, all the principal places to which it takes us; and it makes comments upon them' ('You are now passing historic Poitiers', etc.) (Augé 1995: 97). The same is true of supermarkets, where the shopper wanders around reading texts ('apricots contain calcium'; 'cereals are full of vitamin C'; there are even instructions on how to use unusual ingredients and so forth) which may have relatively little to do with what they actually purchase and later eat.

Augé's non-places are the absolute opposite of the interstitial spaces to which I am referring. Augé's non-places are dystopian, or utopian in a wholly negative sense, in that they are over-determined, totally prescriptive and – at least in the example of the motorway – usually provide an impoverished experience. Interstitial or indeterminate spaces, by contrast, precisely because their purpose is ambiguous or because they are places in between, leading from one more clearly defined place to another, can facilitate imaginative uses by individuals. Thus the flyer, or rather postcard, for the non-places exhibition I mentioned earlier had written on it the following message:

> We are ever increasingly in transit through 'non-places'. Corners that lurk at the edge of
> activity. Passageways where activity occurs but the relationship between use and place
> remains unnamed. Places where names are incidental, meaningless because the need for
> communication – or the passage of time spent – is already deemed to be transient,
> insignificant, minimal, empty. Street corners, bus stops, shopping malls, motorways,
> airport lounges . . .

So, in fact, the anonymous writers or filmmakers of the project merge the two
sorts of space that I have just suggested are polar opposites. They seem to be
looking for a new way in which to articulate another narrative of urban space,
something that is hidden, pre-conscious almost, inarticulate, the secret
experience of the underside of cities. These non-places do not yet have a language. Marc Augé, by contrast, sees the anti-utopia of the non-place as founded
on rhetoric:

> the use of 'basic English' by communications and marketing technologies [and in travel]
> is revealing [because] it is less a question of the triumph of one language over the others
> than of the invasion of all languages by a universal vocabulary [of words such as transit,
> freeway, cashpoint and so on]. What is significant is the need for this generalised
> vocabulary, not the fact that it uses English words. Linguistic enfeeblement . . . is
> attributable more to this generalisation than to subversion of one language by another.
>
> (Augé 1995: 110)

Writers such as Maspero reject the pessimism of this vision of contemporary life.
Zurbrugg (1993: 5) suggests that such pessimism falls into an 'apocalyptic
fallacy', leading to a denunciation of all aspects of postmodern culture.

The novelist Iain Sinclair manages to combine an apocalyptic vision of
London with a relish for the details of the urban landscape, and in his book,
Lights out for the Territory: Nine Excursions into the Secret History of London, he
seeks to excavate some of the meanings of the hidden places or non-places of
the capital. The book begins with a meditation on graffiti writing, which he sees
as a hidden language, 'playful collages of argument and invective, not the publicly displayed, and quietly absorbed papers of the Chinese, but editorials of
madness'. Graffiti, in Sinclair's imagination, constitute an alternative language
bubbling up from the postmodern chaos of the inner city. Everything in the area
he is describing, Hackney, is a fragment: torn bits of posters or newspaper,
amateur advertisement cards in the windows of newsagents, flotsam cast up on
the urban shore, corresponding to the transient lives of immigrants, fugitive East
End criminals, shabby stall holders, Punks, Turkish revolutionaries, Pentecost lists.
And, as he embarks on his walk through the obscurity of the borough, Sinclair
invokes the Situationists and their concept of the dérive or drift. 'The notion', he
writes, 'was to put a crude V into the sprawl of the city, to vandalise dormant
energies by an act of ambulant signmaking. . . . I would transcribe all the pic-
tographs of venom that decorated our near-arbitrary route' (Sinclair 1997: 1). He
would get under the skin of East London in Hackney by cataloguing all the graf-

fiti, every corner shop small-ad and all the sheets of newspaper drifting along the gutters. He would orchestrate them into 'editorials of madness', the unceasing murmur of the dispossessed, the implication being that to notice and record *everything* would be eventually to get at the heart of the hidden city.

Henri Lefebvre's recent writings have explored the experience of the hidden city through what he terms 'Rhythmanalysis' – his way of decoding the language of the urban, which is its sounds: 'Rhythms. Rhythms', he writes in an essay called 'Seen from the Window'. 'They reveal and hide, being much more varied than in music or the so-called civil code of successions, relatively simple texts in relation to the city. Rhythms: music of the city, a picture which listens to itself . . . no camera, no image or sequence of images can show these rhythms' (Lefebvre 1996: 227).

Likewise, Roland Barthes addresses this sense of searching for something unpredictable and unplanned: in *Le Plaisir du Texte* he writes that the reader of a text is looking for jouissance, that orgasmic moment, striven towards but not to be counted upon. As a writer, he too has to look for his reader, without knowing whether he will find him (or her) or where s/he is. 'A space of jouissance is thus created. It is not the reader I need, but the space: the possibility of a dialectic of desire, or an unpredictable jouissance: the knowledge that the dice have not [yet] been thrown, that there is possibility of a game' (Barthes 1994: 1505).

But what has this discussion to do with gender? I find myself more and more resistant to discussing contemporary space in gendered terms, although I am in no doubt of the oppressions that weigh upon the different ethnic and sexual groups and classes of women who in all their diversity inhabit cities. It is as with planning – just as I in no way reject planning and indeed am one of the few who has not turned my back on Marxism and socialism, yet resist the utopianism of planning and its prescriptiveness, so I still have a feminist analysis of women's inequality. Yet I subjectively resist the way in which urban space, from a feminist point of view, tends to be discussed in terms of policy issues, safety, childcare and so on, important as these are – quite apart from being highly relevant to my own and my daughter's lives in the inner city. I no longer want to hear about plans and solutions, because I do not believe we can formulate such ideas until we have heard the susurration of the voices bubbling up from within the hidden city, and understood more about the ways in which so many different kinds of women use the actually existing city.

It seems as if there has been a reversal: through most of modernity it was the masculine voice, the masculine consciousness and the masculine gaze that constructed a utopian vision of city renewal and perfection, with very few exceptions; to women were assigned the domestic, the detailed and to some extent the private or hidden aspects of life. Today, by contrast, is it an accident that all the writers I have cited are men, who search for the hidden secret life of cities (and to some extent, of course, romanticize this search, as Iain Sinclair certainly does), while women emerging into public life are now engaging with large issues of planning, policy and the design of cities?

That is to be applauded – of course it is to be welcomed if women are taking charge of this hugely important aspect of their lives. Yet I return to another favourite quotation, Claude Lévi-Strauss's account of New York in the 1940s: he describes his surprise at finding it to be 'an immense horizontal and vertical disorder ... [and] despite the loftiness of the tallest buildings and the way they were piled up and squeezed together on the cramped surface of an island ... on the edges of these labyrinths the web of the urban tissue was astonishingly slack' (Lévi-Strauss 1987: 261).

It is at these slack edges that the gap in the fabric of the city may be found. The search is for a language – the opposite of the transit lounge language of Augé's non-places – that is adequate to the mystery and uncertainty that is their ever-unfulfilled, romantic promise.

Part VII

Chapter 15: The Time of Architecture

Elizabeth Grosz

How [can] a city engage in philosophy without being destroyed?

(Plato 1974: 497, 153)

What is realized in my history is not the past definite of what was, since it is no more, or even the present perfect of what has been in what I am, but the future anterior of what I shall have been for what I am in the process of becoming.

(Lacan 1977: 86)

The theme of this collection, 'Embodied Utopias', provides me with the opportunity to explore a series of some richly rewarding paradoxes or aporias, which always imply a movement of systems – here systems of reason – beyond their own systematicity, and modes of containment that are unable to quite contain or control that which they draw into their circle of influence. The very title of this collection itself hovers between terms that are tense and uneasy in their relations – and this tension, especially when it expresses itself most acutely in the form of the paradoxical, always provides the strongest of motivations for rethinking categories, terms and assumptions, and for adding complications to perhaps oversimplified frameworks within which those terms were thought. Utopias are the spaces of fantasmatically attainable political and personal ideals, the projection of idealized futures; embodiment, though, is that which has never had its place within utopias. It is not clear whether the phrase, 'embodied utopias', is an oxymoron or not! In this chapter, I want to look at the productive (and perhaps impossible) relations between utopias and embodiment, which link together some elements of architectural discourse and practice (a tradition I know only as an interested outsider) with the political and theoretical concerns of postmodern feminism. I believe that this amalgam of interests – feminist, political, architectural, corporeal – converge on a focal point that has tended to be elided in the history of Western thought, the question of time and futures. So although architecture will be my (perhaps too indirect) object, it will be time that will prove to be my subject.

THE UTOPIC

Discourses of utopia have been with us since the advent of Western philosophy. Plato's *Republic* and *The Laws*, which foreshadow and anticipate Aristotle's *Politics*, provides the basis or ground for the more modern forms that utopic discourses, those structured around ideal forms of political organization, will take in the West. What is significant, and bitterly ironic, about Plato's formulation of the ideal social and political organization is his understanding that the *polis*, the city–state, should be governed by philosopher–kings, under the domination of an order imposed by reason. Like the orderly body, the city–state functions most ably under the rule of reason, the regime of wisdom, for the well-ordered *polis,* like the well-ordered body, operates most harmoniously only in accordance with the dictates of pure reason, and the contemplation of the eternal. This is the basis of Plato's claim that the guardians, rulers of the Republic, need to be those most skilled in reason and the love of truth, yet also tested in the world for their moral character. Their theoretical or abstract reason must be put to the test of worthy concrete practices:

> [N]o perfect city or constitution, and equally no perfect individual, would ever come to be until these philosophers, a few who are not wicked but are now said to be useless, are compelled by chance, whether they wish it or not, to take charge of the city and that city is compelled to obey them.
>
> (Plato 1974: 499b, 155)

More recognizable as a 'modern' template of the utopic than the philosophical oligarchy Plato theorized should rule over the ideal republic is Thomas More's 1516 text, *Utopia*, which is, among other things, a complex and ambivalent sixteenth-century 'treatise on the best constitution of a republic', as More himself describes it. Utopia is the name of an island, which comprises an insulated and relatively self-contained community, space and economy, surrounded by a calm sea; and the people who inhabit this island. Access by foreigners and especially invaders is difficult, for the Utopians are protected by a perilous and rocky harbour, which requires their navigational aid for ships to be safe, guaranteeing the island against the dangers of uninvited entry. The sea that surrounds the island forms an inlet, an interior lake or harbour, a calm and windless space, surrounded and thus protected by dangerous rocks. The harbour inside the island reflects an internalized version of the sea surrounding it, almost like an interiorized mirror representation of its exterior. This calm, harmonious integration is exhibited not only in the climate and location, the geography, of the island, but also in its political organization, its devotion to solemn self-regulation, to the egalitarian distribution of goods, and to modesty, diligence and virtue. Its geography complements, and perhaps enables, its political organization. If the calm harbour reflects the serenity of the sea, the sea functions as emblem of political harmony, for the Utopians live in the best form of commonwealth, though one with its own terrible costs, the intense constraints on personal freedom that seem characteristics of all social contract theorists.

Long recognized as a perplexing and paradoxical enterprise, More's text, like Plato's, involves the postulate of a rationally organized society, which is fundamentally egalitarian in organization,[1] being founded on the notion of communal rather than private property, and collective rather than individual self-interest. This ideal commonwealth, which many claim anticipated the modern welfare state, is also, perhaps by necessity, rigidly authoritarian, hierarchical and intensely personally restrictive. While no one is homeless, hungry, or unemployed, while gold, silver, gems and other material goods hold no greater value than their use in everyday life (gold, for example, is made into chamber pots!), where all individuals are free to meet all their needs, nevertheless they are rigidly constrained in what they are able or encouraged to do. Personal freedom is highly restricted. Utopians are not free to satisfy their desires: debating politics outside the popular assembly is a capital offence; one must get police permission to travel, and even the permission of one's father or spouse in order to take a walk in the countryside. While extolling the virtues of this idealized culture, 'More', the fictional narrator of the two books comprising *Utopia*, enigmatically ends Book 2 by dissociating himself from many of its customs and laws, claiming them absurd and ridiculous, even though he also claims that many others would be worth importing to Europe.

What is significant for our purposes here, though, is the question that intrigued so many of More's commentators: why did More invent a recognizably flawed ideal? The other, more obvious, alternatives – an idealized representation of a perfect commonwealth; or the satire of a bad one – seem more straightforward options. Why invent a non-ideal, or rather, an equivocal ideal? Why compromise and endanger the idealized dimension of the literary and imaginative project with a realism that explains the necessary conditions and consequences of the production of political ideals?

This dilemma is compressed into the very name of that ideal – Utopia. As noted in the introduction to this collection, More's neologism is linguistically ambiguous, the result of two different fusions from Greek roots: the adverb *ou* – 'not' – and the noun *topos* – 'place': no-place. He is also punning on another Greek composite, *eutopia*, 'happy', 'fortunate' or 'good' place. Many commentators have suggested that this pun signals the ideal, or fictional, status of accounts of the perfect society: the happy or fortunate place, the good place, is no place; no place, that is, except in imagination. I would like to suggest a different reading – not: the good place is no place, but rather, no place is the good place. The utopic is beyond a conception of space or place because the utopic, ironically, cannot be regarded as topological at all. It does not conform to a logic of spatiality.

It is thus conceivable, and perhaps even arguable, that the utopic is beyond the architectural. Insofar as architecture is the domain for the regulation and manipulation of made-spaces and places, insofar as its domain or purview has remained geographical, geological, site-specific, location-oriented – that is, insofar as its milieu is spatialized, in the sense of both localized, as well as conceptualized, only in spatial terms. Architecture remains out of touch with the fundamental movement of the utopic, the movement to perfection or to the ideal, which is adequately conceivable only in the temporal dimension, and above all in the temporal modality of the future.

What Plato, More, and virtually every other thinker of utopia share, though the picture each presents of an ideal society fluctuates and varies immensely according to political ideologies, is this: the utopic is always conceived as a *space*, usually an enclosed and commonly isolated space – the walled city, the isolated island, a political and agrarian self-contained organization, and thus a commonwealth. A self-regulating space, autonomous from, though it may function alongside of and in exchange with, other states and regions. The utopic is definitionally conceived in the topological mode, as a place, a space, a locus with definite contours and features. As Margaret Whitford points out, the utopic perpetually verges on the dystopic, the dysfunctional utopia, the more modern these utopic visions become.[2] The atopic, the inverted other of the utopic and its ghostly dystopic accompaniment, is not a place, but rather, a non-place (in its own way, it too is always *ou*-topic), an indeterminate place, but place and space nevertheless.[3]

This is no doubt why the utopic has been a locus of imagination and invention for architects, as well as for political theorists, activists and fiction writers. But this may also help explain why the architectural imaginary that peoples such utopic visions (descriptions of buildings and municipal arrangements figure quite prominently in Plato's, Aristotle's and More's accounts of ideal political regulation) almost invariably produces an architecture of direct control (architecture as that which directly or neutrally facilitates the subject's control over its political and natural environment), an architecture of immense political inflexibility. Until the dimension of time or duration has an impact in the ways in which architecture is theorized and practised, the utopic, with its dual impossibility and necessity, will remain outside architectural reach, and beyond its effect. The utopic is not that which can be planned and built, for that is to imply that it is already an abstract possibility that merely requires a mode of realization. It mistakes a possibility for a virtuality, a preformed structure for a dynamically and organically developing one. This failure to conceive of utopia as a mode of temporality and thus as a mode of becoming is clearly witnessed in the two large-scale 'artificial' cities planned, designed and built according to an abstract plan – Canberra and Brasilia, neither barely representative of utopic design but both planned as communities supporting a civic and political centre, and thus as cities whose architectural conception would facilitate their functioning as the seat of government. Cities, in other words, that have come as close as possible, in their realization, to the abstract and rational plan that governs philosophical utopias. Ironically, of course, both cities have been long recognized, almost since their inception, as both supremely 'practical', as well as largely unliveable, cities, restricted in their capacity for organic growth and for surprise.

Can architecture construct a better future? How can it do so without access to another notion of time than that of projection and planned development (a time in which the future is fundamentally the same as the past, or increases in some formulaic version of the past)? What could a utopic architecture be, if architecture remains grounded in the spatial alone? How, in other words, is architecture, as theory and as practice, able to find its own place in politics, and, above all, its own place in the unpredictable becoming of the movement of time and duration? How can architecture, as the art or science of spatial organization, open itself up to the temporal movements that are somehow still beyond its domain?

THE FUTURE

If Utopia is the good place that is no place, if utopias, by their very nature, involve the fragile negotiation between an ideal mode of social and political regulation and the cost of this that must be borne by the individuals thus regulated, then it is clear that they involve not only the political and social organization of space and power – which Plato and More have recognized and specifically addressed – but also two elements that remain marked, if unremarked upon, in their works: the notion of time as becoming (the utopic as a dimension of the virtual, an admixture of the latency of the past and the indeterminacy of the future, the mode of linkage between an inert past, conceived as potential, and a future not yet in existence); and a conception of the bodies that are the object of utopic, political and temporal speculations. In short, the utopic cradles in the force field composed of several vectors: its 'strange attractors' are triangulated through three processes or systems: (a) the forces and energies of bodies, bodies which require certain material, social and cultural arrangements to function in specific or required ways, and which in turn, through their structuring, and habitual modes, engender and sustain certain modes of political regulation; (b) the pull or impetus of time, which grants a precedence of the future over the past and the present, and which threatens to compromise or undo whatever fixity and guarantees of progress, whatever planning and organization we seek in the present; and (c) the regulation and organization, whether literary or fantasmatic, or pragmatic, of urban and rural spaces of inhabitation.

This triangulation has been rendered less complicated by the common move of dropping out or eliding one of these three terms – usually that represented by time and becoming. It is significant that the question of the future in and of the Republic, the future of the Utopians, remains unaddressed; utopia, like the dialectic itself, is commonly fantasized as the end of time, the end of history, the moment of resolution of past problems. The utopic organization is conceived as a machine capable of solving foreseeable problems through the perfection of its present techniques. This is the image of an ideal society in which time stops, and, as Plato recognized, the timeless sets it. If we explore the plethora of other utopic visions, from Francis Bacon's *New Atlantis*, to the general project of the social contract theorists in the eighteenth century, to Voltaire, Rousseau's *The New Héloïse*, and *The Social Contract*, through to Hegel's *Phenomenology of Mind*, the ideal society, society in its perfection, is represented as the cessation of becoming, the overcoming of problems, a calm and ongoing resolution. While a picture of the future, the utopic is fundamentally that which *has no future*, that place whose organization is so controlled that the future ceases to be the most pressing concern. These utopias function as the exercise of fantasies of control over what Foucault has called 'the event', that which is unprepared for, unforeseeable, singular, unique and transformative, the advent of something new. Indeed it is precisely this idea of newness, creation or advent that the fantasy of utopia, of a perfect and controlled society, is developed to reassure us against (Foucault 1972). Utopias can be understood as further mechanisms or procedures whose function is precisely to provide reassurances of a better future, of the necessity for planning and preparedness, and rational reflection, in the face of an unknowable future.

What utopic visions, both those developed in the past, and those various visions developed today in science fiction and cinema, share – for very few share contents and specific arrangements, though there are common patterns – is the desire to freeze time, to convert the movement of time into the arrangements of space, to produce the future on the model of the (limited and usually self-serving) ideals of the present. The philosopher Michele Le Doeuff argues that this may explain why so many utopian texts are actually double texts, texts with composites, amalgams, with a self-contained fictional representation, which is explained and justified through a theoretical addendum, commonly a text written after the more speculative and fanciful account. If we look at the history of utopic discourses, we can see that from the beginning, there seems to be a coupling of the fictional with the theoretical, without any adequate attempt to modify or transform the fictional or to incorporate the theoretical and justificatory elements into it. To the theoretical disposition of Plato's *Republic*, she counterposes his *Laws*; to Book 2 of *Utopia* must be counterposed the long analysis of private property and theft in contemporary England that comprises Book 1; to Rousseau's *Social Contract* there is *Project de constitution pour la Corse*; to Kepler's science fictional *Somnium* is his theoretical treatise, *Astronomia Nova*. Le Doeuff's explanation of this awkward but prevalent coupling of theory and vision, in brief, is that the theoretical or analytical doublet is written in part to contain the ambiguity, or as she calls it, the polysemic quality, of the visionary text in an attempt to fix its meaning, to provide it a guaranteed reading:

> The point is, in short, that if Utopia had consisted only in its second part, a *de facto* plurality of readings would be possible. But Book I establishes the canonical reading and privileges the political meaning of Book II at the expense of others: as Book I is *essentially* a critique of the social and political organization of England, a denunciation of private property and the English penal system, Book II is taken as being *essentially* a description of the best possible Republic. By writing Book I, More himself provides a principle for decoding his initial text.
>
> (Le Doeuff 1989b: 48–9).

In other words, the function of theoretical doubling of the utopic texts is to contain ambiguity, to control how the text is read, to control the very future that the ideal is designed to protect or ensure. At the very moment when the impulse to project a better future takes form, it attempts to contain that which it invokes, the untidy, unsettling singularity of time, the precedence that temporal flow has over any given image or process, utopic or otherwise. What every utopic model both establishes and paradoxically undermines – why it commonly requires a duplicated theoretical justification – is that the idealized vision puts an end to political problems of the present and projects for itself no role as problem-solving in its future: Utopia has no future, the future has already come as its present (which is why it has no place, but also, even more ironically, no time: the utopic is that which is out of time).

While I do not have the time (or space) here to elaborate in much detail what such a conception of time involves, I have written elsewhere on the notion of duration, virtuality and the architectural field (Grosz 1997a, 1997b). What I can do here is outline some of its most salient elements:

1   Time, or more precisely, duration, is always singular, unique and unrepeatable. Henri Bergson, the great theorist of duration, has suggested that duration is simultaneously both singular and a multiplicity. Each duration forms a continuity, a single, indivisible movement; and yet, there are many simultaneous durations, which implies that all durations participate in a generalized or cosmological duration, which allows them to be described as simultaneous. Duration is the very condition of simultaneity, as well as succession. An event occurs only once: it has its own characteristics, which will never occur again, even in repetition. But it occurs alongside of, simultaneous with, many other events, whose rhythms are also specific and unique. Duration is thus the milieu of qualitative difference.

2   The division of duration – which occurs whenever time is conceptualized as a line, counted, divided into before and after, made the object of the numerical, rendering its analogue continuity into digital or discrete units – transforms its nature; that is to say, reduces it to modes of spatiality. If, as Bergson suggests, space is the field of quantitative differences, of differences of degree, then the counting of time, its linear representation, reduces and extinguishes its differences of kind to replace them with differences of degree.

3   One of the most significant differences of kind within duration (which is commonly misunderstood as a difference of degree) is the distinction between past and present. The past and the present are not two modalities of the present, the past a receded or former present, a present that has moved out of the limelight. Rather, the past and the present fundamentally coexist; they function in simultaneity. Bergson suggests that the whole of the past is contained, in contracted form, in each moment of the present. The past is the virtuality that

the present, the actual carries along with it. The past lives *in time*. The past could never exist if it did not coexist with the present of which it is the past, and thus of every present.[4] The past would be inaccessible to us altogether if we can gain access to it only through the present and its passing. The only access we have to the past is through a leap into virtuality, through a move into the past itself, given that, for Bergson, the past is outside us and that we are in it rather than it located in us. The past exists, but it is in a state of latency or virtuality. We must place ourselves in it if we are to have recollections, memory images.

4   If the present is the actuality whose existence is engendered by the virtual past, then the future remains that dimension or modality of time that has no actuality either. The future too remains virtual, uncontained by the present but prefigured, rendered potential, through and by the past. The future is that over which the past and present have no control: the future is that openness of becoming that enables divergence from what exists. This means that, rather than the past exerting a deterministic force over the future (determinism reduces the future to the present!), the future is that which over-writes or restructures the virtual that is the past: the past is the condition of every future: the future that emerges is only one of the lines of virtuality from the past. The past is the condition for infinite futures, and duration is that flow that connects the future to the past that gave it impetus.

What does this mean for the concept of the utopian and for embodied utopias? That the utopian is not the projection of a future at all, although this is how it is usually understood; rather, it is the projection of a past or present as if it were the future. It is, in fact, a freezing of the indeterminable movement from the past through the future that the present is unable to directly control. Utopian discourses are those texts that attempt to compensate for this indetermination between past and future, and the failure of the present to represent a site of control for this movement to and of the future. The utopian mode seeks a future which itself has no future, a future in which time will cease to be a relevant factor, and movement, change and becoming remain impossible.[5]

BODIES

How do bodies fit into the utopic? In what sense can the utopic be understood as embodied? Here, I want to suggest two contradictory movements. On the one hand, every conception of the utopic, from Plato, through More, to present-day utopians, conceptualizes the ideal commonwealth in terms of the management, regulation, care and ordering of bodies. Each pictures a thoroughly embodied social organization. But on the other hand, there is no space or future, in utopic visions, for the production of a position that acknowledges the sexual, racial and cultural specificity and differential values of its subjects. No utopia has been framed to take account of not only the diversity of subjects, but the diversity of

their utopic visions, that is, to the way in which visions of the ideal are themselves reflections of the specific positions occupied in the present.

All philosophical utopias have dealt with the question of bodies. While they
idealize the potential relations between individual and collective bodies, none of
them advocates a decorporeal or disembodied state. After all, what a social
organization consists in, above all, is the production, regulation and management of bodies through the production of practices, habits, rituals and institutions. The problem is *not* that the various visions of the utopic promulgated over
the last three millennia lack a concern for or interest in the corporeal. Moreover,
it is significant that even the question of relations between the sexes seems to
play a major role in historical representations of the ideal commonwealth.

In well-known passages of Book V of the *Republic*, for example, Plato
expounds on the ideal arrangements between the sexes to ensure the maximal
functioning of the *polis.* His argument is that, just as there are individual differences distinguishing men's capacities and abilities from each other, so there are
individual differences distinguishing women's. There is no reason why the best of
women, like the best of men, should not be educated to the guardian class, and
be rulers of the Republic:

> With a view to having women guardians, we should not have one kind of education to
> fashion the men, and another for the women, especially as they have the same nature to
> begin with.
>
> (Plato 1974: 456e)

Furthermore, Plato suggests that marriage and sexual monogamy should be eliminated, and instead, a controlled, self-constrained sexual and child-raising collective be instituted in their place:

> All these women shall be wives in common to all the men, and not one of them shall live
> privately with any man; the children too should be held in common so that no parent
> shall know which is his offspring, and no child shall know his parent.
>
> (Plato 1974: 456d)

This same concern for the place of women and children, and the status of sexual
relations occupies a good part of the work of More. Because women work
equally alongside of men, there is prosperity. Because twice as many people
work in Utopia as in Europe, the workday is only six hours long. On the other
hand, the rules governing marriage, divorce and sexual relations are strict and
govern a narrow, life-long personal and non-deceptive monogamy. More
explains that the Utopian marital customs may strike Europeans as strange, but
they are more direct and honest:

> In choosing marriage partners they solemnly and seriously follow a custom which
> seemed to us foolish and absurd in the extreme. Whether she be a widow or virgin, the
> bride-to-be is shown naked to the groom by a responsible and respectable matron; and
> similarly, some respectable man presents the groom naked to his prospective bride.

We laughed at this custom, and called it absurd; but they were just as amazed at the folly of all other people. When men go to buy a colt, where they are risking only a little money, they are so cautious that, though the animal is almost bare, they won't close the deal until the saddle and blanket have been taken off, lest there be a hidden sore underneath. Yet in the choice of a mate, which may cause either delight or disgust for the rest of their lives, men are so careless that they leave the rest of the woman's body covered up with clothes . . .

There is extra reason for them to be careful, because in that part of the world they are the only people who practise monogamy, and because their marriages are seldom terminated except by death – though they do allow divorce for adultery or for intolerable offensive behaviour. . .

(More 1975: Book II, 82–3)

There is considerable detail in the texts of all the major thinkers of utopias of various arrangements, some apparently egalitarian, others clearly hierarchized, regarding marital rights and duties, and the sexual and social responsibilities and rights of men, women and children. There is an underlying assumption in them all regarding the fundamental unity and singularity, the neutrality and quasi-universality of the state (excluding slaves/bondsmen). The commonwealth, though it may differentiate them in their roles, nevertheless equalizes them in the protection it appears to offer for their socially validated positions. So, although the question of embodiment, the relations between the sexes and the adjudication of their proper roles are discussed in considerable detail, nevertheless the question of sexual difference has not been adequately raised. Instead of this question, the question of women's place within an apparently neutral but visibly patriarchal and fraternal social order, takes its place – the question of accommodating women within frameworks that have been devised according to what men think is sexually neutral. This may explain the apparent strangeness of More's decree regarding the right of betrothed couples to view each other naked before marriage, as a man would view a horse he was purchasing! Egalitarianism consists in extending to women, or to other cultural minorities, the rights accorded to the dominant group; it does *not* consist in rethinking the very nature of those rights in relation to those groups whom it was originally designed to exclude or constrain. Plato extends to women the same rights he has already deduced for men. The same is true, and even more visibly, in More's text: women remain the same as men insofar as the law, the economy and the judiciary require it; yet they remain men's complements where it suits men![6] In Irigaray's terminology, relations between the sexes have only ever been subjected to a relation of sexual *indifference*, there has been no conceptualization of a *dual sexual symmetry*, or, in other words, any understanding that perhaps women's conceptions of the universal good may differ from men's has yet to be adequately articulated (Irigaray 1985a [1974], 1985b [1977]).

It is Irigaray's claim, and is in many ways relevant to the theme of this collection, that sexual difference is that which has yet to take place, it is that which has staked a place in the future. Sexual difference does not yet exist, and it is possible that it has never existed. In the history of the West, since at least the time of Plato, the ideals of culture, knowledge and civilization have practised a resolute sexual *indifference*, in which the interests of women were seen as parallel or complementary to those of men. The sexes as we know them today, and even the sexes as posed in many feminist visions of a post-patriarchal utopia, have only one model, a singular and universal neutrality. At best, equal participation is formulated. But the idea of sexual difference entails the existence of *at least two* points of view, sets of interests, perspectives, two types of ideal, two modes of knowledge, has yet to be considered. It is, in a sense, beyond the utopian, insofar as the utopian has always been the present's projection of singular and universal ideals, the projection of the present's failure to see its own modes of neutralization. Sexual difference, like the utopic, is a category of the *future anterior*, Irigaray's preferred tense for writing, the only tense that openly addresses the question of the future without, like the utopian vision, pre-empting it. Which is not to say, as I have already intimated, that sexual difference is a utopian ideal (this is Margaret Whitford's claim in her reading of Irigaray) (Whitford 1991: 18–20). On the contrary, because sexual difference is one of the present's ways of conceptualizing its current problems, all the work of sexual difference, its labour of producing alternative knowledges, methods and criteria, has yet to begin. It is beyond the utopian insofar as no vision, narrative or plan of the ideal society, or idealized relations between the sexes, can perform this work of *making difference*: it is entirely of the order of the surprise, the encounter with the new. This is why Irigaray saves herself from the tiresome charges of essentialism and utopianism by refusing to speculate on what this sexual difference might consist in or how it might manifest itself, in seeing that the future for feminism is that which is to be made rather than foreseen or predicted: 'To concern oneself in the present about the future certainly does not consist in programming it in advance but in trying to bring it into existence . . .' (Irigaray, quoted in Whitford 1991: 14).

How, then, can we understand the idea of embodied utopias? What would utopias that consider embodiment be like? And how might they be relevant to the concerns of architecture? Here I have only some suggestions:

1   That architecture itself not be so much concerned with seeking to build, perform or enact ideals, or ideal solutions to contemporary or future problems; indeed, it is a goal-directedness which utopic visions orient us towards, in neglecting the notion of process, precisely because they do not understand the role of time. The solution to the political and social problems of the present, while clearly a good thing for architects to keep in mind in their labours of planning and building, should not be the goal or purpose of either architecture, or politics. Rather, the radical role of the architect is best developed in architectural exploration and invention, in the recognition of the ongoing need for exploration and invention, in recognition of architecture's, and knowledge's roles as experimental practices. Philosophy, architecture, science, are not disciplines which produce answers or solutions, but fields which pose questions, and whose

questions never yield the solutions they seek but which lead to the production of ever more inventive questions. Architecture, along with life itself, moves alongside of, is the ongoing process of negotiating, habitable spaces. Architecture is a set of highly provisional 'solutions' to the question of how to live and inhabit space with others. It is a negotiation with one of the problems life poses to bodies, a spatial question-raising that subjects itself, as all questions and solutions do, to the movements of time and becoming.

2   Too much of politics is devoted to the question of blueprints, plans, preparation for the unexpected. While it is one of the functions of architecture to devise plans, to make blueprints, to prepare in every detail for the future building it is anticipating, this precision and determinacy of planning must not be confused with the kinds of planning that are required for political organization and reorganization, where, as concrete as they may be in conception, they always prove to be indeterminable in their application. An adequate acknowledgement of the vicissitudes of futurity would ensure that we abandon the fantasy of control of the future while not abdicating the responsibility of preparing for a better future than the present.

3   For architecture to have a future in which embodiment plays a self-conscious and positive role, it is crucial that sexual difference have its effects there, as well as in other spheres of life. This is not to be confused with the call for 'gender parity' in the profession. Rather, it is to suggest that in architecture's self-examination and self-reflection, it is crucial to acknowledge that the history of architecture is only one among many possible histories, and the debt that the dominant discourses and practices of architecture owe to the practices and discourses that were either discarded or ignored, or never invented or explored. This is the place that embodiment plays in the history of architecture – the labour of architectural invention, the collective efforts of millennia of architects, builders, engineers, including those whose efforts are not preserved by history and those who were actively excluded from participation. This is to acknowledge that architecture as a discipline is always already a mode of embodiment *and* a mode of the disavowal of a debt to embodiment. That is, the critique of its own phallocentrism is that which architecture must undertake. Such a critique is not to be mistaken for the charges of gender imbalance, which are certainly relevant, but not enough. Architecture, like all other disciplines, needs to come to grips with its own *phallocentrism* (to use Irigaray's phrase), which is to say, its own structures of disavowed debt and obligation, to a recognition that its 'identity', as fluctuating and fragile as it might be, is contingent upon that which it 'others' or excludes. This other is its 'feminine', the virtualities not actualized in the present, the impetus for the future anterior.

4   The relation between bodies, social structures and built living and work environments and their ideal interactions is not a question that can be settled: the

very acknowledgement of the multiplicity of bodies and their varying political interests and ideals implies that there are a multiplicity of idealized solutions to living arrangements, arrangements about collective coexistence, but it is no longer clear that a single set of relations, a single goal or ideal will ever adequately serve as the neutral ground for any consensual utopic form. Utopias are precisely not about consensus but about the enactment of ideals of the privileged, ideals of the government by the few of the many, ideals not derived from consensus but designed to produce or enforce it. In short, ideals need to be produced over and over again, and their proliferation and multiplication is an ongoing process, always a measure of dissatisfaction with the past and present, always the representation of ever-receding futures. The task for architecture, as for philosophy, is not to settle on utopias, models, concrete ideals, but instead to embark on the process of endless questioning.

NOTES

1   While More is insistent on the equality of all, the equal access of all to material goods and the refusal of private property, he also refers to slaves and bondsmen, to those chained or not citizens. It is, like all liberal and egalitarian theorists, an equality made possible only because of the unacknowledged and unpaid labour of the non-citizen, the socially excluded and unequal: 'Bondsmen do the slaughtering and cleaning in these places [outside the city limits]: citizens are not allowed to do such work' (More 1975: Book 2, 57).

2   Utopia is the space where the contradictory inheritance of the Enlightenment appears in one of its clearest terms. Utopias, while not invented in the Enlightenment, certainly flourished in the eighteenth century and persisted into the nineteenth century, when a number of socialist and socialist–feminist utopias proliferated . . . But by the twentieth century, the problems of implementing the ideal state or community have become so obvious that the more characteristic and certainly the most well-known form of the genre would seem to be dystopic: Zamyatin's *We*, Aldous Huxley's *Brave New World*, George Orwell's *1984*.

3   Michele Le Doeuff presents a slightly different understanding of the atopic; while she concurs with the indeterminacy and ambiguity of the term, she wants to link it to an as yet uninformed audience: what distinguishes a utopic from an atopic discourse is the ambiguity of its mode of address:

> *Atopos* means that which has no place, but also that which is bizarre, extravagant or strange. An atopia is a text which cannot immediately be given one single correct meaning by its reader . . . A work is atopian if it finds no circle of witnesses or readers already able to receive it. That is to say, also, that it manifests its author's singularity. The text is his own (and he further asserts his mastery of the work by retrieving it into univocity, by operating a reprise of his text) and is shareable only at the cost of a series of mediations.
>
> (Le Doeuff 1989b: 54–5)

For Le Doeuff, though her point is not merely semantic or classificatory, this means that Plato, More, Bacon, Rousseau and others, must be considered more atopic than utopic. As an example of utopic thinking, she cites Marx and Engels, for whom the structure of self-justificatory writing seems irrelevant:

> Marx and Engels do not have to provide instructions for the use of the *Communist Manifesto*. Its political meaning is clear: that is to say, already shared by the group it addresses, the activists of the Communist League. Moreover Marx and Engels do not present themselves as its authors, but as spokesmen. All these factors go together.
>
> (Le Doeuff 1989b: 55)

While I would agree with Le Doeuff's distinction between texts which attempt to contain their own polysemy and those which do not, nonetheless, a different distinction needs to be drawn for my purposes here: there is a significant difference between those discourses which provide concrete images of an ideal future (from Plato to Marx and contemporary feminism), and those discourses which, while directed to a future preferable to our present, refuse to characterize or represent its concrete features (Nietzsche, Deleuze, Irigaray), and can only specify elements it would *not* contain.

4   The past and the present do not denote two successive moments, but two elements which coexist: One is the present, which does not cease to pass, and the other is the past, which does not cease to be but through which all presents pass ... The past does not follow the present, but on the contrary, is presupposed by it as the pure condition without which it would not pass. In other words, each present goes back to itself as past.

(Deleuze 1988: 59)

5   This timelessness is what More shares with Plato:

> So I reflect on the wonderfully wise and sacred institutions of the Utopians, who are so well governed by so few laws. Among them virtue has its rewards, yet everything is shared equally, and all men live in plenty. I contrast them with the many other nations, none of which, though all are constantly passing new ordinances, can ever order its affairs satisfactorily.
>
> (More 1975: Book 1, 38)

6   Cf. More's description of cooking and eating arrangements:

> planning the meal, as well as preparing and cooking food, is carried out by the women alone, with each family taking its turn ... The men sit with their backs to the wall, the women on the outside, so that if a woman has a sudden qualm or pain, such as occasionally happens during pregnancy, she may get up without disturbing the others, and go off to the nurses.
>
> (More 1975: 58)

Bibliography

'A place Walt would call home.' (1995) *Celebration Chronicle*, summer 2.

Ackelsberg, M.A. (1984) '*Mujeres Libres* and the role of women in anarchist revolution', in R. Rohrlich and E. Hoffman Baruch (eds) *Women in Search of Utopia: Mavericks and Mythmakers*, New York: Schocken Books.

Adams, H. (1918) *The Education of Henry Adams,* Boston and New York: Houghton Mifflin Co. Available online: http://xroads.virginia.edu/~HYPER/hadams/eha25.html.

Adams, J. (1896) 'What a great city might be – a lesson from the White City', *The New England Magazine* 14: 3–13.

Addams, J. *et al.* (1969a [1893]) 'The objective value of a social settlement', in *Philanthropy and Social Progress*, Maryland: McGrath Publishing Company.

Addams, J. (1969b [1893]) 'The subjective necessity for social settlements', in *Philanthropy and Social Progress*, Maryland: McGrath Publishing Company.

Addams, J. (1981 [1910]) *Twenty Years at Hull House*, NY: Penguin Books.

Aden, R. (1999) *Popular Stories and Promised Lands: Fan Cultures and Symbolic Pilgrimages*, Tuscaloosa, AL: University of Alabama Press.

Alberti, L.B. (1988 [1485]) *On the Art of Building in Ten Books*, trans. J. Rykwert, N. Leach and R. Tavernor, Cambridge, MA and London: MIT Press.

Albisetti, J. (1988) *Schooling German Girls and Women: Secondary and Higher Education in the Nineteenth Century*, Princeton: Princeton University Press.

Anderson, W. (1997) 'The trespass speaks: white masculinity and colonial breakdown', *American Historical Review*, December: 1343–70.

Annual Report: Celebration Development of Regional Impact (1997, March) Bowyer-Singleton & Associates, Inc., n.p.

'Ansprache' (1912) 'Ansprache von Frau Hedwig Heyl', *Deutscher Lyceum Club* 8, 2a: 72–3.

'A.P.' (1915) 'Das Viktoria-Studienhaus. Ein neues Studentinnenheim in Charlottenburg', *Neue Bahnen* 50, 18: 142–3.

Architectural Review (1955a) 'Subtopia', vol. 117, May 1955, 365.

Architectural Review (1955b) 'Agents', vol. 117, May 1955, 371.

Arcidi, P. (1992) 'Housing for women: safely linked, Amadala Crossing, Edison, New Jersey', *Progressive Architecture* 73, 8: 64–5.

Aries, P. and Duby, G. (eds) (1987) *A History of Private Life*, Cambridge, MA: Belknap Press of Harvard University Press.

Asendorf, C. (1993) *Batteries of Life: On the History of Things and their Perception in Modernity*, trans. D. Reneau, Berkeley: University of California Press.

Askew, M. (1994) *Interpreting Bangkok: the Urban Question in Thai Studies*, Bangkok: Chulalongkorn University Press.

Augé, M. (1995) *Non-Places: Introduction to an Anthropology of Supermodernity*, London: Verso.

Austen, I. (2000) 'Studies reveal a rush of older women to the web', *New York Times*, 29 June 2000.

Avenir du Tonkin, 4 December 1937: 7e; 11 December 1937: 4e; 18 December 1937: 4e.

Bachelard, G. (1964) *The Poetics of Space*, trans. M. Jolas, New York: Orion Press.

Baker, G.H. (1996) *Le Corbusier: The Creative Search*, New York: Van Nostrand Reinhold.

Banham, R. (1984) *The Architecture of the Well-Tempered Environment*, Second Edition, Chicago: University of Chicago Press.

Banlang Khamasundara (1984) *Maps of Bangkok: AD 1888–1931,* Bangkok: Royal Thai Survey Department.

Barrows, S. (1981) *Distorting Mirrors: Visions of the Crowd in Late Nineteenth-Century France,* New Haven: Yale University Press.

Barthes, R. (1994 [1966–1973]) 'Le Plaisir du Texte', in *Oeuvres Completes*, vol. 2, Paris: Éditions du Seuil.

Baudelaire, C. (1986) *The Painter of Modern Life*, New York: Da Capo Press, Inc.

Beecher, C.E. and Stowe, H. B. (1975 [1869]) *The American Woman's Home, or Principles of Domestic Science*, New York: J.B. Ford & Co; rpt. with introduction by J. Van Why, Hartford: Stowe-Day Foundation.

Behnisch-Kappstein, A. (1916) 'Wohnung und Frau', *Welt der Frau*, no. 24: 380–1.

Benhabib, S. (1992) 'Models of public space: Hannah Arendt, the liberal tradition, and Jürgen Habermas', in C. Calhoun (ed.) *Habermas and the Public Sphere*, Cambridge, MA: MIT Press.

Benjamin, W. (1968) *Illuminations,* New York: Schocken Books.

Benjamin, W. (1978) 'Paris, capital of the nineteenth century', in *Reflections: Essays, Aphorisms, Autobiographical Writings*, New York: Schocken Books.

Benjamin, W. (1999) *The Arcades Project*, Cambridge: Harvard University Press.

Bennett, L. and Palmer, J. (1997) *Experiencing Computer Mediated Communication on the Internet – Does Gender Still Equal Difference,* Online. Available http://www.imago.com.au/WOV/papers/gender.htm (20 March 1999).

Berlant, L. (1991) *The Anatomy of National Fantasy: Hawthorne, Utopia, and Everyday Life*, Chicago and London: The University of Chicago Press.

Berlant, L. (1994) ' '68, or something', *Critical Inquiry* 21.

Berlant, L. (1995) 'The Queen of America goes to Washington City: Harriet Jacobs, Frances Harper, Anita Hill', in M. Moon and C. Davidson (eds) *Subjects and Citizens*, Durham, NC: Duke University Press.

Berman, M. (1988) *All That is Solid Melts into Air: The Experience of Modernity*, New York: Penguin Books.

Bertolo, D. (1997) *FT2K*, Online. Available http://www.turbulence.org/Works/FT2K (20 March 1999).

Bestor, A.E., Jr. (1950) *Backwoods Utopias*, Philadelphia: University of Pennsylvania Press.

Billotey, P. (1929) *L'Indochine en zigzags,* Paris: Albin Michel.

Biondi, J. (1992) *Les Anticolonialistes (1881–1962)*, Paris: Robert Laffont.

Bissell, W. (1999) 'Camera Zanzibar', *Public Culture* 11, 1.

Blair, C., Jeppeson, M.S. and Pucci, Jr., E.P. (1991) 'Public memorializing in postmodernity: The Vietnam veterans memorial as prototype', *Quarterly Journal of Speech* 77: 263–88.

Bloch, E. (1996) *The Utopian Function of Art and Literature, Selected Essays*, Cambridge, MA: MIT Press.

Bloch, E. (2000 [1919]) *The Spirit of Utopia*, trans. A. Nassar, Stanford, CA: Stanford University Press.

Bloch, E. and Adorno, T. (1996) 'Something's missing: a discussion between Ernst Bloch and Theodor W. Adorno on the contractions of utopian longing', in E. Bloch, *The Utopian Function of Art and Literature, Selected Essays*, Cambridge, MA: MIT Press.

Bloomer, K. and Moore, C. (1977) *Body, Memory, and Architecture,* New Haven: Yale University Press.

Blueprint for health (1997) The Celebration Company.

Boetticher, E. von. (1915) 'Heimstätten für Frauen', *Berliner Frauenclub von 1900* 3, 10: 5–7.

Bois, Y.-A. and Krauss, R.E. (1997) *Formless: A User's Guide*, New York: Zone Books.

Borchert, J. (1980) *Alley Life in Washington: Family, Community, Religion and Folklife in the City, 1850–1970*, Urbana: University of Illinois Press.

Boudon, P. (1972) *Lived-In Architecture: Le Corbusier's Pessac Revisited,* London: Lund Humphries.

Boyer, P. (1978) *Urban Masses and Moral Order in America*, Cambridge, MA: Harvard University Press.

'Bridge over troubled water.' (1972) *Architect's Journal* 156, 39: 680–3.

Bridges, H.J. (1936) 'Chicago's greatest woman: Jane Addams', an address to the Chicago Ethical Society.

Brieux, E. (1910) *Voyage aux Indes et en Indo-Chine*, Paris: Ch. Delagrave.

Brocheux, P. and Hémery, D. (1995) *Indochine: la Colonisation Ambiguë (1858–1954)*, Paris: Editions la Découverte.

Brooks, H.A. (1997) *Le Corbusier's Formative Years,* Chicago: University of Chicago Press.

Brooks, P. (1993) *Body Work: Objects of Desire in Modern Narrative*, Cambridge, MA: Harvard University Press.

Brooks, S. and Stryker, B. (1998) *DissemiNET,* Online. Available http://www.wexarts.org/thefold/disseminet (20 March 1999).

Buci-Glucksman, C. (1987) 'Catastrophic utopia: the feminine as allegory of the modern', in C. Gallagher and T. Laqueur (eds) *The Making of the Modern Body*, Berkeley: University of California Press.

Buck-Morss, S. (2000) *Dreamworld and Catastrophe: The Passing of Mass Utopia in East and West*, Cambridge, MA: MIT Press.

Bunting, H. (1997) *Own, Be Owned or Remain Invisible,* Online. Available http://www.irational.org/heath/_readme.html (20 March 1999).

Burgin, V., Donald, J. and Kaplan, C. (eds) (1989) *Formations of Fantasy*, London: Routledge.

Burney, F. (1968 [1778]) *Evelina or the History of a Young Lady's Entrance into the World*, Oxford: Oxford University Press.

Burnham, D. (1902) 'White City and capital city', *Century* 63: 62–3.

Bush-Brown, H. (1899) 'New York City monuments', *Municipal Affairs* 3: 602–12.

Butler, J. (1993) *Bodies That Matter: On the Discursive Limits of 'Sex'*, London: Routledge.

Buttimer, A. (1980) 'Home, reach, and the sense of place', in A. Buttimer and D. Seamon (eds) *The Human Experience of Space and Place*, New York: St Martin's Press.

Calhoun, C. (ed.) (1992) *Habermas and the Public Sphere*, Cambridge, MA: MIT Press.

Candee, H. (1927) *New Journeys in Old Asia: Indo-China, Siam, Java, Bali,* New York: Frederick A. Stokes Company.

Celebration Company (1995). *Celebration Pattern Book*, Orlando, FL: Celebration Company.

'Celebration home buyers select their dream homes' (1996) *Celebration Chronicle*, Spring 1, 3.

'Celebration is focus of project to improve health nationwide' (1997) *Celebration Chronicle*, Summer 2.

Celebration: American town taking shape in Central Florida (1997) The Celebration Company.

Çelik, Z. (1996) 'Gendered spaces in colonial Algiers', in D. Agrest, P. Conway and L.K. Weisman (eds) *The Sex of Architecture*, New York: Harry Abrams.

Century (1902) 'Civic improvement as a phase of patriotism', *The Century* 63: 793.

Charities (1905) 'To wipe Washington alleys off the map', *Charities* 13: 960.

Cheang, S.L. (1998–9) *Brandon,* Online. Available http://brandon.guggenheim. org (20 March 1999).

ChickClick. (1997–) *chickclick site,* Online. Available http://www.chickclick.com (20 March 1999).

Chivas-Baron, C. (1925) 'Madame Hoa's husbands', in *Three Women of Annam*, 207. New York: Frank-Maurice (Originally published as *Trois femmes annamites*, Paris, 1922).

Chivas-Baron, C. (1927) *Confidences de métisse*, Paris: Eugène Fasquelle.

Chivas-Baron, C. (1929) *La femme français dans les colonies*, Paris: Larose.

Chmielewski, W., Ker, L. and Klee-Hartzell, M. (eds) (1993) *Women in Spiritual and Communitarian Societies in the United States*, Syracuse: Syracuse University Press.

Choay, F. (1997 [1980]) *The Rule and the Model: On the Theory of Architecture and Urbanism*, Cambridge, MA: MIT Press.

Churchill, H. (1927) *New Journeys in Old Asia: Indo-China, Siam, Java, Bali*, New York: Frederick A. Stokes Company.

Clancy-Smith, J. and Gouda, F. (eds) (1998) *Domesticating the Empire: Race, Gender, and Family Life in French and Dutch Colonialism,* Charlottesville: University Press of Virginia.

Colomina, B. (1996) 'Battle Lines: E.1027', in D. Agrest, P. Conway, L. K. Weisman (eds) *The Sex of Architecture,* New York: Harry Abrams.

Colomina, B. (1997) 'Where are we?', in E. Blau and N.J. Troy (eds) *Architecture and Cubism,* Cambridge, MA: Centre Canadien d'Architecture & MIT Press.

'Community gets connected' (1997, Winter) *Celebration Chronicle*: 8.

Conklin, A. (1998) *A Mission to Civilize: The Republican Idea of Empire in France and West Africa, 1895–1930*, Stanford, CA: Stanford University Press.

Connell, R.W. (1987) *Gender and Power: Society, the Person and Sexual Politics*, Palo Alto, CA: Stanford University Press.

Coontz, S. (1992) *The Way We Never Were: American Families and the Nostalgia Trap*, New York: Basic Books.

Corre, A. (1894) *L'Ethnographie Criminelle, d'apres les Statistiques Judiciaires Recueillies dans les Colonies Françaises*, Paris: C. Reinwald et Cie.

County of Fairfax, Virginia (1991) *Zoning Ordinance Chapter 112 of the 1976 Code of the County of Fairfax, Virginia*, Tallahassee: Municiple Code Corporation.

County of Fairfax, Virginia (1993) *Public Facilities Manual*. Fairfax, County of Fairfax.

Crocker, R.H. (1992) *Social Work and Social Order: The Settlement Movement in Two Industrial Cities, 1889–1930,* Urbana, IL: University of Illinois Press.

Da Costa Meyer, E. (1996) 'La Donna è Mobile: Agoraphobia, Women, and Urban Space', in D. Agrest, P. Conway and L. Weisman, (eds) *The Sex of Architecture*, New York: Harry N. Abrams, Inc., 141-156.

Dandekar, H. (ed.) (1993) *Shelter, Women, and Development: First and Third World Perspectives*, Ann Arbor: George Wahr Publishing Co.

Davis, M. (1990) *City of Zuartz*, London: Verso.

de Certeau, M. (1984a [1974]) *The Practice of Everyday Life*, trans. S. Rendall, Berkeley, CA: University of California Press.

de Certeau, M. (1984b) 'Walking in the city', in M. de Certeau, *The Practice of Everyday Life*, trans. S. Rendall, Berkeley, CA: University of California Press.

de Certeau, M. (1989) *Heterologies: Discourse on the Other*, Minneapolis: University of Minnesota Press.

de Certeau, M. (2000) *The Certeau Reader*, Graham Ward (ed.), Oxford: Blackwell Publishers.

Declaration of Covenants (1997) The Celebration Company, 2 January 1997.

Deleuze, G. (1988) *Bergsonism*, trans. H. Tomlinson and B. Habberjam, New York: Zone Books.

Deleuze, G. and Guattari, F. (1987) *A Thousand Plateaus: Capitalism and Schizophrenia,* Minneapolis: University of Minnesota Press.

Denison House Reports (DH) (1912) *Denison House: The College Settlement in Boston. Annual Report for the Year Ending October 1, 1912,* Boston.

Denison House Reports (DH) (1916) *Denison House: The College Settlement in Boston. Annual Report for the Year Ending October 1, 1916,* Boston.

Derrida, J. (1973) *Speech and Phenomena and Other Essays on Husserl's Theory of Signs*, Evanston: Northwestern University Press.

Derrida, J. (1978) *Edmund Husserl's Origin of Geometry: An Introduction*, Stony Brook, NY: Nicolas Hays, Ltd.

Derrida, J. (1994) *Specters of Marx,* London and New York: Routledge.

Deutsch, S. (2000) *Women and the City: Gender, Space, and Power in Boston, 1870–1940*, Oxford and New York: Oxford University Press.

Deutscher Lyceum-Klub (1910) 'Satzungen', Berlin. Club statutes in the files 'Beschickung von Kunst und Gewerbe Ausstellungen', Rep. 120E, XVI, 1. 8. vol. 9 (1911–1912), Geheimes Staatsarchiv Preußischer Kulturbesitz, Berlin.

Deutscher Lyceum-Klub (1911) 'Der Deutscher Lyceum-Klub e.V.', Berlin. Brochure in the files 'Beschickung von Kunst und Gewerbe Ausstellungen', Rep. 120E, XVI, 1. 8. vol. 9 (1911–1912), Geheimes Staatsarchiv Preußischer Kulturbesitz, Berlin.

Dibbell, J. (1993) 'A rape in cyberspace', *Village Voice,* New York. 23 December 1993. Online. Available http://www.levity.com/julian/bungle_vv.html (15 November 2000).

Dickinson, G. (1997) 'Memories for sale: nostalgia and the construction of identity in Old Pasadena', *Quarterly Journal of Speech* 83: 1–27.

Di Franco, A. (1992) 'I'm no heroine', in *Imperfectly*, Buffalo, NY: Righteous Babe Records.

'Disney's sinless city'. (1996) *Boston Globe*, 25 February, 60.

Dölle, G. (1997) *Die (unheimliche) Macht des Geldes: Finanzierungsstrategien der bürgerlichen Frauenbewegung in Deutschland zwischen 1865 und 1933*, Siegener Frauenforschungsreihe, Sabine Hering (ed.) vol. 2, Frankfurt am Main: dipa-Verlag.

Douglas, M. (1966) *Purity and Danger: An Analysis of Concepts of Pollution and Taboo*, New York and Washington: Frederick A. Praeger, Publishers.

Downtown Celebration architectural walking tour (1997). The Celebration Company.

Draper, M. (1995) 'Exploring the influence of a virtual body on spatial awareness', M.Sc. Diss., University of Washington.

Duany, A. and Plater-Zyberk, E. (1994) 'The Neighborhood, the District and the Corridor', in P. Katz (ed.) *The New Urbanism*, New York: McGraw-Hill.

Duany, A. and Plater-Zyberk, E. (1995, Spring) 'The second coming of the American small town', *Historic Preservation Forum*: 30–45.

DuBois, P. (1988) *Sowing the Body: Psychoanalysis and the Ancient Representation of Women,* Chicago: University of Chicago Press.

Dumm, T. (1994) *United States*, Ithaca and London: Cornell University Press.

Dunn, A. (1996) 'Language: final frontier for the true global network', in *New York Times: CyberTimes*, 25 December 1996 Online. Available http://adaweb.walkerart.org/influx/muntadas/nytlang.html (20 March 1999).

Durel, P. (1898) *La femme dans les colonies Françaises*, Paris: J. Dulon.

Durkheim, E. (1964 [1893]) *The Division of Labour in Society*, New York: The Free Press.

Durtain, L. (1930) *Dieux blancs, hommes jaunes*, Paris: Flammarion.

'E.H.' (1912) 'Die Frau in Haus und Beruf', *Die Welt*, no. 24: 475–9.

Eisenstein, Z. (1998) *Global Obscenities: Patriarchy, Capitalism, and the Lure of Cyberfantasy*, New York: New York University Press.

Elizabeth Peabody House (EPH), Boston (1897) *First Annual Report of the Elizabeth Peabody House: Report for the Year 1896*, Boston: Thomas Todd Co.

Elizabeth Peabody House (EPH), Boston (1900) *Fourth Annual Report of the Elizabeth Peabody House: Report for the Year 1899*, Boston: Thomas Todd Co.

Elizabeth Peabody House (EPH), Boston (1903) *Seventh Annual Report of the Elizabeth Peabody House: Report for the Year 1902*, Boston: Thomas Todd Co.

Elizabeth Peabody House (EPH), Boston (1906) *Tenth Annual Report of the Elizabeth Peabody House: Report for the Year 1905*, Boston: Thomas Todd Co.

Elizabeth Peabody House (EPH), Boston (1908) *Twelfth Annual Report of the Elizabeth Peabody House: Report for the Year 1907*, Boston: Thomas Todd Co.

Elizabeth Peabody House (EPH), Boston (1909) *Thirteenth Annual Report of the Elizabeth Peabody House: Report for the Year 1908*, Boston: Thomas Todd Co.

Elizabeth Peabody House (EPH), Boston (1911) *Fifteenth Annual Report of the Elizabeth Peabody House: Report for the Year 1910*, Boston: Thomas Todd Co.

Elizabeth Peabody House (EPH), Boston (1913) *Seventeenth Annual Report of the Elizabeth Peabody House: Report for the Year 1912*, Boston: Thomas Todd Co.

Elizabeth Peabody House (EPH), Boston (1915) *Nineteenth Annual Report of the Elizabeth Peabody House: Report for the Year 1914*, Boston: Thomas Todd Co.

Enstam, E.Y. (1998) *Women and the Creation of Urban Life: Dallas, Texas, 1843–1920*, College Station: Texas A&M University Press.

Erickson, C. (1999) *neighborhood WATCH*, Online. Available http://christa.art.sunysb.edu/watch (20 March 1999).

Erickson, C., Brooks, S. and Stryker, B. (1997) *INVERTIGO*, Online. Available http://christa.art.sunysb.edu/invertigo (20 March 1999).

États généraux du féminisme 30–31 mai 1931. Exposition coloniale internationale Paris (1931), Paris: Beaumont.

'Events underway.' (1997, Winter) *Celebration Chronicle*: 3.

Ezra, E. (2000) *The Colonial Unconscious: Race and Culture in Interwar France,* Ithaca: Cornell University Press.

Farrère, C. (1908 [1905]) *Les Civilisés*, Paris: Société d'Editions Littéraires et Artistiques.

Farrère, C. (1925) *Une jeune fille voyagea*, Paris: E. Flammarion.

Fishel, T.V. (1999) *Romances of the Sixth Reign: Gender, Sexuality, and Siamese Nationalism*, in P.A. Jackson and N.M. Cook (eds) *Genders & Sexualities in Modern Thailand*, Chiang Mai: Silkworm Books.

Fishman, R. (1987) *Bourgeois Utopias: The Rise and Fall of Suburbia,* New York: Basic Books.

Fitzgerald, F. (1986) *Cities on a Hill: A Journey through Contemporary American Cultures*, New York: Simon and Schuster.

Fleury, M. (1930) 'Les névroses urbaines', *Les Cahiers de la Republique des lettres des sciences et des arts*, 106.

Flower, J. (1996, January 20) 'Downhome technopia', *New Scientist*: 33–6.

Forrester Sprague, J. (1991) *More than Housing: Lifeboats for Women and Children*, Boston: Butterworth Architecture.

Foster, L. (1991) *Women, Family, and Utopia: Communal Experiments of the Shakers, the Oneida Community, and the Mormons*, Syracuse: Syracuse University Press.

Foucault, M. (1972) 'The discourse on language', in *The Archaeology of Knowledge*, New York: Harper Colophon.

Foucault, M. (1979) *Discipline and Punish*, New York: Random House.

Foucault, M. (1982) 'Space, knowledge, and power,' *Skyline*, rpt. in P. Rabinow (ed.) (1984) *The Foucault Reader*, New York: Pantheon Books.

Foucault, M. (1986) 'Of other spaces: utopias and heterotopias', *Diacritics* 16: 22–7.

Frank, A.G. (1998) *Reorient: Global Economy in the Asian Age,* Berkeley, CA: University of California Press.

Frank, R. (1994–6) *Hermes Mistress,* Online Documentation. Available http://www.regina-frank.de/level2/hermes.level2.html (20 March 1999).

Frantz, D. and Collins, C. (1999) *Celebration U.S.A.: Living in Disney's Brave New Town*, New York: Henry Holt and Company.

Fraser, N. and Gordon, L. (1997) 'Decoding "dependency": inscriptions of power in a keyword of the U.S. welfare state', in M.L. Shanley and U. Narayan (eds) *Reconstructing Political Theory: Feminist Perspectives*, University Park, PA: The Pennsylvania State University Press.

'Frauenheimstätten' (1913) 'Frauenheimstätten', *P.F.H.* [Pestalozzi-Fröbel-Haus] *II Zeitung,* July. 8–10.

Freedman, A. (1992) 'Nurturing independence', *Progressive Architecture* 73, 8: 61–3.

Freud, S. (1965) *The Interpretation of Dreams*, New York: Avon Books.

Freud, S. (1989) *Civilization and Its Discontents*, New York: W.W. Norton & Company.

Friedberg, A. (1993) *Window Shopping: Cinema and the Postmodern*, Berkeley: University of California Press.

Friedlaender, T. (1917) 'Haus Ottlie von Hansemann', *Deutscher Lyceum-Club* 13, 1: 13–14.

Frisby, D. and Featherstone, M. (1997) *Simmel on Culture*, London: Sage.

Furstenberg, F. (1992) 'Daddies and Fathers: men who do for their children and men who don't', in F. Furstenberg et al. (eds) *Caring and Paying: What Fathers and Mothers Say About Child Support*, New York: Manpower Research Development Corp.

Garcia, F. (n.d.) *Harriet Tubman & The Harriet Tubman House of United South End Settlements in Boston, Massachusetts.* Pamphlet, n.p.

Garreau, J. (1991) *Edge City: Life on the New Frontier*, New York: Anchor Books, Doubleday.

Gearheart, S. (1985) *The Wanderground*, London: The Women's Press.

'Genossenschaft' (1914) 'Die Genossenschaft "Die Frauenwohnung" ', *Frauenkapital – eine werdende Macht* 21: 18.

Ghirardo, D. (1996 [1984]) 'The architecture of deceit', in K. Nesbitt (ed.) *Theorizing A New Agenda for Architecture,* New York: Princeton Architectural Press, pp. 384–9.

Gibson, W. (1984) *Neuromancer,* New York: ACE Press.

Giedion, S. (1982) *Space, Time and Architecture: The Growth of a New Tradition,* Cambridge, MA: Harvard University Press.

Gilens, M. (1996) 'Race and poverty in America: public misperceptions about the American news media', *Public Opinion Quarterly* 60: 515–41.

Gillette, H. (1995) *Between Justice and Beauty: Race, Planning, and the Failure of Urban Policy in Washington, D.C.*, Baltimore: The Johns Hopkins University Press.

Gilloch, G. (1996) *Benjamin and the City,* Cambridge: Polity Press.

Gilman, C.P. (1899, 1994) *Women and Economics: The Economic Factor between Men and Women as a Factor in Social Revolution,* Boston: Small Maynard, rpt. New York: Prometheus Books.

Gilman, C.P. (1979 [1915]) *Herland,* New York: Pantheon Books.

Gilman, C.P. (1997 [1916]) *With Her in Ourland – a Sequel to Herland,* New York: Praeger.

Girard, R. (1993) *Violence and the Sacred*, Baltimore: Johns Hopkins University Press.

Goffman, E. (1959) *The Presentation of Self in Everyday Life*, Garden City, NY: Doubleday.

Gómez-Peña, G. (1996) *The New World Border: Prophesies, Poems, and Loqueras for the End of the Century,* San Francisco: City Lights.

Gómez-Peña, G. (1998) 'Visual activists: Chicano art at the end of the century', performance at *New Millenium, New Humanities,* 28 March 1998, SUNY, Stony Brook.

Gómez-Peña, G. and Sifuentes, R. (1996) *Temple of Confessions,* Online. Available http://www.echonyc.com/~confess (20 March 1999).

Gómez-Peña, G., Sifuentes, R. and Luna, J. (1995). *The Shame-Man and the El Mexican't Meet the CyberVato,* Online Documentation. Available http://rice-info.rice.edu/projects/CyberVato (20 March 1999).

Goncourt. E. *et al.* (1889) *Les Types de Paris,* Paris: Plon.

Gordon, L. (1994) *Pitied but Not Entitled: Single Mothers and the History of Welfare, 1890–1935*, New York: Free Press.

Goscha, C. (1995) *Vietnam or Indochina: Contesting Concepts of Space in Vietnamese Nationalism, 1887–1954,* Copenhagen: Nordic Institute of Asian Studies.

Graphics, Visualization, and Usability Center (1999) *GUV 10th WWW User Survey*, Online. Available http://www.gatech.edu/user_surveys/survey-1998–10/tenthreport.html (15 November 2000).

Gravelle, C. (1913) *Enquête sur la Question des Métis, Revue Indochinoise.* January, 31–43.

Green, C.M. (1962) *Washington: A History of the Capital, 1800–1950*, Princeton: Princeton University Press.

Green, C.M. (1967) *The Secret City: A History of Race Relations in the Nation's Capital*. Princeton: Princeton University Press.

Greenslade, W. (1994) *Degeneration, Culture and the Novel 1880–1940*, Cambridge: Cambidge University Press.

Greer, N.R. (1985) 'The homeless: an urban crisis of the 1980s', *Architecture: The AIA Journal* 74, 7: 56–9.

Greer, N.R. (1988) *The Creation of Shelter,* Washington, DC: American Institutes of Architects.

Grosz, E. (1990) *Sexual Subversions: Three French Feminists*, Sydney: Allen & Unwin.

Grosz, E. (1994) *Volatile Bodies: Toward A Corporeal Feminism,* Bloomington and Indianapolis: Indiana University Press.

Grosz, E. (1995) *Space, Time, and Perversion: Essays on the Politics of Bodies,* New York: Routledge.

Grosz, E. (1997a) 'Cyberspace, virtuality and the real: some architectural reflections', in C. Davidson (ed.) *ANYbody*, Cambridge, MA: The MIT Press, pp. 108–17.

Grosz, E. (1997b) 'The future of space: toward an architecture of invention', in 'The Virtual House' issue of *ANY*, 19, pp. 12–16.

Grosz, E. (2001) 'The time of architecture', in *Embodied Utopias: Gender, Social Change, and the Modern Metropolis,* London: Routledge.

Groth, P. (1994) *Living Downtown: The History of Residential Hotels in the United States*, Berkeley, CA: University of California Press.

Grumbach, A. (1978) *France, les laboratoires de l'architecture,* London: Architectural Design Magazine.

Guerrilla Girls (1995) *Internet Poster,* Online. Available http://www.guerrillagirls.com/posters/internetposter.html (20 March 1999).

Günther, S., Jachmann, C. and Schmidt-Thomsen, H. (1986) *The History of Women Architects: About the History of Women Architects and Designers in the Twentieth Century: A First Survey*, trans. M. Stanley, Berlin: UIFA.

Gutheim, F. (1977) *Worthy of the Nation: The History of City Planning for the National Capital*, Washington, DC: The Smithsonian Institution Press.

Habermas, J. (1991 [1962]) *The Structural Transformation of the Public Sphere*, Cambridge, MA: MIT Press.

Hacking, I. (1998) *Mad Travelers: Reflections on the Reality of Transient Mental Illnesses,* Charlottesville: University Press of Virginia.

Hahn, H. (1997) *Street Picturesque: Advertising in Paris, 1830–1914*, PhD diss., University of California at Berkeley.

Hall, P. (1988) *Cities of Tomorrow,* Oxford: Blackwell.

Hanke, R. (1998) 'Theorizing masculinity with/in the media', *Communication Theory* 8(2), 183–203.

Haraway, D. (1991) 'A cyborg manifesto: science, technology, and socialist feminism in the late twentieth century', *Simians, Cyborgs, and Women: the Reinvention of Nature*, New York: Routledge.

Harder, A. (1916) 'Ein Heim für studierende Frauen in Berlin', *Die Welt der Frau* 36: 563–6.

Harris, S. and Berke, D. (eds) (1997) *Architecture of the Everyday,* Princeton: Princeton Architectural Press.

Harrison, S. and Dourish, P. (1996) 'Re-placing space: the roles of place and space in collaborative environments', in *Proceedings of ACM Conference, Computer Supported Cooperative Work CSCW '96,* Boston, MA.

Harry, M. (1912) *L'Indo-Chine,* Vincennes: Les Arts Graphiques.

Harry, M. (1913) *Petites epouses*, 7th ed., Paris: Calmann-Levy.

Hayden, D. (1976) *Seven American Utopias: The Architecture of Communitarian Socialism, 1790–1975,* Cambridge, MA: MIT Press.

Hayden, D. (1980) 'What would a non-sexist city be like? Speculations on housing, urban design, and human work', in C. Stimpson *et al.* (eds) *Women and the American City*, Chicago: University of Chicago Press.

Hayden, D. (1981) *The Grand Domestic Revolution: A History of Feminist Designs for American Homes, Neighborhoods, and Cities*, Cambridge, MA: MIT Press.

Hayden, D. (1984) *Redesigning the American Dream: The Future of Housing, Work, and Family Life*, New York: W.W. Norton.

Hayden, D. (1995) *Power of Place: Urban Landscapes as Public History*, Cambridge, MA: MIT Press.

Heatherington, K. (1997) *The Badlands of Modernity*, New York: Routledge.

Hegel, G.W.F. (1993) *Introductory Lectures on Aesthetics*, London: Penguin Books.

Heidegger, M. (1961) *An Introduction to Metaphysics*, Garden City, NY: Anchor Books, Doubleday & Co, Inc.

Heuß, T. (1912) 'Die Frauenausstellung in Berlin', *Die Hilfe* 18, 11: 170–1.

Higginbotham, E.B. (1992) 'African–American women's history and the metalanguage of race', *Signs* 17, 2: 251–74.

Hill, E.D. (1982, July) 'The place of the future: Louis Marin and his Utopiques', *Science Fiction Studies*: 167–79.

Hillier, B. and Hanson, J. (1984) *The Social Logic of Space,* Cambridge: Cambridge University Press.

Hoesch, K. (1995) *Ärztinnen für Frauen: Kliniken in Berlin, 1877–1914*, Stuttgart: J.B. Metzler.

Holbé, T. (1916) *Métis de Cochinchine. Revue Anthropologique.* v. 26, December.

Holbrook, A.S. (1970 [1895]) 'Map notes and comments', in Residents of Hull-House, *Hull-House Maps and Papers*, New York: Arno Press, Inc.

Hooper, B. (1998) 'The poem of male desires: female bodies, modernity, and "Paris, Capital of the Nineteenth Century" ', in L. Sandercock (ed.) *Making The Invisible Visible: A Multicultural Planning History*, Berkeley: University of California Press.

Horowitz, H.L. (Winter 1983–4) 'Hull-House as women's space', *Chicago History*, XII: 40–55.

Hoskin, J. (2000) *Subways, Skytrains, and a City Redefined,* Bangkok: Curiosa.

Huffman, K.R. and Wohlgemuth, E. (1997) *Face Settings* Online. Available http://thing.at/face (20 March 1999).

Hunt, C.L. (1912) *The Life of Ellen H. Richards, 1842–1911*, Boston: Whitcomb and Barrows.

Huyssen, A. (1995) *Twilight Memories: Marking Time in a Culture of Amnesia*, New York: Routledge.

Ichenhaeuser, E. (1910) 'Weibliche Arzte [sic] und Frauenkrankenhäuser unter Leitung weiblicher Ärzte', *Die Welt der Frau* 39: 611–14.

Ichenhaeuser, E. (1911) 'Frauenklubs', *Die Welt der Frau* 46: 727–9.

Ichenhaeuser, E. (ed.) (1913) *Was die Frau von Berlin wissen muß*, Berlin: Herbert Loesdau.

Ingraham, C. (1998) *Architecture and the Burdens of Linearity*, New Haven: Yale University Press.

Irigaray, L. (1985a [1974]) *Speculum of the Other Woman*, trans. G.C. Gill, Ithaca, NY: Cornell University Press.

Irigaray, L. (1985b [1977]) *This Sex Which Is Not One*, trans. C. Porter with C. Bunker, Ithaca, NY: Cornell University Press.

Isn't this reason enough for Celebration? (1997) The Celebration Company: n.p.

Jackson, J.B. (1984) *Discovering the Vernacular Landscape,* New Haven, CT: Yale University Press.

Jackson, P.A. (1995) *Dear Uncle Go: Male Homosexuality in Thailand,* Bangkok: Bua Luang Books.

Jackson, S. (2000) *Lines of Activity: Performance, Historiography, Hull-House Domesticity,* Ann Arbor: University of Michigan Press.

Jacobs, J. (1961) *The Death and Life of Great American Cities,* New York: Random House.

Jacoby, R. (1999) *The End of Utopia: Politics and Culture in an Age of Apathy,* New York: Basic Books.

Jaguaribe, B. (1999) 'Modernist ruins: narratives and architectural forms', *Public Culture: Society for Transnational Cultural Studies, Alter/Native Modernities,* D. Gaonkar, Guest Editor, 11, 1: 294–312.

Jameson, F. (1981) *The Political Unconscious: Narrative as a Socially Symbolic Act,* Ithaca, NY: Cornell University Press.

Jameson, F. (1991) *Postmodernism, Or, The Cultural Logic of Late Capitalism,* Durham: Duke University Press.

Jamieson, T. (1999) 'The city on the screen', *The Herald,* 1 February, Glasgow.

Jane Addams Memorial Collection, Special collections, University of Illinois at Chicago.

Jencks, C. (1973) *Le Corbusier and the Tragic View of Architecture,* Cambridge, MA: Harvard University Press.

Jones, K. (1993) *Compassionate Authority: Democracy and the Representation of Women,* New York and London: Routledge.

Joyeux, C. and Sicé, A. (1937*) Précis de Médecine Coloniale,* Paris: Masson et Cie.

Jung, E. (1901) *La Vie Européenne au Tonkin,* Paris: Ernest Flammarion.

Karatani, K. (1995) *Architecture as Metaphor: Language, Number, Money,* Cambridge, MA: MIT Press.

Karger, H. (1987) *The Sentinels of Order: A Study of Social Control and the Minneapolis Settlement House Movements, 1915–1950,* Lanham, MD: University Press of America.

Katz, M. (1989) *The Undeserving Poor: From the War on Poverty to the War on Welfare,* New York: Pantheon Books.

Kelley, F. (1898) 'Hull House', *New England Magazine* XVII: 550–66.

Kelley, F. (1986 [1927]) 'I go to work', in K.K. Sklar (ed.) *The Autobiography of Florence Kelley,* Chicago: Charles H. Kerr Publishing Company.

Kern, S. (1983) *The Culture of Space and Time 1880–1918,* Cambridge, MA: Harvard University Press.

Kipnis, A. (1995) '"Face": an adaptable discourse of social surfaces', *Positions 3:* 119–21.

Kitsch, S. (2000) *Higher Ground: From Utopianism to Realism in American Feminist Thought and Theory,* Chicago: University of Chicago Press.

Knapp, T. and Schumacher, M. (eds) (1988) 'Commentary', in Westphal's *Die Agoraphobie,* New York: University Press of America, p. 43.

Knibiehler, Y. and Goutalier, R, (1985) *La Femme au Temps des Colonies,* Paris: Stock.

Koolhaas, R. and Mau, B. (1998 [1996]) *S, M, L, XL,* New York and London: The Monacelli Press.

Korr, J. (1997) 'A proposed model for cultural landscape study', *Material Culture* 29, 3: 1–18.

Kostoff, S. (1991) *The City Shaped: Urban Patterns and Meanings Through History,* Boston: Little, Brown and Company.

Kozak, R. (1993) 'Community and the new urban village: requirements, problems and solutions to siting domestic abuse shelters and transitional housing', *Interchange* 7: 15–21.

Krauss, R. (1983) 'Sculpture in the expanded field', in Hal Foster (ed.) *The Anti-Aesthetic: Essays on Postmodern Culture,* Seattle, Washington: Bay Press, pp. 31–42.

Krempl, S. and Dominguez, R. (2000) 'Email interview with Ricardo Dominguez, a pioneer of net activism and one of the founders of the electronic disturbance theater', *Telepolis,* Germany. 16 February 2000. Online. Available http://www.heise.de/tp/english/inhalt/te/5801/1.html (15 November 2000).

Kriehn, G. (1899) 'The city beautiful', *Municipal Affairs* 3: 594–601.

Krier, L. (1980) *Counter Projects,* Brussels: Les Archives.

Krier, R. (1979) *Urban Space,* London: Academy Editions.

Kristeva, J. (1982) *Powers of Horror: An Essay on Abjection*, trans. L.S. Roudiez, New York: Columbia University Press.

Kroker, A. and Weinstein, M.A. (1994) 'Global algorithm 1.4: the theory of the virtual class', excerpt from *DataTrash: The Theory of the Virtual Class*, New York: St Martin's Press. Online. Available http://www.ctheory.com/ga1.4–theory_virtual.html (15 November 2000).

Kunstler, J. (1993) *The Geography of Nowhere: The Rise and Decline of America's Man-Made Landscape*, Simon & Schuster. New York: Touchstone.

Kusno, A. (2000) *Behind the Postcolonial: Architecture, Urban Space and Political Cultures in Indonesia,* New York: Routledge.

L'Illustration, 23 May 1931.

La Jolla Institute. (1999, January 23) *Does Place Matter?* Online. Available HTTP: http://www.lajollainstitute.org/Forum/edgecity.htm.

Lacan, J. (1977) *Écrits. A Selection*, trans. A. Sheridan, London: Tavistock.

Ladd, D. (1999) 'Squatting is a political right', in *intellectualcapital.com,* Online. Available http://intellectualcapital.com/issues/issue247/item5339.asp (10 June 1999).

'Lakeside park offers fun and relaxation.' (1996) *Celebration Chronicle*, Fall. 7.

Lange, L. (1979) 'The function of equal education in Plato's Republic and Laws', in L.M.G. Clark and L. Lange (eds) *The Sexism of Social and Political Theory: Women and Reproduction from Plato to Nietzsche*, Toronto: University of Toronto Press.

Lavin, S. (1992) *Quatremere De Quincy and the Invention of a Modern Language of Architecture*, Cambridge, MA: MIT Press.

Lawson, C. (1995) 'When you wish upon a home', *New York Times*, 16 November. C1, C6.

Le Bon, G. (1887) 'Ethnographie: L'Algérie et les idées régnantes en France en matière de colonisation', in *Revue Scientifique*: 15.

Le Bon, G. (1912) *La Psychologie politique*, Paris: Ernest Flammarion.

Le Bon, G. (1924) *The Psychology of Peoples: Its Influence on Their Evolution*, New York: G. E. Stechert & Co.

Le Brusq, A. (1999) *Vietnam, à Travers l'architecture Coloniale,* Paris: Patrimoines et Medias.

Le Corbusier (1947) *When the Cathedrals Were White,* New York: McGraw Hill.

Le Corbusier (1948) *Concerning Town Planning*, New Haven: Yale University Press.

Le Corbusier (1957) *The Chapel at Ronchamp*, New York: Frederick A. Praeger Publishers.

Le Corbusier (1967) *The Radiant City,* New York: Orion Press.

Le Corbusier (1968) *Modular 2,* Cambridge, MA: MIT Press.

Le Corbusier (1973*) The Modular,* Cambridge, MA: MIT Press.

Le Corbusier (1986) *Towards a New Architecture,* New York: Dover Publications.

Le Corbusier (1987a) *Aircraft,* Paris: Fondation Le Corbusier.

Le Corbusier (1987b) *The City of Tomorrow and its Planning,* New York: Dover Publications.

Le Corbusier (1991) *Journey to the East,* Cambridge, MA: MIT Press.

Le Corbusier (1998) *The Decorative Art of Today,* London: The Architectural Press.

Le Corbusier (1999) *Talks With Students From the Schools of Architecture,* New York: Princeton Architectural Press.

Le Doeuff, M. (1989a) 'Daydream in Utopia', in *The Philosophical Imaginary*, trans. Colin Gordon, Stanford: Stanford University Press, pp. 21–8.

Le Doeuff, M. (1989b) 'The polysemy of atopian discourse', in *The Philosophical Imaginary*, trans. Colin Gordon, Stanford: Stanford University Press, pp. 45–56.

Leavitt, J. (1984) 'The shelter plus issue for single parents', *Women and Environments* 6, 20: 16–20.

Lebel, R. (1931) *Histoire de la Littérature Coloniale en France*, Paris: Librairie Larose.

Lee, J. (1988) 'Paradise limited: An interview with Leo Marx by Judith Yaross Lee', *Invention & Technology*: 34–9.

Lee, Leo Ou-Fan (1999) 'Shanghai modern: reflections on urban culture in China in the 1930s', in *Public Culture: Society for Transnational Cultural Studies*, *Alter/Native Modernities*, D. Gaonkar, Guest Editor, 11, 1.

Lefebvre, H. (1971) *Everyday Life in the Modern World*, trans. S. Rabinovitch, New York: Harper and Row.

Lefebvre, H. (1991) *The Production of Space*, trans. D. Nicholson-Smith, Oxford, UK and Cambridge, MA: Basil Blackwell Ltd.

Lefebvre, H. (1996) 'Seen from the window' and 'Rhythmanalysis of Mediterranean cities', in H. Lefebvre, *Writings on Cities*, trans. and ed., E. Kofman and E. Lebas, Oxford: Blackwell, pp. 219–27 and 228–40.

Lemann, N. (1996) 'Kicking in Groups', *Atlantic Monthly*, April. 22–4.

Les Français peints par eux-mêmes, 8 vols., Paris: Cumer.

Lévi-Strauss, C. (1987) *The View From Afar*, Harmondsworth: Penguin.

Levitas, R. (1990) *The Concept of Utopia*. Syracuse: Syracuse University Press.

Levy, H.F. (1992) *Fiction of the Home Place*, Jackson, MS: University Press of Mississippi.

Levy-Rathenau, J. (10 March 1910) 'Unsre deutschen Frauenklubs und ihre Leistungen', *Frauen-Fortschritt*: 3.

Lewis, P. (1979) 'Axioms for reading the landscape: some guides to the American scene', in D.W. Meinig (ed.) *The Interpretation of Ordinary Landscapes: Geographical Essays*, New York: Oxford University Press.

Ley, D. (1989) 'Modernism, post-modernism and the struggle for place', in J.A. Agnew and J.S. Duncan (eds) *The Power of Place: Bringing Together Geographical and Sociological Imaginations,* Boston: Unwin Hyman.

L'Illustration (1931), special issue on colonial exposition, 23 May.

Lincoln House (LH) (1899) *Lincoln House Bulletin 1899*, Boston.

Lincoln House (LH) (1902) *Lincoln House Report for 1902*, Boston.

Lincoln House (LH) (1903) *Lincoln House Report for 1903*, Boston.

Lincoln House (LH) (1904) *Lincoln House Report for 1904*, Boston.

Lincoln House (LH) (1905) *Lincoln House Report for 1905*, Boston.

Lincoln House (LH) (1906) *Lincoln House Report for 1906*, Boston.

Lincoln House (LH) (1907) *Lincoln House Report for 1907*, Boston.

Lincoln House (LH) (1910) *Lincoln House Report for 1910*, Boston.

Linn, J.W. (1935) *Jane Addams: A Biography*, New York: D. Appleton-Century Company.

Lissak, R. (1989*) Pluralism and Progressives: Hull House and the New Immigrants, 1890–1919,* Chicago: University of Chicago Press.

Logan, W. (1994) 'Hanoi townscape: symbolic imagery in Vietnam's capital,' M. Askew and W. Logan, (eds). In *Cultural Identity and Urban Change in Southeast Asia: Interpretative Essays,* Geelong, Victoria: Deakin University Press.

Logan, W. (2001) *Hanoi: Biography of a City,* Seattle: University of Washington Press.

Loos, A. (1998) *Ornament and Crime: Selected Essays*, Riverside, CA: Ariadne Press.

Lovejoy, A. and Boas, G. (1997) *Primitivism and Related Ideas in Antiquity,* Baltimore: Johns Hopkins Press.

'Lyzeumklub' (1905) 'Der Lyzeumklub', *Die Frau* 12, 12: 752–5.

Majupuria, T.C. (1993) *Erawan Shrine and Brahma Worship in Thailand*, Bangkok: Craftsman Press.

Malleret, V. (1934) *L'Exotisme indochinois dans la litterature française depuis 1860*, Paris: Larose.

Marin, L. (1984 [1973]) *Utopics: Spatial Play*, trans. R.A. Vollrath, Atlantic Highlands, NJ: Humanities Press.

Marin, L. (1998 [1980]) 'Toward a theory of reading in the visual arts: Poussin's "The Arcadian Shepherds" ', in D. Preziosi (ed.) *The Art of Art History: A Critical Anthology*, Oxford: Oxford University Press.

Marks, M.B. (1900) 'Among the workers: Jane Addams, of Hull House', *Good Housekeeping*, November: 31.

Markus, T.A. (1993) *Buildings and Power: Freedom and Control in the Origin of Modern Building Types*, New York: Routledge.

Marpeau, B. (2000) *Gustave Le Bon: Parcours d'un Intellectuel 1841–1931,* Paris: CNRS Editions.

Martial, R. (1942) *Les Métis. Nouvelle étude sur les migrations, le mélange des races, le métissage, la retrempe de la race française et la révision du code de la famille*, Paris: Flammarion.

Marx, L. (1964) *The Machine in the Garden: Technology and the Pastoral Ideal in America*, New York: Oxford University Press.

Maspero, F. (1994) *Roissy Express*, London: Verso.

Mazey, M.E. and Lee, D.R. (1983) *Her Space, Her Place: A Geography of Women*, Washington, DC: Association of American Geographers.

McClintock, A. (1995) *Imperial Leather: Race, Gender, and Sexuality in the Colonial Context*, New York, London: Routledge.

McGaw, J.A. (1987) 'Women and the history of American technology', in S. Harden and J.F. O'Barr (eds) *Sex and Scientific Inquiry,* Chicago: University of Chicago Press.

McGrath, B. and C. Weisz (eds) (2000) *New Urbanisms/New Workplace: Yonkers Nepperhan Valley,* New York: Columbia Books on Architecture.

McLuhan, M. (1964) *Understanding Media: The Extensions of Man,* New York: McGraw-Hill.

Meinig, D.W. (1979) 'The beholding eye: ten versions of the same scene', in D.W. Meinig (ed.) *The Interpretation of Ordinary Landscapes: Geographical Essays*, New York: Oxford University Press.

Mencher, S. (1974) *Poor Law to Poverty Program: Economic Security Policy in Britain and the United States,* Pittsburgh: University of Pittsburgh Press.

Mensch, E. (1912) 'An Damen wird nicht vermietet', *Die Deutsche Frau* 2, 37: 7–8.

Mills, C. (1993) 'Myths and meanings of gentrification', in J. Duncan and D. Ley (eds), *Place/Culture/Representation*, London: Routledge.

Mitchell, W. J. (1995) *City of Bits,* Cambridge, MA: MIT Press.

Moore, C. (1902a) 'The improvement of Washington City, first paper', *The Century* 63: 621–8.

Moore, C. (1902b) 'The improvement of Washington City, second paper', *The Century* 63: 747–57.

Moore, C. (1929) *The Life and Times of Charles McKim*, Cambridge, MA: The Riverside Press.

More, T. (1975 [1515]) *Utopia*, Cambridge: Cambridge University Press.

Moresco, M.E. (1911) 'De la condition des métis et de l'attitude des Gouvernements à leur égard', in *Compte rendu de la session tenue à Brunswick. Institut Colonial Internationale*, v. 2: 453.

Morris, P. (1997) 'Design of Celebration', *Celebration Journal* 1, 37–44.

Morris, R.C. (1994) *Three Sexes and Four Sexualities: Redressing the Discourses on Gender and Sexuality in Contemporary Thailand*, in *Positions*, 2, 1, Durham: Duke University Press.

Morton, P. (2000) *Hybrid Modernities: Architecture and Representation at the 1931 Colonial Exposition,* Paris, Cambridge, MA: MIT Press.

Mosley, L. (1990) *Disney's World,* Chelsea, MI: Scarborough House.

Mulder, N. (1996) *Inside Southeast Asia: Religion, Everyday Life, Cultural Change,* Chiang Mai, Thailand: Silkworm Books.

Muller, P. (1981) *Contemporary Suburban America,* Englewood Cliffs, NJ: Prentice-Hall.

Mumford, L. (1961) *The City in History,* New York: Harcourt, Brace & World, Inc.

Muntadas, A. (1994) *FileRoom,* Online. Available http://www.fileroom.org (20 March 1999).

Muntadas, A. (1996) *On Translation* Online. Available http://adaweb.walkerart.org/influx/muntadas (20 March 1999).

Murdoch, I. (1982 [1954]) *Under the Net,* Harmondsworth: Penguin Books.

National Archives n.1, Hanoi, Mairie de Hanoi E9 383.

National Research Council (1991) *Thailand from Space,* Bangkok: National Research Council.

Nead, L. (1992) *The Female Nude: Art, Obscenity, and Sexuality,* London: Routledge.

Negroponte, N. (1995) *Being Digital,* New York: Knopf.

Nordau, M. (1993 [1892]) *Degeneration,* Lincoln: University of Nebraska Press.

Norindr, P. (1997) *Phantasmatic Indochina: French Colonial Ideology in Architecture, Film, and Literature,* Durham: Duke University Press.

Noury, J. (1992) *L'Indochine en cartes postales avant l'ouragan: 1900–1920,* Mercues, France: Publi-Fusion Editeur.

Ohlert, A. (1912) 'Das Lehrerinnenheim in Hamburg', *Frauen-Rundschau* 13, 11: 238–9.

Old Boys Network (1997) *Old Boys Network site,* Online. Available http://www.obn.org (20 March 1999).

Ong, W.J. (1982) *Orality and Literacy: The Technologizing of the Word,* London: Routledge.

Ong, W.J. (1986) 'Writing is a technology that restructures thought', in G. Baumann (ed.) *The Written Word: Literacy in Transition,* Oxford: Clarendon Press.

Ono, K.A. and Sloop, J.M. (1995) 'The critique of vernacular discourse', *Communication Monographs* 62: 19–46.

Orwell, G. (1934) *Burmese Days,* New York: Harper & Brothers.

Osborne, M. (1990) 'Fear and fascination in the tropics: A reader's guide to French fiction on Indo-China', in R. Winks and J. Rush (eds) *Asia in Western Fiction,* Manchester: Manchester University Press.

Ozenfant (1952) *Foundations of Modern Art,* New York: Dover.

Ozenfant and Jeanneret (n.d.) *La Peinture Moderne,* Paris: Les Editions G. Cres and Cie.

Pasuk Phongpaichit and Baker, C. (1995) *Thailand: Economy and Politics,* Kuala Lumpur: Oxford University Press.

Pasuk Phongpaichit and Baker, C. (2000) *Thailand's Crisis,* Chiang Mai: Silkworm Books.

Paterson, N. (1998) *Stock Market Skirt*, Online Documentation. Available http://www.bccc.com/nancy/skirt.html (20 March 1999).

Penley, C. and Ross, A. (1991) 'Cyborgs at large: interview with Donna Haraway', in *Technoculture*, Minneapolis: University of Minnesota Press.

Petit, M. (ed.) (1902) *Les Colonies françaises* v.2, Paris: Larousse.

Picket fences. (1997) *Celebration Journal* 1: 53–5.

Piercy, M. (1979 [1976]) *Woman on the Edge of Time,* London: The Women's Press.

Piercy, M. (1992) *Body of Glass,* Harmondsworth: Penguin [published as *He, She and It* (1991) New York: Knopf].

Pile, S. (1994) 'Masculinism, the use of dualistic epistemologies and third spaces', *Antipode* 26: 255–77.

Pile, S. (1996) *The Body and the City: Psychoanalysis, Space and Subjectivity*, London and New York: Routledge.

Plant, S. (1996) 'Feminizations: reflections on women and virtual reality', in Leeson, L.H (ed.) *Clicking In,* Seattle: Bay Press.

Plant, S. (1997) *Zeros and Ones*, New York: Doubleday.

Plato (1974) *The Republic*, trans. G.M. Gude, Indianpolis: Hackett Publishing Co.

Pochhammer, M. (1913) 'Berliner Wohnungsverhältnisse', in Eliza Ichenhaeuser (ed.) *Was die Frau von Berlin wissen muß*, Berlin: Herbert Loesdau.

Pond, A.B. (1902a) 'The Settlement House I', *Brickbuilder* 1: 140–5.

Pond, A.B. (1902b) 'The Settlement House III', *Brickbuilder* 11: 178–85.

Poovey, M. (1998) 'The production of abstract space', in S. Aiken *et al.* (eds) *Making Worlds: Gender, Metaphor, Materiality*, Tucson: The University of Arizona Press.

Price-Chalita, P. (1994) 'Spatial metaphor and the politics of empowerment: Mapping a place for feminism and postmodernism in geography?', *Antipode* 26: 236–54.

Putnam, R.D. (1995) 'Bowling alone: America's declining social capital', *Journal of Democracy* 6, 1: 65–78.

Putnam, R.D. (2000) *Bowling Alone: The Collapse and Revival of American Community*, New York: Simon & Schuster.

Queer Arts. (1996–) *Queer Arts Resources,* Online. Available http://www.queer-arts.org (20 March 1999).

Rajchman, J. (1998) *Constructions*, Cambridge, MA: The MIT Press.

Rappaport, E.D. (2000) *Shopping for Pleasure: Women in the Making of London's West End*, Princeton: Princeton University Press.

Ratigan, M. (1946) *A Sociological Survey of Disease in Four Alleys in the National Capital*, Washington, DC: The Catholic University of America Press.

Rauschenbusch, W. (1912) *Christianizing and Social Order*, New York: Macmillan.

Read, A. (ed.) (2000) *Architecturally Speaking: Practices of Art, Architecture and the Everyday,* London and New York: Routledge.

Redmond, W. (1998) *Wondering into Thai Culture,* Bangkok: Redmondian Insight Enterprises.

Relph, E. (1987) *The Modern Urban Landscape*, London and Sydney: Croom Helm.

Reps, J.W. (1965) *The Making of Urban America,* Princeton: Princeton University Press.

Reps, J.W. (1967) *Monumental Washington: The Planning and Development of the Capital Center*, Princeton: Princeton University Press.

Reston, J. (1941) 'L'Enfant's capital – and boomtown, too', in R. Ginger (ed.) *Modern American Cities*, Chicago: Quadrangle Books.

Revon, M. (1924) *Claude Farrère: Son oeuvre, portrait et autographe*, Paris: La Nouvelle Revue Critique.

Robinson, J. (1970) *Modern Civic Art or The City Made Beautiful*, New York: Arno Press.

Rochefort, D.A. (1981) 'Progressive and social control perspectives on social welfare', *Social Service Review* 55 (December): 568–92.

Rosaldo, M.Z. (1974) 'Woman, culture, and society: a theoretical overview', in M.Z. Rosaldo and L. Lamphere (eds) *Woman, Culture, and Society,* Stanford, CA: Stanford University Press.

Rose, G. (1993) *Feminism & Geography: The Limits of Geographical Knowledge,* Minneapolis, MN: University of Minnesota Press.

Rosenberg, R. (1982) *Beyond Separate Spheres: Intellectual Roots of Modern Feminism*, New Haven, CT: Yale University Press.

Ross, A. (1999) *The Celebration Chronicles: Life, Liberty, and the Pursuit of Property Values in Disney's New Town*, New York: Ballantine Books.

Rossi, A. (1982) *Architecture of the City,* Cambridge, MA: MIT Press.

Rothschild, J. (ed.) (1999) *Design and Feminism: Re-Visioning Spaces, Places, and Everyday Things,* New Brunswick, NJ: Rutgers University Press.

Rouvier, C. (1986) *Les Idées Politiques de Gustave Le Bon,* Paris: Presses Universitaires de France.

Rowe, C. and Koeter, F. (1978) *Collage City,* Cambridge: MIT Press.

Rowe, C. and Slutzky, R. (1963) 'Transparency: literal and phenomenal,' *Perspecta* 8: 45–54.

RTMark (1997–) *rtmark.com,* Online. Available http://www.rtmark.com (15 November 2000).

RTMark (2000) *RTMark Annual Report*, Online. Available http://rtmark.com/2000.html (30 December 2000).

Rykwert, J. (1976) *The Idea of a Town: The Anthropology of Urban Form in Rome, Italy and the Ancient World,* London: Faber and Faber.

Said, E. (1979) *Orientalism*, New York: Vintage Books, Random House.

Saigon Times (2000) 1–2000 (430), January 1.

Saigon Times Weekly (1999), no. 46, 1999 (423), November 13.

Salomon, A. (1899) 'Frauenklubs', *Centralblatt des Bundes Deutscher Frauenvereine* 1, 16: 124–6.

Schonfield, K. (2000) *Walls Have Feelings: Architecture, Film and the City,* London and New York: Routledge.

Schor, N. (1992) 'Cartes Postales: representing Paris 1900', *Critical Inquiry* 18, 2: 188–244.

Schneider, R. (1997) *The Explicit Body in Performance,* London and New York: Routledge.

Schneider, W. (1990) 'The eugenics movement in France 1890–1940, M. Adams (ed.)' In *The Wellborn Science: Eugenics in Germany, France, Brazil, and Russia,* New York: Oxford University Press, 69–109.

Schwartz, V. (1998) *Spectacular Realities: Early Mass Culture in Fin-de-Siècle Paris*, Berkeley: University of California Press.

Sedway Cook Associates (1990) *Comprehensive Plan: Reedy Creek Improvement District*, December.

Seigfried, C.H. (1996) *Pragmatism and Feminism,* Chicago: University of Chicago Press.

Sennett, R. (1971) *The Uses of Disorder: Personal Identity and City Life,* Harmondsworth: Penguin.

Sennett, R. (1978) *The Fall of Public Man*, New York: Vintage Books.

Sennett, R. (1994) *Flesh and Stone: The Body and the City in Western Civilization*, New York and London: W.W. Norton Company.

Sidel, M. (1998) *Old Hanoi*, Oxford and New York: Oxford University Press.

Siebenmorgen, A. (1995) 'Die Geschichte des Internationalen Lyceum-Clubs Berlin e.V. 1905–1995', Festschrift, Berlin: Internationaler Lyceum-Club Berlin.

Siebers, T. (ed.) (1994) *Heterotopia: Postmodern Utopia and the Body Politic*, Ann Arbor: University of Michigan Press.

Silverman, K. (1992) *Male Subjectivity at the Margins*, New York: Routledge.

Simmel, G. (1970) 'The metropolis and mental life', in D. Levine (ed.) *On Individuality and Social Forms: Selected Writings*, Chicago: The University of Chicago Press.

Sinclair, I. (1997) *Lights Out for the Territory: Nine Excursions into the Secret History of London*, London: Granta.

Sitwell, O. (1939) *Escape With Me! An Oriental Sketch-Book*, London: Macmillan & Co.

Sklar, K.K. (1985) 'Hull House in the 1890s: a community of women reformers', *Signs* 10, 658–677.

Sklar, K.K. (1990) 'Who funded Hull House?', in K.D. McCarthy (ed.) *Lady Bountiful Revisited: Women, Philanthropy, and Power*, New Brunswick: Rutgers University Press.

Slotkin, R. (1992) *Gunfighter Nation: The Myth of the Frontier in Twentieth-Century America*, New York: HarperCollins.

Smith, C. (1995) *Urban Disorder and the Shape of Belief: The Great Chicago Fire, The Haymarket Bomb, and the Model Town of Pullman*, Chicago: University of Chicago Press.

Smith-Rosenberg, C. (1985) *Disorderly Conduct: Visions of Gender in Victorian America*, New York: Oxford University Press.

Snyder, A. (1972) *Dauntless Women in Childhood Education 1856–1931*, Washington, DC: Association for Childhood Education International.

Soja, E.W. (1995) 'Hetertopologies: A remembrance of other spaces in the citadel-LA', in S. Watson and K. Gibson (eds) *Postmodern Cities and Spaces*, Oxford, UK: Blackwell Publishers.

Solomon, M.H. (1977) Oral Memoir, 3 vols. William E. Weiner Oral history Library of the American Jewish Committee. Schlesinger Library, Radcliffe College, Cambridge, MA.

Sorkin, M. (ed.) (1992) *Variations on a Theme Park: The New American City and the End of Public Space*, New York: Hill and Wang.

South End House (SEH) (1910) *South End House 1910: Democracy Domesticated,* Boston.

Spencer-Wood, S.M. (1987) 'A survey of domestic reform movement sites in Boston and Cambridge, ca. 1865–1905', *Historical Archaeology* 21, 2: 7–36.

Spencer-Wood, S.M. (1991) 'Towards an historical archaeology of materialistic domestic reform', in R.M. McGuire and R. Paynter (eds) *The Archaeology of Inequality*, Oxford: Basil Blackwell.

Spencer-Wood, S.M. (1994a) 'Diversity in 19th century domestic reform: relationships among classes and ethnic groups', in E.M. Scott (ed.) *Those 'Of Little Note': Gender, Race and Class in Historical Archaeology,* Tucson: University of Arizona Press.

Spencer-Wood, S.M. (1994b) 'Turn-of-the-century women's organizations, urban design, and the origin of the American playground movement', *Landscape Journal* 13, 2: 125–38.

Spencer-Wood, S.M. (1996) 'Feminist historical archaeology and the transformation of American culture by domestic reform movements, 1840–1925', in L.A. De Cunzo and B.L. Herman (eds) *Historical Archaeology and the Study of American Culture*, Knoxville: Winterthur Museum & University of Tennessee.

Spencer-Wood, S.M. (1997) 'Feminism and pragmatism', paper presented at the annual meetings of the American Anthropological Association, Washington, DC.

Spencer-Wood, S.M. (1999a) 'The world their household: changing meanings of the domestic sphere in the nineteenth century', in P.M. Allison (ed.) *The Archaeology of Household Activities: Gender Ideologies, Domestic Spaces and Material Culture*, London: Routledge.

Spencer-Wood, S.M. (1999b) 'Gendering power', in T.L. Sweely (ed.) *Manifesting Power: Gender and the Interpretation of Power in Archaeology*, London: Routledge.

Spencer-Wood, S.M. and Baugher, S. (2001) 'Introduction and historical context for the archaeology of nineteenth-century institutions for reform: asylums and prisons', *International Journal of Historical Archaeology* 5, 1.

Spivak, G.C. (1990) *The Post-Colonial Critic: Interviews, Strategies, Dialogues*, London: Routledge.

Stack, C. (1974) *All Our Kin: Strategies for Survival in a Black Community*, New York: Harper and Row.

Stansell, C. (1986) *City of Women: Sex and Class in New York, 1789–1860,* New York: Knopf.

Stanton, L. (ed.) (1985) *North Bennet Street School: A Short History 1885–1985*, Boston: Chadis Printing.

Sternberg, G. (1908) *Report of the Committee on Building Model Homes*, Washington, DC: The President's Homes Commission.

Stoler, A. (1991) 'Carnal knowledge and imperial power: gender, race and morality in colonial Asia', in *Gender at the Crossroads of Knowledge: Feminist Anthropology in the Postmodern Era*, Berkeley: University of California Press.

Stoler, A. (1995) *Race and the Education of Desire: Foucault's* History of Sexuality *and the Colonial Order of Things*, Durham: Duke University Press.

Stoler, A. (1997) 'Sexual affronts and racial frontiers: European identities and the cultural politics of exclusion in colonial Southeast Asia', in F. Cooper and A. Stoler (eds) *Tensions of Empire: Colonial Cultures in a Bourgeois World*, Berkeley: University of California Press.

Stone, A.R. (1995) *The War of Desire and Technology at the Close of the Machine Age,* Cambridge, MA: MIT Press.

Stratigakos, D.M. (1999) 'Skirts and scaffolding: women architects, gender, and design in Wilhelmine Germany', PhD diss., Bryn Mawr College.

Stropp, E. (1913) 'Berliner Frauenklubs', in Eliza Ichenhaeuser (ed.) *Was die Frau von Berlin wissen muß*, Berlin: Herbert Loesdau.

Sudjic, D. (1992) *The 100 Mile City*, London: André Deutsch Limited.

Suleri, S. (1992) *The Rhetoric of English India*, Chicago: The University of Chicago Press.

Szuberla, G. (1977) 'Three Chicago settlements: their architectural form and social meaning', *Journal of the Illinois Historical Society* LXX: 114–29.

Tannenbaum, N. (1999) *Buddhism, Prostitution and Sex*, in P.A. Jackson and N.M. Cook (eds) *Genders & Sexualities in Modern Thailand,* Chiang Mai: Silkworm Books.

Taylor, G. (1935) 'Jane Addams, the great neighbor', *Survey Graphic.*

Tehan, R. (2000) RL3045: *Internet and E-Commerce Statistics: What They Mean and Where to Find Them on the Web*, Online. Available http://www.cnie.org/nle/st-36.html (15 November 2000).

'The doctor is in' (1996) *Celebration Chronicle*, Fall: 6.

Theweleit, K. (1987) *Male Fantasies, Volume 1: Women, Floods, Bodies, History*, Minneapolis: University of Minnesota Press.

Thompson, V. (1937) *French Indo-China*, New York: Macmillan.

Thongchai Winichakul, (1994). *Siam Mapped: A History of the Geo-Body of a Nation,* Honolulu: University of Hawaii Press.

Time (1995) Volume 146, No. 1, 3 July 1995.

Todorov, T. (1993) *On Human Diversity: Nationalism, Racism, and Exoticism in French Thought*, Cambridge: Harvard University Press.

Toulmin, S. (1990) *Cosmopolis: The Hidden Agenda of Modernity*, Chicago, IL: The University of Chicago Press.

Trujillo, N. (1991) 'Hegemonic masculinity on the mound: media representations of Nolan Ryan and American sports culture', *Critical Studies in Mass Communication* 8, 3: 290–308.

Tschumi, B. (1998) *Architecture and Disjunction*, Cambridge, MA: MIT Press.

Tschumi, B. (2000) 'Six concepts', in A. Read (ed.) *Architecturally Speaking: Practices of Art, Architecture and the Everyday,* London and New York: Routledge, pp. 155–76.

Turner, P. (1965) 'Introduction', in More, T., *Utopia,* New York: Penguin Books.

Under Construction (1996) The Celebration Company: n.p.

Ungers, O.M. (1982) *Morphologie-City Metaphors*, Koln: Verlag der Buchhandlung, W. Korig, New York: J. Rietman.

Urry, J. (1995) *Consuming Places*, London: Routledge.

US Department of Commerce (2000) 'Retail e-commerce sales in third quarter 2000 increased', *Commerce News*. Washington, DC. Online. Available http://www.census.gov/mrts/current.html (15 November 2000).

US House of Representatives (1914) *Certain Alleys in the District of Columbia*. Hearing before the House Committee on the District of Columbia. 63 Cong. 2 Sess. March 13 and 18, 1914. Washington, DC: Government Printing Office.

US National Telecommunications and Information Administration (1999) *Falling Through the Net: Defining the Digital Divide*. Online. Available http://www.ntia.doc.gov/ntiahome/fttn99/contents.html (15 November 2000).

US Senate (1902) Hearing on the bill (S. 3244) creating a commission for the condemnation of insanitary buildings in the District of Columbia. March 12, 1902.

US Senate (1914) *Inhabited Alleys in the District of Columbia*. Hearing of the United States Senate Subcommittee on the District of Columbia. Thursday, May 7, 1914. Washington, DC: Government Printing Office.

Van Esterik, P. (1999) 'Repositioning Gender, Sexuality, and Power in Thai Studies', in P.A. Jackson and N.M. Cook (eds) *Genders & Sexualities in Modern Thailand,* Chiang Mai: Silkworm Books.

Vanderbilt, T. (1995) 'Revolt of the nice: Edge City, capital of the 21st century', in *The Baffler*.

'Vereinigung' (1911) 'Die Vereinigung für moderne Frauenwohnungen', *Die Deutsche Frau* 1, 30: 7.

'Vereinigung' (1914) 'Die Vereinigung für Frauenwohnungen', *Frauenkapital – eine werdende Macht*, Geschäftliche Notizen section, 5: 20.

Verges, F. (1999) *Monsters and Revolutionaries: Colonial Family Romance and Métissage*, Durham: Duke University Press.

Vesna, V. (1996) *Bodies Inc.*, Online. Available http://www.bodiesinc.ucla.edu (15 November 2000).

Vidler, A. (1987) *The Writing of the Walls*, New York: Princeton Architectural Press.

Vidler, A. (1991) 'Agoraphobia: spatial estrangement in Georg Simmel and Siegfried Kracauer', *New German Critique* 54: 31–45.

Vidler, A. (1993) 'Bodies in space/subjects in the city: psychopathologies of modern urbanism', *Differences* 5: 31–51.

Vitruvius (1960) *The Ten Books On Architecture*, New York: Dover Publications, Inc.

VNS Matrix (1991–7) Online. Available http://sysx.apana.org.au/artists/vns (15 November 2000).

Von Moos, S. (1987) *L'Esprit Nouveau, Le Corbusier Et L'Industrie 1920–1925.* Exhibition Catalogue, Les Musées de la Ville de Strasbourg, 29 Septembre au 31 Octobre, Berlin: Ernst and Sohn.

Wall, A. (1995) 'Dispersed cities', in *The Periphery, Architectural Design No. 88*, London: Academy Editions.

Walter, L. (1912) 'Berliner Klubs', *Elegante Welt* 3: 4–6.

Warner, S.B. (1972) *The Urban Wilderness: A History of the American City*, New York: Harper & Row.

Weeks, L. (1999, September 7). 'Can a Planned Community Approach the Utopian Ideal? In Celebration, Fla., It's a Question That Hits Close to Home.' *Washington Post*: C01.

Weiss, G. (1999) *Body Images: Embodiment as Intercorporeality*. New York: Routledge.

Weller, C. (1909) *Neglected Neighbors: Stories of Life in the Alleys, Tenements, and Shanties of the National Capital*, Philadelphia: John C. Winston Company.

Werth, L. (1926) *Cochinchine*, Paris: F. Rieder et Cie.

Whitford, M. (1991) *Luce Irigaray. Philosophy in the Feminine*, London and New York: Routledge.

Wigley, M. (1995a) *The Architecture of Deconstruction: Derrida's Haunt,* Cambridge, MA: MIT Press.

Wigley, M. (1995b) *White Walls, Designer Dresses: The Fashioning of Modern Architecture,* Cambridge, MA: MIT Press.

Wilding, F. and Critical Art Ensemble. (1998) 'Notes on the political conditions of cyberfeminism', Online. Available http://critical-art.net/lectures/fem.html (15 November 2000).

Williams, L.F. (1991) 'The machine at utopia's center', in M.S. Cummings and N.D. Smith (eds) *Utopian Studies III*, Lanham, MD: University Press of America.

Williams, M. (1995) 'Disney Plans Ideal Town', *Atlanta Journal – Constitution*, 18 November: E7.

Wilson, C. (1995) 'Celebration puts Disney in reality's realm', *USA Today*, 18 November: A1.

Wilson, E. (1991) *The Sphinx in the City: Urban Life, the Control of Disorder, and Women*, Berkeley and Los Angeles: University of California Press.

Wilson, W.H. (1989) *The City Beautiful Movement*, Baltimore: Johns Hopkins University Press.

Winkelmann, E. (1914) 'Erläuterungsbericht zum Neubau Berlinerstrasse 37/38', Charlottenburg City Hall, archive of the 'Wohnungswesen' department.

Winter, E. (1994) *The Development of Social Welfare in Britain,* Buckingham: Open University Press.

Wolff, J. (1991) 'Women and the modern city: reflections on the flâneuse', Online. Available http://www.bunkler.com.pl/klub/janet_text.html (15 November 2000).

Wölfflin, H. (1994) 'Prolegomena to a psychology of architecture', in H.E. Mallgrave (ed.) *Empathy, Form, and Space: Problems in German Aesthetics 1873–1893*, Santa Monica, CA: Getty Center for the History of Art and the Humanities.

Wood, A. and Adams, T. (1998) 'Embracing the machine: Quilt and quilting as community-building architecture,' in B. Ebo's (ed.) *Cyberghetto or Cybertopia? Race, Class, and Gender on the Internet*, Praeger/Greenwood Press.

Wood, E. (1913) 'Four Washington alleys', *Survey* 31: 44–6.

Woods, R.A. (ed.) (1898) *The City Wilderness: A Settlement Study by Residents and Associates of the South End House*, Boston: Houghton-Mifflin.

Woods, R.A. (1923) *The Neighborhood in Nation-Building,* Boston: Houghton Mifflin.

Woods, R.A. and Kennedy, A. J. (eds) (1911) *Handbook of Settlements,* Philadelphia: William L. Fell Co.

Wright, G. (1991) *The Politics of Design in French Colonial Urbanism,* Chicago: University of Chicago Press.

Young, I. (1990) *Justice and the Politics of Difference*, Princeton: Princeton University Press.

Young, I. (1997) *Intersecting Voices: Dilemmas of Gender, Political Philosophy, and Policy*, Princeton: Princeton University Press.

Zueblin, C. (1905) *A Decade of Civic Development*, Chicago: University of Chicago Press.

Zurbrugg, N. (1993) *The Parameters of Postmodernism*, London: Routledge.

Index

Page numbers in *italic* refer to figures and illustrations